The
Mulberry Tree

'The Bowen terrain cannot be demarcated on any existing map . . . Since I started writing, I have been welding together an inner landscape, assembled anything but at random.'

Pictures and Conversations

THE MULBERRY TREE

Writings of Elizabeth Bowen

Selected and introduced by
HERMIONE LEE

To
Eudora Welty

Published by Virago Press Limited 1986
41 William IV Street
London WC2N 4DB

This collection Copyright © 1986 by Curtis Brown Ltd.,
London, Literary Executors of the Estate of the late
Elizabeth Bowen.

This selection, introduction and notes Copyright © 1986 by
Hermione Lee.

British Library Cataloguing in Publication Data

Bowen, Elizabeth
  The Mulberry tree: writings of
  Elizabeth Bowen.
  1. Bowen, Elizabeth, *1899–1973*——
  Biography   2. Authors, English——Biography
  I. Title   II. Lee, Hermione
  823'.912   PR6003.06757Z/

  ISBN 0-86068-527-6

Typeset by Wyvern Typesetting Ltd. of Bristol
and printed and bound by Anchor Brendon Ltd.
of Tiptree, Essex.

Contents

List of Illustrations

(*between pages 182 and 183*)

Acknowledgements

The editor and publishers are grateful to Spencer Curtis Brown for permission to reprint material from the Elizabeth Bowen estate; to the Harry Ransom Humanities Research Center, The University of Texas at Austin; to the University of Sussex Library, and to the librarian of the William Plomer Collection of the University of Durham Library (Palace Green Section) for permission to publish Elizabeth Bowen's letters. The editor is particularly grateful to Finlay Colley for permission to use unpublished letters and photographs in his possession, to Terence Kilmartin of the *Observer* for permission to reproduce a review and an extract from a letter, to Elizabeth North for information about Downe House, to Ursula Owen for her patience and advice, and to John Barnard.

Preface

Elizabeth Bowen is best known for her novels and short stories. But, like Henry James and Virginia Woolf, two writers she greatly admired, she was prolific and versatile. She wrote a history of her Anglo-Irish family, *Bowen's Court*, books about Rome and Dublin, a guide to 'English Novelists', and a very large number of essays, prefaces and reviews. She was a generous letter writer, a frequent broadcaster, and a regular visitor to writing classes at American universities. This edition is selective, drawing mainly on her three volumes of non-fiction, and also on previously uncollected material. The best of this writing makes an essential companion to her novels and stories. It is a form of autobiography; it illuminates other writers, and it discloses her own methods, choices of subject and 'sources of inspiration'.

All writers, Elizabeth Bowen believed, have their own peculiar 'terrain', or inner 'climate' which can be recognised from book to book beneath apparent shifts in subject or style. In her own novels and stories, that 'terrain' (a favourite word) or interior landscape is vivid and coherent, and is shaped, essentially, by a preoccupation with loss, betrayal and dislocation. Places, which are of the utmost importance to her, are always moral indices of character. The setting may be a big house in Ireland, or a south coast sea-front in wartime, a bombed London flat or an out-of-season hotel: it is always the stage for a conflict of will between romantic innocents, driven to extremes by expectation and desire, and the dispossessed or disenchanted, those who have had to give up 'picnicking in Eden'. These are very often comic confrontations – Elizabeth Bowen's mannered, elegant, edgy style is a humorist's tool, and the fiction, like the essays and reviews, can be marvellously funny – but the comedy expresses a severe judgement on a diminished society.

This inner terrain has its sources in childhood. The critic's task, Elizabeth Bowen says, is to locate and describe the writer's core, or essential subject, and very often, in her opinion, the core will turn out to be a kind of childishness, as though what makes the writer is the part that never grows up.

Concentration on any one writer's work almost always ends by exposing a core of naivety – a core which, once it has been laid bare, seems either infantile or august. There is little *inner* complexity, after all: the apparent outer complexity of the art has been little more than the effort towards expression. Somewhere within the pattern, somewhere behind the words, a responsive, querying innocence stays intact. ('The Roving Eye')

When Elizabeth Bowen writes about her childhood, which she does frequently – in 'Pictures and Conversations', a late unfinished autobiographical sketch; in '*She*', a tribute to an early influence, and in the books about her family, *Bowen's Court* and *Seven Winters* – her reminiscences are always bound up with her sense of herself as a writer. Born in Dublin in 1899, the only child of Protestant Anglo-Irish parents, she was brought up among the 'darkening Georgian façades' of the city and in the classic impersonality of Bowen's Court, the family house in north-east Cork. At the age of seven, a family tragedy uprooted her. Her father, Henry Cole Bowen, a lawyer, had a breakdown through overwork and developed anaemia of the brain. The doctors advised that he should be separated from his family, so, while he stayed in Ireland, Elizabeth and her mother went to live in England, where 'Bitha' was provided for by an assortment of protective Anglo-Irish aunts and well-balanced English boarding-schools in Kent. Any security, though, was fragile. Her father recovered in 1911, but her mother died of cancer when she was thirteen.

Elizabeth Bowen's adult life was more stable, less itinerant, than her childhood. She began writing when she was twenty and had her first volume of stories, *Encounters*, published in 1923, the same year that she married Alan Cameron, then working for the Ministry of Education in Northampton. After two years they moved to Oxford, and then, in 1935, to a house in Regent's Park. Until the 1950s, Elizabeth Bowen divided her time between London and Ireland. But the later part of her life resembled her childhood in its unfixedness. After the death of Alan Cameron and the sale of Bowen's Court, she spent a great deal of time in America and lived again in Oxford and Kent. She died in 1973.

For the novelist, Elizabeth Bowen believes, there is no escaping first impressions. And, as with Graham Greene's childhood fascination for Marjorie Bowen's *The Viper of Milan*, or V. S. Naipaul's first taste of Conrad, reading plays a vital part in those formative influences. 'I feel certain that if I *could* read my way back, analytically, through the books of my childhood, the clues to everything could be found.' Rider Haggard's *She* provides a splendid example of a turning-point in her early imaginative life. To the bored twelve-year-old, longing for primary colours and undiscovered countries, *She*, with its moon-blanched ruined city (to be used in the story 'Mysterious Kôr') acted as an intoxicant. The novel confirmed an already latent idea of 'obstination': 'Want anything hard enough, long enough, and it must come your way. This did strike deep: it came up like a reinforcement, because in my day, my childhood, all polite education was against the will.'

This conflict, between society and the will, was to be the subject of much of her fiction: it is one of the ingredients of the 'Bowen terrain', which has its sources in that childhood reading of *She*. Similarly, the voluptuous feeling for place, the interest in people who don't belong (spies, orphans, passionate criminals), the keen eye for absurd manners, the love of dramatic journeys, can all be attributed to early experiences. But she doesn't merely hark back to or re-enact the events of her childhood, as in the novel *The Little Girls*. She is also interested in the idea of childishness. The fiction is full of retarded overgrown juveniles (Eva Trout is a late example), reckless innocents, characters who haven't found ways of compromising with adult society. In *The Death of the Heart*, a disabused novelist remarks that we each keep 'battened down inside' us a sort of 'lunatic giant' whose 'knockings and batterings' only a few of us can hear. As a critic, Bowen is always quick to notice the writer who still gives ear to his 'lunatic giant' – as when she pinpoints the 'sublimated infantilism' of Le Fanu's *Uncle Silas* or the legacy of Dickens's or Trollope's miserable childhood.

In all the retrospective essays about childhood, Bowen is ironically alert to the possibility that 'the most powerful of my memories are only half true'. In 'Coming to London', for instance, she describes the blurring between the real city and imagined versions of it; in 'Out of a Book' she shows how literary and lived experiences are amalgamated in the mind. In old age, she became increasingly preoccupied with the 'oblique and selective' action of memory. Her last two novels, both of which draw on her childhood, demonstrate the powerful influence of Proust: his belief (referred to in the Preface to *The Last September*) that 'it is those periods of existence which are lived through . . . carelessly, unwillingly or in boredom, that most often fructify into art', and his ideas about involuntary recall, *déjà vu*, and the relation between the imagination and time. 'Imagining oneself to be remembering,' the novelist says in *Eva Trout*, 'more often than not one is imagining: Proust says so.'

Her fascination with the treacherous 'bend back' of memory is part of a political antipathy for the modern world, a Burkean conservatism which is most apparent when she is writing about the history of the Anglo-Irish or the wartime and post-war climate of feeling in England. At its crudest, this takes the form of a preference for stately homes and good manners – 'the unwary civility of the old world, privilege, ease, grace', as she calls it in a review of Rosamond Lehmann – over middle-brow provincialism, best-selling novels full of sex, blocks of flats and housing estates, and the unwelcome successors to Mr Churchill, described in a letter to William Plomer of 1945 as 'little middle-class Labour wets with their old London School of Economics ties and their women'. This snobbishness is less off-putting when seen as the unsympathetic side of her Anglo-Irishness. The essay on 'The Big House', like the book on Bowen's Court, persuasively describes the 'humanistic, classic and dis-ciplined' idea of living which the eighteenth-century Ascendancy builders expressed in their houses. It is their lack of self-conscious-ness and self-absorption which Elizabeth Bowen most relishes: 'What is fine about the social idea is that it means the subjugation of the personal to the impersonal. In the interest of good manners and good behaviour people learned to subdue their own feelings.'

That classic impersonality is what attracts her to Jane Austen, who seems to her to set up 'Elegance and Propriety' against the encroach-ments of gothic extravagance and 'fancy', and above all to Flaubert, whose 'self-control' and 'coldness' she explicitly opposes to the excesses of Romanticism. Flaubert resisted what she sees, histori-cally, as the slide from the 'main healthy abstract' of the eighteenth century, via the Romantic elevation of the 'I', to what she calls in *Bowen's Court* 'the dire period of Personal Life'. The break-up of classical humanism and social decorum into fantasy and egotism leads ultimately, she thinks, to the wars of the twentieth century. 'Today [1942] the mutilated frontiers of Europe show the outcome of the romantic obsession. From the declamation on the eve of the duel to the Nazi monologue it has not really been such a far cry.'

Elizabeth Bowen's personal vision of contemporary life, which she repeatedly characterizes as dislocated, dispossessed and denatured, was confirmed on a vast scale by the Second World War. Her idea of a spiritual disinheritance was now made brutally palpable. *Bowen's Court* graphs the disastrous plunge from a decorous, stable 'aesthetic of living' 'to 1939'; her wartime short stories and essays, written at

the same time, describe with hallucinatory clearness a diminished life
lived under conditions of violent abnormality. Over and over again,
her characters voice the sense of loss: 'There's been a stop in our
senses and in our faculties that's made everything around us so much
dead matter.' 'How are we to live without natures? . . . So much
flowed through people; so little flows through us . . . All we can do is
imitate love or sorrow.' Writing, as she says in her preface to *The
Demon Lover*, is a form of resistance to this loss of selfhood: fictions,
ghosts, memories, and imaginary terrains become more real than the
'real' world.

In the post-war essays and the late novels, she dwells more than
ever on the cauterization of feeling in modern civilization ('What
fails in the air of our present-day that we cannot breathe it?') and on
the dubious attraction of retreats into fantasy and nostalgia. Like the
heroine of *A World of Love*, she feels that 'her time, called hers
because she was required to live in it and had no other, was in bad
odour, and no wonder . . . too much had been going on for too long.'
Her distaste for 'the anaesthetized and bewildered present' extends
to an uneasiness about contemporary fiction, where she finds 'an
increasing discrepancy between facts, or circumstances, and feeling,
or the romantic will', and an increasing compulsion to back off from
the nullity of modern life into 'the better days'. Many of the essays of
the early '50s reiterate her distrust of 'the bend back', not less
because she herself is a prey to it. The radio play on Trollope, stories
such as 'The Happy Autumn Fields' and 'Ivy Gripped the Steps', the
retrospective essays, the wistful references to Dickens in *Eva Trout*,
show how drawn she is by the consolatory (if illusory) stability of the
past, its richness and slowness, its dependability. 'We're homesick
for anything right-and-tight,' says the young soldier in *Anthony
Trollope*, 'we long for what's ordinary.' Like her contemporaries,
she hankers for 'memoirs, biographies, old diaries found in old
desks, agreeable works of history, rich historical novels'. But escap-
ism and fantasy, and what she describes severely as 'the sickly
dominance of nostalgia in our talk, writing and reading' are to be
resisted. Her reviews are dotted with critiques of 'vague romanti-
cized feeling', 'the subjective landscape', 'the cult of nostalgia'. She
requires instead (even as early as 1936 and 1941) the 'detachment'
exemplified by Joyce, 'the coldness Flaubert desired', a freedom
'from self-interest, from obsession, from nostalgia, from arbitrary
loyalties', 'emotion implied (not merely written up)'. Impersonality
and disengagement are everywhere recommended, for herself as
much as for others. 'I am dead against art's being self-expression,'

she says, looking back on her own stories, and attempting to view her own work with as much 'cold familiarity' as possible. The modern writers she most admires – Ivy Compton-Burnett, Katherine Mansfield, Henry Green, Cyril Connolly – are those who seem most in control of their personal experience.

So a consistent paradox can be perceived. Whether the subject is Anglo-Ireland, or the war, or modern fiction, or her own past, there is, characteristically, a convergence of sensation and detachment. In her own temperament, as she describes it, a satirical self-awareness is superimposed on a sensation-hungry romanticism, to produce 'a career of withstood emotion'. In her relation to society, as compared with Graham Greene's and V. S. Pritchett's in *Why Do I Write?*, the usual conflict between individualism and discipline manifests itself: the writer is 'solitary and farouche', has a duty, like a spy, to be 'disloyal' to the state, and should not be asked to join in communal activities: 'My books *are* my relation to society.' At the same time, there is a pressure to behave with some 'decorum', and not to 'contribute to anarchy'. In her fiction, melodramatic, gothic materials – spies and ghosts, adulterers and runaways, murderers and suicides – pull against the control of a mannered style, just as her fanatical innocents (Portia in *The Death of the Heart*, or Emmeline in *To The North*, or Leopold in *The House in Paris*) batter themselves against a knowing, compromised, grown-up world.

In her critical essays and prefaces, the pull between dispassion and sensation is most clearly seen when she is writing about short stories, her own and others'. She is firm about the responsibility of the short story: it must be '*necessary*', and it must have 'a valid central emotion', as with a lyric poem. That central emotion should be 'austere, major' and have 'implicit dignity'; and there must be 'exact and impassive' narration. But, at the same time, the short story admits extremes which are forbidden to the novel, 'with its calmer, stricter, more orthodox demands'. It is a kind of free zone, allowing for 'what is crazy about humanity'. She considers it 'unethical' to bring the supernatural into her novels; but the stories are full of hallucinations and strange 'psychological weather'.

The emphasis here on a writer's responsibility to the choice of subject and form is reminiscent of Henry James's theory of fiction. Elizabeth Bowen's loosely humanistic definition of the novel as 'the non-poetic statement of a poetic truth' in 'Notes on Writing a Novel' and elsewhere (where plot, character, settings and dialogue are all seen to interact, and strong statements are made about 'the validity of the truth the novel is to present') seem to be indebted to James's belief in 'the perfect dependence of the "moral" sense of a work of art on the amount of felt life concerned in producing it'. She emulates James, Flaubert, Proust and Virginia Woolf in her attempts to analyse and define, as coldly as possible, what makes writing and what writing does. But, characteristically, impersonal explication is applied to processes which are admitted to be obscure and involuntary. In 'The Writer's Peculiar World' she distinguishes between 'intellectual novelists' who consciously change their faiths or theories or subjects, and 'intuitive writers' whose loyalties and preoccupations are 'involuntary and inborn'. Clearly, she thinks of herself as the intuitive sort. But for any kind of writer, there are areas which are not susceptible to cold analysis. Plot 'is not a matter of choice' but what the novelist is 'driven to' after the accumulation of 'a mass of subjective matter . . . impressions received, feelings about experience, distorted results of ordinary observation'. Characters are not made but '*found*': 'They reveal themselves slowly to the novelist's perception,' she says, echoing Virginia Woolf, 'as might fellow-travellers seated opposite one in a very dimly-lit railway carriage.' Settings, too are 'assembled – out of memories which, in the first place, may have had no rational connection with one another'. Still, what the writer does with this often inexplicable material can be rigorously and dispassionately analysed. To penetrate to what underlies and accounts for the writer's peculiar terrain, whether her own or another's, is the impulse of all Elizabeth Bowen's critical, biographical and personal writings.

ESSAYS

Introduction

Elizabeth Bowen's novels and stories are full of desolate, self-conscious children whose secret imaginative lives are always under pressure from the socialized expectations of the adult world. Henrietta and Leopold in *The House in Paris* and the children in the story 'The Tommy Crans' are the most touching examples of these, but there is also, long before *The Little Girls*, a whole parade of daunting schoolgirls: over-enthusiastic Cordelia in *The Hotel*, spotty, witchlike, vengeful Maud in *A World of Love*, the fiendish motherless child in 'Maria', who is 'having her character "done for her" at school', the wretched Hermione in 'The Easter Egg Party' ('I feel just as if I was dead, and I do want to go home') and the sophisticated boarders in *Friends and Relations*:

> The girls at Mellyfield developed very early a feeling for character. They were interested in their own personalities, which they displayed, discussed, and altered. They . . . read psychology to each other on Sunday afternoons. Everyone knew, for instance, that Jenna's insincerity arose from a nervous opposition to circumstance; that Marise to live at all would have to break down her overpowering sense of order, that Hester since she was six had ruined all her friendships by her intolerance and that Ludmilla must be ignored when she squeaked at games because of a bad heredity.

The sources of these gleeful caricatures are on show in Elizabeth Bowen's essays. 'On Not Rising to the Occasion' is a splendid retrospect of her Edwardian childhood embarrassments and over-anxieties; 'Coming to London' sympathetically reconstructs her intense fantasy life and her Anglo-Irish 'blend of impatience and evasiveness' about 'all things English'. And 'The Mulberry Tree', her contribution to Graham Greene's collection of essays *The Old School* (1934), an account of her wartime boarding school, Downe House in Kent (run by the formidably realistic and charming Olive Willis), provides a fine example of the close relation between her childhood experience and her fictional subjects. The brilliant social comedy of the essay is a blueprint for all her close observation of adolescent behaviour and English class-marks.

Her feeling for place, which she regarded as her most important quality ('Am I not manifestly a writer for whom places loom large?') pervades those childhood essays. Kent, Ireland and London (her three 'terrains') are constantly being written up. 'The Big House', with its haunting, tender evocation of the life of the demesne 'in its circle of trees', and its wry appraisal of the decline of the Anglo-Irish, makes an excellent companion-piece to *Bowen's Court* and to the Irish novels, *The Last September* and *A World of Love*. It is rather more surprising to find a matter-of-fact, realistic political essay, written for *The Spectator* in 1941, which sets out to correct English misapprehensions about conditions in neutral Ireland. 'Eire' came out of Elizabeth Bowen's wartime work for the Ministry of Information, which enabled her to travel to Ireland to report on attitudes to the war. For all its factuality, though, it lets some characteristically Bowenish tones slip through, as when she notes 'the sense of a ban on *feeling*, in a country in which feeling naturally runs high'. 'London, 1940' shares that sensitivity to wartime unreality and dislocation. Elizabeth Bowen's house in Clarence Terrace, Regent's Park, was bombed in 1940 and again in 1944: over and over again – in this essay, in *The Heat of the Day*, in *The Demon Lover* short stories – she evokes the hallucinatory atmosphere of the Blitz. Like Graham Greene's *The Ministry of Fear*, or Henry Green's *Caught*, or the eyewitness accounts in Angus Calder's *The People's War*, her writing gives us, as Anthony Burgess said in a review of *The Heat of the Day*, 'the very feel and smell of London in the 1940s'.

The acuteness and immediacy of the pieces on childhood and places also characterizes her essays on writers and writing. These are very much of their time. 'Notes on Writing a Novel', for instance, now seems rather old-fashioned, with its blithe talk of characters as 'pre-existing' forces, and its belief in unbreakable rules for fiction. For all this, it is a shrewd and illuminating piece, and has the sort of sensible perceptiveness we find in her judgements on other writers. Her fine long essay on Katherine Mansfield is very sympathetic: she writes especially feelingly about Mansfield's courage, of the risks inherent in her aesthetic vision, and of her wonderfully 'glass-transparent' style.

As a deracinated writer harking back to her childhood in New Zealand, Mansfield seemed a kindred spirit to Elizabeth Bowen; she says of her art that it grew 'not only from memory but from longing'. Bowen's preoccupation with those two overlapping states of mind is evident in many of the 1950s essays about the relationship between the past and the present. The perilous attractions of nostalgia, the lure not of the past itself but of 'our own illusion . . . the idea of the past' is one of her essential subjects. It seems appropriate, then, to begin with her essay on her schooldays.

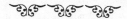

THE MULBERRY TREE

[Downe House]

The house with a shallow front lawn, swagged in July with Dorothy Perkins roses, stood back from a tarmac road outside the Kentish village of Downe. The main block, three stories high, had a white pillared portico and a dado of ivy, looking friendly and undistinguished. It contained classrooms and bedrooms for about sixty girls, the staff study and the dining-room. To the left facing the porch (as we seldom had time to do) was a stable-yard, to the right, a warren of painted iron buildings – gymnasium, music-rooms, washrooms – twisted off at an angle, parallel with the road. A low trellis of ivy concealed these windows.

The back of the house, one portion curving out in a deep bay, faced a lawn flanked each side by heavily treed paths, tunnels in summer. A bed of azaleas outside the senior study french window made the summer term exotic. Features of this lawn landscape were an old mulberry tree with an iron belt and a mound with a large ilex, backed by evergreen shrubs, on which Shakespeare plays were acted. It was usual during rehearsals to pluck and chew the leaves of the ilex tree. We girls were for ever masticating some foreign substance, leaves of any kind, grass from the playing fields, paper, india rubber, splinters from pencil-ends or the hems of handkerchiefs. In the course of my three years at school both the ilex and mulberry trees took on an emotional significance; under the mulberry a friend whose brother at that time captained the Winchester eleven, and who was herself our only overhand bowler, criticized my behaviour on an occasion, saying I had done something that was not cricket. The lawn gave on a meadow crossed by a path to the playing field: beyond the school boundary, meadows and copses rolled off into Kent pleasantly. In summer there was a great smell of hay. I remember also one June a cuckoo that used to flap round the school roof, stout, squawking and losing its mystery. It has taken years for me to reinstate cuckoos. The Cudham valley was said to be a great place for nightingales, but we girls can never have walked there at the right time. . . . From across country, features of this rather odd and imposing back view of the house were its very white window-frames, a glass veranda on to which the drawing-room debouched and a modern addition, one side, in the form of a kind of chalet, from whose balcony I played Jezebel with a friend's teddy bear.

The survival of such childish inanimate pets was encouraged by fashion; several dormitory beds with their glacial white quilts were encumbered all day and shared nightly with rubbed threadbare teddy bears, monkeys or in one case a blue plush elephant. Possibly this seemed a good way to travesty sentiment: we cannot really have been idiotic girls. A friend of mine wore a carved ivory Chinese dog round her neck on a gold cord for some days, then she was asked to wear this inside her djibbah. A good deal of innocent fetishism came to surround these animals; the mistress of the blue elephant used to walk the passages saying: 'You must kiss my elephant.' Photos of relatives, sometimes quite distant but chosen for their good appearance, the drawings of Dulac, Medici prints and portraits of Napoleon, Charles I, Rupert Brooke, Sir Roger Casement or Mozart lent advertising touches of personality to each cubicle's walls, slung on threads from the frieze-rail and flapping and tapping in an almost constant high wind from the open windows. The ever difficult business of getting oneself across was most pressing of all at this age: restricted possessions, a uniform dictated down to the last detail and a self-imposed but rigid emotional snobbishness shutting the more direct means of self-expression away. Foibles, mannerisms we therefore exaggerated most diligently.

If anyone said 'You are always so such-and-such' one felt one had formed a new intimacy and made one's mark. A good many young women were led to buffoon themselves. It seemed fatal not to be at least one thing to excess, and if I could not be outstandingly good at a thing I preferred to be outstandingly bad at it. Personality came out in patches, like damp through a wall.

The dormitories were called bedrooms, and we had little opinion of schools where the bedrooms were called dormitories. Ours were in fact the bedrooms of a fair-sized country house, divided into from four to six cubicles. The window cubicles went to the best people, who were sometimes terribly cold at nights; the door cubicle went to the youngest inhabitant, who could hold everyone up if her sense of decency were over-acute. 'You *can't* come through,' she would shout; 'I am indecent.' The niceties of curtain-drawing and of intrusion varied from bedroom to bedroom, according to temper, but we always closed our curtains to say our prayers. No embarrassment surrounded the saying of prayers at this school; in fact it would have been more embarrassing to have left them unsaid. Whom one sleeps with is always rather important, and ill-assorted companions could cast a gloom over the term. There was always one rather quiet girl who patiently wished herself elsewhere, lurked a good deal behind her curtains and was afraid to speak. As in a railway carriage, one generally disliked one's companions less after some time. The tone of a bedroom would be, of course, set by the noisiest girl, who talked most freely about her private affairs. As one began to realize that bedroom lists for a term were drawn up on a psychological basis, the whole thing became more interesting. Great friends were not put together and we were not allowed into each other's bedrooms, but it was always possible to stand and talk in the door, with one toe outside. Assignations for serious or emotional talks connected themselves with the filling of hot-water-bottles and water cans at a tap outside the bathrooms, when one was otherwise ready for bed. Girls of a roving disposition with a talent for intimacy were always about this passage. A radiator opposite this tap was in demand in winter; one could lean while one talked and warm the spine through the dressing-gown. The passage was dim-lit, with wobbly gas brackets, and it was always exciting to see who had got there first. The radiator was near the headmistress's door, and she would disperse any group she came out and found. It irritated her to see us being girlish in any way. We cannot really have been emotional girls; we were not highly sexed and any attractions had an aesthetic, snobbish, self-interested tinge. Conversations over the radiator were generally about art, Roman Catholicism, suicide, or how impossible somebody else had been. At nine o'clock a bell rang from the matron's room and we all darted back to our bedrooms and said our prayers.

I first went to this school in September 1914. We unpacked our trunks in a cement passage outside the gymnasium and carried our things upstairs. The school must have re-assembled with an elating sense of emergency, but as I was new I was not conscious of this. Everything seemed so odd that the war was dwarfed, and though one had been made to feel that one was now living in history, one's own biography was naturally more interesting. I found my school-fellows rather terse and peremptory, their snubbing of me had a kind of nobility: whether this arose from the war's or my own newness I did not ask: as I had been told that this was a very good school it was what I had been led to expect. A squad of troops marching past in the dark on the tarmac road, whistling, pointed the headmistress's address to us in the gymnasium that first night of term. Wind kept flapping the window cords on their pulleys, the gas jets whistled and the girls drawn up by forms in resolute attitudes looked rather grim. The headmistress stated that it did not matter if we were happy so long as we were good. At my former school the headmistress had always said she knew we should be good as long as we were happy. That sounded sunnier. But in my three years at this school I learnt to define happiness as a kind of inner irrational exaltation having little to do with morals one way or the other. That night in the gymnasium I felt some apprehension that my character was to be lopped, or even forcibly moulded, in this place, but this came to be dispelled as the term wore on. The war having well outlasted my schooldays, I cannot imagine a girl's school without a war. The moral stress was appalling. We grew up under the intolerable obligation of being fought for, and could not fall short in character without recollecting that men were dying for us. During my second year, the *Daily Mail* came out with its headline about food-hogs, and it became impossible to eat as much as one wished, which was to over-eat, without self-consciousness. If the acutest food shortage had already set in, which it had not, meals would really have been easier. As it was, we *could* over-eat, but it became unfeeling to do so. The war dwarfed us and made us morally uncomfortable, and we could see no reason why it should ever stop. It was clear, however, that someone must have desired it, or it would not have begun. In my first term, we acted a pageant representing the Allies for the headmistress's birthday, and later sang songs of the epoch, such as 'We don't want to lose you, but . . .' at a concert in the village, in our white muslin Saturday evening frocks. Most eligible fighters had, however, by this time gone to the war and we can only have made their relatives more hysterical. An excellent bun supper was provided by the village committee, and some of us over-ate.

I do not remember ever discussing the war among ourselves at school. Possibly some of the girls may have done so, but I had a sense of inferiority owing to having no brothers and not taking in a daily paper. Though, seated beside one of the staff at meals one would say: 'Aren't the French doing splendidly?' or 'Isn't it awful about the Russians?' The Danish music mistress, however, had melancholia and we were not allowed to mention the war at her table. I do not think it was so much the war that made her melancholic as her unhappy friendship with the violin mistress; any attempt to make conversation with her was the last straw. She looked extraordinarily like Hamlet, and as she was a neutral I always resented her taking up this attitude about the war ... If a girl's brother were killed or wounded we were all too much embarrassed to speak of it. Though death became familiar, it never became less awkward: if heroic feeling ran low in us I think this was because the whole world's behaviour seemed to be travestying our own: everywhere, everyone was behaving as we were all, at our ages, most anxious not to behave. Things were being written and said constantly that would have damned any one of us: the world seemed to be bound up in a tragic attack of adolescence and there seemed no reason why we should ever grow up, since moderation in behaviour became impossible. So we became in contradistinction violently precious, martyrized by our own good taste. Our morbidity was ingrowing. I cannot, either, remember discussing men. Possibly the whole sex had gloomy associations. One or two of the girls fell in love in the holidays, but something in the atmosphere made it impossible to talk of this naturally without seeming at once to make copy of it. All the same, I and my friends all intended to marry early, partly because this appeared an achievement or way of making one's mark, also from a feeling it would be difficult to settle to anything else until this was done. (Like passing the School Certificate.) Few of my friends anticipated maternity with either interest or pleasure, and though some have since become mothers it still seems inappropriate. Possibly, however, we were not natural girls. We may have discussed love, but I do not remember how. The future remained very hazy and insecure. We were not ambitious girls, though we all expected to distinguish ourselves in some way. Not one of us intended to be L.O.P.H. (Left On Pa's Hands). We lived, however, intensively in the present; when the present became over-powering there was an attic-loft over the bedroom ceilings in the main buildings, with sacks and a cistern in it, where an enterprising person could go and weep. Less fastidious people wept in their cubicles.

We were not in love with each other at all continuously, or, as far as I know, with the staff at all. A certain amount of emotion banked up in the holidays, when letters became important. During the school day we all looked violently plain: school uniform, even djibbahs, cannot expect to suit everyone; red wrists stuck out of our cuffs and our hair (short hair was not at that time the prevailing fashion) was so skinned back that our eyes would hardly shut. After games we charged indoors, stripped, rubbed down, put on stays and private clothes, released our front hair and became a little more personable. On Saturday nights, in modified evening dresses, quite a certain amount of glamour set in. In the week, curvilinear good looks were naturally at a discount and a swaggering, nonchalant air cut the most ice. If you were not good at games the best way of creating an atmosphere was to be good at acting. We acted a good deal. On Saturday afternoons, one or two people who could play the piano emotionally had séances in the music rooms. All this was the best we could put up in the way of romance. All the same, one or two people contrived to keep diaries, moon round the garden alone and be quite unhappy.

Competitive sociability and team spirit were rather well united at my school by the custom of picking up tables. The first day of term seven seniors shut themselves up and, by rotative bidding, each picked up from the rest of the school a team of about eight for her table at meals. Each team moved round each week to the next of the seven dining-room tables, each table presided over by one of the staff. The object of each team was to make the most conversation possible, and to be a success: girls were therefore picked with a view to chattiness, desirability, tact, table manners, resource and charm. Certain unfortunate girls were never in demand, and the screams of seniors repudiating them could sometimes be heard from the other end of the garden. It was a great thing to be at the head of the most patently animated table in the dining-room. Many of us have grown up to be good hostesses. If a girl sat just eating on without saying anything the head of the table would kick at her, if within reach. So that young nervous girls got into a way of saying almost anything. The great thing was to amuse the mistress whose table it was, and keep her smiling constantly: each girl had to take it in turns to do this. There was a French table and a German table: the games mistress was usually difficult to talk to. The headmistress sometimes received our remarks with irony, and was inclined to say 'Quite . . .' The table rule bound us only for breakfast and dinner; at tea and supper we sat with whom we liked, few of the staff were present and very merry we were. Quarrels, if any, sometimes occurred at this time.

The other great social occasion was Saturday evening (as I have said). We danced (we thought) rather glamorously in the gymnasium to a piano, and dances were often booked up some days ahead. On summer Saturday evenings we walked round the garden between dances, feeling unlike ourselves. The garden was long, with lime trees and apple trees and long grass with cuckoo flowers in it: it looked very beautiful in the late evening light, with the sound of the piano coming out through the gymnasium door. On winter Saturday evenings we danced more heartily, in order to keep warm. The staff filed in in evening dresses and sat on a platform, watching the dancing, and occasionally being asked to dance, with expressions of animation which, now that I look back, command my respect.

Lessons must have occupied a good deal of our time, but I remember very little of this. What I learnt seems to have been absorbed into my system, which shows how well taught I was. I used to sit riveting, or trying to rivet, the mistress's eye, but must otherwise have been pretty passive. I spent an inordinate amount of time over the preparation for some lessons; the rest of my preparation time went by in reading poetry or the Bible or looking up more about the facts of life in the *Encyclopaedia Britannica*. We were morbidly honourable girls and never spoke to each other at preparation or in our bedrooms after the lights were out. I often wonder whether in after life one has not suffered from an overstrained honour from having been too constantly put upon it in youth, and whether the espionage one hears of in foreign schools might not have kept one's sense of delinquency more enduringly active. In these ways, we were almost too good to last. We did not pass notes either, though one of my friends, just back from a day in London, once wrote on the margin of her rough note book, and pushed across to me, that Kitchener had been drowned. Perhaps the occasion may have excused the breach. I simply thought, however, that she was pulling my leg. . . . Games were compulsory and took up the afternoon: it did not matter being bad at them so long as you showed energy. At lacrosse, girls who could run would pound up and down the field; those who could not gripped their crosses fiercely and stalked about. Lacrosse is such a fierce game that I wonder we all lived through it. Hockey, though ungainly, is not nearly so perilous. The only real farce was cricket, a humiliating performance for almost all. I never thought worse of anyone for being good at games so long as she was not unattractive in other ways; one or two of the games committee had, however, an air of having no nonsense about them that was depressing. We were anything but apathetic about matches: when a match was played away the returning team would, if victorious, begin to cheer at a given turn of the road; we all sat with straining ears; if the charabanc rolled up in silence we knew the worst. Our team so often won that I should like to think we had given them moral support.

The literary society was presided over by the headmistress, of whom I should like to place it on grateful record that she did definitely teach me how not to write. There were gardens to garden in, if you had nothing more personal to do in your spare time, and, because of the war, there was haymaking in season. Two or three of the girls who had formed the idea that they wished to be engineers in after life spent a good deal of time looking through the windows of the engine room at the light plant and water-pumping machine; sometimes they were let in by the geography mistress to help her oil the thing. The geography mistress was a Pole, who had built the chapel as well as all the other modern additions to the school. The chapel was put up during my second year and dedicated by the Bishop of Rochester: a friend of mine pointed out to me during the service that the Bishop's sleeves were not white but of very pale pink lawn, and I have had no opportunity since to correct this impression: perhaps it was not incorrect. The chapel was approached by a dark, draughty and rather impressive arcade from the gymnasium. There were no cases of religious mania or any other obsession while I was at school.

Seeing *Mädchen in Uniform*, and reading more sensitive people's impressions of their school life, makes me feel that either my old school was prosaic or that I was insensitive. A toughish, thick child, I did not in fact suffer in any way. My vanity would have been mortified anywhere and my heart was at that age really all over the place. At my old school there was nothing particular to conform to, and the worst that can be said of it is that I got no kick out of not conforming to anything. I was only too well understood, and when I left school my relations complained that my personality had made rapid and rank growth. I talked too much with a desperate self-confidence induced perhaps by competitive talking at meals. I say with deference to the susceptibilities of possible other essayists in this book [*The Old School*] that I consider my old school an exceedingly good one. If girls ought really to be assembled and taught, I can think of no better way of assembling and teaching them. No one dragooned us; in the course of three years I never once heard the expression *esprit de corps* and we were never addressed as future mothers. The physical discomfort was often extreme but (I am prepared to believe now that its details escape me) salutary. I regret that my palate has been blunted for life by being made to finish up everything on my plate, so that when I dine out with a gourmet my manner becomes exceedingly artificial. I was taught not only how not to write (though I still do not always write as I should) but how not, if possible, to behave, and how not to exhibit feeling. I have not much idea what more than ten people at my school were like, so cannot well generalize about our type or mentality. No one of my companions betrayed my affections, corrupted me, aggravated my inferiority complex, made me wish I had more money, gave me a warp for life or did anything that is supposed to happen at schools. There is nothing I like better than feeling one of a herd, and after a term or two I began to feel firmly stuck in.

Memory is, as Proust has it, so oblique and selective that no doubt I see my school days through a subjective haze. I cannot believe that those three years were idyllic: days and weeks were no doubt dreary and squalid on end. I recall the most thundering disappointments and baulked ambitions, but those keep repeating themselves throughout after life. I do not desire to live those three years again, but I should be exceedingly sorry to have them cut out of my past. Some years after I left, the house, after so much pounding and trampling, began to wear out; the school moved and the building has been reinstated as some kind of shrine, for Charles Darwin lived there for some years and died there, I believe, too. Our Morris wallpapers have been all stripped off and the white woodwork grained: the place now rather seriously and unsatirically reconstructs a late Victorian epoch. Our modern additions have been pulled down; the geography mistress has re-erected the chapel, the gymnasium, the lavatories and the music-rooms elsewhere. When I revisited the place, only the indestructible cement flooring of these remained. To indulge sentiment became almost impossible. I have never liked scientific people very much, and it mortifies me to think of them trampling reverently around there on visiting days, thinking of Charles Darwin and ignorant of my own youth.

1934

LONDON, 1940

Early September morning in Oxford Street. The smell of charred dust hangs on what should be crystal pure air. Sun, just up, floods the once more innocent sky, strikes silver balloons and the intact building-tops. The whole length of Oxford Street, west to east, is empty, looks polished like a ballroom, glitters with smashed glass.

Down the distances, natural mists of morning are brown with the last of smoke. Fumes still come from the shell of a shop. At this corner where the burst gas main flaming floors high made a scene like a hell in the night, you still feel heat. The silence is now the enormous thing – it appears to amaze the street. Sections and blocks have been roped off; there is no traffic; the men in the helmets say not a person may pass (but some sneak through). Besides the high explosives that did the work, this quarter has been seeded with timebombs – so we are herded, waiting for those to go off. This is the top of Oxford Street, near where it joins the corner of Hyde Park at Marble Arch.

We people have come up out of the ground, or out from the bottom floors of the damaged houses: we now see what we heard happen throughout the night. Roped away from the rest of London we seem to be on an island – when shall we be taken off? Standing, as might the risen dead in the doors of tombs, in the mouths of shelters, we have nothing to do but yawn at each other or down the void of streets, meanwhile rubbing the smoke-smart deeper into our eyes with our dirty fists. . . . It has been a dirty night. The side has been ripped off one near block – the open gash is nothing but dusty, colourless. (As bodies shed blood, buildings shed mousey dust.) Up there the sun strikes a mirror over a mantelpiece; shreds of a carpet sag out over the void. An A.R.P. man, like a chamois, already runs up the debris; we stare. The charred taint thickens everyone's lips and tongues – what we want is bacon and eggs, coffee. We attempt little sorties – 'Keep BACK, please! Keep OFF the street!' The hungry try to slake down with smoking. 'PLEASE – that cigarette *out*! Main gone – gas all over the place – d'*you* want to blow up London?' Cigarette trodden guiltily into the trodden glass. We loaf on and on in our cave-mouths; the sun goes on and on up. Some of us are dressed, some of us are not: pyjama-legs show below overcoats. There are some Poles, who having lost everything all over again sit down whenever and wherever they can. They are our seniors in this experience: we cannot but watch them. There are two or three unmistakable pairs of disturbed lovers – making one think 'Oh yes, how odd – love.' There are squads of ageless 'residents' from aquarium-like private hotels just round the corner. There are the nomads of two or three nights ago who, having been bombed out of where they were, pitched on this part, to be bombed out again. There is the very old gentleman wrapped up in the blanket, who had been heard to say, humbly, between the blasts in the night, 'The truth is, I have outlived my generation . . .' We are none of us – except perhaps the Poles? – the very very poor: our predicament is not a great predicament. The lady in the fur coat has hair in two stiff little bedroomy grey plaits. She appeals for hair-pins: most of us have short hair – pins for her are extracted from one of the Poles' heads. Girls stepping further into the light look into pocket mirrors. 'Gosh,' they say remotely. Two or three people have, somehow, begun walking when one time-bomb goes off at Marble Arch. The street puffs itself empty; more glass splinters. Everyone laughs.

It is a fine morning and we are still alive.

This is the buoyant view of it – the theatrical sense of safety, the steady breath drawn. We shall be due, at tonight's siren, to feel our hearts once more tighten and sink. Soon after black-out we keep that date with fear. The howling ramping over the darkness, the lurch of the barrage opening, the obscure throb in the air. We *can* go underground – but for this to be any good you have to go very deep, and a number of us, fearful of being buried, prefer not to. Our own 'things' – tables, chairs, lamps – give one kind of confidence to us who stay in our own paper rooms. But when tonight the throb gathers over the roof we must not remember what we looked at this morning – these fuming utter glissades of ruin. No, these nights in September nowhere is pleasant. Where you stay is your own choice, how you feel is your fight.

However many people have crowded together, each has, while air whistles and solids rock, his or her accesses of solitude. We can do much for each other, but not all. Between bomb and bomb we are all together again: we all guess, more or less, what has been happening to all the others. Chatter bubbles up; or there is a cosy slumping sideways, to doze. Fear is not cumulative: each night it starts from scratch. On the other hand, resistance becomes a habit. And, better, it builds up a general fund.

Autumn seems a funny time to be bombed. By nature it is the hopeful start of the home year. The colours burning in the trees and weed-fires burning in the gardens ought to be enough. Autumn used to be a slow sentimental fête, with an edge of melancholy – the children going back to school, the evenings drawing in. Windows lit up earlier. Lanes in the country, squares in the city crisp with leaves. (This year, leaves are swept up with glass in them.) In autumn, where you live touches the heart – it is the worst time not to be living anywhere. This is the season in which to honour safety.

London feels all this this year most. To save something, she contracts round her wounds. Transport stoppages, roped-off districts, cut-off communications and 'dirty' nights now make her a city of villages – almost of village communes. Marylebone is my village. Friends who live outside it I think about but seldom see: *they* are sunk in the life of their own villages. We all have new friends: our neighbours. In Marylebone, shopping just before the black-out or making for home before the bombers begin to fill up the sky, we say, 'Well, good luck!' to each other. And every morning after the storm we go out to talk. News comes filtering through from the other villages. They say St John's Wood had it worse than we did. Camden Town, on the other hand, got off light. Chelsea, it seems, was hot again. They say they brought 'one' down on Paddington Green. Has anybody been over to Piccadilly? A man from Hampstead was here a minute ago; he said . . . Mrs X is a Pimlico woman; she's quite upset. Anybody know how it was in Kilburn? Somebody had a letter from Finsbury Park.

For one bad week, we were all turned out on account of time-bombs: exiled. We camped about London in other villages. (That was how I happened to be in Oxford Street, only to be once more dislodged from there.) When we were let home again we were full of stories, spent another morning picking up all the threads. The fishmonger said he had caught sight of me buying milk in Paddington. 'What, you were there too?' I asked. 'No,' he replied, 'I've got Finchley people; I was only over in Paddington looking after a friend.' We had all detested our week away: for instance, I had been worrying about my typewriter left uncovered in the dust blowing through our suddenly-emptied house; the fishmonger had been worrying about all that fish of his in the frig. with the power off. It had been necessary for several of us to slip through the barricades from time to time in order to feed cats.

Regent's Park where I live is still, at the time of writing, closed: officially, that is to say, we are not here. Just inside the gates an unexploded bomb makes a boil in the tarmac road. Around three sides of the Park, the Regency terraces look like scenery in an empty theatre: in the silence under the shut façades a week's drift of leaves flitters up and down. At nights, at my end of my terrace, I feel as though I were sleeping in one corner of a deserted palace. I had always placed this Park among the most civilized scenes on earth; the Nash pillars look as brittle as sugar – actually, which is wonderful, they have not cracked; though several of the terraces are gutted – blown-in shutters swing loose, ceilings lie on floors and a premature decay-smell comes from the rooms. A pediment has fallen on to a lawn. Illicitly, leading the existence of ghosts, we overlook the locked park.

Through the railings I watch dahlias blaze out their colour. Leaves fill the empty deck-chairs; in the sunshine water-fowl, used to so much attention, mope round the unpeopled rim of the lake. One morning a boy on a bicycle somehow got inside and bicycled round and round the silence, whistling 'It's a Happy, Happy Day.' The tune was taken up by six soldiers digging out a bomb. Now and then everything rips across; a detonation rattles remaining windows. The R.E. 'suicide squad' detonate, somewhere in the hinterland of this park, bombs dug up elsewhere.

We have no feeling to spare.

1950

THE BIG HOUSE

Big houses in Ireland are, I am told, very isolated. I say 'I am told' because the isolation, or loneliness, of my own house is only borne in on me, from time to time, by the exclamations of travellers when they arrive. 'Well,' they exclaim, with a hint of denunciation, '*you* are a long way from everywhere!' I suppose I see this the other way round: everywhere seems to have placed itself a long way from me – if 'everywhere' means shopping towns, railway stations or Ireland's principal through roads. But one's own point of departure always seems to one normal: I have grown up accustomed to seeing out of my windows nothing but grass, sky, tree, to being enclosed in a ring of almost complete silence and to making journeys for anything that I want. Actually, a main road passes my gates (though it is a main road not much travelled); my post village, which is fairly animated, is just a mile up the hill, and a daily bus, now, connects this village with Cork. The motor car demolishes distances, and the telephone and wireless keep the house knit up, perhaps too much, with the world. The loneliness of my house, as of many others, is more an effect than a reality. But it is the effect that is interesting.

When I visit other big houses I *am* struck by some quality that they all have – not so much isolation as mystery. Each house seems to live under its own spell, and that is the spell that falls on the visitor from the moment he passes in at the gates. The ring of woods inside the demesne wall conceals, at first, the whole demesne from the eye: this looks, from the road, like a *bois dormant*, with a great glade inside.

Inside the gates the avenue often describes loops, to make itself of still more extravagant length; it is sometimes arched by beeches, sometimes silent with moss. On each side lie those tree-studded grass spaces we Anglo-Irish call lawns and English people puzzle us by speaking of as 'the park'. On these browse cattle, or there may be horses out on grass. A second gate — (generally white-painted, so that one may not drive into it in the dark) — keeps these away from the house in its inner circle of trees. Having shut this clanking white gate behind one, one takes the last reach of avenue and meets the faded, dark-windowed and somehow hypnotic stare of the big house. Often a line of mountains rises above it, or a river is seen through a break in woods. But the house, in its silence, seems to be contemplating the swell or fall of its own lawns.

The paradox of these big houses is that often they are not big at all. Those massive detached villas outside cities probably have a greater number of rooms. We have of course in Ireland the *great* houses — houses Renaissance Italy hardly rivals, houses with superb façades, colonnades, pavilions and, inside, chains of plastered, painted saloons. But the houses that I know best, and write of, would be only called 'big' in Ireland — in England they would be 'country houses', no more. They are of adequate size for a family, its dependants, a modest number of guests. They have few annexes, they do not ramble; they are nearly always compactly square. Much of the space inside (and there is not so much space) has been sacrificed to airy halls and lobbies and to the elegant structure of staircases. Their façades (very often in the Italian manner) are not lengthy, though they may be high. Is it height — in this country of otherwise low buildings — that got these Anglo-Irish houses their 'big' name? Or have they been called 'big' with a slight inflection — that of hostility, irony? One may call a man 'big' with just that inflection because he seems to think the hell of himself.

These houses, however, are certainly not little. Let us say that their size, like their loneliness, is an effect rather than a reality. Perhaps the wide, private spaces they occupy throw a distending reflection on to their walls. And, they were planned for spacious living — for hospitality above all. Unlike the low, warm, ruddy French and English manors, they have made no natural growth from the soil — the idea that begot them was a purely social one. The functional parts of them — kitchens and offices, farm-buildings, outbuildings — were sunk underground, concealed by walls or by trees: only the stables (for horses ranked very highly) emerged to view, as suavely planned as the house. Yet, in another sense, the most ornate, spacious parts of these buildings *were* the most functional – the steps, the halls, the living-rooms, the fine staircases – it was these that contributed to society, that raised life above the exigencies of mere living to the plane of art, or at least style. There was a true bigness, a sort of impersonality, in the manner in which the houses were conceived. After an era of greed, roughness and panic, after an era of camping in charred or desolate ruins (as my Cromwellian ancestors did certainly) these new settlers who had been imposed on Ireland began to wish to add something to life. The security that they had, by the eighteenth century, however ignobly gained, they did not use quite ignobly. They began to feel, and exert, the European idea – to seek what was humanistic, classic and disciplined.

It is something to subscribe to an idea, even if one cannot live up to it. These country gentlemen liked sport, drink and card-playing very much better than they liked the arts – but they religiously stocked their libraries, set fine craftsmen to work on their ceilings and mantelpieces and interspersed their own family portraits with heroi-cized paintings of foreign scenes. Outdoors there was at first a good deal of negligence, but later one planned and planted demesnes. . . . All this cost money: many of these genial builders died badly in debt and left their families saddled with mansions that they could ill afford. Then, decline set in almost at once. A more modest plan of living would have made, in the end, for very much more peace: big houses that had begun in glory were soon only maintained by struggle and sacrifice. Sons were recalled from college, or never went there; daughters, undowered, stayed unwed; love-marriages had to be interdicted because money was needed to prop the roof. Husbands and wives struggled, shoulder to shoulder, to keep the estate anything like solvent, or, in the last issue, to hold creditors off; their children grew up *farouches*, haughty, quite ignorant of the outside world. And in this struggle for life, a struggle that goes on everywhere, that may be said, in fact, to *be* life itself, and should not therefore have anything terrible about it, the big house people were handicapped, shadowed and to an extent queered – by their pride, by their indignation at their decline and by their divorce from the countryside in whose heart their struggle was carried on. They would have been surprised to receive pity. I doubt, as a matter of fact, that they ever pitied themselves: they were obsessed, and to a degree exalted. They had begun as conquerors and were not disposed to let that tradition lapse. These big house people admit only one class-distinction: they instinctively 'place' a person who makes a poor mouth.

It is, I think, to the credit of big house people that they concealed their struggles with such nonchalance and for so long continued to throw about what did not really amount to much weight. It is to their credit that, with grass almost up to their doors and hardly a sixpence to turn over, they continued to be resented by the rest of Ireland as being the heartless rich. Now this myth has broken down: I think everyone knows that life is not all jam in the big house. Nowadays, what I hear most commented on is the apparent futility of the sacrifice. New democratic Ireland no longer denounces the big house, but seems to marvel at it. Why fight to maintain life in a draughty barrack, in a demesne shorn of most of its other land, a demesne in which one can hardly keep down the thistles, far from neighbours, golf links, tennis clubs, cinemas, buses, railways, shops? 'What do you *do* all day? Isn't it very lonely? Do servants stay with you? Can you keep warm in winter? Isn't it very ghostly? How do you do your shopping?'

To most of these questions it would be hard to give a concrete and satisfactory answer. To some few of the big houses wealth and security have returned – or one should say had returned, for the war attacks these again. But in the majority life maintains itself by a series of fortuities. As I have heard many occupants say: 'I have no idea how we live, but we do.' Such people not only live but enjoy life. To the keeping afloat of the household not only the family but the servants contribute ingenuity and goodwill. As on a ship out at sea, there is a sense of community. There is also – and this, I think, is the strength of such households – a very great feeling of independence: in the big house one does not feel overlooked; one lives by one's own standards, makes one's own laws and does not care, within fairly wide limits, what anybody outside the demesne wall thinks. This may tend to exaggerate, to the point of absurdity, the family's individual point of view: there are a thousand legends of eccentricity. But it does also make for a sort of hardiness and absence of social fear. And ennui, that threat to life in Ireland, is kept at bay by the constant exigencies, some of them unexpected, of the house and place. (This was not so in the more prosperous days – 'Beautiful as it is, much as I love it,' wrote one of George Moore's ancestors about Moore Hall, 'I have not been able to exclude ennui from its precincts.') No, life in the big house, in its circle of trees, is saturated with character: this is, I suppose, the element of the spell. The indefinite ghosts of the past, of the dead who lived here and pursued this same routine of life in these walls add something, a sort of order, a reason for living, to every minute and hour. This is the order, the form of life, the tradition to which big house people still sacrifice much.

From the point of view of the outside Irish world, does the big house justify its existence? I believe it could do so now as never before. As I said, the idea from which these houses sprang was, before everything, a social one. That idea, although lofty, was at first rigid and narrow – but it could extend itself, and it must if the big house is to play an alive part in the alive Ireland of today. What is fine fine about the social idea is that it means the subjugation of the personal to the impersonal. In the interest of good manners and good behaviour people learned to subdue their own feelings. The result was an easy and unsuspicious intercourse, to which everyone brought the best that they had – wit, knowledge, sympathy or personal beauty. Society – or, more simply, the getting-together of people – was meant to be at once a high pleasure and willing discipline, not just an occasion for self-display. The big, or big-seeming, rooms in the big houses are meant for just such pleasures of intercourse. They are meant for something more creative, and gayer, than grumbles, gossip or the tearing to pieces of acquaintances' characters. 'Can we not', big, half-empty rooms seem to ask, 'be, as never before, sociable? Cannot we scrap the past, with its bitter-nesses and barriers, and all meet, throwing in what we have?'

There are difficulties – expensive 'entertainment', for instance, cannot be given now. The distances *are* great – and an impalpable barrier stands between city and country Ireland. But there are buses and there are bicycles; we all eat and drink a good deal less, and would not find it any shame in a host not to offer what he has not got. The world around us is moving so rapidly that it is impossible to be dull-minded; we should all, more than ever, have a great deal to say; every newcomer, with his point of view, becomes an object of quite magnetic interest. Symbolically (though also matter-of-factly) the doors of the big houses stand open all day; it is only regretfully that they are barred up at night. The stranger is welcome, just as much as the friend – the stranger, in fact, *is* the friend if he does not show himself otherwise. But who ever walks in? Is it suspicion, hostility, irony that keep so much of Ireland away from the big house door? If this lasts, we impoverish life all round. Or is it the fear that, if one goes into the big house, one will have to be 'polite'? Well, why not *be* polite – are not humane manners the crown of being human at all? Politeness is not constriction; it is a grace: it is really no worse than an exercise of the imagination on other people's behalf. And are we to cut grace quite out of life?

The big house has much to learn – and it must learn if it is to survive at all. But it also has much to give. The young people who are taking on these big houses, who accept the burden and continue the struggle are not content, now, to live for themselves only; they will not be content, either, to live 'just for the house'. The young cannot afford to be stupid – they expect the houses they keep alive to inherit, in a changed world and under changed conditions, the good life for which they were first built. The good in the new can add to, not destroy, the good in the old. From inside many big houses (and these will be the survivors) barriers are being impatiently attacked. But it must be seen that a barrier has two sides.

1940

EIRE

Difficulties arising from the position of Eire have been on the increase since the start of the war, without being, on either side of the water, at all comprehensively understood. It has been difficult for the people of Britain to see Eire's declaration of neutrality, and resolute abiding by her neutrality, as anything but a passively hostile and in some senses rather inhuman act. They are puzzled by Eire's apparent failure to realize the magnitude of the issues at stake, and puzzled to find a country that cared so much for freedom refusing to add her effort to freedom's war. Pigheadedness, ostrichism, childishness, apathy as to the fate of civilization and even a dishonourable timidity have been charges levelled at Eire from this side. Pictures of Eire existing in indifferent comfort, under a British protection she does not recognize, cannot, as the rigours of war heighten, fail to present themselves to the British mind. The British popular press does not allow such pictures to lapse: the blaze of Dublin city lights (almost Broadway, after the darkness here) suggest an unfeeling ostentation, and hams, steaks and butter are given luscious prominence by journalists who, on flying visits to Dublin, failed to obtain the desired interviews. The number of Germans at present in Eire, their social acceptability and their power were, until lately (when exact figures were given) exaggerated with a good deal of busyness. That the effect of all this has not been more inflammatory is only because Britain, at this juncture, has not much idle angry feeling to spare. But misstatements about Eire, in irresponsible columns, have a serious aspect: they hamper those responsible men who, at both sides of the water, work to maintain an equable atmosphere in which negotiations between the two countries may be carried on. If Anglo-Irish relations stand, as they must stand, this present strain, there are great hopes of something pacific and durable. Time and tact, on which there are many demands already, must go to disposing of rumours hostile to this.

Britain – that is to say, the mass of people in Britain – is not only in the dark as to Eire's intentions, but doubts, apparently, the validity of her will. It is true that a thinking minority in Eire holds that the country would, in her own interests, have done better to enter the war, on the British side, in the autumn of 1939. This reflective opinion, quietly held, is distinct from the emotional opinion of former Unionists, with their tradition of service under the British flag. But this minority recognizes its own extreme smallness. It also holds that Eire, having declared for neutrality, is at this stage in no position to alter her policy. So this minority has to be ruled out: it does not now hope or wish to effect a change. That the overwhelming wish of the people of Eire was in 1939, and is still, for neutrality is an indisputable fact. In Mr de Valera's declaration sounded the almost unanimous voice of his people – a people to whom the *positive* aspects of peace were newer, and seemed more essential, than Britain may realize. The decision – of which the momentousness was recognized – was made on behalf of a people young in political life, not yet adult in citizenship, now only just on the upgrade after internal strife and in no sense fit or ready to enter war. But the decision was not wholly grounded in weakness: it had one aspect of an assertion of strength. It was Eire's first major independent act. As such it had, and keeps, a symbolic as well as moral significance – a significance that identifies, for the people, Eire's neutrality with her integrity. Eire feels as strongly, one might say as religiously, about her neutrality as Britain feels about her part in the war. She has invested in it her natural consciousness. She has taken a stand – a stand, as she sees it, alone. All this should be kept in view when one asks oneself how the Irish, given their disposition, can embrace what seems from the outside such a colourless, timid and negative policy.

Hopes of immunity – and among the unthinking people, which means most of the people, these at the start were many – have been dashed with a sureness that ought to satisfy Eire's most savage critics at this side. Any hopes of war-profit were early dispelled. The country grasped slowly the fact known to its Government – that not only would no one be richer for all this but that one would need all one's energies to survive at all. At present Eire suffers, in all senses, and while her deprivations are far less than Britain's, they have to be met without the heroic stimulus that comes from participation in war. She is outside every circuit; she has not an admirer; she is conscious of a cold draught of disapprobation from what she has taken to be America's friendly shore. The suspension of travel between Eire and Britain sets up an abnormal isolation, of which the effects are felt in all departments of life. Accustomed, whether as Eire or Ireland, to being much visited, not only by sportsmen and tourists but by people of cultural sympathies and enquiring mind, the country does not like segregation. Eire's immense sociability, her natural bent to the stranger makes this loss more vital than it might appear. And Eire is as hard to leave, just now, as she is to enter: claustrophobia is the threat to every civilized mind. Society, localized, becomes very intensive: opinions rapidly come to boiling-point. On top of this, the countrysides have been immobilized and the cities slowed down by the disappearance of petrol: private cars – other than those of priests, clergy and doctors – are off the roads; and in the bus services that join up whole tracts of trainless country there have been severe cuts, and threats of more. More adjusted than she had realized to modern tempo, Eire finds it hard to go back to the old.

If this isolation, of and throughout Eire, results in an apparently arrogant hardening of attitude, who can wonder? It is in Eire's power, in the long-term sense, to justify her neutrality: she well may. But, temporarily, some of the measures she takes to guard it are having a rather dwarfing effect. The Censorship is an outstanding example. There is freedom of public speech, but no freedom of reporting. No home criticism of Eire's neutrality, or suggestion that this ever could or should be abandoned, is allowed mention by the press. No award or honour to any Irishman serving with H.M. Forces is allowed to be mentioned – in newspapers – so that, virtually, the hero's country is debarred from its natural pride in him. (The exodus of young Irishmen to enlist, across the Border or across the Channel, has not been stopped; it is officially ignored. The numerous Irishmen serving with the Army, Navy or Air Force may re-enter Eire on leave, in civilian clothes.) Leading articles on the course of the war have to affect a cautious colourlessness – one may deplore no outrage and praise no victory. This does not, one is bound to admit, impair the dispassionate shrewdness of many comments: there have been times in Britain when one could have wished for a more dispassionate press. But the general effect is – the sense of a ban on *feeling*, in a country in which feeling naturally runs high. And, more serious, there is an inhibition of judgement that cannot be good for human development. No fact (with regard to Europe) is withheld, but facts are denied moral context. In the cinemas, the omission of all war scenes from the newsreels gives one the feeling of an invented world – one may watch social functions (not connected with war effort), trotting-races in the sunny Dominions, and one may still watch America drill, and the American warplanes take to the sky. No film drama featuring or hinging on the present war (or even, I understand, the 1914 war) may be shown. And, inevitably, *The Dictator* is not on view. Exception having been taken by the French and German Ministries to Mr Lennox Robinson's dramatization of *Boule de Suif*, the play was withdrawn from the Gate Theatre. As against this, English books on the war and on wartime political theory are available at bookshops and libraries, and English newspapers and periodicals can be obtained on order. *Picture Post* is in constant demand. Shortly, a watch is kept on anything that could be taken as propaganda. But, owing to the (still) common language, the British view of the war is represented, while the German, except in random talk, is not. On the whole, Eire's sequestration from Europe is (for her) the principal ill of her neutrality: it may go to create a national childishness, a lack of grasp on the general scheme of the world.

Compassionate feeling towards war victims there has been no attempt to check: this not only finds all but official expression, but has a number of outlets. The bombing of British civilians inspires horror and pity that are a good deal more than perfunctory. The Coventry raid, in particular, made a profound impression: one southern county raised, by subscription, a mobile canteen for Coventry. (It must be remembered that the name of Coventry has stood out in Eire ever since the I.R.A. bomb affair, and the executions that followed.) There is a wish, particularly in country places, to receive children from England – and this wish extends beyond the children already received – who have been, so far, limited to those of Irish connections or birth. The wish to house British children is more than purely compassionate; it embodies the hope for a future better relationship. 'If the children grew up together,' a countryman said, 'the two countries might grow to be better friends.'

Any German influence in Eire has, very largely, a cultural source. The Nazi encouragement of folk culture runs parallel to activities in Eire that date from the start of the Gaelic League, and the Nazi revivals of racial history and myth, the organizations of *Heimkunst* and song and dance are sometimes held up as a model. Educationists wishing for progress on these lines are impressed. The cultivated middle-class Irish traveller has tended to overshoot Britain: one meets an impregnable ignorance of any advance in British social conditions. To many serious people of the new Eire, at odds with the fatalism of their own land, the Nazi briskness, race-culture and application of method showed (at least until recently) only its admirable side. Also, to the obstructed youth of Eire the idealization of youth makes its appeal. (As against this, there is the temperamental dislike of regimentation in any form.) Again, the Nazi sweep-forward in the first year of the war had, for the imagination of an inactive country, Martian impressiveness – though against this stood the stigma of cruelty. I have met no one who entertained the idea that Eire could really profit from Axis victory – to most minds it seems clear that she would in the end suffer. Factions who might expect to gain for Eire from a severe limitation of Britain's power do not seem to welcome the idea of the concomitant – extension of Axis power to the Irish shore.

Materially, neutral Eire in wartime is far from being the home of comfort and ease. Shortage and insecurity are felt everywhere. Any original fools' paradise is being rapidly broken up. The De Valera government is not unrealistic with regard to home affairs; Mr Lemass, Minister for Supplies, and Dr Ryan, Minister of Agriculture, have issued a succession of biting home truths, directed at self-delusion in any form. Eire has been, and continues to be, warned: not only are luxuries out of the question, but she must look to herself only for her necessities. It is the last hard application of *Sinn Fein*. The situation is grave, and may become desperate if there is not a response in solid national effort. Outside the huge extension of compulsory tillage there is a drive for digging. The acute coal shortage has raised the slogan 'Cut more turf' – but there is a danger that one may strip the bogs. Lack of raw material for the industries threatens unemployment on an alarming scale. The cost of living goes up. Tea is to be closely rationed – and one has to know Eire to know how much this is felt. Butter is (in fact) short – owing to a severe drought in the summer and to reduction, for tillage, of grazing lands. The crowning threat to the country is the outbreak of foot-and-mouth disease – the worst in this century. The stoppage of petrol, by emptying shopping towns, hits trade all round. Everywhere there is sombreness, and anxiety. But there is, with this, a growth of the sense of responsibility, an abandonment of the idea of privilege. Parish Councils work for co-operation, for emergency action, for mutual aid. Factions have come together, and national unity is more than a phrase. The Army shows, with regard to the size of the population, imposing figures; the size and zeal of the Local Security Force – whose junior group has been taken over for training by the Army command – shows citizen readiness to defend the land. While the rights of Eire's neutrality may be questioned, the conviction behind it must be believed.

1941

NOTES ON WRITING A NOVEL

PLOT

ESSENTIAL.   THE PRE-ESSENTIAL.

Plot might seem to be a matter of choice. It is not. The particular plot for the particular novel is something the novelist is driven to. It is what is left after the whittling-away of alternatives. The novelist is confronted, at a moment (or at what appears to be the moment: actually its extension may be indefinite) by the impossibility of saying what is to be said in any other way.

He is forced towards his plot. By what? By 'what is to be said'. What is 'what is to be said'? A mass of subjective matter that has accumulated – impressions received, feelings about experience, distorted results of ordinary observation, and something else – x. This matter is *extra* matter. It is superfluous to the non-writing life of the writer. It is luggage left in the hall between two journeys, as opposed to the perpetual furniture of rooms. It is destined to be elsewhere. It cannot move till its destination is known. Plot is the knowing of destination.

Plot is diction. Action of language, language of action.

Plot is story. It is also 'a story' in the nursery sense = lie. The novel lies, in saying that something happened that did not. It must, therefore, contain uncontradictable truth, to warrant the original lie.

Story involves action. Action towards an end not to be foreseen (by the reader) but also towards an end which, having *been* reached, must be seen to have been from the start inevitable.

Action by whom? The Characters (see CHARACTERS). Action in view of what, and because of what? The 'what is to be said'.

What about the idea that the function of action is to *express* the characters? This is wrong. The characters are there to provide the action. Each character is created, and must only be so created, as to give his or her action (or rather, contributory part in the novel's action) verisimilitude.

What about the idea that plot should be ingenious, complicated – a display of ingenuity remarkable enough to command attention? If more than such a display, what? Tension, or mystification towards tension, are good for emphasis. For their own sakes, bad.

Plot must further the novel towards its object. What object? The non-poetic statement of a poetic truth.

Have not all poetic truths been already stated? The essence of a poetic truth is that no statement of it can be final.

Plot, story, is in itself un-poetic. At best it can only be not anti-poetic. It cannot claim a single poetic licence. It must be reasoned – only from the moment when its none-otherness, its only-possibleness has become apparent. Novelist must always have one foot, sheer circumstantiality, to stand on, whatever the other foot may be doing. (N.B. – Much to be learnt from story telling to children. Much to be learnt from the detective story – especially non-irrelevance. (See RELEVANCE).)

Flaubert's '*Il faut intéresser*'. Stress on manner of telling: keep in mind, 'I will a tale *unfold*'. Interest of watching a dress that has been well packed unpacked from a dress-box. Interest of watching silk handkerchief drawn from conjuror's watch.

Plot must not cease to move forward. (See ADVANCE.) The *actual* speed of the movement must be even. *Apparent* variations in speed are good, necessary, but there must be no actual variations in speed. To obtain those apparent variations is part of the illusion-task of the novel. Variations in texture can be made to give the effect of variations in speed. Why are *apparent* variations in speed necessary? *(a)* For emphasis. *(b)* For non-resistance, or 'give', to the nervous time-variations of the reader. Why is *actual* evenness, non-variation, of speed necessary? For the sake of internal evenness for its own sake. Perfection of evenness = perfection of control. The evenness of the speed should be the evenness inseparable from tautness. The tautness of the taut string is equal (or even) all along and at any part of the string's length.

CHARACTERS

Are the characters, then, to be constructed to formula – the formula pre-decided by the plot? Are they to be drawn, cut out, jointed, wired, in order to be manipulated for the plot?

No. There is no question as to whether this would be right or wrong. It would be impossible. One cannot 'make' characters, only marionettes. The manipulated movement of the marionette is not the 'action' necessary for plot. Characterless action is not action at all, in the plot sense. It is the indivisibility of the act from the actor, and the inevitability of *that* act on the part of *that* actor, that gives action verisimilitude. Without that, action is without force or reason. Forceless, reasonless action disrupts plot. The term 'creation of character' (or characters) is misleading. Characters pre-exist. They are *found*. They reveal themselves slowly to the novelist's perception – as might fellow-travellers seated opposite one in a very dimly-lit railway carriage.

The novelist's perceptions of his characters take place *in the course of the actual writing of the novel*. To an extent, the novelist is in the same position as his reader. But his perceptions should be always just in advance.

The ideal way of presenting character is to invite perception.

In what do the characters pre-exist? I should say, in the mass of matter (see PLOT) that had accumulated before the inception of the novel.

(N.B. – the unanswerability of the question, from an outsider: 'Are the characters in your novel invented, or are they from real life?' Obviously, neither is true. The outsider's notion of 'real life' and the novelist's are hopelessly apart.)

How, then, is the pre-existing character – with its own inner spring of action, its contrarieties – to be made to play a pre-assigned rôle? In relation to character, or characters, once these have been contemplated, *plot* must at once seem over-rigid, arbitrary.

What about the statement (in relation to PLOT) that 'each character is created in order, and only in order, that he or she may supply the required action'? To begin with, strike out 'created'. Better, the character is *recognised* (by the novelist) by the signs he or she gives of unique capacity to act in a certain way, which 'certain way' fulfils a need of the plot.

The character is there (in the novel) for the sake of the action he or she is to contribute to the plot. Yes. But also, he or she exists *outside* the action being contributed to the plot.

Without that existence of the character outside the (necessarily limited) action, the action itself would be invalid.

Action is the simplification (for story purposes) of complexity. For each one act, there are an *x* number of rejected alternatives. It is the palpable presence of the alternatives that gives action interest. Therefore, in each of the characters, while he or she is acting, the play and pull of alternatives must be felt. It is in being seen to be capable of alternatives that the character becomes, for the reader, valid.

Roughly, the action of a character should be unpredictable before it has been shown, inevitable when it has been shown. In the first half of a novel, the unpredictability should be the more striking. In the second half, the inevitability should be the more striking.

(Most exceptions to this are, however, masterpiece-novels. In *War and Peace, L'Education Sentimentale* and *La Recherche du Temps Perdu,* unpredictability dominates up to the end.)

The character's prominence in the novel (pre-decided by the plot) decides the character's range – of alternatives. The novelist must allot (to the point of rationing) psychological space. The 'hero', 'heroine' and 'villain' (if any) are, by agreement, allowed most range. They are entitled, for the portrayal of their alternatives, to time and space. Placing the characters in receding order to their importance to the plot, the number of their alternatives may seem to diminish. What E. M. Forster has called the 'flat' character has no alternatives at all.

The ideal novel is without 'flat' characters.

Characters must *materialize* – i.e., must have a palpable physical reality. They must be not only see-able (visualizable); they must be to be felt. Power to give physical reality is probably a matter of the extent and nature of the novelist's physical sensibility, or susceptibility. In the main, English novelists weak in this, as compared to French and Russians. Why?

Hopelessness of categoric 'description'. Why? Because this is static. Physical personality belongs to action: cannot be separated from it. Pictures must be in movement. Eyes, hands, stature, etc., must appear, and only appear, *in play*. Reaction to physical personality is part of action – love, or sexual passages, only more marked application of this general rule.

(Conrad an example of strong, non-sexual use of physical personality.)

The materialization (in the above sense) of the character for the novelist must be instantaneous. It happens. No effort of will – and obviously no effort of intellect – can induce it. The novelist can *use* a character that has not yet materialized. But the unmaterialized character represents an enemy pocket in an area that has been otherwise cleared. This cannot go on for long. It produces a halt in plot.

When the materialization *has* happened, the chapters written before it happened will almost certainly have to be recast. From the plot point of view, they will be found invalid.

Also, it is essential that for the reader the materialization of the character should begin early. I say begin, because for the *reader* it may, without harm, be gradual.

Is it from this failure, or tendency to fail, in materialization that the English novelist depends so much on engaging emotional sympathy for his characters?

Ruling sympathy out, a novel must contain at least one *magnetic* character. At least one character capable of keying the reader up, as though he (the reader) were in the presence of someone he is in love with. This is not a rule of salesmanship but a pre-essential of *interest*. The character must do to the reader what he has done to the novelist – magnetize towards himself perceptions, sense-impressions, desires.

The unfortunate case is, where the character has, obviously, acted magnetically upon the author, but fails to do so upon the reader.

There must be combustion. Plot depends for its movement on internal combustion.

Physically, characters are almost always copies, or composite copies. Traits, gestures, etc., are searched for in, and assembled from the novelist's memory. Or, a picture, a photograph or the cinema screen may be drawn on. Nothing physical can be *invented*. (Invented physique stigmatizes the inferior novel.) Proust (in last volume) speaks of this assemblage of traits. Though much may be lifted from a specific person in 'real life', no person in 'real life' could supply everything (physical) necessary for the character in the novel. No such person could have just that exact degree of physical intensity required for the character.

Greatness of characters is the measure of the unconscious greatness of the novelist's vision. They are 'true' in so far as he is occupied with poetic truth. Their degrees in realness show the degrees of his concentration.

SCENE –

IS A DERIVATIVE OF PLOT. GIVES ACTUALITY TO PLOT

Nothing can happen nowhere. The locale of the happening always colours the happening, and often, to a degree, shapes it.

Plot having pre-decided what is to happen, scene, scenes, must be so found, so chosen, as to give happening the desired force.

Scene, being physical, is, like the physical traits of the characters, generally a copy, or a composite copy. It, too, is assembled – out of memories which, in the first place, may have had no rational connection with one another. Again, pictures, photographs, the screen are sources of supply. Also dreams.

Almost anything drawn from 'real life' – house, town, room, park, landscape – will almost certainly be found to require *some* distortion for the purposes of the plot. Remote memories, already distorted by the imagination, are most useful for the purposes of scene. Unfamiliar or once-seen places yield more than do familiar, often-seen places.

Wholly invented scene is as unsatisfactory (thin) as wholly invented physique for a character.

Scene, much more than character, is inside the novelist's conscious power. More than any other constituent of the novel, it makes him conscious *of* his power.

This can be dangerous. The weak novelist is always, compensatorily, scene-minded. (Jane Austen's economy of scene-painting, and her abstentions from it in what might be expected contexts, could in itself be proof of her mastery of the novel.)

Scene is only justified in the novel where it can be shown, or at least felt, to act upon action or character. In fact, where it has dramatic use.

Where not intended for dramatic use, scene is a sheer slower-down. Its staticness is a dead weight. It cannot make part of the plot's movement by being shown *in play*. (Thunderstorms, the sea, landscape flying past car or railway-carriage windows are not scene but *happenings*.)

The deadeningness of straight and prolonged 'description' is as apparent with regard to scene as it is with regard to character. Scene must be evoked. For its details relevance (see RELEVANCE) is essential. Scene must, like the characters, not fail to materialize. In this it follows the same law – instantaneous for the novelist, gradual for the reader.

In 'setting a scene' the novelist directs, or attempts to direct, the reader's visual imagination. He must allow for the fact that the reader's memories will not correspond with his own. Or, at least, not at all far along the way.

DIALOGUE

MUST (1) FURTHER PLOT. (2) EXPRESS CHARACTER.
Should not on any account be a vehicle for ideas for their own sake.
Ideas only permissible where they provide a key to the character who
expresses them.

Dialogue requires more art than does any other constituent of the
novel. Art in the *celare artem* sense. Art in the trickery, self-justifying
distortion sense. Why? Because dialogue must appear realistic
without being so. Actual realism – the lifting, as it were, of passages
from a stenographer's take-down of a 'real life' conversation –
would be disruptive. Of what? Of the illusion of the novel. In 'real
life' everything is diluted; in the novel everything is condensed.

What are the realistic qualities to be imitated (or faked) in novel
dialogue? – Spontaneity. Artless or hit-or-miss arrival at words used.
Ambiguity (speaker not sure, himself, what he means). Effect of
choking (as in engine): more to be said than can come through.
Irrelevance. Allusiveness. Erraticness: unpredictable course.
Repercussion.

What must novel dialogue, behind mask of these faked realistic
qualities, really be and do? It must be pointed, intentional, relevant.
It must crystallize situation. It must express character. It must
advance plot.

During dialogue, the characters confront one another. The confrontation is in itself an occasion. Each one of these occasions,
throughout the novel, is unique. Since the last confrontation, something has changed, advanced. What is being said is the effect of
something that has happened; at the same time, what is being said *is
in itself something happening*, which will, in turn, leave its effect.

Dialogue is the ideal means of showing what is between the
characters. It crystallizes relationships. It *should*, ideally, so be
effective as to make analysis or explanation of the relationships
between the characters unnecessary.

Short of a small range of physical acts – a fight, murder, love-
making – dialogue is the most vigorous and visible inter-action of
which characters in a novel are capable. Speech is what the characters *do to each other*.

Dialogue provides means for the psychological materialization of
the characters. It should short-circuit description of mental traits.
Every sentence in dialogue should be descriptive of the character
who is speaking. Idiom, tempo, and shape of each spoken sentence
should be calculated by novelist, towards this descriptive end.

Dialogue is the first case of the novelist's need for notation from real life. Remarks or turns of phrase indicatory of class, age, degree of intellectual pretension, *ideés reçues*, nature and strength of governing fantasy, sexual temperament, persecution-sense or acumen (fortuitous arrival at general or poetic truth) should be collected. (N.B. – Proust, example of this semi-conscious notation and putting to use of it.)

All the above, from *class* to *acumen*, may already have been established, with regard to each character, by a direct statement by the novelist to the reader. It is still, however, the business of dialogue to show these factors, or qualities in play.

There must be present in dialogue – i.e., in each sentence spoken by each character – *either (a)* calculation, or *(b)* involuntary self-revelation.

Each piece of dialogue *must* be 'something happening'. Dialogue *may* justify its presence by being 'illustrative' – but this secondary use of it must be watched closely, challenged. Illustrativeness can be stretched too far. Like straight description, it then becomes static, a dead weight – halting the movement of the plot. The 'amusing' for its *own* sake, should above all be censored. So should infatuation with any idiom.

The functional use of dialogue for the plot must be the first thing in the novelist's mind. Where functional usefulness cannot be established, dialogue must be left out.

What is this functional use? That of a bridge.

Dialogue is the thin bridge which must, from time to time, carry the entire weight of the novel. Two things to be kept in mind – *(a)* the bridge is there to permit *advance, (b)* the bridge must be strong enough for the weight.

Failure in any one piece of dialogue is a loss, at once to the continuity and the comprehensibility of the novel.

Characters should, on the whole, be under rather than over articulate. What they *intend* to say should be more evident, more striking (because of its greater inner importance to the plot) than what they arrive at *saying*.

ANGLE

The question of *angle* comes up twice over in the novel.

Angle has two senses – *(a)* visual *(b)* moral.

(a) Visual Angle. This has been much discussed – particularly I think by Henry James. Where is the camera-eye to be located? (1) In

the breast or brow of *one* of the characters? This is, of course, simplifying and integrating. But it imposes on the novel the limitations of the 'I' – whether the first person is explicitly used or not. Also, with regard to any matter that the specific character does not (cannot) know, it involves the novelist in long cumbrous passages of cogitation, speculation and guesses. E.g. – of any character other than the specific (or virtual) 'I' it must always be 'he appeared to feel', 'he could be seen to see', rather than 'he felt', 'he saw'. (2) In the breast or brow of a succession of characters? This is better. It *must*, if used, involve very careful, considered division of the characters, by the novelist, in the *seeing* and the *seen*. Certain characters gain in importance and magnetism by being only *seen*: this makes them more romantic, fatal-seeming, sinister. In fact, no character in which these qualities are, for the plot, essential should be allowed to enter the *seeing* class. (3) In the breast or brow of omniscient story-teller (the novelist)? This, though appearing naive, would appear best. The novelist should retain right of entry, at will, into any of the characters: their memories, sensations and thought-processes should remain his, to requisition for appropriate use. What conditions 'appropriateness'? The demands of the plot. Even so, the novelist must not lose sight of point made above – the gain in necessary effect, for some characters, of their remaining *seen* – their remaining closed, apparently, even to the omniscience of the novelist.

The cinema, with its actual camera-work, is interesting study for the novelist. In a good film, the camera's movement, angle and distance have all worked towards one thing – the fullest possible realization of the director's idea, the completest possible surrounding of the subject. Any trick is justified if it adds a statement. With both film and novel, plot is the pre-imperative. The novelist's relation to the novel is that of the director's relation to the film. The cinema, cinema-going, has no doubt built up in novelists a great authoritarianism. This seems to me good.

(b) Moral Angle. This too often means, pre-assumptions – social, political, sexual, national, aesthetic, and so on. These may all exist, sunk at different depths, in the same novelist. Their existence cannot fail to be palpable; and their nature determines, more than anything else, the sympatheticness or antipatheticness of a given novel to a given circle of readers.

Pre-assumptions are bad. They limit the novel to a given circle of readers. They cause the novel to act immorally *on* that given circle. (The lady asking the librarian for a 'nice' novel to take home is, virtually, asking for a novel whose pre-assumptions will be identical with her own.) Outside the given circle, a novel's pre-assumptions must invalidate it for all other readers. The increasingly bad smell of most pre-assumptions probably accounts for the growing prestige of the detective story: the detective story works on the single, and universally acceptable, pre-assumption that an act of violence is anti-social, and that the doer, in the name of injured society, must be traced.

Great novelists write without pre-assumption. They write from outside their own nationality, class or sex.

To write thus should be the ambition of any novelist who wishes to state poetic truth.

Does this mean he must have no angle, no moral view-point? No, surely. Without these, he would be (*a*) incapable of maintaining the *conviction* necessary for the novel (*b*) incapable of *lighting* the characters, who to be seen at all must necessarily be seen in a moral light.

From what source, then, must the conviction come? and from *what* morality is to come the light to be cast on the characters?

The conviction must come from certainty of the validity of the truth the novel is to present. The 'moral light' has not, actually, a moral source; it is moral (morally powerful) according to the strength of its power of revelation. Revelation of what? The virtuousness or non-virtuousness of the action of the character. What is virtue in action? Truth in action. Truth by what ruling, in relation to what? Truth by the ruling of, and in relation to, the inherent poetic truth that the novel states.

The presence, and action, of the poetic truth is the motive (or motor) morality of the novel.

The direction of the action of the poetic truth provides – in fact, *is* – the moral angle of the novel. If he remains with that truth in view, the novelist has no option as to his angle.

The action, or continuous line of action, of a character is 'bad' in so far as it runs counter to, resists, or attempts to deny, the action of the poetic truth. It is predisposition towards such action that constitutes 'badness' in a character.

'Good' action, or 'goodness' in the character from predisposition towards such action, is movement along with, expressive of and contributory to, the action of the poetic truth.

If the novelist's moral angle is (*a*) decided by recognition of the poetic truth, and (*b*) maintained by the necessity of stating the truth by showing the truth's action, it will be, as it should be, impersonal. It will be, and (from the 'interest' point of view) will be able to stand being, pure of pre-assumptions – national, social, sexual, etc.

(N.B. – 'Humour' is the weak point in the front against pre-assumptions. Almost all English humour shows social (sometimes, now, backed by political) pre-assumptions. (Extreme cases – that the lower, or employed, classes are quaint or funny – that aristocrats, served by butlers, are absurd. National pre-assumptions show in treatment of foreigners.)

ADVANCE

It has been said that plot must advance; that the underlying (or inner) speed of the advance must be even. How is this arrived at?

(1) Obviously, first, by the succession, the succeedingness, of events or happenings. It is to be remembered that *everything* put on record at all – an image, a word spoken, an interior movement of thought or feeling on the part of a character – is an event or happening. These proceed out of one another, give birth to one another, in a continuity that must be (*a*) obvious, (*b*) unbroken.

(2) Every happening cannot be described, stated. The reader must be made to feel that what has not been described or stated has, none the less, happened. How? By the showing of subsequent events or happenings whose source *could* only have been in what has not actually been stated. Tuesday is Tuesday by virtue of being the day following Monday. The stated Tuesday must be shown as a derivative of the unstated Monday.

(3) For the sake of emphasis, time must be falsified. But the novelist's consciousness of the subjective, arbitrary and emotional nature of the falsification should be evident to the reader. Against this falsification – in fact, increasing the force of its effect by contrast – a clock should be heard always impassively ticking away at the same speed. The passage of time, and its demarcation, should be a factor in plot. The either concentration or even or uneven spacing-out of events along time is important.

The statement 'Ten years had passed', or the statement, 'It was now the next day' – each of these is an event.

(4) Characters most of all promote, by showing, the advance of the plot. How? By the advances, from act to act, in their action. By their showing (by emotional or physical changes) the effects both of action and of the passage of time. The diminution of the character's alternatives shows (because it is the work of) advance – by the end of a novel the character's alternatives, many at the beginning, have been reduced to almost none. In the novel, everything that happens

happens either *to* or *because* of one of the characters. By the end of the novel, the character has, like the silk worm at work on the cocoon, spun itself out. Completed action is marked by the exhaustion (from one point of view) of the character. Throughout the novel, each character is expending potentiality. This expense of potentiality must be felt.

(5) Scene promotes, or contributes to, advance by its *freshness*. Generically, it is fresh, striking, from being unlike the scene before. It is the new 'here and now'. Once a scene ceases to offer freshness, it is a point-blank enemy to advance. Frequent change of scene *not* being an imperative of the novel – in fact, many novels by choice, and by wise choice, limiting themselves severely in this matter – how is there to continue to be freshness? By means of ever-differing presentation. Differing because of what? Season of year, time of day, effects of a happening (e.g., with house, rise or fall in family fortunes, an arrival, a departure, a death), beholding character's mood. At the first presentation, the *scene* has freshness; afterwards, the freshness must be in the *presentation*. The same scene can, by means of a series of presentations, each having freshness, be made to ripen, mature, to actually advance. The *static* properties in scene can be good for advance when so stressed as to show advance by contrast – advance on the part of the characters. Striking 'unchangingness' gives useful emphasis to change. Change should not be a factor, at once, in *both* scene and character: either unchanged character should see, or be seen, against changed scene, or changed character should see, or be seen, against unchanged scene. *Two* changes, obviously cancel each other out, and would cancel each other's contribution to the advance of plot.

RELEVANCE

Relevance – the question of it – is the headache of novel-writing.

As has been said, the model for relevance is the well-constructed detective story: nothing is 'in' that does not tell. But the detective story is, or would appear to be, simplified by having *fact* as its kernel. The detective story makes towards concrete truth; the novel makes towards abstract truth.

With the detective story, the question 'relevant to *what?*' can be answered by the intelligence. With the novel, the same question must constantly, and in every context, be referred to the intuition. The intelligence, in a subsequent check over, may detect, but cannot itself put right, blunders, lapses or false starts on the part of the intuition.

In the notes on Plot, Character, Scene and Dialogue, everything has come to turn, by the end, on relevance. It is seen that all other relevances are subsidiary to the relevance of the plot – i.e., the relevance to itself that the plot demands. It is as contributory, in fact relevant, to plot that character, scene and dialogue are examined. To be perfectly contributory, these three must be perfectly relevant. If character, scene or dialogue has been weakened by anything irrelevant *to itself*, it can only be imperfectly relevant – which must mean, to a degree disruptive – to the plot.

The main hope for character (for each character) is that it should be magnetic – i.e., that it should *attract* its parts. This living propensity of the character to assemble itself, to integrate itself, to make itself in order to *be* itself will not, obviously, be resisted by the novelist. The magnetic, or magnetizing, character can be trusted as to what is relevant *to itself*.The trouble comes when what is relevant to the character is found to be not relevant to the plot. At this point, the novelist must adjudicate. It is possible that the character may be right; it is possible that there may be some flaw in the novelist's sense of what is relevant to the plot.

Again, the character may, in fact must, decide one half of the question of relevance in dialogue. The character attracts to itself the right, in fact the only possible, idiom, tempo and phraseology for *that* particular character in speech. In so far as dialogue is *illustrative*, the character's, or characters', pull on it must not be resisted.

But in so far as dialogue must be 'something happening' – part of action, a means of advancing plot – the other half of the question of dialogue-relevance comes up. Here, the pull from the characters may conflict with the pull from the plot. Here again the novelist must adjudicate. The recasting and recasting of dialogue that is so often necessary is, probably, the search for ideal compromise.

Relevance in scene is more straightforward. Chiefly, the novelist must control his infatuation with his own visual power. No non-contributory image, must be the rule. Contributory to what? To the mood of the 'now', the mood that either projects or reflects action. It is a good main rule that objects – chairs, trees, glasses, mountains, cushions – introduced into the novel should be stage-properties, necessary for 'business'. It will be also recalled that the well-set stage shows many objects *not* actually necessary for 'business' – but that these have a right to place by being descriptive – explanatory. In a play, the absence of the narrating voice makes it necessary to establish the class, period and general psychology of the characters by means of objects that can be seen. In the novel, such putting of objects to a descriptive (explanatory) use is excellent – alternative to the narrator's voice.

In scene, then, relevance demands either usefulness for action or else explanatory power in what is shown. There is no doubt that with some writers (Balzac, sometimes Arnold Bennett) categoricalness, in the presentation of scene, is effective. The aim is, usually, to suggest, by multiplication and exactitude of detail, either a scene's material oppressiveness or its intrinsic authority. But in general, for the purposes of most novelists, the number of objects genuinely necessary for explanation will be found to be very small.

Irrelevance, in any part, is a cloud and a drag on, a weakener of, the novel. It dilutes meaning. Relevance crystallises meaning.

The novelist's – any writer's – object is, to whittle down his meaning to the exactest and finest possible point. What, of course, is fatal is when he does not know what he does mean: he has no point to sharpen.

Much irrelevance is introduced into novels by the writer's vague hope that at least some of this *may* turn out to be relevant, after all. A good deal of what might be called provisional writing goes to the first drafts of first chapters of most novels. At a point in the novel's progress, relevance becomes clearer. The provisional chapters are then recast.

The most striking fault in work by young or beginning novelists, submitted for criticism, is irrelevance – due either to infatuation or indecision. To direct such an author's attention to the imperative of relevance is certainly the most useful – and possibly the only – help that can be given.

1945

OUT OF A BOOK

I know that I have in my make-up layers of synthetic experience, and that the most powerful of my memories are only half true.

Reduced to the minimum, to the what did happen, my life would be unrecognizable by me. Those layers of fictitious memory densify as they go deeper down. And this surely must be the case with everyone else who reads deeply, ravenously, unthinkingly, sensuously, as a child. The overlapping and haunting of life by fiction

began, of course, before there was anything to be got from the
printed page; it began from the day one was old enough to be told a
story or shown a picture book. It went on up to the age when a
bookish attitude towards books began to be inculcated by education.
The young person is then thrown out of Eden; for evermore his brain
is to stand posted between his self and the story. Appreciation of
literature is the end of magic: in place of the virgin susceptibility to
what is written he is given taste, something to be refined and trained.

Happily, the Eden, like a natal climate, can be unconsciously
remembered, and the magic stored up in those years goes on
secreting under today's chosen sensations and calculated thoughts.
What entered the system during childhood remains; and remains
indistinguishable from the life of those years because it *was* that
greater part of the life. Probably children, if they said what they
thought, would be much franker about the insufficiency of so-called
real life to the requirements of those who demand to be really alive.
Nothing but the story can meet the untried nature's need and
capacity for the whole. Of course one cannot narrow down children
to the reading child; but I could not as a child, and I cannot now,
conceive what the non-reading child must be like inside. Outdoor
children were incomprehensible to me when I was their age, and I
still find them dull; I could not, and cannot, find out what makes
them do what they do, or why they like what they like; and of such
children now they are grown up I can only say that I cannot conceive
what they remember, if they do remember – for how can even the
senses carry imprints when there was no story? The non-reading
active children were not stupid; they had their senses. Nor was it the
clever children who read most, or who were at any rate the ones who
inhaled fiction – quite apart there were always the horrible little
students, future grown-ups, who pursued knowledge. The light-
headed reading child and the outdoor child had more in common (in
fact, the life of sensation) than either had with the student. Readers
of my kind were the heady ones, the sensationalists – recognizing one
another at sight we were banded together inside a climate of our
own. Landscapes or insides of houses or streets or gardens, outings
or even fatigue duties all took the cast of the book we were
circulating at the time; and the reading made of us an electric ring.
Books were story or story-poetry books: we were unaware that there
could be any others.

Some of the heady group remained wonderfully proof against
education: having never graduated these are the disreputable grown-
ups who snap up shiny magazines and garner and carry home from

libraries fiction that the critics ignore. They read as we all once read –
because they must: without fiction, either life would be insufficient
or the winds from the north would blow too cold. They read as we all
read when we were twelve; but unfortunately the magic has been
adulterated; the dependence has become ignominious – it becomes
an enormity, inside the full-sized body, to read without the brain.
Now the stories they seek go on being children's stories, only with
sex added to the formula; and somehow the addition queers everything. These readers, all the same, are the great malleable bulk, the
majority, the greater public – hence best-sellers, with their partly
artful, partly unconscious play on a magic that has gone stale. The
only above-board grown-up children's stories are detective stories.

No, it is not only our fate but our business to lose innocence, and
once we have lost that it is futile to attempt to picnic in Eden. One
kind of power to read, or power that reading had over us, is gone.
And not only that: it is a mistake to as much as re-open the books of
childhood – they are bare ruined choirs. Everything has evaporated
from those words, leaving them meaningless on the page. This is the
case, for me, even with Dickens – I cannot read him now because I
read him exhaustively as a child. Though I did not in those years read
all his books, I cannot now read any that I did not read then – there is
no more oxygen left, for me, anywhere in the atmosphere of his
writing. The boredom I seem to feel as I pursue the plots is, really, a
flagging of my intellect in this (by me) forever used up and devitalized
air. I came to an end with Dickens when I had absorbed him into
myself.

Yes, one stripped bare the books of one's childhood to make
oneself – it is inevitable that there should be nothing left when one
goes back to them. The fickleness of children and very young persons
shocks their elders – children abandon people, for instance, without
a flicker, with a simplicity that really ought not to be hurting: the
abandoned one has been either a 'best' friend or an object of hero-
worship, and the more emotionally fruitful and fanciful the relationship, the more complete the break. 'Where is So-and-so these days? I
don't seem to have heard anything about him (or her) for a long time.
Haven't you two got any more plans?' – 'Oh, I can't be bothered.'
What applies to people applies to books, and for the same reason:
everything that was wanted has been taken; only the husk or, still
worse, mortifying repetition remains. The child is on the make –
rapacious, mobile and single-minded. If the exhausted book survives
physical abandonment – being given away or left out in the garden in
the rain – it languishes on in its owner's indifferent keeping;

however, once memory and sentiment have had time to set in and gather about it, it is safe. I still keep a row of books I loved as a child – but I neither wish nor dare to touch them.

What do I mean by those books making myself? In the first place, they were power-testing athletics for my imagination – cross-country runs into strange country, sprints, long and high jumps. It was exhilarating to discover what one could feel: the discovery itself was an advance. Then, by successively 'being' a character in every book I read, I doubled the meaning of everything that happened in my otherwise constricted life. Books introduced me to, and magnified, desire and danger. They represented life, with a conclusiveness I had no reason to challenge, as an affair of mysteries and attractions, in which each object or place or face was in itself a volume of promises and deceptions, and in which nothing was impossible. Books made me see everything that I saw either as a symbol or as having its place in a mythology – in fact, reading gave bias to my observations of everything in the between-times when I was not reading. And obviously, the characters in the books gave prototypes under which, for evermore, to assemble all living people. This did not by any means simplify people for me; it had the reverse effect, and I was glad that it should – the characters who came out of my childish reading to obsess me were the incalculable ones, who always moved in a blur of potentialities. It appeared that nobody who mattered was capable of being explained. Thus was inculcated a feeling for the dark horse. I can trace in all people whom I have loved a succession from book characters – not from one only, from a fusion of many. 'Millions of strange shadows on you tend.'

Also the expectation, the search, was geographic. I was and I am still on the look out for places where something happened: the quivering needle swings in turn to a prospect of country, a town unwrapping itself from folds of landscape or seen across water, or a significant house. Such places are haunted – scenes of acute sensation for someone, vicariously me. My identity, so far as I can pin it down at all, resides among these implacable likes or dislikes, these subjections to magnetism spaced out between ever-widening lacunae of indifference. I feel certain that if I *could* read my way back, analytically, through the books of my childhood, the clues to everything could be found.

The child lives in the book; but just as much the book lives in the child. I mean that, admittedly, the process of reading is reciprocal; the book is no more than a formula, to be furnished out with images out of the reader's mind. At any age, the reader must come across:

the child reader is the most eager and quick to do so; he not only lends to the story, he flings into the story the whole of his sensuous experience which from being limited is the more intense. Book dishes draw saliva to the mouth; book fears raise gooseflesh and make the palms clammy; book suspense makes the cheeks burn and the heart thump. Still more, at the very touch of a phrase there is a surge of brilliant visual images: the child rushes up the scenery for the story. When the story, as so often happens, demands what has not yet come into stock, indefatigable makeshifts are arrived at – as when a play that calls for elaborate staging is performed by an enterprising little company with scanty equipment and few drop-scenes. Extension (to draw an iceberg out of a fishmonger's ice-block) or multiplication (to make a thin, known wood into a trackless forest) goes on. For castles, gorges, or anything else spectacular out of art or nature, recollections of picture postcards, posters or travel albums are drawn on; and, of course, the child today has amassed a whole further scenic stock from the cinema. This provision of a convincing *where* for the story is a reflex.

For the child, any real-life scene that has once been sucked into the ambiance of the story is affected, or infected, forever. The road, cross-roads, corner of a wood, cliff, flight of steps, town square, quayside or door in a wall keeps a transmuted existence: it has not only given body to fiction, it has partaken of fiction's body. Such a thing, place or scene cannot again be walked past indifferently; it exerts a pull and sets up a tremor; and it is to indent the memory for life. It is at these points, indeed, that what I have called synthetic experience has its sources. Into that experience come relationships, involving valid emotion, between the child reader and book characters; a residuum of the book will be in all other emotions that are to follow.

In reverse, there are the real-life places – towns, seaports, suburbs of London – unknown to the child, though heard of, which become 'real' through being also in books. For instance, after *David Copperfield* I could not hear either Dover or Yarmouth mentioned, in the most ordinary context, without excitement: I had a line on them. Towns that were in books, and the routes between them travelled by characters, stood out in relief on the neutral map of England. Not a Londoner, I was continuously filling in and starring my map of the environs – at Richmond lived Sir Percy, the Scarlet Pimpernel, and his wife Marguerite, who fainted into a bed of heliotrope in her riverside garden; at Highgate, the Steerforths and Rosa Dartle; at Blackheath and Lewisham, the E. Nesbit children. When I came to read 'Kipps', I was made dizzy by the discovery that I had, for years, been living in two places, Hythe and Folkestone, that were in a book. Historic places one was taken to see meant no more and no less to me than this; history was fiction – it took me a long time to be able to see that it gained anything further from being 'true'.

Though not all reading children grow up to be writers, I take it that most creative writers must in their day have been reading children. All through creative writing there must run a sense of dishonesty and of debt. In fact, is there such a thing, any more, as creative writing? The imagination, which may appear to bear such individual fruit, is rooted in a compost of forgotten books. The apparent choices of art are nothing but addictions, pre-dispositions: where did these come from, how were they formed? The aesthetic is nothing but a return to images that will allow nothing to take their place; the aesthetic is nothing but an attempt to disguise and glorify the enforced return. All susceptibility belongs to the age of magic, the Eden where fact and fiction were the same; the imaginative writer was the imaginative child, who relied for life upon being lied to – and how, now, is he to separate lies from his consciousness of life? If he be a novelist, all his psychology is merely a new parade of the old mythology. We have relied on our childhoods, on the sensations of childhood, because we mistake vividness for purity; actually, the story was there first – one is forced to see that it was the story that apparelled everything in celestial light. It could lead to madness to look back and back for the true primary impression or sensation; those we did ever experience we have forgotten – we only remember that to which something was added. Almost no experience, however much simplified by the distance of time, is to be vouched for as being wholly my own – *did* I live through that, or was I told that it happened, or did I read it? When I write, I am re-creating what was created for me. The gladness of vision, in writing, is my own gladness, but not at my own vision. I may see, for instance, a road running uphill, a skyline, a figure coming slowly over the hill – the approach of the figure is momentous, accompanied by fear or rapture or fear of rapture or a rapture of fear. But who and how is this? Am I sure this is not a figure out of a book?

1946

THE BEND BACK

Contemporary writing retreats from the present-day. Or such, at any rate, is the charge against it. One may suggest that readers are not so docile as to be led where they do not want to go. In making the past their subject, writers respond instinctively to a general wish – they react to, voice, what is in the air around them. Nostalgia is not a literary concoction, it is a prevailing mood – to which, it may be, writers yield too much. Evidently the mood is not confined to a small, hyper-aesthetic or sentimental circle. It must be widespread – for, novels set back in time, picturesque biographies, memoirs, diaries dated long ago, books about old homes, collections of family letters from generations back, are now in universal demand. The past has become identified with what in Ireland we call 'the better days'. Imagination finds it a golden terrain.

What is the matter with us, it may be asked, that we cannot acclimatize ourselves to our own time – to the days in which we are called upon to live? Does our century fail us, or we it? This is 1951, a year in which to reflect: our century has run just half of its course. Has it been from the first mistrusted, cold-shouldered by its children? No, now one comes to think of it, far from that. We have had, for instance, out of America, out of Europe, a fine literature of contemporary sensation. And, the century *was* sung in, during its first decade, in a flush of zest for its progress, its immunity from the older ills, its delights, its ameliorations and its discoveries. In that dawn – as a child of the period may remember – it was considered glory to be alive. 'The better days', if one needed them, were the future. But confidence was broken by 1914: from then on, decline of love for the present went with the loss of faith in it. After 1918, the artist, by general assent, took up the attitude of the critical exile, the psychologically displaced person. Therefore, although that literature of contemporary sensation was produced, it was to remain a literature of sensation only – cerebrally brilliant, but skin-deep, ultimately bodiless in that it lacked soul. Between the world's two wars, that literature ran its course; its failure being that it could not either root down deeply into the imagination or touch the heart. Mystery, loyalty, tenderness shrivelled under its ray. Bright lights glared round the vacuum left by a disillusionment. The key was sophistication –

from which, though fascinated, human nature felt a sort of recoil.

Now, after a second war, with its excoriations, grinding impersonality, obliteration of so many tracks and landmarks, heart and imagination once more demand to be satisfied – to be fed, stabilised, reassured, taught. The demand is, that writers should re-instate the idea of life as liveable, lovable. Can this demand be met only by recourse to life in the past? It at present seems so.

Are we to take it that our own time has been, from the point of view of its inhabitants, irreparably injured – that it shows some loss of vital deficiency? What fails in the air of our present-day that we cannot breathe it; or, at any rate, breathe it with any joy? Why cannot the confidence in living, the engagement with living, the prepossession with living be re-won? One must have the life-illusion. For our forefathers, life seemed to generate the illusion as it went along – however testing the struggle, however harsh the days, people had an attachment to the familiar, an equable attitude to the unknown. The pious called this God's grace. Can it, in our generation, be our fate to see the grace give out, the illusion die? In order to live, we must love life, in one or another form. Do we compromise in this matter of loving life by loving it at one remove – in the past?

There are two routes back to 'the better days': that of direct and that of factitious memory. The former leads to one's own past: childhood. But even direct memory needs stimulants – so, evocative literature plays its part. Witness the multiplication, in almost every country, every language, of books about childhood written for grown-ups. Such books, at their best, recapture sensation in its ideal purity by restoring to us the early morning. We are made to behold a landscape just after sunrise, a tract in which every feature not only stands up gleaming but casts a shadow which is unique, distinct. For the child (or so it appears now) everything was an adventure or a drama; at the same time, there were spaces of lyric happiness. Nothing – or so our re-awakened memory tells us – nothing in childhood went to loss. The semi-mystical topography of childhood seems to be universal, for all who revisit it find the same: the stream, the woods, the thicket hideout, the beach or estuary, the attic or the old barn, the toyshop, the grandmother's treasure box, the 'haunted house', and so on. To the city, even, childhood imparted the elemental mysteries, threats and promises of a countryside: submerged rivers were to be sensed underneath the pavements, elemental rock in the flanks of walls. Best of all, there was emotional simplicity – rebellions perhaps, but (we think) no conflicts. And, framing the whole picture, we see security.

The vocabulary summoned up to recall childhood is, like its topography, universal. The images summoned up are clear-coloured, sensory and, above all, comforting. Books about childhood, having evolved a language common to almost every heart, create meeting-places, valuable common ground, points of contact upon which all types of people can and do converge. In the sharing of pleasure in such books, isolating distances between adult and adult are broken down – just as friends or lovers advance in intimacy by speaking to one another of their younger days. Can one wonder that the author of such a book establishes immediate, almost telepathic, communication with his readers? His subject was general, but he has touched in each reader upon a special chord. In an age when change works so fast, when each change spells so much obliteration, and when differentiation between person and person becomes less, each one of us clings to personal memory as a life-line. One might say, one invests one's identity *in* one's memory. To re-live any moment, acutely, is to be made certain that one not only was but is. Desire to be reminded may be a modern symptom, but it deserves respect: woe to those who abuse it.

The other route to the past (or idea of the past) is factitious memory. That is to say, by art we are made to seem to remember that which we have not actually known. To an extent, the writer of any fiction must bring factitious memory into play. But for the biographer colouring in the background of a long-dead person, or for the novelist pitching his story back in time, the induction of such memory is of first importance. It is a case, here, not of the personal past, which may be evoked, but of the historic past, which must be created – i.e., re-created in terms of art. The reader, led into an unfamiliar region of time, must have a key to his whereabouts slipped to him – as unostentatiously as possible. He must be made to feel familiar with where he is; and, familiarity only grows with liking. The historic landscape – with all that this comprehends in the way of speech, dress, manners, customs, architecture, passions, psychology – must be made not only convincing but attractive. The reader desires to marvel, and must be allowed to marvel; but he desires also to understand. The temptation at once to simplify and stage-light the past of their particular choice seems, for many biographers and historical novelists, irresistible: it is probably less a temptation than an unconscious impulse. A foreign region of time needs, for the average reader, to be 'presented' – which is to say, sympathetically shown. What might be harsh, alien, formidable or shocking about its elements has to be toned down. And, above all, the reader needs to have the illusion that the characters – whether in the biography or the historical novel – are, in spite of picturesque superficial differences, his contemporaries. Contemporaries happier than himself in that they inhabit a golden climate.

The air of the past in the story seems to the visitor crystal clear – unclouded by doubts, hesitations or dullness. And here is major suspense instead of minor anxieties. There is (as there was in childhood) heroic simplification; everything shapes to drama. Colour and beauty, passion and richness, pay themselves out liberally to the hungering reader; moreover, by being in company with those who, either by birth or character, are 'the great', he has human status (including, unconsciously, his own) magnified for him, raised to a higher plane. Intrinsically, the appeal of the past is moral – here are displayed, in action, virtues of boldness we had dreaded to lose. In responding to them, the reader, with gladness, feels the stir of something dormant within himself.

The past of centuries back – with its Courts and rivalries, brocades and jewels, glimmer of corridors, stretches of heath or forest – may be the more spectacular: the 'near' past holds, however, an ultimately more disturbing appeal.

That past is only just over the frontier of living memory; it is the epoch of our immediate forebears. It is the youth of our parents, the prime of our grand-parents and great-grand-parents, which most subtly seem to have stolen our hearts away. A particular spell is exercised by the nineteenth century; while we may think ourselves lucky in being clear of the tabus and restrictions of Victorianism, we hanker after its solidness, its faith, its energetic self-confidence, its domestic glow. America has, to look back on, the dauntless hardiness of the pioneer days; England dwells on a picture of exuberance in a settled scene – unspoiled countrysides, tribes of ruddy-faced children raised in manors, parsonages, farmhouses, cottages with roses over the porch. Victorian relics which come to us – the cameo brooch, the fluted pink vase, the family album, the beaded footstool – seem to carry locked in themselves some virtue. That day-before yesterday represents at once the last and the best of the old order.

So it seems. . . . We must not shy at the fact that we cull the past from fiction rather than history, and that art, out of the very necessity to compose a picture, cannot but eliminate, edit – and so, falsify. Raw history, in its implications, is unnerving; and, even so, it only chronicles the survivors. A defeat accompanied every victory; faiths failed; millions went under leaving behind no trace. If the greater part of the past had not been, mercifully, forgotten, the effect upon our modern sensibility would be unbearable: it would not be only injustice and bloodshed that we should have to remember but the dismay, the apathy, the brutalising humiliations of people for whom there was no break. How few, all down history, have been the favoured few – of the past as a whole we might say, 'We are well out of it!' The human dilemma, the dilemma inherent in being human, was at no time less than it is now. As things are, the past is veiled from us by illusion – our own illusion. It is that which we seek. It is not the past but the idea of the past which draws us.

To say that the idea has been planted upon us, that the illusion has been knowingly stimulated, would not be quite true. There *has* been considerable literary exploitation – which might (or might not) be defended by saying that readers who expose their daydreams to exploitation deserve no better. But among serious writers there has been no conspiracy – if these turn to the past it is because they are themselves magnetized to the subject. The writer's subject, once found (or, more exactly, once it has found him) inevitably kindles the matter and manner of his writing. Creative art has one sort of fault in its strength: it cannot but illuminate, intensify and to a degree transmute what it dwells upon. The writer may not mean to idealize; but his vision, acting upon the reader, has that effect. What might be called involuntary idealization is most marked in our day, when so much prose shows a poetic trend – when, indeed, in our writing romanticism has all but reached the high-water mark. The romantic never has cared for things as they are.

This invites reflection. Do we, perhaps, consider our love for the past to be a more alarming, because more strictly contemporary, symptom than it is? Looking back through romantic literature – poetry, novels, essays – do we not trace an unbroken nostalgic vein? At what time has the imaginative, sentient human being ever been at home in his surroundings? Have not poets immortalized themselves by their expression of the immortal longing? Have not children been influenced from the start by those classic openings of fairy tales, the 'once upon a time' and the 'a long time ago'? Where one did not crave other times, one craved other lands – the unexplored, the distant, the little-known. Mythical regions once held mythical promise. Now, the whole world is mapped out in routes and railways, networked by press and radio: there are no 'other lands', only other countries – of which we know too much. Accordingly, we have shifted our desire for the ideal 'elsewhere' from space to time. In itself the desire is not new.

Not new – but in us so widespread, so conscious, so articulate that we have come to ask ourselves if it be a malady. It may be aggravated to malady-point by our disrelish for and uneasiness in the present – the aching, bald uniformity of our urban surroundings, their soulless rawness. Where is the eye to linger, where is fancy to dwell? No associations, no memories have had time to gather around the new soaring blocks of flats, the mushroom housing-estates. And, will they ever do so? – where shall they find a foothold? Nothing rustles, nothing casts a feathery shadow: there is something frightening about the very unhauntedness of 'functional' rooms. Atmosphere has been conditioned out of the air. Nor even, among all this oppressiveness of brick and concrete, do we feel secure – all this, in a split second, could become nothing. Nor, stacked and crowded upon one another in our living and moving, do we feel in contact: personal isolation has increased.

As creatures of feeling, we register this dismay. Is it not, all the same, something to *be* a creature of feeling? Our power to idealize, to desire, spells life in us. We perceive the past in terms of vital glittering moments; but, if we had not in ourselves experienced such moments, how should we recognise them? Can one really envisage that which one has not (in one form or another) known? Unconsciously, we have built up our idea of the past out of contemporary images and sensations, at their most delightful. It is something to have accumulated that store – we cannot have fared so badly, after all! What of our unacknowledged debt to the present-day?

Is this an age of frustration – or simply one in which many more people ask more of life? Education, literacy, discussion, aesthetic experiences of all kinds, have widened the boundaries of our self-consciousness. At its best, democracy breeds the sentient person – it is in the nature of such a person to seek fulfilment. His mind, his heart, his senses stand tuned in, waiting for intimations. We are more aware than were our forefathers of dissatisfactions – may this not, however, mean that awareness, rather than dissatisfactions, has increased? We give more expression to longings because we grow more articulate. More and more of us are being cast in the mould of those to whom no present time ever has been ideal. Yet, our predecessors not only came to terms with their own existence but extracted pleasure from it – of that we have evidence, not only major art but in the letters, journals, memoirs which come our way. All those sublime moments, great or little, were victories – one must remember that. Out of existence, with all its imperfections, mankind has continued to forge something. Are we to lose that art by which, in the past, people triumphed over *their* present-day?

Let us examine the stuff of our own time to see if, through it also, there does not run some gold vein. It is our writers who must begin the search, but how are they to lead if we will not follow? Our time, being part of all time, holds within it something essential which needs divining, perceiving. Let us await the writer who, by genius in that, can touch awake the genius in us.

1950

DISLOYALTIES

'Isn't disloyalty as much the writer's virtue', asks Graham Greene, 'as loyalty is the soldier's?' Taken out of its context, the remark is startling: it has place in a triangular correspondence, in which the contemporary artist's relation to society is discussed. From the letters, whose range is fairly wide, emerge two main topics: attitude and morality. Graham Greene, expanding the sentence quoted, goes on to say, 'Loyalty confines us to accepted opinions: loyalty forbids us to comprehend sympathetically our dissident fellows; but disloyalty encourages us to roam experimentally through any human mind; it gives to the novel the extra dimension of sympathy.'

Few novelists, few understanding critics would dispute this, upon a second thought. The public may hesitate for a while longer – do we not, it may be inquired, look to creative writers to be the guardians and spokesmen of human values? Do they propose to swerve, to betray, default? On his side, the writer might and probably should agree that human values are his concern, and that in so far as to register and to voice these makes him their guardian, he is their guardian. But the point is, also, that for him they are neither abstractions nor standing points; he perceives them to be in their nature not fixed but shifting. He cannot but be aware of the endlessness of human variation and dissonance, the doublings and twistings of mankind under the grip of circumstance and the pressure of life. The novelist's subject is not society, not the individual as a social unit, but the individual as he himself is, behind the social mask. As such, his peculiarities are infinite. If the novel is to continue vital, the 'extra dimension of sympathy' must be found.

This, a writer's concept of writers' virtue, may seem to conflict with the concept held by the public mind. Never has loyalty, on the face of it, been ranked higher than it is today: it has come to be an essential of our survival – so much so that to fail in any adherence undermines, it is felt, some part of civilization. It should be noted that Graham Greene does not denounce adherences or attack their merit – is not the *soldier's* virtue loyalty? What he has pointed out is, the danger to the writer of anything which may exercise a restrictive and ultimately a blinding hold. His ideal is, to be at once disabused and susceptible, and for ever mobile. This is not easily come at; for, indeed, the writer has in an even greater degree than his fellow man the disposition to be attached – ideas, creeds, persons and ways of life first magnetize then begin to absorb him. By temperament he has a high potential of that extreme of loyalty, fanaticism. To break off any adherence involves dismay, pain, loneliness and the sense of loss. It is not for him a matter of infidelity but of abstinence – one cannot be clear enough as to the distinction between the two. In turning away from resting-places, from lighted doorways, to pursue his course into darker country, he carries with him a burden of rejected alternatives and troubling regrets. Graham Greene is advocating the harder road.

Restrictive loyalties, with their danger, vary in their temptation to the writer according to his personal cast or temperament. The division of novelists into types or kinds is misleading; so many cannot be classed. No creative person is purely intellectual – one may, however, distinguish the intellectual novelist, building upon a framework of ideas, from the aesthetic-intuitive, working mainly on memories and impressions. In one case, the seat of integrity is the brain; in the other, feeling. For the former are involved constant speculation, cognizance of his own day, scrutiny of current science and thought, consideration of history, measurement of experience. For such a mind, the arrival at any position is important, and abandonment of it constitutes a crisis. Each time the writer disengages himself, convulsively, from a faith or theory, he spreads – and knows that he spreads – disarray in his readers' ranks: he has gainsaid the demand for stability. Does he not, then, it is asked, know his own mind? It is his own mind – and perhaps that only – with its demands and exactions and refusals to compromise, that he knows. He has once more imperilled good faith out of the need for truth – which for ever shifts and changes its form in front of him. It is when he seems most to be trusted that he mistrusts himself – may not his apparent arrival at any standpoint mean no more than a slackening-down of his faculties?

The accounted disloyalties of the thinking writer are at least overt, clear-cut and definite: they manifest themselves in the public view and have taken place, where he himself is concerned, well over the watermark of consciousness. Those of the intuitive writer are more subtle, gradual, and are moreover to him the more disturbing in that they may be evident only to himself. For in this case the sphere of the art is feeling. The artist of this kind is often the child of a background, the product of an intensive environment – racial, local or social. What he creates takes character from his own strongly personal and often also inherited sense of life. His loyalties are involuntary and inborn – not, like the intellectual's of his choice or seeking – and are the more powerful for that. Psychologically if not actually he is a regionalist, in his work relying not only for subject but for atmosphere, texture, colour and flavour upon the particular enclave which has given him birth. In return for the inspiration he owes pieties; his ancestor-worship – however much this may seem to be diluted by irony – is fundamental. His sensibility, during the first of his working years, repays its sheltering by making impressive aesthetic growth. He has not yet touched the limits or felt the remoteness of his peculiar world.

This cannot continue: gradually the pulse of the art flags, and the writer knows it; or else, he notices in his work that other death symptom which is repetition. Now is the time to make the break, to strike out, to establish at any price the new vital outside communication. He has exhausted his native air – can his imagination learn to breathe another? This crisis, simultaneously felt in his personal being (because of debts and affections) and his aesthetic being is the crux of the feeling writer's career. He cannot free himself from the hereditary influences without the sense of outraging, injuring and betraying them – virtually, it appears to him, he must cease to honour his father and his mother. From the moment he has perceived this, there is no choice – the matter decides itself according to whether he is or is not a valid writer. To the outside world, the effect and outcome of the struggle is not at once apparent – all that may be observed is a hardening or harshening of the manner, or an unexpected tension between the writer and his accustomed subject – for he has not necessarily forsaken the old scenes; what has happened is that he sees them newly. Only the rare reader or the perceptive critic is able to detect the transition book.

The disloyalties of the writer, evidently, are not a privilege; they are a test and a tax. They are the inverse of an ultimate loyalty – to the pursuit, the search, the range of the exploration, the hope of the 'extra dimension', wherein lies truth.

1950

THE ROVING EYE

How, and why, does the writer find the subject – *his* subject, which germinates into play or story, poem or novel? Is this a matter of chance, or of expert calculation? The question, natural enough, is not easy to answer in natural terms – hence, the growth around literary art of a myth or mystery. Writers are not secretive, but they are shy – shy behind the façade they learn to put up, and most shy about what is most simple to them. The fact is, they are of a childishness which could seem incredible, and which is more than half incredible to their thinking selves. The childishness is necessary, fundamental – it involves a perpetual, errant state of desire, wonder, and unexpected reflex. The writer, unlike his non-writing adult friend, has no predisposed outlook; he seldom observes deliberately. He sees what he did not intend to see; he remembers what does not seem wholly possible. Inattentive learner in the schoolroom of life, he keeps some faculty free to veer and wander. His is the roving eye.

By that roving eye is his subject found. The glance, at first only vaguely caught, goes on to concentrate, deepen; becomes the vision. Just what *has* he seen, and why should it mean so much? The one face standing forward out of the crowd, the figure in the distance crossing the street, the glare or shade significant on a building, the episode playing out at the next table, the image springing out of a phrase of talk, the disproportionate impact of some one line of poetry, the reverberation after a street accident or tiny subjective echo of a huge world event, the flare-up of visual memory or of sensuous memory for which can be traced no reason at all – why should this or that be of such importance as to bring all else to a momentous stop? Fate has worked, as in a falling in love – the writer, in fact, first knows he has found his subject by finding himself already obsessed by it. The outcome of obsession is, that he writes – rationalization begins with his search for language. He must (like the child who cannot keep silent) share, make known, communicate what he has seen, or knows. The urgency of what is real to him demands that it should be realized by other people.

It might, it appears, be said that writers do not find subjects: subjects find them. There is not so much a search as a state of open susceptibility. Can, and still more should, the state deliberately be maintained? At the outset it is involuntary, unconscious; when it is less so it loses some of its worth. 'Relax, become blank, be passive' – should one advocate that? No, surely: nothing can happen to an inactive man; life shuns and experience forsakes him. Temperamentally, the writer exists on happenings, on contacts, conflicts, action and reaction, speed, pressure, tension. Were he a contemplative purely, he would not write. His moments of intake are inadvertent; not only that, but they may occur in what seems the very heart of the mêlée. How, then, and in what sense is he to pull out? How shall he keep unstaled his peculiar inner faculty for experience, his awareness of *the* experience, his susceptibility?

The essential is that he be not imposed upon. He must know his own – that is, when it comes to subject. Truth is in his eye, in that roving eye: there are, and should never cease to be, unmistakable moments of recognition. Yet such moments may be daunting and unacceptable – '*Must* this be my subject?' the writer sighs. He is not so young, perhaps; he foresees with dismay endless demands and challenges, a required break with all he knows of technique, a possible inadequacy of his powers, cold critics, a baffled public, a drop in sales. Can there be no alternative? There are, of course, a dozen: lively, factitious, tempting – the deflected writer writes with sinister ease: what he has lost, or that he is lost himself, he may if he is fortunate never know. But the true, abandoned subject takes its revenge.

The outward, apparent tie between writer and subject is not fortuitous. Background, origin, circumstance, the events of life may be found to account, clearly enough, for a writer's trend and predispositions – his choice of scene, his pitch of mood or his view of persons. A man's whole art may be rendered down, by analysis, to variations upon a single theme. A novelist's cast of characters may, from book to book, seem to be repetitions of one another. Or, regional colour lends a sort of rich, enchanted monotony to an entire output. Recurrence of images, the shape and blend of style give to individual writing a sort of signature. But all that is not *subject*: subject remains apart – an inexplicable factor, an inner choice for which no external can yet account. The child, almost any child, is born with the hope that the universe is somehow to be explained: it may be, the writer does not outlive that hope – here and there his eye passes, from clue to clue. Through subject, he offers his explanation. But can he say so – how be as simple as that?

It is for the critic, perhaps, to perceive, and say.

Concentration on any one writer's work almost always ends by exposing a core of naïvety – a core which, once it has been laid bare, seems either infantile or august. There is little *inner* complexity, after all: the apparent outer complexity of the art has been little more than the effort towards expression. Somewhere within the pattern, somewhere behind the words, a responsive, querying innocence stays intact. There is, there must be, always the husk of thought. Intellectually, the writer ought to desire and must expect to confront in his critic one who is his intellectual match; it may be, his intellectual senior. Mind meets mind: style must stand up to hard analysis; structure at once reveals and defies its faults; method is there to sustain query; imagery is to be sifted through. All the same, there comes a point in the judgement process when intellect brings itself to a natural stop: the final value is rated by intuition. The vital test is the sense of truth in the vision – its clearness, its spontaneity, its authority. In the case of the giant writer there is no doubt; though there lingers an element of surprise – Balzac and Tolstoy, Faulkner and Mauriac confound as well as command us, by their discoveries. Unsuspected meaning in everything shines out; yet, we have the familiar re-sheathed in mystery. Nothing is negative; nothing is commonplace. For is it not that the roving eye, in its course, has been tracing for us the lineaments of a fresh reality? Something has been beheld for the first time.

1952

ON NOT RISING TO THE OCCASION

Rising to the occasion: I do not remember that it was ever *called* that. No, I am sure it was not. There was no name for what one was asked to do – in a way, this made it all the more ominous. A name, the grown-ups may have thought, would have made too much of it – pandered too much to juvenile self-importance. Children, in my Edwardian childhood, were decidedly played down rather than played up. 'Just be natural' – they used to say, before the occasion; 'nobody wants you to show off.' What a blow to ambition – what a slap in the face! 'Be natural'; really, what a demand!

PLEASURE, GRATITUDE AND SYMPATHY

I could scent an occasion coming, a mile away. Everybody was going to be implicated in something tricky. Socially, 'they' were about to turn on the heat. It could be some primitive embarrassment was coming a shade nearer the surface than the grown-ups liked. This could have left me cold – *had* they left me out. But no, on what is known as an 'Occasion', children are useful. One was to be on tap. One would be on view. One would be required, and tensely watched. One would have to express, to register, something *extra*. Pleasure: 'Aunt Emmeline is coming, you know, today: do show her how happy you are to see her.' Gratitude, for a present or a party: 'And don't just mumble "Thank you": do smile, too!' Sympathy, with a grief: 'Look, here's poor Mrs X coming down the street: you need not *say* anything, just let her *see* you're sorry!' Interest, in anything that a senior chose to explain to one, tell one or point out to one. Enthusiasm, for anything one was caused to see – scenery, famous or noble persons, some dreary, intricate curio from the East.

React, child! Demonstrate! That was all they wanted. It was not unreasonable, really – a child like a stuck pig *is* a dreadful sight. I do not want, at all, to give the impression that my childhood was an emotional forcing-house, or, still more, an unduly social one. It was not such a bad preparation for after life. People are always going to expect one to react, in some way: no harm in learning to be quick off the mark. And reactions must be appropriate, not excessive. This cannot be drilled into the young too soon ... or, can it? The Edwardians considered not. Today, I hear, many differ from them: there are some, aren't there, who go so far as to hold that children should not say 'Thank you' unless they do feel a surge of spontaneous gratitude, or 'Sorry' – when they tread on anyone's toe – unless they are truly stabbed by remorse. I do not think I can go into the rights and wrongs of it. I imagine there must be in each generation some children uneasily conscious of what is wanted, and uneasily certain they must fall short. They either cannot or will not deliver the goods.

Would this be recalcitrance, or plain nervousness? In me, it was a mixture of both – plus a wary dread of 'going too far'. If one crossed the very fine line, if one *went* too far, one's behaviour fell into the 'showing off' class. To celebrate the arrival of a visitor by whooping, prancing, clashing imaginary cymbals together over one's head was considered hysterical and excessive – I once tried it. And effusiveness, in the matter of gratitude, was, I was to discover, another error.

'Thank you, Mrs Robinson, so very, very much for the absolutely wonderful LOVELY party!' 'Well, dear,' my hostess would say with a frigid smile, 'I'm afraid it was hardly so wonderful as all *that*.' And, 'Who was that gushing little thing?' I could practically hear her say it, as I left the room. To this day I remember – and still with blushes, mortification – the awful number of marks that I overshot. After each excess, I had periods of stand-offish caution; I had to resort to the stodgy gruffness of manner allowed, I had seen, to little boys.

I connect so many occasions with stage-fright, paralysing self-consciousness, all but impotence. And, let me be clear, this was far from shyness. I was not a retiring child – I should not at all have liked to be banished from the scene of activity. I had dreams of glory in which I behaved conspicuously well, well to the point of evoking comment. But alas, in real life for a child to behave 'well' meant – above all things – never to be conspicuous. An occasion is an orderly grown-up concept, an affair of a thousand-and-one rules. The accustomed actors are old stagers; it is only the child who must walk on without having been rehearsed; though, still, with enough instructions to make it nervous. You see, the poor child is in the picture, but not the centre of it – unless of course, it is at its own birthday party. The child dithers somewhere round the margin.

In my long-ago childhood, it was important what grown-ups thought. They were the censors, the judges. Today, they have less prestige, they have abdicated from power, gone down in status: in some families, they seem like a fallen upper-class. Children, like freedmen going round in gangs, are rather more, today, in each others' power. Well, I say 'more', but honestly, looking back, I see that this gang-formation did go on in my childhood also: as an underworld, blinked at by the eye of authority. We children put one another to drastic tests. There was, for one thing, the dire 'I dare you . . .' Tree and roof climbing to the extremest heights, blindfold acrobatics on bicycles, one-leg hopping along the tops of walls, balance on parapets over deep railway cuttings – these were the *sine qua non*. I daresay they are today? All the same, physical ordeals were less scorching than non-stop criticism. At day school, we kept a narrow watch on each other – the glances shot from desk to desk in the classroom, and we trailed each other down the streets when we started home. Forever we were keeping each other up to the mark, without committing ourselves by saying what the mark *was*; and this amounted, I see now, to a continuous rising to an occasion which – unlike others – never came to an end.

Friendships, for instance, were exacting: they involved the almost daily exchange of secrets which had to be of a horrific magnitude, and so did plans for Saturday afternoons. This was Folkestone: there was the switchback railway, there was the outdoor roller skating rink, but we looked for something more desperate and more original. Keeping tryst with the dearest friend of the moment, it was fatal not to produce a bright idea. The search – for some reason – always devolved on me. I was forever devising, racking my brains and fancy, tying myself into knots, to think something up. The approach of a Saturday afternoon loomed over me far more darkly than school work.

'Well,' the friend would say, 'so what *are* we going to do?' A suspicious pause; 'or haven't you thought?'

'Oh yes, I have!'

'I hope it's not something silly.'

Thus encouraged, I would unfold my plan. 'That does not sound much fun,' she would remark. 'Still, it's too late to think of anything else, so I s'pose we may as well try. Come on.'

An un-thrilling Saturday could cool off a friendship. Folkestone in 1910 was dressy, law-abiding, and well patrolled; the amount of things children could do – bring off without being shouted at – was limited. Bye-laws, prohibiting almost everything, were posted up and down the Leas and along the woodsy paths of the undercliff. Oh, that initiative – why was *I* forced to take it? Yes, it took one's contemporaries, it took other children, to put that particular pressure on one. 'You put yourself out too much about your friends!' my mother would declare as, fagged-out, white in the face, I came tottering back to her through the Folkestone dusk. 'Why not let them amuse you, for a change, sometimes?' And indeed in my own mind I often wondered.

Would the strain become less as I grew older? No: on the contrary. When I was fourteen, fifteen, the dress-problem raised its ugly head. It was necessary to look nice, as well as be nice. Still more, it was necessary to look 'suitable'. But, my heavens, suitable to what? For life was to bristle, from now on, with unforeseeable occasions. In advance, these were daydream occasions: I dressed accordingly. In those days, the teenager was unguided. Fashion, now so kind to that age-group, took no account of us. So, trial-and-error it was, for me. Outcome: errors. The rose-pink parasol with which I all but poked out somebody's eye at a cricket match; the picture hat in which I attended a country lunch-party – only to be taken out ratting by my host; the ornamental muslin, with blue bows, in which I turned up at a grown-up beach picnic – *that* I disposed of by slipping off a rock into the sea. The splash was big, though the sea was shallow. The crisis obliterated my frock. Was my accident quite accidental? I cannot answer.

Yes, I think as a child I did better with my back to the wall – in extreme situations, among strangers. Whatever strangers could do to me, they could not bite, and there was the hope I might never meet them again. It was my near ones, my dear ones, the fond, the anxious, the proud-of-me, who set up the inhibition. I could not endure their hopes; I could not bear to fail under loving eyes. I detested causing a disappointment. Perhaps I exaggerated the disappointment? Perhaps I did less badly than I imagined? You see, it mattered too much. I shall never know. For how does one rise – fully, ever – to an occasion?

1956

A LIVING WRITER:
KATHERINE MANSFIELD

If Katherine Mansfield were living, she would this year be sixty-eight. Is this fact out of accord with our idea of her? Sometimes it may be that an early death so fixes our image of a person that we cannot envisage him as older. Youth comes to seem an attribute of the personality – in the case of a beautiful woman or romantic artist, both of which Katherine Mansfield was, this happens particularly often. Yet in the case of Katherine Mansfield it becomes particularly wrong. For one thing, we lose much and deny her something if we altogether banish her in imagination from the place she could have had in our own time. For another, she had no desire whatever to be 'spared' life or anything further it could bring. Useless as it is to lament her going, let us not forget she would have stayed if she could, and fought to do so with savage courage.

She could not have lived as she was; she was far too ill. To restore health, at the stage her illness had reached, would have taken a miracle – she sought one. Could that have been granted, a fresh start, one can think of few people more fitted than Katherine Mansfield to have aged without decline, ignominy, or fear. One can picture her at sunset, but not in twilight. Born with good nerve, she had learned comprehensive courage, and in a hard school. In spite of setback after setback, she was already on her way towards equilibrium. Her spirit was of the kind which does not die down. Her beauty, even, was of the enduring kind, hardy and resolute in cast as it was mysterious in atmosphere – nor need one imagine her without the peculiar personal magic she emanated: a magic still so much part of her legend. Already she was 'old' in imagination – up to any age, would she not have been young in temperament?

She was drawn to old people, seeing them as victors. They stood to her for vision, and for the patience she so impatiently longed to have. (She was aware, of course, also of ancient monsters.) Is it too much to say that she envied old age, and the more so as her own hopes of attaining it grew slender? But one does not waste desire on the unlikely: her real need was pressing, and grew obsessive – she needed time, time in which to achieve 'a body of work'. By now, she would have had thirty-four years more. Enough? I suspect that in the extreme of her desperation she would have been content to compound for ten. There is never enough of the time a writer wants – but hers was cut so short, one is aghast. The more one salutes the fulfilment in her work, the more one is awed by its stretching promise. The perfectedness of the major pieces sets up anguish that there could not be more of them. Equally, I may say that a fellow writer cannot but look on Katherine Mansfield's work as interrupted, hardly more than suspended, momentarily waiting to be gone on with. Page after page gives off the feeling of being still warm from the touch, fresh from the pen. Where is she – our missing contemporary?

As it was, she died in January 1923, late one evening, in her bare room in the community at Fontainebleau. One's impression, from her husband's account, is that the end when it did come took her by surprise: she had been beginning again to expect life. And from then on everything, purged of dross of falseness, was to have been different. She was thirty-four, young as a woman, as an artist at the beginning of her maturity – that is, she had entered into her full powers without being yet certain how to command them.

It is with maturity that the really searching ordeal of the writer begins. Maturity, remember, must last a long time. And it must not be confused with single perfections, such as she had accomplished without yet having solved her abiding problems. She had had throughout no guide but her own light, nothing outside to check by, no predecessor. Chekhov was her ally, but not authority. In her field, Katherine Mansfield worked by herself.

She had, when she went to Fontainebleau, reached a crisis both in regard to life and regard to art. She had undergone an intense revulsion against her existence as it had come to be, and against her writing as she now saw it. Conflicts and the sickness they had set up, mistrusts the sickness in turn engendered, made it all but impossible for her to go forward. Essential as it was for her to have faith, she repudiated faith based on self-deception. She had come to look on herself, and with that her work, as in danger of being rotted by unreality. She sought nothing less than rebirth.

In her journal, at the close of her final August, she puts on record her part in a conversation:

> I began by telling him how dissatisfied I was with the idea that Life must be a lesser thing than we were capable of imagining it to be. I had the feeling that the same thing happened to nearly everybody I knew and whom I did not know. No sooner was their youth, with the little force and impetus characteristic of youth, done, than they stopped growing. At the very moment that one felt that now was the time to gather oneself together, to use one's whole strength, to take control, to be an adult, in fact, they seemed content to swap the darling wish of their hearts for innumerable little wishes. Or the image that suggested itself to me was that of a river flowing away in countless little trickles over a dark swamp.
>
> . . . Sooner or later, in literature at any rate, there sounded an undertone of deep regret. There was an uneasiness, a sense of frustration. One heard, one thought one heard, a cry that began to echo in one's own being: 'I have missed it. I have given up. This is not what I want. If this is all, then Life is not worth living.'
>
> But I *know* it is not all. How does one know that? Let me take the case of K.M. She has led, ever since she can remember, a very typically false life. Yet, through it all, there have been moments, instants, gleams, when she has felt the possibility of something quite other.

By October of 1922, Katherine Mansfield became convinced that there must be a miracle or nothing. She made up her mind to enter the community, to subject herself to its physical rigours for the sake of inner regeneration. The step was taken against the advice and wishes of her friends. On the eve, she wrote in her journal:

How can you hesitate? Risk! Risk anything! Care no more for the opinion of others, for those voices. Do the hardest thing on earth for you. Act for yourself. Face the truth.

True, Chekhov didn't. Yes, but Chekhov died. And let us be honest. How much do we know of Chekhov from his letters? Was that all? Of course not. Don't you suppose he had a whole longing life of which there is hardly a word? Then read the final letters. He has given up hope. If you desentimentalize those final letters they are terrible. There is no more Chekhov. Illness has swallowed him.

. . . Now, Katherine, what do you mean by health? And what do you want it for?

Answer: By health I mean the power to live a full, adult, living, breathing life in close contact with what I love – the earth and the wonders thereof – the sea – the sun. All that we mean when we speak of the external world. I want to enter into it, to be part of it, to live in it, to learn from it, to lose all that is superficial, and acquired in me and to become a conscious direct human being. I want, by understanding myself, to understand others. I want to be all that I am capable of becoming. . . .

Then I want to *work*. At what? I want so to live that I may work with my hands and my feeling and my brain. I want a garden, a small house, grass, animals, books, pictures, music. And out of this, the expression of this, I want to be writing. (Though I may write about cabmen. That's no matter.)

But warm, eager, living life – to be rooted in life – to learn, to desire to know, to feel, to think, to act. That is what I want. And nothing else. That is what I must try for.

*

'Katherine Mansfield's death, by coming so early, left her work still at the experimental stage.' This could be said – but would it be true? To me, such a verdict would be misleading. First, her writing already *had* touched perfection a recognizable number of times; second, she would have been bound to go on experimenting up to the end, however late that had come. One cannot imagine her settling down to any one fixed concept of the short story – her art was, by its very nature, tentative, responsive, exploratory. There are no signs that she was casting about to find a formula: a formula would, in fact, have been what she fled from. Her sense of the possibilities of the story was bounded by no hard-and-fast horizons: she grasped that it is imperative for the writer to expand his range, never contract his method. Perception and language could not be kept too fresh, too alert, too fluid. Each story entailed a beginning right from the start, unknown demands, new risks, unforeseeable developments. Often, she worked by trial-and-error.

So, ever on the move, she has left with us no 'typical' Katherine Mansfield story to anatomize. Concentrated afresh, each time, upon expression, she did not envisage technique in the abstract. As it reached her, each idea for a story had inherent within it its own shape: there could be for it no other. That shape, it was for her to perceive, then outline – she thought (we learn from her letters and journal) far more of perception than of construction. The story *is* there, but she has yet to come at it. One has the impression of a water-diviner, pacing, halting, awaiting the twitch of the hazel twig. Also, to judge from her writings about her writing, there were times when Katherine Mansfield believed a story to have a volition of its own – she seems to stand back watching it take form. Yet this could not happen apart from her; the story drew her steadily into itself.

All of her pieces, it seems clear, did not originate in the same order. Not in all cases was there that premonitory stirring of an idea; sometimes the external picture came to her first. She found herself seized upon by a scene, an isolated incident or a face which, something told her, must *have* meaning, though she had yet to divine what the meaning was. Appearances could in themselves touch alight her creative power. It is then that we see her moving into the story, from its visual periphery to its heart, recognizing the 'why' as she penetrates. (It could seem that her great scenic New Zealand stories came into being by this process.) Her failures, as she uncompromisingly saw them, together with her host of abandoned fragments, give evidence of the state of mind she voices in anguished letters or journal entries – the sensation of having lost her way. She could finish a story by sheer craftsmanship but only, later, to turn against the results.

Able and fine as was her intelligence, it was not upon that that she depended: intuitive knowing, vision, had to be the thing. She was a writer with whom there could be no secondary substitute for genius: genius was vision. One might speak of her as having a burning gaze. But she faced this trouble – vision at full intensity is not by nature able to be sustained; it is all but bound to be intermittent. And for Katherine Mansfield those intermittences set up an aesthetic disability, a bad, an antipathetic working condition. Under such a condition, her work abounded, and well she knew it, in perils peculiar to itself. She dreaded sagging of tension, slackening of grip, flaws in interior continuity, numbness, and, most of all, a sort of synthetic quality which could creep in. She speaks of one bad day's work as 'scrappy and dreamy'. Dreaminess meant for her, dilution.

Subjects, to be ideal for Katherine Mansfield, had to attract, then hold, her power called vision. There occurred a false dawn, or false start, when a subject deceived her as to its possibilities – there were those which failed her, I feel, rather than she them. We must consider later which kind or what range of subject stood by her best, and why this may have been so. There was not a subject which did not tax her – raising, apart from anything else, exacting problems of treatment, focus, and angle. Her work was a succession of attempts to do what was only just not impossible. There is danger that in speaking of 'attempts' one should call to mind those which have not succeeded: one forgets the no less attempt which is merged in victory. Katherine Mansfield's masterpiece stories cover their tracks; they have an air of serene inevitability, almost a touch of the miraculous. (But for the artist, remember, there are no miracles.) Her consummate achievements soar, like so many peaks, out of the foothills of her working life – spaced out, some nearer together in time than others. One asks oneself why the artist, requited thus, could not have been lastingly reassured, and how it could have happened that, after each, troughs of frustration, anxiety, dereliction should have awaited her once again?

The truth was, she implacably cut the cord between herself and any completed story. (She admits, in the journal: 'It took me nearly a month to "recover" from *At the Bay*. I made at least three false starts. But I could not get away from the sound of the sea, and Beryl fanning her hair at the window. These things would not *die down*.') She must not look back; she must press forward. She had no time to form a consistent attitude to any one finished story: each stood to her as a milestone, passed, not as a destination arrived at. Let us say, she reacted to success (if in Katherine Mansfield's eyes there was such a thing) as others react to failure: there seemed to be nothing left but to try again.

To be compelled to experiment is one thing, to be in love with experiment quite another. Of love for experiment for its own sake, Katherine Mansfield shows not a sign. Conscious artist, she carries none of the marks of the self-consciously 'experimental' writer. Nothing in her approach to people or nature is revolutionary; her story-telling is, on its own plane, not much less straightforward than Jane Austen's. She uses no literary shock tactics. The singular beauty of her language consists, partly, in its hardly seeming to *be* language at all, so glass-transparent is it to her meaning. Words had but one appeal for her, that of speakingness. (In her journal we find noted: 'The *panting* of a saw.') She was to evolve from noun, verb, adjective, a marvellous sensory notation hitherto undreamed of outside poetry; nonetheless, she stayed subject to prose discipline. And her style, when the story-context requires, can be curt, decisive, factual. It is a style generated by subject and tuned to mood – so flexible as to be hardly *a* style at all. One would recognize a passage from Katherine Mansfield not by the manner but by the content. There are no eccentricities.

Katherine Mansfield was not a rebel, she was an innovator. Born into the English traditions of prose narrative, she neither revolted against these nor broke with them – simply, she passed beyond them. And now tradition, extending, has followed her. Had she not written, written as she did, one form of art might be still in infancy. One cannot attribute to Katherine Mansfield the entire growth, in our century, of the short story. Its developments have been speedy, inspired, various; it continues branching in a hundred directions many of which show her influence not at all. What she did supply was an immense impetus – also, did she not first see in the story the ideal reflector of the day? We owe to her the prosperity of the 'free' story: she untrammelled it from conventions and, still more, gained for it a prestige till then unthought of. How much ground Katherine Mansfield broke for her successors may not be realized. Her imagination kindled unlikely matter; she was to alter for good and all our ideas of what goes to make a story.

*

To make a selection has not been easy. In *The Short Stories of Katherine Mansfield* (Alfred A. Knopf, 1937) we have her output: eighty-eight stories, of which twenty-six are unfinished. The first whole story, *The Tiredness of Rosabel*, was written when she was twenty; the last completed one, *The Canary*, dates from the summer before her death. The time span is, thus, fourteen years.

The dimensions of this, our present volume [*Thirty-Four Short Stories* by Katherine Mansfield, Collins, 1957], limit me to thirty-four stories only. Obviously there could have been more had I chosen shorter ones – but, I decided, to sacrifice longer stories would have been an injustice to the author, all of whose masterpieces required space.

To have left out masterpieces would, no less, also have been unjust to the readers to whom this volume will go. Well known as may be these major stories, they cannot be read too often or known too well. Here, accordingly, are *The Little Governess, Prelude, At the Bay, Bliss, Je ne parle pas francqis, Picture, The Man Without a Temperament, The Stranger, The Daughters of the Late Colonel, The Garden Party,* and, for all it is unfinished, *Six Years After.*

Next I looked for stories to be examples of Katherine Mansfield's ways of seeing or feeling; of her satire, sympathy, or favouritisms; or of her supremacy as a story-teller. *The Modern Soul, Psychology, Sun and Moon, Mr Reginald Peacock's Day, This Flower, Revelations, The Young Girl, Life of Ma Parker, Mr and Mrs Dove, An Ideal Family, Miss Brill, Marriage à la Mode, The Doll's House,* and again unfinished, *The Doves' Nest* and *Father and the Girls* make a bid for inclusion under those headings. They may be found unequally good; one or two are not even her second-best work. But each of them, I would contend, exhibits some characteristic of hers and of hers only.

Room was left (at the cost of exclusions I regretted) for the early work, with its harshnesses, its first glints of authority, and, most interesting of all, its alternatives – what kind of writer was she to be? This, as with other highly gifted young persons, did not immediately decide itself. Writers today at their own beginning must want to see how Katherine Mansfield began, and how the themes of her future work were already like reefs under the surface. *The Tiredness of Rosabel* was the first of what were to be a succession of daydream stories: apart from its interest as that, one would hardly claim for *Rosabel* that it is better than any average story turned out today by a twenty-year-old member of a writing group. Twenty-year-old Katherine Mansfield worked unaided by friendly criticism, and without the incitement of group discussion. And recall that in 1908 the idea of writing a story *about* a daydream was in itself novel – a daring break with accepted pattern. And how many *Rosabel* tales today would have been written at all but for Katherine Mansfield? Today her influence operates at more than one remove – that is to say, students who have not read her and may know hardly more of her than her name show in their own writing an unconscious debt.

Some of my choices bring me dead up against the author's stated feeling. 'I couldn't have *The Woman at the Store* reprinted, *par example,*' she protested to her husband in 1920, when she was deciding upon the list of her stories first to appear in book form. Yet *The Woman at the Store* (date, 1912) is here. I have put it in because I like it: it shows the touch of one of the earlier, possible Katherine Mansfields who, as time went on, was to be crowded out. In this it differs from *Ole Underwood*, which far more foreshadows the Katherine Mansfield the world was to come to know – *Ole Underwood* is an early 'injustice' story. Both are set in New Zealand, and their flavour and vigour raise a question – could she have made a regional writer? Did she, by leaving her own country, deprive herself of a range of associations, of inborn knowledge, of vocabulary? She never did, as we know, return to New Zealand as a mature woman: it took its toll of her in dreams, broodings, and often a tortuous homesickness. New Zealand was to return to Katherine Mansfield, but not before she had travelled a long way.

Sun and Moon she regarded, apparently, as a lapse. This story had origin in a night's dream, transcribed while the vividness lasted. I overrule her objections to *Sun and Moon* because it epitomizes one theme of hers, almost one obsession: wrecking of illusion. The flawless, famous *Bliss* has that theme on an adult plane – yet *Bliss*, for all its accomplishment, is to me one of her few disagreeable stories. In the more roughly written *The Doll's House*, illusion triumphs – 'I seen the little lamp'. Disagreeableness, a compulsive brooding upon the ugly, appears in the collection of German stories, the 1912 *In a German Pension*. Two out of that volume, *The Baron* and *The Modern Soul*, are here. I do not care for them, but to have left them out would have given an incomplete picture of Katherine Mansfield. She had, though she tried more and more to curb it, a terrifying faculty for contempt.

One cannot, I think, discuss this artist's work in terms of ordinary progress. One is, rather, aware of greatened deepening and heightening. She taxed herself more rather than less as she went on – she herself remarked the loss of her first facility. The rate at which she abandoned stories shows (apart from the dislocations of sickness) how ever more demanding her art became: at the start she had asked less of it, or it less of her. That burning gaze of hers, her vision, gained in intensity: by the end almost nothing it turned on remained opaque. Her interpretations became more searching – what was spiritually happening to Katherine Mansfield gives signs of itself in the stories, one by one. Her art followed her being's, it would seem, inevitable course. Very important indeed is the continuity, and I therefore feel it very important that the stories be given in the right time-order. John Middleton Murry, her husband, established this (as nearly as could be done) for the 1937 collected edition – departing from it, he tells us, at one point only: *At the Bay*, conceived as a continuation of *Prelude*, is placed by him immediately after *Prelude*, though actually it was written four years later. I have, in arranging my selection, kept to the Middleton Murry order, abiding by his allowable one change.

To select is a grievous responsibility, because it involves representation also. In reducing eighty-eight stories to thirty-four, there is danger of giving untrue proportion to the 'body' of Katherine Mansfield's work. Stories I have had to omit could have given further significance to those chosen – for there is no doubt that short stories by the same hand do have a bearing on one another. They enhance, they throw light on each other; together they acquire composite meaning. Also, stories fall into groups according to scene, mood, subject: each masterpiece, planetlike, has satellites. In making my choice, it becomes my business to give you no two Katherine Mansfield stories of the same kind, in order to give you as many kinds as possible. Her range was wide, and I want to stress that. How her manner varied – yes, to the point, as said, of never having hardened in *a* manner – I also want to bring to your notice. Working on these lines has entailed, alas, the isolating of almost every story from its creative surround – that is, from others which led either up to or away from it. The transitions, the subconscious links between story and story have had to go. To be forced to disturb relationships makes one, often, more conscious of their reality.

*

I have touched on Katherine Mansfield's alternatives: the evidences, that is, in her early stories that she could have been a writer of more than one kind. Alternations went on throughout her working life. In her letters appears a brusque, formidable, masculine streak, which we must not overlook in the stories. Her art has backbone. Her objectiveness, her quick, sharp observations, her adept presentations – are these taken into account enough? Scenically, how keen is her eye for the telling detail! The street, quayside, café, shop interior, tea-time terrace, or public garden stand concretely forward into life. She is well documented. Her liking for activity, for the crowd at play, for people going about their work, her close interest in process and occupation, give an extra vitality to stories. Admire the evening Chinamen in *Ole Underwood*, or Alice, the servant in *At the Bay*, taking tea with Mrs Stubbs of the local store.

She engraves a scene all the more deeply when it is (as few of her scenes are not) contributory to a mood or crisis. Here, at the opening of *The Voyage*, are the awarenesses of a little girl going away with her grandmother after her mother's death:

The Picton boat was due to leave at half-past eleven. It was a beautiful night, mild, starry, only when they got out of the cab and started to walk down the Old Wharf that jutted out into the harbour, a faint wind blowing off the water ruffled under Fenella's hat, and she had to put up a hand to keep it on. It was dark on the Old Wharf, very dark; the wool sheds, the cattle trucks, the cranes standing up so high, the little squat railway engine, all seemed carved out of solid darkness. Here and there on a rounded woodpile, that was like the stalk of a huge black mushroom, there hung a lantern, but it seemed afraid to unfurl its timid, quivering light in all that blackness; it burned softly, as if for itself.

Fancifulness, fantastic metaphor, play more part in her London (as opposed to New Zealand) scene-setting. Less seems taken for granted. *The Wrong House* (not in this selection) furnishes one example. Here, in a residential backwater, an unloved old woman looks out of a window:

It was a bitter autumn day; the wind ran in the street like a thin dog; the houses opposite looked as though they had been cut out with a pair of ugly steel scissors and pasted on to the grey paper sky. There was not a soul to be seen.

This factual firmness of Katherine Mansfield's provides a ballast, or antidote, to her other side – the high-strung susceptibility, the almost hallucinatory floatingness. Nothing is more isolated, more claustrophobic than the dream-fastness of a solitary person – no one knew the dangers better than she. Yet rooted among those dangers was her genius: totally disinfected, wholly adjusted, could she have written as she did? Perhaps there is no such thing as 'pure' imagination – all air must be breathed in, and some is tainting. Now and then the emotional level of her writing drops: a whimsical, petulant little-girlishness disfigures a few of the lesser stories. Some others show a transferred self-pity. She could not always keep up the guard.

Katherine Mansfield was saved, it seems to me, by two things – her inveterate watchfulness as an artist, and a certain sturdiness in her nature which the English at their least friendly might call 'colonial'. She had much to stand out against. She was in danger of being driven, twice over, into herself – by exile to begin with, then by illness. In London she lived, as strangers are wont to do, in a largely self-fabricated world.

She lived, indeed, exactly the sort of life she had left New Zealand in hopes of finding. Writers and intellectuals surrounded her – some merely tempestuous, some destructive. She accustomed herself to love on a razor's edge. Other factors made for deep insecurity. She and her husband were agitatingly and endlessly short of money; for reasons even other than that they seemed doomed to uproot themselves from home after home. As intelligentsia, they were apt to be preyed upon by the intelligentsia-seeking sub-*beau monde* – types she was to stigmatize in *Bliss* and again in *Marriage à la Mode*. Amid the etherealities of Bloomsbury she was more than half hostile, a dark-eyed tramp. For times at a stretch there was difficulty as to the placing of her stories; individually, their reception was uncertain: no full recognition came till the volume *Bliss*. In England she moved, one gets the impression, among nothing but intimates or strangers – of family, familiar *old* friends, neighbours, girlhood contemporaries there were none. Habits, associations were lacking also: here was a background without depth, thwarting to a woman's love of the normal. From this parched soil sprang the London stories.

To a degree it was better, or always began by being better, in the South of France. She felt a release among Mediterranean people and the Midi light reminded her of New Zealand's. It was at Bandol, late in 1915, that she began *The Aloe*, original version of *Prelude*, and thereby crossed a threshold. At Bandol was suffered the agony out of which the story had to be born. She had come to Bandol to be alone with loss: her brother Chummie, over with the army from New Zealand, had been killed fighting in France. His last leave had been spent with Katherine in London. That same month, late at night in her sea-facing hotel room, she wrote in her journal:

The present and future mean nothing to me, I am no longer 'curious' about people; I do not wish to go anywhere; and the only possible value that anything can have for me is that it should put me in mind of something that happened or was when we were alive.

'Do you remember, Katie?' I hear his voice in the trees and flowers, in scents and light and shadow. Have people, apart from these far-away people, ever existed for me? Or have they always failed me and faded because I denied them reality? Supposing I were to die as I sit at this table, playing with my Indian paperknife, what would be the difference? No difference. Then why don't I commit suicide? Because I feel I have a duty to perform to the lovely time when we were both alive. I want to write about it, and he wanted me to. We talked it over in my

little top room in London. I said: I will just put on the front
page: To my brother Leslie Heron Beauchamp. Very well: it
shall be done.

That winter, though she had other maladies, tuberculosis had not
declared itself. When it did, South of France winters became
enforced. War continued, the wind whistled, *volets* clattered, the
Mediterranean sea turned to black iron. She burned, shivered,
coughed, could not bear herself, wrote, wrote, wrote. The years
1919–20 brought the Italian nightmare, Ospedaletti. These weeks,
months, in cut-price hotels, ramshackle villas, were twice over exile,
exile with doubled force. One man's letters from London were the
lifeline, and letters did not invariably come. Who can measure the
power of that insatiable longing we call homesickness? Home, now
she was torn from it, became hers in London. She thought of the
yellow table, the Dresden shepherdess, the kitten Wingley – growing
up without her. Loneliness, burning its way into Katherine
Mansfield, leaves its indelible mark upon her art.

She wrote the august, peaceful New Zealand stories. They would
be miracles of memory if one considered them memories at all –
more, they are what she foresaw them as: a reliving. And, spiritually
as in art, they were her solution. Within them fuse the two Katherine
Mansfields: the sturdy soul and the visionary are one. The day-to-
day receives the full charge of poetry.

And now one and now another of the windows leaped into light.
Someone was walking through the empty rooms carrying a
lamp. From a window downstairs the light of a fire flickered. A
strange beautiful excitement seemed to stream from the house in
quivering ripples.

This is the child Kezia's first, late-night sight of the Burnells' new
home. Katherine Mansfield the artist is also home-coming.

*

The writer was a woman of strong feeling. How quick were her
sympathies, vehement her dislikes, total her angers, penitent her
forgivingness, letters and journal show. If we had not these, how
much would we know of her from her stories? Impersonality cannot
but be the aim of a writer of anything like her calibre, and she fought
to keep her stories clear of herself. But, human temperament and its
workings being her subject, how could she wholly outlaw her own?
And temperament played in her work an essential part – it was to

provide as it were the climate in which ideas grew and come to flower. That throughout years of her creative life Katherine Mansfield was a sick woman, and that tuberculosis engenders a special temperament, or intensifies the one there already, must be allowed for. It has been more than allowed for – there is danger, in her case as in Keats's, that the medical history be overstressed. We are to marvel at the persistent strength with which Katherine Mansfield the artist threw off the sick-room. She was conscious only of her vocation – she *was* to write, she wrote, and wrote as she did. It may be that brutalities on the part of fate made her the more feel singled out, set apart. The battering at her health accounts for the inequalities of her accomplishment: that there was any trace of the pathological in the art itself, I imagine nobody could assert.

She was not by nature dispassionate. In the New Zealand, the 'far-away people' stories, conflict seems stilled – there is an overruling harmony, the seer come to rest with the seen. Katherine Mansfield's ethics and partisanships come through far more in the English pieces (possibly because of their thinner fabric) and in some of those set in the South of France – though in *The Young Girl* and *The Doves' Nest* we again have a shining impartiality. She loved righteousness and hated iniquity: what, for her, constituted those two? She was on the side of innocence and honour: honesty, spontaneity, humbleness, trustfulness and forbearingness distinguish characters she is fond of. No less could she embody what she detested: cruelty or heartlessness, affectation, neurotic indulgence, cowardice, smugness. Indignation at injustice, from time to time, makes her no less inflammatory a writer than Charles Dickens. She concerns herself with bad cases rather than bad systems: political awareness or social criticism do not directly express themselves in the stories. How hard is her bearing against oppressors, how tender her leaning towards victims! Unimaginativeness, with regard to others, seemed to her one of the grosser sins. The denial of love, the stunting of sorrow, or the cheating of joy was to her not short of an enormity – she had an intense regard for the human birthright.

How good is Katherine Mansfield's character-drawing? I have heard this named as her weak point. I feel one cannot insist enough upon what she instinctively grasped – that the short story, by reason of its aesthetics, is not and is not intended to be the medium either for exploration or long-term development of character. Character cannot be more than *shown* – it is there for use, the use is dramatic. Foreshortening is not only unavoidable, it is right. And with Katherine Mansfield there was another factor – her 'stranger' outlook on so much of society. I revert to the restrictedness of her life in England, the eclecticism of her personal circle. She saw few people, saw them sometimes too often. This could account for her tendency to repeat certain types of character. This restless New Zealand woman writing of London deals with what was more than half a synthetic world: its denizens *are* types, and they remain so – to the impoverishment of the London stories. The divorce of the intelligentsia from real life tends to be with her an obsessive subject – aggravated more than she knew, perhaps, by her sense of being far from her home base. Her sophisticates are cut out sharply, with satire; they are animated, expressive but two-dimensional.

In the South of France stories, characters are subsidiary to their environment; they drift like semi-transparent fish through the brilliantly lighted colours of an aquarium. Here, Katherine Mansfield's lovely crystallization of place and hour steals attention away from men and women. Could *she* not bear to examine these winter visitors – idle, half-hearted and non-indigenous? Tense Anglo-Saxons, they contrast with physically equable busy natives – beauty cheats them, Nature withholds her secret. Patient is the husband without a temperament; true is Miss Brill to her fur necktie; the young girl is a marvel of young hauteur. Yet these three, even, no more than brush one's memory: the South of France stories are about moods.

Katherine Mansfield, we notice, seldom outlines and never dissects a character: instead, she causes the person to expose himself – and devastating may be the effect. The author's nominal impassivity is telling. I should not in the main call her a kind writer, though so often she is a pitiful one. Wholly benevolent are her comedies: high spirits, good humour no less than exquisite funniness endear to us *The Daughters of the Late Colonel, The Doves' Nest, The Singing Lesson*. Nor is the laugh ever against a daydreamer.

The New Zealand characters are on a quite other, supreme level. They lack no dimension. Their living-and-breathing reality at once astonishes and calms us: they belong to life, not in any book – they existed before stories began. In their company we are no longer in Katherine Mansfield's; we forget her as she forgot herself. The Burnells of *Prelude, At the Bay* and *The Doll's House* are a dynasty. Related, though showing no too striking family likeness, are the conversational Sheridans of *The Garden Party*. Of Burnell stock, graver and simplified, are elderly Mr and Mrs Hammond of *The Stranger* – Katherine Mansfield's equivalent of James Joyce's *The Dead*. Alike in Burnells, Sheridans, and Hammonds we feel the almost mystic family integration. Husbands and fathers are convincing; men give off an imposing masculinity. These men, women, old women, young girls, children are in a major key. I do not claim that the New Zealand stories vindicate Katherine Mansfield's character-drawing – the *drawing* is not (to my mind) elsewhere at fault. What she fails at in the European stories is full, adult character-*realization* – or, should one say, materialization? Her Londoners are guessed at, her New Zealanders known. As to the Burnells, she had information of the kind not gained by conscious experience. Writing of these people, she dwells upon them – her art grew not only from memory but from longing.

The New Zealand stories are timeless. Do the rest of the Katherine Mansfield stories 'date'? I find there is some impression that they do – an impression not, I think, very closely checked on. To an extent, her work shows the intellectual imprint of her day, many of whose theories, tenets, preoccupations seem now faded. It is the more nearly *mondaine*, the 'cleverer' of her stories which wear least well. Her psychology may seem naïve and at times shallow – after all, she was young; but apart from that much water has flowed under bridges in thirty years. *Bliss, Psychology* and *Je ne parle pas français* (technically one of her masterpieces) give out a faintly untrue ring. And one effect of her writing has told against her: it was her fate to set up a fashion in hypersensitivity, in vibratingness: it is her work in this vein which has been most heavily imitated, and travesties curdle one's feeling for the original. The idea of her as a literary Marie Laurencin, sponsor of a brood of gazelle-eyed heroines, tends too much to be a prevailing one. In fact, in her verve, raciness, husky sensuous poetry, life-likingness, and sense of the moment's drama, she is more often sister to Berthe Morisot.

She wrote few love stories; those she did, today seem distant, dissatisfying. Staking her life on love, she was least happy (I think) with love in fiction. Her passionate faith shows elsewhere. *Finesses*, subtleties, restless analysis, cerebral wary guardedness hallmark the Katherine Mansfield lovers. Was this, perhaps, how it was in London, or is this how Londoners' *amours* struck young New Zealand? She had left at the other side of the world a girlhood not unlike young Aunt Beryl's: beaux, waltzes, muslin, moonlight, murmuring sea. . . . We revert to that entry near the close of her journal: 'Take the case of K.M. She has led, ever since she can remember, a very typically false life. Yet, through it all, there have been moments, instants, gleams, when she felt the possibility of something quite other.'

The stories are more than moments, instants, gleams: she has

given them touches of eternity. The dauntless artist accomplished, if
less than she hoped, more than she knew. Almost no writer's art has
not its perishable fringes: light dust may settle on that margin. But
against the core, the integrity, what can time do? Katherine
Mansfield's deathless expectations set up a mark for us: no one has
yet fulfilled them. Still at work, her genius rekindles faith; she is on
our side in every further attempt. The effort she was involved in
involves us – how can we feel her other than a contemporary?

1956

COMING TO LONDON

All through my childhood, London had a fictitious existence for me.
It loomed darkly somewhere at the other side of the water; I thought
of it (when at all) as an entity, at once magnetic and dangerous. It
was, from all I heard, a city into which no one ventured alone, and
which was to be entered only after preparation and wary forethought. It stood for the adult, and so much so that there should be
children in London seemed unimaginable – in fact that there should
be people of any kind was only a secondary idea: I pictured the thing
as a mass of building, a somehow impious extreme of bulk and
height in whose interstices was fog. I first crossed the city when I first
crossed the sea, when I was four: it must have been winter, we
arrived after dark and were driven as hurriedly as possible from
Euston to some other terminus in a cab. The street lamps, seeming
dimmer than Dublin's, showed us to be in the continuous bottom of
a chasm, among movement conveying a sense of trouble, and which
one suspected rather than saw. My mother for a minute put down a
window, saying, as though in extenuation, 'London has a smell of its
own.' But this, like all else given off, was non-human.

I do not know when, at what later date, I came to know that the
sun shone there – that is to say, there also – or when I took in that
this, like some planet, also must be taken to be inhabited. If I had
been an American child instead of an Anglo-Irish one, it is possible
that London, from being farther in the distance, would have been
more clear-cut as an idea: I should have had some rational notion of
it, instead of being infested by it imaginatively. As it was, it was like a
hand too near my eyes. Nobody ever told me about London, or

explained to me what or why it was – I was assumed, I suppose, to have been born knowing. This may have come from the Anglo-Irish ambivalence as to all things English, a blend of impatience and evasiveness, a reluctance to be pinned down to a relationship – one which, all the same, nobody could have conceived of life without. So for what seems a long time London remained partly a not quite convincing fiction, partly a symbol of ambiguity, partly an overcast physical fact. Even when my mother and I went to live in the south of England we almost never took the train to the capital. Though we knew *of* quite a number of people who lived in London, we visited only one or another aunt or my mother's godmother, to whom we glued ourselves onward from Charing Cross. My mother knew she would lose her way. For my part, each time I looked for London it had jiggled itself into a different pattern. Nothing like a picture was to be formed.

The picture, when it did form, came out of books – as I could not read easily till I was over seven, and did not begin to read novels till I was ten, it came late. It was composite, geographically wrong and intensely vivid, pieced together out of Dickens, E. F. Benson, E. Nesbit, Galsworthy, Conan Doyle and of course Compton Mackenzie. I also read many Edwardian novels in which Park Lane featured, and for some reason I saw this overhanging the Thames (really more like Riverside Drive overhanging the Hudson in New York). This envisaged London gained on me something of the obsessive hold of a daydream; it invested itself with a sensuous reality – sounds, smells, motes of physical atmosphere – so powerful as to have been equalled since by almost no experience of so-called reality. Even the weather was dramatic: fogs impenetrable, summers Mediterranean, sunsets lurid and nights gothic with pitchblack shadows. And I endowed London with extremes of fashion and wealth, alongside which lay sinister squalor. Fancy was slow to encompass the middle reaches. This romanticist's London I have never extirpated from my heart – and, like a renewed vision it does now and then, even now, reappear. Probably the magic of a city, as of a person, resides in its incapacity to be known, and the necessity therefore that it should be imagined.

Imaginative writing, fiction, was my only data for London till I was nearly twenty. Bayswater was the first region to project into my personal life, for here lived two or three of my friends at boarding-school, whom I used to visit on my way across London at the beginnings or ends of term. Theirs were the first doors I ever saw opening upon interiors – which themselves never seemed quite credible, or at any rate wholly everyday. Leaving my friends behind, I realized that their existences while apart from me were almost literally a closed book, and went back to books capable of being opened – that is, actual ones. Nothing made full sense to me that was not in print. Life seemed to promise to be intolerable without full sense, authoritative imaginative knowledge. Feeling what a book could do, and what indeed only a book *could* do, made me wish to write: I conceived of nothing else as worth doing. At the same time, what attributes were required? Could one be a writer and not a demigod? I became most anxious to be in the presence of one or two, not so much I think out of curiosity as in the hope that virtue proceeded from them. Oh to be at least in the outer precincts, whatever came of it.

In these days I cannot believe it possible that anybody should live to the age of nineteen without having encountered an author. At Folkestone a disastrous cold in the head had prevented my setting eyes on Baroness Orczy; E.V. Lucas's daughter was at my school, but when he came there I was never around. My County Cork home was eighty-five miles away from Edith Somerville's, but that was a distance, before motor cars. At last, near Limerick, at my father's wedding to my stepmother I met her magnificent brother, Stephen Gwynn – talk with him confirmed me in my idea: generally, authors lived in London. So back I went, this time with intention. As a sort of disguise, I worked at the L.C.C. School of Art in Southampton Row, near which trams rushed up out of the earth. My Earls Court lodgings had the merit of being round the corner from Lilley Road, mentioned in *Sinister Street*. When I moved in, theatrical autumn sunshine bathed this first part of London I was on domestic terms with, and thin blonde leaves drifted through the air. . . . The year after, I changed my locale, going to live with a great-aunt in Queen Anne's Gate. My existence there, beautiful as it was, seemed to be missing in one dimension – unaccountably, I had not yet found Westminster in a story. It was too bad that Virginia Woolf had not by then written *Mrs Dalloway*.

The winters of 1919, '20 and '22 run together: I cannot always remember which was which. (1921, I was in Italy.) The London of then – I mean, the London I sought – could not have been kinder to that most awkward of creatures, a literary aspirant. Looking back, I fancy that there were, then, more aspirants, fewer very young authors. Not one of the great I met asked me why I was not at a university, as no doubt I should have been. At Oxford or Cambridge, I expect I should have talked about ideas; in London I was careful to keep my mouth shut, listening to talkers like a spy. Apart from schoolfriends I met again, I had not much interest in my contemporaries – I could only think about The Elect. My idea of contemporary artists was a sacerdotal one. I had read their work not only with absorption but a kind of piety; everything but their appearances was known to me. (The putting of authors' photographs on book-jackets was not then, for better or worse, in practice.) I could not wait to be where they moved and spoke.

The big orange *London Mercury* was the dominating magazine. The Poetry Bookshop was a *foyer*: upstairs, after dark, in a barn-like room, I listened to Ezra Pound reading aloud what was hypnotically unintelligible to me by the light of one candle. The beginning of my life as the greater part of it has been since was when I was asked to tea to meet Rose Macaulay at the University Women's Club: this I owed to her friend, my headmistress, Olive Willis. In youth, and I suppose always, it is kindness with a touch of imaginative genius that one rates most highly: this I had from Rose. She lit up a confidence I had never had: having written stories, I showed them to her. With her I met Naomi Royde-Smith, then editing *The Saturday Westminster*: it was in those pages that a story of mine first appeared in print. But something more: there were Naomi's and Rose's memorable evening parties – Thursdays, I think. I went, supported by Mary Hope Allen. Inconceivably, I found myself in the same room as Edith Sitwell, Walter de la Mare, Aldous Huxley; and I know there were others. I remember almost unearthly electric light broken on brocade-angular folds of one poet's dress, and her benevolence (she was talking about something lost under a sofa) and the graven face and shining cavern eyes of the other. Of Aldous Huxley I was most nearly frightened, through no fault of his. But alas these images, and so many since, cast themselves on the screen as a silent film: I have a wonderful visual memory but a poor verbal one. I recall little or anything that has been at any time *said* – the sense and atmosphere of a conversation, yes, but the words no. And all things considered, this is a tragedy.

I suppose that literary London then was, as it is now, multicellular. That was not a thing a young provincial was likely to realize. Many of the older writers I know now, it could have been possible to meet then. In one or two cases, D. H. Lawrence, Katherine Mansfield, it was then or never: I never did meet them – but then, I hardly knew them till they were dead. My relations with London were discontinuous: for twelve years after I married I did not live there. I went to London, off and on, for a day or two at a time: strictly I think that these recollections should be called 'Going [not Coming] to London'. It was a matter of sporadic approaches, different and shifting centres of interest. I lived through the 1920s without being aware of or taking part in them: they were a placid decade of my own existence. I recall successions of parties, each of which may have stood for a further phase or a change of focus. New planets were appearing in the sky. I recall with gratitude John Strachey's 1924 literary-editorship of *The Spectator*. Cyril Connolly, whose first novel to review for *The New Statesman* had been the first novel I had written, I met at the house of Miss Ethel Sands: later, there were Cyril's and Jean's deeply enjoyable parties in the King's Road. I did not know Virginia Woolf or T. S. Eliot till I met them both at Lady Ottoline Morrell's, in Gower Street, in the early '30s. . . . I can give the sensations of my protracted London half-life better than I can give the facts: the scrappiness and subjective vagueness of this record are inherent in its attempt at truth. I *came* to London, with any finality, only when we came to live there, in 1935, in Regent's Park — and by then first impressions were over. The attraction of Regent's Park, the immediate sense that this place was habitable, were due to its seeming something out of (or in) a book. And throughout seventeen years, it did never wholly emerge from art. It was much as I had fancied London would be.

1956

PREFACES

Introduction

In the foreword to *Afterthought*, her 1962 collection of essays and prefaces, Elizabeth Bowen explained her choice of title by saying: 'The only criticism of which I am capable is a form of afterthought.' It is a remark which fits in with her preoccupation with time and memory and with the dangerous attractions of looking back. When she writes about her own work, however, whether long afterwards (as in the 1952 Preface to *The Last September* of 1929) or soon after (as in the 1945 Postscript to the wartime stories, *The Demon Lover*), retrospection never makes for sentiment or nostalgia. With one touching exception, where she admits that *The Last September* (itself a retrospective novel) 'of all my books is nearest my heart', she criticizes her past self with 'cold familiarity'. Old favourites among her stories fail 'under the test of austere re-reading', and the early manner of *Encounters* (1923) is coolly appraised for its 'blend of precocity and naivety'. 'At the beginning, I over-wrote.' So the prefaces interestingly illustrate the way her mind works, as well as casting light on the sources of her writing: the visual 'germ' behind most of the stories, the 'resistance-fantasies' necessary in wartime, the Proustian belief that only in 'afterthought' is experience thoroughly perceived.

Her prefaces about writers for whom she felt a strong affinity confirm her belief that the best criticism can be 'creative'. Space prevents the inclusion of some of these (on Flaubert and Trollope, who come in elsewhere in this selection, and on Mrs Gaskell and William Sansom), but the three best, I think, are here. They are a retrospective piece on *Orlando*, by her friend Virginia Woolf, comparing the reactions to the book amongst Elizabeth Bowen's contemporaries when it first came out in 1928 (they thought it élitist and whimsical) to its standing in 1960, when it could be seen as a necessary rebellion against solemnity, and a precursor to *The Waves*; a marvellously sympathetic account of Antonia White's *Frost in May*, a 'minor classic' about a convent school education, which interests her, characteristically, for its clash between romantic personality and closed-in discipline; and the preface to Sheridan Le

Fanu's *Uncle Silas*, which is Elizabeth Bowen's outstanding critical essay. The novel's 'psychological weather', its 'voluptuousness' and 'claustrophobia', its 'oblique suggestive art' and 'negligent virtuosity' are brilliantly described, with an acuteness which says as much about her own writing as about Le Fanu's. She guesses, quite correctly, that *Uncle Silas* is 'an Irish story transposed to an English setting', and uses the same sort of trick in her story 'The Happy Autumn Fields', where we are not told that the vanished Victorian pastoral, evoked by a London woman in a bombed flat, is meant to be County Cork. She pinpoints the 'infantilism' of Le Fanu's novel, the childishness of his heroine, Maud Ruthyn, who shows, like a 'bride of Death', the 'acquiescence of the predestined person'. In that, Maud is like her own doomed innocents, Emmeline in *To the North* or Portia in *The Death of the Heart*. And she writes extremely well about Le Fanu's indirect insinuations of violence, a technique she exploits in alarming, edgy stories such as 'The Cat Jumps' and 'The Demon Lover'. In 'Pictures and Conversations' she would attribute a powerful influence to the Anglo-Irish 'peculiarities' of 'Le Fanu and Edgeworth novels', among others. This preface locates that influence very precisely.

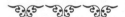

THE DEMON LOVER

The stories in the collection entitled *The Demon Lover* were written in wartime London – between the spring of 1941 and the late autumn of 1944. They were written for the magazines or papers in which they originally appeared. During these last years, I did not always write a story when I was asked for one; but I did not write any story that I was not asked for. For at the same time I have been writing a novel; and sometimes I did not want to imperil its continuity. Does this suggest that these *Demon Lover* stories have been in any way forced or unwilling work? If so, that is quite untrue. Actually, the stimulus of being asked for a story, and the compulsion created by having promised to write one were both good – I mean, they acted as releases. Each time I sat down to write a story I opened a door; and the pressure against the other side of that door must have been very great, for things – ideas, images, emotions – came through with force and rapidity, sometimes violence. I do not say that these stories wrote themselves – aesthetically or intellectually speaking, I found the writing of some of them very difficult – but I was never in a moment's doubt as to *what* I was to write. The stories had their own momentum, which I had to control. The acts in them had an authority which I could not question. Odd enough in their way – and now some seem very odd – they were flying particles of something enormous and inchoate that had been going on. They were sparks from experience – an experience not necessarily my own.

During the war I lived, both as a civilian and as a writer, with every pore open; I lived so many lives, and, still more, lived among the packed repercussions of so many thousands of other lives, all under stress, that I see now it would have been impossible to have been writing only one book. I want my novel, which deals with this same time, to be enormously comprehensive. But a novel must have form; and, for the form's sake, one is always having to make relentless exclusions. Had it not been for my from-time-to-time promises to write stories, much that had been pressing against the door might have remained pressing against it in vain. I do not feel I 'invented' anything I wrote. It seems to me that during the war the overcharged subconsciousnesses of everybody overflowed and merged. It is because the general subconsciousness saturates these stories that they have an authority nothing to do with me.

These are all wartime, none of them *war*, stories. There are no accounts of war action even as I knew it – for instance, air raids. Only one character – in 'Mysterious Kôr' – is a soldier; and he only appears as a homeless wanderer round a city. These are, more, studies of climate, war-climate, and of the strange growths it raised. I see war (or should I say feel war?) more as a territory than as a page of history: of its impersonal active historic side I have, I find, not written. Arguably, writers are always slightly abnormal people: certainly, in so-called 'normal' times my sense of the abnormal has been very acute. In war, this feeling of slight differentiation was suspended: I felt one with, and just like, everyone else. Sometimes I hardly knew where I stopped and somebody else began. The violent destruction of solid things, the explosion of the illusion that prestige, power and permanence attach to bulk and weight, left all of us, equally, heady and disembodied. Walls went down; and we felt, if not knew, each other. We all lived in a state of lucid abnormality.

Till the proofs came, I had not re-read my stories since they were, singly, written. When I read them straight through as a collection, I was most struck by what they have in common. This integrates them and gives them a cumulative and collective meaning that no one, taken singly, has by itself. *The Demon Lover* is an organic whole: not merely a collection, but somehow – for better or worse – a book. Also, the order in which the stories stand – an order come at, I may say, casually – seems itself to have a meaning, or to add a meaning, I did not foresee. We begin with a hostess who has not learned how with grace to open her own front door; we end with a pair of lovers with no place in which to sleep in each other's arms. In the first story, a well-to-do house in a polite square gives the impression of having been organically dislocated by shock; in the last, a pure abstract empty timeless city rises out of a little girl's troubled mind. Through the stories – in the order in which they are here placed – I find a rising tide of hallucination. The stories are not placed in the time-order in which they they were first written – though, by chance, 'In the Square', placed first here, *is* the first in the book I wrote, in a hot, raid-less patch of 1941 summer, just after Germany had invaded Russia.

The hallucinations in the stories are not a peril; nor are the stories studies of mental peril. The hallucinations are an unconscious, instinctive, saving resort on the part of the characters: life, mechanized by the controls of wartime, and emotionally torn and impoverished by changes, had to complete itself in *some* way. It is a fact that in Britain, and especially in London, in wartime many people had strange deep intense dreams. 'Whatever else I forget about the war,' a friend said to me, 'I hope I may never forget my own dreams, or some of the other dreams I have been told. We have never dreamed like this before; and I suppose we shall never dream like this again.' Dreams by night, and the fantasies – these often childishly innocent – with which formerly matter-of-fact people consoled themselves by day were compensations. Apart from them, I do not think that the *desiccation*, by war, of our day-to-day lives can be enough stressed. The outsize World War news was stupefying: headlines and broadcasts came down and down on us in hammerlike chops, with great impact but, oddly, little reverberation. The simple way to put it was: 'One cannot take things in.' What was happening was out of all proportion to our faculties for knowing, thinking and checking up. The circumstances under which ordinary British people lived were preposterous – so preposterous that, in a dull way, they simplified themselves. And all the time we knew that compared with those on the Continent we in Britain could not be said to suffer. Foreign faces about the London streets had personal pain and impersonal history sealed up behind the eyes. All this pressure drove egotism underground, or made it whiten like grass under a stone. And self-expression in small ways stopped – the small ways had been so very small that we had not realized how much they amounted to. Planning fun, going places, choosing and buying things, dressing yourself up, and so on. All that stopped. You used to know what you were like from the things you liked, and chose. Now there was not what you liked, and you did not choose. Any little remaining choices and pleasures shot into new proportion and new value: people paid big money for little bunches of flowers.

Literature of the Resistance has been steadily coming in from France. I wonder whether in a sense all wartime writing is not resistance writing? Personal life here, too, put up its own resistance to the annihilation that was threatening it – war. Everyone here, as is known, read more: and what was sought in books – old books, new books – was the communicative touch of personal life. To survive, not only physically but spiritually, was essential. People whose homes had been blown up went to infinite lengths to assemble bits of themselves – broken ornaments, odd shoes, torn scraps of the curtains that had hung in a room – from the wreckage. In the same way, they assembled and checked themselves from stories and poems, from their memories, from one another's talk. Outwardly, we accepted that at this time individual destiny became an obsession in every heart. You cannot depersonalize persons. Every writer during this time was aware of the personal cry of the individual. And he was aware of the passionate attachment of men and women to every object or image or place or love or fragment of memory with which his or her destiny seemed to be identified, and by which the destiny seemed to be assured.

The search for indestructible landmarks in a destructible world led many down strange paths. The attachment to these when they had been found produced small worlds-within-worlds of hallucination – in most cases, saving hallucination. Writers followed the paths they saw or felt people treading, and depicted those little dear saving illusory worlds. I have done both in *The Demon Lover* stories.

You may say that these resistance-fantasies are in themselves frightening. I can only say that one counteracts fear by fear, stress by stress. In 'The Happy Autumn Fields', one finds a woman projected from flying-bombed London, with its day-and-night eeriness, into the key emotional crisis of a Victorian girlhood. In 'Ivy Gripped the Steps', a man in the early '40s peers through the rusted fortifications and down the dusty empty perspectives of a seaside town at the Edwardian episode that has crippled his faculty for love. In 'The

Inherited Clock', a girl is led to find the key to her own neurosis inside a timepiece. The past, in all these cases, discharges its load of feeling into the anaesthetized and bewildered present. It is the 'I' that is sought – and retrieved at the cost of no little pain. And the ghosts – definite in 'Green Holly', questionable (for are they subjective purely?) in 'Pink May', 'The Cheery Soul' and 'The Demon Lover' – what part do they play? They are the certainties. The bodiless foolish wanton, the puritan other presence, the tipsy cook with her religion of English fare, the ruthless young soldier lover unheard of since 1916: hostile or not, they rally, they fill the vacuum for the uncertain 'I'.

I am sorry that my stories do not contain more 'straight' pictures of the wartime scene. Such pictures could have been interesting: they *are* interesting in much of the brilliant reportage that exists. I know that, in these stories, the backgrounds, and sometimes the circumstances, are only present by inference. Allow for the intensely subjective mood into which most of the characters have been cast. Remember that these impulsive movements of fantasy are by-products of the non-impulsive major routine of war. These are between-time stories – mostly reactions from, or intermissions between, major events. They show a levelled-down time, when a bomb on your house was as inexpedient but not more abnormal than a cold in your head. There was an element of chanciness and savageness about everything – even, the arrival at a country house for Christmas. The claustrophobia of not being able to move about freely and without having to give account of yourself – not, for instance, being able to visit a popular seaside resort, within seventy miles of London, between 1940 and 1944 – appears in many: notably, in 'Ivy Gripped the Steps'. The ghostly social pattern of London life – or, say, the conventional pattern one does not easily break, and is loath to break because it is 'I'-saving – appears in the vacant politeness of 'In the Square', and in the inebriate night-club conversation, and in 'Careless Talk'. These are ways in which some of us did go on – after all, we had to go on *some* way. And the worthless little speaker in 'Pink May' found the war made a moratorium for her married conscience. Yes, only a few were heroic purely: and see how I have not drawn the heroic ones! But everyone was pathetic – more than they knew. Owing, though, to the thunder of those inordinate years, we were shaken out of the grip of our own pathos.

In wartime, even in Britain, much has been germinating. *What*, I do not know – who does, yet, know? – but I felt the germination; and feel it, here and there, in these stories now that I read them through. These are received impressions of happening things; impressions that stored themselves up and acquired force without being analysed or considered. These, as wartime stories, are at least contemporary – twenty, forty, sixty years hence they may be found interesting as documents, even if they are found negligible as art. This discontinuous writing, nominally 'inventive', is the only diary I have kept. Transformed into images in the stories, there *may* be important psychological facts: if so, I did not realize their importance. Walking in the darkness of the nights of six years (darkness which transformed a capital city into a network of inscrutable canyons) one developed new bare alert senses, with their own savage warnings and notations. And by day one was always making one's own new maps of a landscape always convulsed by some new change. Through it all, one probably picked up more than can be answered for. I cannot answer for much that is in these stories, except to say that I know they are all true – true to the general life that was in me at the time. Taken singly, they are disjected snapshots – snapshots taken from close up, too close up, in the middle of the *mêlée* of a battle. You cannot *render*, you can only embrace – if it means embracing to suffocation-point – something vast that is happening right on top of you. Painters have painted, and photographers who were artists have photographed, the tottering lace-like architecture of ruins, dark mass-movements of people, and the untimely brilliance of flaming skies. I cannot paint or photograph like this – I have isolated, I have made for the particular, spot-lighting faces or cutting out gestures that are not even the faces or gestures of great sufferers. This is how I am, how I feel, whether in war or peacetime; and only as I am and feel can I write. As I said at the start, though I criticize these stories now, afterwards, intellectually, I cannot criticize their content. They are the particular. But through the particular, in wartime, I felt the high-voltage current of the general pass.

1945

Uncle Silas
by Sheridan Le Fanu

Uncle Silas is a romance of terror. Joseph Sheridan Le Fanu lets us know that he expanded it from a short story (length, about fifteen pages) which he wrote earlier in his literary life and published, anonymously, in a magazine – under the title of *A Passage in the Secret History of an Irish Countess*. As he does not give the name of the magazine I have not, so far, been able to trace the story. I should make further efforts to do so could I feel that its interest was very great: its initial interest, that is to say, *qua* story. It holds, it is true, the germ of the later novel – or, at least, of its plot. But about that plot itself there is little new. The exterior plot of *Uncle Silas* is traditional, well worn by the time Le Fanu took up his pen. What have we? The Wicked Uncle and the Endangered Heir. I need not point out the precedents even in English history. Also, this is the Babes in the Wood theme – but in *Uncle Silas* we have only one babe – feminine, in her late adolescence, and, therefore, the no less perpetual Beauty in Distress. Maud Ruthyn has her heroine-proto-type in a large body of fiction which ran to excess in the gothic romances but is not finished yet – the distraught young lady clasping her hands and casting her eyes skyward to Heaven: she has no other friend. . . . No, it is hard to see that simply uncle and niece, her sufferings, his designs, compressed, as they were at first, into a number of pages so small as to limit 'treatment' (Le Fanu's *forte*) could have made up into anything much more than the conventional magazine story of the day.

What *is* interesting is that Le Fanu, having written the story, should have been unable, still, to discharge its theme from his mind. He must have continued, throughout the years, to be obsessed, if subconsciously, by the niece and uncle. More, these two and their relationship to each other became magnetic to everything strangest and most powerful in his own imagination and temperament. The resultant novel, our *Uncle Silas*, owes the pressure, volume and spiritual urgency which make it comparable to *Wuthering Heights* to just this phenomenon of accretion. Accretion is a major factor in art. Le Fanu could not be rid of the niece and uncle till he had built around them a comprehensive book.

Something else draws my interest to the original story: its heroine, by the showing of the title, was Irish, by marriage if not birth. Joseph Sheridan Le Fanu (1814–73, grand-nephew of Sheridan the dramatist) was Irish; or rather Anglo-Irish. And *Uncle Silas* has always struck me as being an Irish story transposed to an English setting. The hermetic solitude and the autocracy of the great country house, the demonic power of the family myth, fatalism, feudalism and the 'ascendency' outlook are accepted facts of life for the race of hybrids from which Le Fanu sprang. For the psychological background of *Uncle Silas* it was necessary for him to invent nothing. Rather, he was at once exploiting in art and exploring for its more terrible implications what would have been the norm of his own heredity. Having, for reasons which are inscrutable, pitched on England as the setting for *Uncle Silas*, he wisely chose the north, the wildness of Derbyshire. Up there, in the vast estates of the landed old stock, there appeared, in the years when Le Fanu wrote (and still more in the years of which he wrote: the early 1840s) a time lag – just such a time lag as, in a more marked form, separates Ireland from England more effectually than any sea.

Le Fanu was not, in his generation, alone in seeing the possibilities of the country house from the point of view of drama, tension and mystery. We may comment on 'atmosphere': almost all the Victorians who were novelists used it without fuss. Wilkie Collins, for instance, wrings the last drop of effect from the woodgirt Hampshire mansion in *The Woman in White*, with its muffling, oppressive silence and eerie lake. The castles, granges and lonely halls back through romantic fiction are innumerable. One might, even, say that Le Fanu showed himself as traditional, or unoriginal, in his choice of setting as in his choice of plot. Only, while his contemporaries, the by then urbanized Victorian English, viewed the ancestral scene from the outside, the Irishman wrote out of what was in his bones.

Uncle Silas is, as a novel, Irish in two other ways: it is sexless, and it shows a sublimated infantilism. It may, for all I know, bristle with symbolism; but I speak of the story, not of its implications – in the story, no force from any one of the main characters runs into the channel of sexual feeling. The reactions of Maud, the narrator-heroine, throughout are those of a highly intelligent, still more highly sensitive, child of twelve. This may, to a degree, be accounted for by seclusion and a repressive father – but not, I think entirely: I should doubt whether Le Fanu himself realized Maud's abnormality as a heroine. She is an uncertain keyboard, on which some notes sound clearly, deeply and truly, others not at all. There is no question, here, of Victorian censorship, with its suggestive gaps: Maud, on the subject of anything she does feel, is uninhibited, sometimes disconcerting. And equally, in the feeling of people round her we are to take it that, child-like, she misses nothing. The distribution of power throughout the writing is equal, even: the briefest scene is accorded brimming sensuous content. We must in fact note how Maud's sensuousness (which is un-English) disperses, expends itself through the story in so much small change. She shows, at every turn, the carelessness, or acquiescence, of the predestined person: Maud is, by nature, a bride of Death. She delays, she equivocates, she looks wildly sideways; she delights in fire and candlelight, bedroom tea-drinking, cosy feminine company, but her bias is marked. The wind blowing her way from the family mausoleum troubles our heroine like a mating cry. Her survival after those frightful hours in the locked bedroom at Bartram-Haugh is, one can but feel, somewhat ghostly: she has cheated her Bridegroom only for the time being. Her human lover is colourless; her marriage – unexceptionable as to level and in felicity – is little more than the shell of a happy ending. From the parenthesis in her 'Conclusion' (Maud writes down her story after some years of marriage) we learn that her first child dies.

Is, then, *Uncle Silas* 'morbid'? I cannot say so. For one thing, morbidity seems to me little else than sentimentality of a peculiar tint, and nothing of that survives in the drastic air of the book. For another, Maud is counterpoised by two other characters, her unalike cousins Monica Knollys and Milly Ruthyn, who not only desire life but are its apostles. And, life itself is painted in brilliant colours – colours sometimes tantalizing, as though life were an alternative out of grasp, sometimes insidious, disturbing, as though life were a temptation. I know, as a matter of fact, of few Victorian novels in which cosiness, gaiety and the delights of friendships are so sweetly rendered or play such a telling part. Le Fanu's style, translucent, at once simple and subtle, is ideal for such transitions. He has a genius for the unexpected – in mood as well as event. One example – a knowing twist of his art – is that Maud, whose arrival at Bartram-Haugh has been fraught with sinister apprehension, should, for the first few months, delight in her uncle's house. After Knowl – overcast, repressive, stiff with proprieties – Bartram-Haugh seems to be Liberty Hall. She runs wild in the woods with her cousin Milly; for the first time, she has company of her own age. Really, it is the drama of Maud's feelings, the heightening of conflict in her between hopes and fears, rather than the melodrama of her approaching fate, which ties one to *Uncle Silas*, page after page, breathless, unwilling to miss a word.

*

Le Fanu either felt or claimed to feel uneasy as to the reception of *Uncle Silas*. He mentions the genesis of the novel, not for its interest as a creative fact, but in order to clear himself, in advance, of the charge of plagiarism: his long-ago short story had been anonymous. And, in the same 'Preliminary Word' he enters a plea that the novel be not dismissed as 'sensation' fiction. *Uncle Silas* was published in 1864: the plea would not be necessary today. Sensationalism, for its own sake, does, it is true, remain in poor repute; but sensation (of the kind which packs *Uncle Silas*) is not only not disdained, it is placed in art. The most irreproachable pens, the most poetic imaginations pursue and refine it. The status of the psychological thriller is, today, high. *Uncle Silas* was in advance of, not behind, its time: it is not the last, belated gothic romance but the first (or among the first) of the psychological thrillers. And it has, as terror-writing, a voluptuousness not approached since. (It was of the voluptuousness in his own writing that Le Fanu may, really, have been afraid.) The novel, like others of its now honoured type, relies upon suspense and mystification: I should be doing wrong to it and the reader were I to outline the story or more than hint at its end. To say that a rich, lonely girl is placed, by her father's will, in charge of an uncle who, already suspected of one murder, would be the first to profit by her death is, I think, at once sufficient and fair. But, the real suspense of the story emanates from the characters; it is they who keep the tale charged with mystery. The people in *Uncle Silas* show an extraordinary power of doubling upon or of covering their tracks. Maud seldom knows where she stands with any of them; neither do we. They are all at one remove from us, seen through the eyes of Maud. The gain to a story of this nature of being told in the first person is obvious (but for the fact that the teller, for all her dangers, must, we take it, survive, in order to tell the tale). All the same, it is not to this device that Le Fanu owes the main part of his effects – you and I, as readers, constantly intercept glances or changes in tones of voice that Maud just notes but does not interpret aright. No, Maud has little advantage over you or me. Temperamentally, and because of her upbringing, she is someone who moves about in a world of strangers. She is alternately blind and unnecessarily suspicious. Her attitude towards every newcomer is one of fatalistic mistrust; and this attitude almost, but not quite (which is subtle) communicates itself to the reader. We do not, for instance, know, for an unreasonably but enjoyably long time, whether Milly, for all her rustic frankness, may not at heart be a Little Robber Girl, or Lady Knollys a schemer under her good nature.

> You perceive [says Maud] that I had more spirit than courage. I think I had the mental attributes of courage; but then I was but an hysterical girl, and in so far neither more nor less than a coward.
>
> No wonder I distrusted myself; no wonder my will stood out against my timidity. It was a struggle, then; a proud, wild struggle against constitutional cowardice.
>
> Those who have ever had cast upon them more than their strength seems framed to bear – the weak, the aspiring, the adventurous in will, and the faltering in nerve – will understand the kind of agony which I sometimes endured.

And later, on receiving comforting news:

> You will say then that my spirits and my serenity were quite restored. Not quite. How marvellously lie our anxieties, in filmy layers, one over the other! Take away that which has lain on the upper surface for so long – the care of cares – the only one, as it seemed to you, between your soul and the radiance of Heaven – and straight you find a new stratum there. As physical science tells us no fluid is without its skin, so does it seem with this fine medium of the soul, and those successive films of care that form upon its surface on mere contact with the upper air and light.

Who are the characters whom, in *Uncle Silas*, this at once nervous and spirited girl confronts? There is her father, Austin Ruthyn of Knowl, scion and reigning head of an ancient family, wealthy, recluse, widower, given up to Swedenborgian religion. There is Mr Ruthyn's spiritual director Dr Bryerly – 'bilious, bewigged, black-eyed' – whose nocturnal comings and goings seem to bode no good. There is Mr Ruthyn's first cousin Lady Knollys, woman of the world, who comes to stay at Knowl and interests herself in Maud. There is Maud's French governess Madame de la Rougierre, who, arriving early on in the story, gibbers in moonlight outside the drawing-room window.

Half-way through, story and heroine cross sixty miles of country. Austin Ruthyn is dead: his place in Maud's life is taken by his younger brother Silas, of Bartram-Haugh – reformed rake, widower and, again, religious recluse. Silas's marriage to a barmaid had dealt the first, though not yet the worst, blow to Ruthyn family pride. Children of the marriage are Milly ('a very rustic Miranda,' her father says) and Dudley, a sinister Tony Lumpkin. In the Bartram-Haugh woods dwell an ill-spoken miller and his passionate daughter. . . . In both great houses there is the usual cast of servants – at Knowl, correct, many and reassuring; at Bartram-Haugh few and queer. On from this point, characterization, in any full sense, stops: we are left with 'types', existing, solely and flatly, for the require-ments of the plot. A fortune-hunting officer, three clergymen, two lawyers and a thoughtful peer, Maud's future husband, come under this heading.

That last group, uninspired and barely tinted in, represents Le Fanu's one economy. In the main, it could be a charge against him that too many of the characters in *Uncle Silas* are overcharged, and that they break their bounds. There is abnormal pressure, from every side; the psychic air is often overheated. And all the time, we must remember, this is a story intended to be dominated by the figure of one man: Uncle Silas. All through, Uncle Silas meets competition. He is, I think, most nearly played off the stage by Madame de la Rougierre. Apart from that he is (as central character) at a disadvan-tage: *is* he, constantly, big enough for his own build-up? Is there or is there not, in scenes in which he actually appears, a just perceptible drop into anticlimax? Le Fanu, in dealing with Uncle Silas, was up against a difficulty inherent in his kind of oblique, suggestive art. He has overdrawn on his Silas in advance. In the flesh, Uncle Silas enters the story late: by this time, his build-up has reached towering heights. It is true that most of the time at Bartram-Haugh he remains off stage, and that those intervals allow of batteries being recharged. At Knowl, still only a name, he was ever-present – in the tormented silences of his brother, the hinting uneasy chatter of Lady Knollys, and Maud's dreams.

I don't [Lady Knollys admits, to Maud] understand metaphysics, my dear, nor witchcraft. I sometimes believe in the supernatural, and sometimes I don't. Silas Ruthyn is himself alone, and I can't define him because I don't understand him. Perhaps other souls than human are sometimes born into the world, and clothed in flesh. It is not only about that dreadful occurrence, but nearly always throughout his life; early and late he has puzzled me. . . . At one time of his life I am sure he was awfully wicked – eccentric indeed in his wickedness – gay, frivolous, secret and dangerous. At one time I think he could have made poor Austin do almost anything; but his influence vanished with his marriage, never to return again. No; I don't understand him. He has always bewildered me, like a shifting face, sometimes smiling, but always sinister, in an unpleasant dream.

Here is Maud, on arrival at Bartram-Haugh, fresh from her first meeting with her uncle:

When I lay down in my bed and reviewed the day, it seemed like a month of wonders. Uncle Silas was always before me; the voice so silvery for an old man – preternaturally soft; the manner so sweet, so gentle; the aspect smiling, suffering, spectral. It was no longer a shadow; I had now seen him in the flesh. But, after all, was he more than a shadow to me? When I closed my eyes I saw him before me still, in necromantic black, ashy with a pallor on which I looked with fear and pain, a face so dazzlingly pale, and those hollow, fiery, awful eyes! It sometimes seemed to me as though the curtain had opened, and I had seen a ghost.

'What a sweet, gentle, insufferable voice he has!' exclaims, later, Lady Knollys, who, for Maud's sake, has tried to reopen relations with Bartram-Haugh. And, towards the end, we hear the beleaguered Maud: 'There were the sensualities of the gourmet for his body, and there ended his human nature, as it seemed to me. Through that semi-transparent structure I thought I could now and then discern the light or glare of his inner life. . . . Was, then, all his kindness but a phosphoric radiance covering something colder and more awful than the grave?'

Of the French governess, what is one to say? She is Uncle Silas's rival or counterpart. She is physical as opposed to metaphysical evil. No question of 'semi-transparent structure' here – the Frenchwoman is of the rankest bodily coarseness: one can smell her breath, as it were, at every turn. In the *Uncle Silas* atmosphere, bleached of sex, she is no more woman than he is man; yet, somehow, her marelike coquetry – that prinking with finery and those tales of lovers – is the final, grotesque element of offence. As a woman, she can intrude on the girl at all points. She is obscene; and not least so in the alternate pinchings and pawings to which she subjects Maud. While the uncle gains in monstrousness by distance, the governess gains in monstrousness by closeness.

Madame de la Rougierre is unhandicapped by a preliminary build-up: she enters the story without warning and makes growth, page by page, as she goes along. Le Fanu, through the mouths of his characters, is a crack marksman in the matter of epithets: nothing said of the governess goes wide. He had, it is true, with this Frenchwoman a great vein to work on: with Wilkie Collins and Dickens he could exploit the British concept of the foreigner as sinister. Her broken English (with its peculiar rhythm, like no other known broken English, specially coined for her) further twists, in speech, the thoughts of her hideous mind. Like Uncle Silas, Madame de la Rougierre is, morally, of an unrelieved black: considering how much we are in her company it is wonderful that she does not become monotonous – the variations Le Fanu *has* contrived to give her are to be admired. 'When things went well,' we are told, 'her soul lighted up into sulphureous good-humour.' The stress is most often upon this woman's mouth – a 'large-featured, smirking phantom' is Maud's first view of her, through the drawing-room window. We have her 'wide, wet grin'. She would 'smile with her great carious teeth'.

This creature's background is never fully given. Indeed, her engagement, as his daughter's companion, by Mr Ruthyn of Knowl, is, with his obstinate tolerance of her presence, one of the first anomalies of the plot.

*

Uncle Silas, as a novel, derives its power from an inner momentum. In the exterior plot there are certain weaknesses, inconsistencies and loose ends. In this regard, the book has about it a sort of brilliant – nay, even inspired – amateurishness; a sort of negligent virtuosity in which Le Fanu shows his race. This may be the reason why *Uncle Silas* has never yet quite made the popular grade. It has not so far, that is to say, moved forward from being a favourite book of individual people into the rank of accepted Victorian classics.

It cannot, I think, be said that most Victorian novels are guiltless of loose ends. But, in their elaborate plots with their sub-structures, crowds of characters and varied, shifting scenes, there is usually more to distract the eye: reader as well as author may well overlook something. *Uncle Silas* is, in this matter, defenceless in its simplicity: it has no sub-plots and contains comparatively few people. The writing is no less simple: this, its beauty apart, is its great virtue. The effect of the simplicity is, that every sentence of Le Fanu's – or, at least, its content – incises itself deeply upon one's memory: one can forget not the slightest hint or statement or question. And, the excitingness of the story keeps one on the stretch, at once watchful and challenging, like a child listener. Like the child, one finds oneself breaking in, from time to time, with: 'But – ? . . . But, I thought you *said* –?'

The omissions or inconsistencies of the plot are not psychological; they are practical or mechanical. They do not, to my mind, detract from or injure the real story, because they are not on its reallest plane. However, there they are. I do not feel it to be the function of this Introduction to point them out to the reader in advance – I intend, therefore, only to mention one, which could hardly escape the most careless eye. *Who* was the concealed witness who relayed to Maud the conversation between Madame de la Rougierre and Dudley Ruthyn at Church Scarsdale? A witness who must, by the way, have been no less observant and subtle than Maud herself, for no inflection, gesture or glance is lost. We are never told who it is. The most likely bid is Tom Brice, the girl Beauty's lover and, at one time, Dudley's hanger-on. Tom might have told Beauty, who might have told Maud. But the account does not sound as though it had come through the mouths of two peasants. . . . Elsewhere, the fact that the degree and origin of the Frenchwoman's relationship with the Bartram-Haugh Ruthyns is never stated may worry some readers. We are left to infer that she was, already, their agent from before the time she arrived at Knowl.

The plot is obfuscated (sometimes, one may say, helpfully) by an extraordinary vagueness about time. This is a book in which it is impossible to keep a check on the passage of weeks, months, years. The novel is dominated by one single season in whose mood it is pitched: autumn. Practically no other season is implied or named. (Yes, we have a Christmas visit to Elvaston, and a mention, elsewhere, of January rain. And after Madame de la Rougierre's departure from Knowl Maud, in the joy of her release, is conscious of singing birds and blue skies – but those could be in September.) The whole orchestral range of the novel's weather is autumnal – tranced dripping melancholy, crystal morning zest, the radiance of the magnified harvest moon, or the howl and straining of gales through not yet quite leafless woods. The daylight part of Maud's drive to her uncle's house is through an amber landscape. The opening words of the novel are, it is true, 'It was winter. . . .' But our heroine, contradictory with her first breath, then adds: 'the second week in November'. By this reckoning Maud, in telling Lady Knollys that Madame de la Rougierre had arrived at Knowl 'in February' is incorrect. The Frenchwoman, we had been clearly told, arrived 'about a fortnight' after the opening scene. . . . No, there is nothing for it: one must submit oneself to Le Fanu's hypnotizing, perpetual autumn. One autumn merges into another: hopeless to ask how much has happened between! Yet always, against this nebulous flow of time stand out the moments – each unique, comprehensive, crystal, painfully sharp.

The inner, non-practical, psychological plot of *Uncle Silas* is, I suggest, faultless: it has no inconsistencies. The story springs from and is rooted in an obsession, and the obsession never looses its hold. Austin Ruthyn of Knowl, by an inexorable posthumous act, engages his daughter's safety in order to rescue his brother's honour. Or rather, less Silas's honour than the family name's. Silas Ruthyn is a man under a cloud: he has never yet been cleared of a charge against him. Austin's having committed Maud to his brother's keeping is to demonstrate, to the eyes of a hostile world, his absolute faith in his brother's innocence. By surviving years under his lonely roof, Maud, whose next heir he is, is to vindicate Silas. Maud has, during her father's lifetime, agreed in principle to the trust. (She has still, be it said, to hear the terms of the will, and to learn the full story of Silas from Lady Knollys.)

> I think [Austin says to his daughter] little Maud would like to contribute to the restitution of her family name. . . . The character and influence of an ancient family is a peculiar heritage – sacred but destructible; and woe to him who either destroys or suffers it to perish.

Call this *folie de grandeur*, or a fanaticism of the Almanach de Gotha. It is the extreme of a point of view less foreign to Le Fanu than to his readers. It was a point of view that they, creatures of an industrialized English nineteenth century, were bound to challenge, and could deride. It could only hope to be made acceptable, as mainspring and premise of his story, by being challenged, criticized – even, by implication, derided – in advance, and on behalf of the reader, by a person located somewhere inside the story. The necessary mouthpiece is Dr Bryerly. Dr Bryerly's little speech to Maud is a piece of, as it were, insurance, on Le Fanu's part. 'There are people', remarks Dr Bryerly, 'who think themselves just as great as the Ruthyns, or greater; and your poor father's idea of carrying it by a demonstration was simply the dream of a man who had forgotten the world, and learned to exaggerate himself by his long seclusion.' True – and how effective. The reader's misgivings, his fear of being implicated in something insanely disproportionate, have been set at rest. He is now prepared to lean back and accept, as Le Fanu wished, the idea on one – but that a great – merit purely: its validity for the purposes of the tale.

One more comment, before we leave the plot. In the disposition of characters (including what I have called functional types) about the field of the story, Le Fanu shows himself, as a novelist, admirably professional, in a sense that few of his contemporaries were. Not a single, even the slightest, character is superfluous; not one fails to play his or her part in the plot, or detains us for a second after that part is played. One or two (such as the house party guests at Elvaston) are merely called in to act on Maud's state of mind. But Maud's mind, we must remember, reflects, and colours according to its states, the action of the interior plot. No person is in the story simply to fill up space, to give the Victorian reader his money's worth, or to revive flagging interest – Le Fanu, rightly, did not expect interest to flag.

*

The background, or atmosphere, needs little discussion: in the first few pages one recognizes the master-touch. The story of *Uncle Silas* is, as I have indicated, as to scene divided between two houses: Knowl and Bartram-Haugh. The contrast between the two houses contributes drama. Knowl, black and white, timbered, set in well-tended gardens, is a rich man's home. It is comfortable; fires roar in the grates; pictures and panelling gleam; the servants do all they should. As against this, Knowl is overcast, rigid, haunted: Mr Ruthyn is closeted with dark mysteries; there are two ghosts, and, nearby, the family mausoleum, in which Maud's young mother lies and to which her father is to be carried under the most charnel circumstances of death.

Maud, sitting with Lady Knollys after Austin's death, hears the wind come roaring her way through the woods from the mausoleum. The wind, Lady Knollys can but point out, comes, too, from the more really threatening direction of Bartram-Haugh. Uncle Silas's house, already the scene of one violent death, is, beforehand, invested with every terror. Bartram-Haugh, as first seen, demands a John Piper drawing:

I was almost breathless as I approached. The bright moon shining fully on the white front of the old house revealed not only its highly decorated style, its fluted pillars and doorway, rich and florid carving and balustraded summit, but also its stained and mossgrown front. Two giant trees, overthrown at

last by the recent storm, lay with their upturned roots, and their
yellow foliage still flickering on the sprays that were to bloom
no more, where they had fallen, at the right side of the
courtyard, which, like the avenue, was tufted with weeds and
grass.

'The mind is', as Maud elsewhere remarks, 'a different organ by
night and by day.' Next morning's awakening is reassuring – a
wakening to bright morning through bare windows, a cheerful
breakfast, superb if neglected stretches of parkland, a blackberrying
walk. Exploration, with Milly, of whole closed derelict floors and
internal galleries brings only a fleeting memory of the ill-fated
Charke. The psychological weather of those first Bartram-Haugh
chapters is like the out-of-doors weather: gay and tingling. Till Milly
is sent away, nothing goes wholly wrong.

From *that* point, the closing in is continuous. The ruined rooms,
the discovery of the ogress-governess in hiding, introduce the beginning of the end. . . . All through Le Fanu's writing, there is an ecstatic
sensitivity to light, and an abnormal recoil from its inverse, darkness.
Uncle Silas is full of outdoor weather – we enjoy the rides and glades,
cross the brooks and stiles, meet the cottagers and feel the enclosing
walls of two kingdom-like great estates. Though static in ever-
autumn, those scenes change: there is more than the rolling across
them of clouds or sunshine. Indeed we are looking at their reflection
in the lightening or darkening mirror of Maud's mind.

*

Uncle Silas is a romance of terror, written more than eighty years
ago. Between then and now, human susceptibilities have altered –
some may have atrophied, others developed further. The terror-
formula of yesterday might not work today. Will *Uncle Silas* act on
the modern reader?

I think so, and for several reasons. Le Fanu's strength, here, is not
so much in his story as in the mode of its telling. *Uncle Silas*, as it is
written, plays on one constant factor – our childish fears. These leave
their work at the base of our natures, and are never to be rationalized
away. Two things are terrible in childhood: helplessness (being in
other people's power) and apprehension – the apprehension that
something is being concealed from us because it is too bad to be told.
Maud Ruthyn, vehicle of the story, is helpless apprehension itself, in
person: this is what gets under our skin. Maud, simplified (in the
chemical sense, reduced) for her creator's purpose, is, we may tell

ourselves, an extreme case. She has a predisposition towards fear: we are to watch her – and be her – along her way towards the consummation of perfect terror – just as, were this a love story, we should be sharing her journey towards a consummation of a different kind. Proust has pointed out that the predisposition to love creates its own objects: is this not true of fear? At the start Maud, in her unconscious search, experiments with Dr Bryerly: she fears him. He acts as the forecast shadow of Uncle Silas – and, that he may play this rôle for the first act, he is given all the necessary trappings. Then, the Doctor discloses a character in point-blank reverse: he is level-headed, a man of daylight, unfailing good counsellor, champion, friend. But by that time, what the Doctor is does not matter: using the love–fear analogy, he is an off-cast love. He has been superseded by Uncle Silas, past whom Maud has no further to look.

Maud had suspected in Dr Bryerly a supernatural element of evil: his influence on her father appeared malign. This brings us to another terror-ingredient: moral dread. Should one call this timeless, or is it modern? Let us say, it is timeless, but that its refinement in literature has been modern. (By modern I mean, modern at the best.) Henry James inspired, and remains at the head of, a whole school of moral horror stories – I need not point out that it is the stench of evil, not the mere fact of the supernatural, which is the genuine horror of *The Turn of the Screw*. Our ancestors may have had an agreeable–dreadful reflex from the idea of the Devil or a skull-headed revenant popping in and out through a closed door: we need, to make us shiver, the effluence from a damned soul. In *Uncle Silas*, there is no supernatural element in the ordinary sense – the Knowl ghosts exist merely to key Maud up. The genuine horror is in the non-natural. Lady Knollys, in her chatter, suggests that Silas may be a non-human soul clothed in a human body.

What Maud dreads, face to face with Silas, is not her own death.

Physically, Maud's nerve is extremely good. She stands up to Madame de la Rougierre, to whom her reactions are those of intense dislike, repugnance and disdain. She is frightened only of what she cannot measure, and she has got the governess taped. With the same blend of disdain and clear-sightedness, she stands up to Dudley. She shows, I think, remarkable nonchalance in re-exploring the top rooms alone, in the late dusk, after Milly's departure. As the plot thickens round her and door after door clangs to, she shows herself fanatically disposed, up to the very last minute, to give her uncle the benefit of the doubt. Were she, in fact, a goose or weakling, the story would lack the essential tension: *Uncle Silas* would fail. As it is, we have the impact of a crescendo of hints and happenings on taut, hyper-controlled and thus very modern nerves. *Is* there to be a breaking-point? If so, why, how, when? That, not the question of Maud's bodily fate, sets up the real excitement of *Uncle Silas*.

The let-up, the pause for recuperation, even the apparent solicitude: these are among the sciences of the torture chamber. The victim must regain his power to suffer fully. The let-ups in *Uncle Silas* – the fine days, the walks, the returned illusions of safety – are, for Maud and the reader, artfully timed. Nothing goes on for long enough either to dull you or to exhaust itself. And the light, the open air, the outdoor perspective enhance, by contrast, the last of the horror-constants – claustrophobia. On the keyboard of any normal reader *Uncle Silas* will not, I think, fail to strike one or another note: upon the claustrophobic it plays a fugue. The sense of the tightening circle, the shrinking and darkening room. . . .

Just as the outer plot of *Uncle Silas* is traditional, or unoriginal, Le Fanu does draw also, for fear or horror, out of the traditional bag of tricks – the lonely ruinous house, the closed rooms, the burning eyes, the midnight voices, the hired assassins, and so on. Maud herself, exploring Bartram-Haugh in the dusk, has in mind the romances of Mrs Radcliffe. The induction of misery and despair preparatory to slaughter is Elizabethan. . . . In so far as *Uncle Silas* uses physical horror, the use is extremely sophisticated: Maud's quick and almost voluptuous reactions to sound, sight, touch and smell make her the perfect reagent. The actual sound of a murder, a messy butchery, has probably never, in any gangster story, been registered as it is here.

*

The function of an Introduction is, I think, to indicate the nature of a book and to suggest some angles for judgment. That judgment the reader himself must form. *Uncle Silas* will, in this new edition, reach, among others, a generation of readers who have grown up since the novel was last in print. They may read into it more than I have found. That it will have meaning for them I do not doubt.

1947

Frost in May
by Antonia White

Frost in May is a girls' school story. It is not the only school story to be a classic; but I can think of no other that is a work of art. What, it may be wondered, is the distinction? A major classic is necessarily also a work of art. But a book may come to be recognized as a minor classic by right of virtues making for durability – vigour, wideness, kindness, manifest truth to life. Such a book gathers something more, as the years go on, from the affection that has attached to it – no question of its aesthetic value need be raised. A work of art, on the other hand, may and sometimes does show deficiency in some of the qualities of the minor classic – most often kindness. As against this, it brings into being unprecedented moments; it sets up sensation of a unique and troubling kind.

School stories may be divided and subdivided. There is the school story proper, written for school-age children; and the school novel, written for the grown-up. There is the pro-school school story and the anti-school – recently almost all school novels have fallen into the latter class. *Tom Brown's Schooldays* has a host of dimmer descendants, all written to inculcate manliness and show that virtue pays. *Stalky and Co.* fits into no classification: one might call it an early gangster tale in a school setting. The Edwardian novelist's talent for glamorizing any kind of society was turned by E. F. Benson and H. A. Vachell on two of the greater English public schools. The anti-school school novel emerged when, after the First World War, intellectuals captured, and continued to hold, key positions along the front of fiction. A few, too few, show a sublime disinfectedness that makes for comedy, or at least satire. In the main, though, the hero of the anti-school novel is the sombre dissentient and the sufferer. He is in the right: the school, and the system behind it, is wrong. From the point of view of art, which should be imperturbable, such novels are marred by a fractious or plangent note. Stephen Spender's *The Backward Son*, not thus marred, is a work of art; but I should not call it strictly a school novel – primarily it is a study of temperament.

To return to the school story proper (written for young people), those for boys are infinitely better than those for girls. The curl-tossing tomboys of the Fourth at St Dithering's are manifestly and insultingly unreal to any girl child who has left the nursery; as against this, almost all young schoolgirls devour boys' school books, and young boys, apparently, do not scorn them. For my own part, I can think of only one girls' school story I read with pleasure when young, and can re-read now – Susan Coolidge's *What Katy Did at School*. As a girls' school *novel* (other than *Frost in May*) I can only think of Colette's *Claudine à l'École*.

I began by calling *Frost in May* a school story. By subsequent definition it is a school novel – that is to say, it is written for grown-ups. But – which is interesting – Antonia White has adopted the form and sublimated, without complicating, the language of the school story proper. *Frost in May* could be read with relish, interest and excitement by an intelligent child of twelve years old. The heroine, Nanda Grey, is nine when she goes to Lippington, thirteen when, catastrophically, she leaves. She is in no way the born 'victim' type – she is quick-witted, pleasing, resilient, normally rather than morbidly sensitive. Call her the high-average 'ordinary' little girl. She is not even, and is not intended to be, outstandingly sympathetic to the reader: the scales are not weighted on her behalf. We have Nanda's arrival at Lippington, first impressions, subsequent adaptations, apparent success and, finally, head-on crash. *Frost in May* deviates from the school-story formula only in not having a happy ending. We are shown the school only through Nanda's eyes – there is no scene from which she is off stage. At the same time there is no impressionistic blurring, none of the distortions of subjectivity: Lippington is presented with cool exactness. Antonia White's style as a story-teller is as precise, clear and unweighty as Jane Austen's. Without a lapse from this style Antonia White traverses passages of which the only analogy is to be found in Joyce's *Portrait of the Artist as a Young Man*.

The subject of this novel is in its title – *Frost in May*. Nanda shows, at the start, the prim, hardy pink-and-white of a young bud. What is to happen to her – and how, or why?

Of the two other girls' school books named, one is American and the other French. *Frost in May* is English – but English by right only of its author's birth and its geographic setting. Lippington is at the edge of London. But it is a convent school – of a Roman Catholic order which Antonia White calls 'the Five Wounds'. Its climate is its own; its atmosphere is, in our parlance, international. Or, more properly, as one of the girls put it, 'Catholicism isn't a religion, it's a nationality'. A Lippington girl is a Child of the Five Wounds; she may by birth be French, German, Spanish or English, but that is secondary. Also the girls here show a sort of family likeness: they are the daughters of old, great Catholic families, the frontierless aristocracy of Europe; they have in common breeding as well as faith. From Spanish Rosario, Irish Hilary and French-German Léonie the rawness of English Protestant middle-class youth is missing. Initially, Nanda is at a twofold disadvantage, never quite overcome. Her father is a convert; she herself was received into the Catholic Church only a year before her arrival at Lippington. And, she is middle-class, her home is in Earl's Court. There is one Protestant here, but she is aristocratic; there are two other middle-class girls, but they come of Catholic stock.

Lippington is a world in itself – hermetic to a degree possible for no lay school. It contains, is contained in, and represents absolute, and absolutely conclusive, authority. Towards what aim is that authority exercised? On the eve of the holiday that is to celebrate the canonization of the foundress of the Order, the Mistress of Discipline addresses the school:

> 'Some of that severity which to the world seems harshness is bound up in the school rule which you are privileged to follow. . . . We work today to turn out, not accomplished young women, nor agreeable wives, but soldiers of Christ, accustomed to hardship and ridicule and ingratitude.'

What are the methods?

> As in the Jesuit Order every child was under constant observation, and the results of this observation were made known by secret weekly reports to Mother Radcliffe and the Superior. . . .

How did one child, Nanda, react to this?

> Nanda's rebelliousness, such as it was, was directed entirely against the Lippington methods. Her faith in the Catholic Church was not affected in the least. If anything, it became more robust.

Nonetheless, when, at thirteen, Nanda is faced by her father with the suggestion that she should leave Lippington to receive a more workaday education elsewhere, her reaction is this:

> She was overwhelmed. . . . Even now, in the shock of the revelation of her dependence, she did not realise how thoroughly Lippington had done its work. But she felt blindly she could only live in that rare, intense element; the bluff, breezy air of that 'really good High School' would kill her.

And, elsewhere:

> In its [Lippington's] cold, clear atmosphere everything had a
> sharper outline than in the comfortable, shapeless, scrambling
> life outside.

That atmosphere and that outline, their nature, and the nature of
their power over one being, Nanda, are at once the stuff and the
study of *Frost in May*. They are shown and felt. The result has been
something intense, sensuous, troubling, semi-miraculous – a work of
art. In the biting crystal air of the book the children and the nuns
stand out like early morning mountains. In this frigid, authoritarian,
anti-romantic Catholic climate every romantic vibration from
'character' is, in effect, trebled. *Frost in May* could, for instance, go
down to time on the strength, alone, of Léonie de Wesseldorf –
introduced, in parenthesis almost, but living from the first phrase, on
page 78. Momentum gathers round each sequence of happenings
and each event – the First Communion, the retreat, the canonization
holiday, Mother Francis's death, the play for the cardinal, the
measles idyll. . . . Lyricism – pagan in the bonfire scene, sombre on
the funeral morning – gains in its pure force from the very
infrequency of its play. . . . Art, at any rate in a novel, must be
indissolubly linked with craft: in *Frost in May* the author's handling
of time is a technical triumph – but, too, a poetic one.

The *interest* of the book is strong, though secondary; it is so strong
that that it should be secondary is amazing. If you care for controversy, the matter of *Frost in May* is controversial. There exists in the
mind of a number of English readers an inherited dormant violence
of anti-Popery: to one type of mind *Frost in May* may seem a gift too
good to be true – it is. Some passages are written with an effrontery
that will make the Protestant blink – we are very naïve. As a school
Lippington does, of course, run counter to the whole trend of English
liberal education: to the detached mind this is in itself fascinating.
The child-psychologist will be outraged by the Lippington attitude to
sex and class. Nanda's fate – one might almost feel, Nanda's doom –
raises questions that cannot be disposed of easily, or perhaps at all.
This book is intimidating. Like all classics, it acquires further
meaning with the passage of time. It was first published in 1933:
between then and now our values, subconscious as well as conscious,
have been profoundly changed. I think it not unlikely that *Frost in
May* may be more comprehensible now than it was at first.

1948

ENCOUNTERS

These stories, the first of mine to be published, were written when I was between twenty and twenty-three. Their arrangement is that of the first edition, 1923, as to which I was helped by Frank Sidgwick, my first publisher. The order happens to be, roughly, chronological, though I do not think either of us had that in mind.

I must have re-read *Encounters* several times when the original copy reached my hands: to have failed to be dazzled by print would have been unnatural. (Not one of the stories had ever 'appeared' before; all magazine editors had rejected them.) Since that summer, I had not read the collection through till I undertook this much later edition's preface. By now, I ought to be old enough to control those split, heated or tangled feelings aroused in writers by their very early work. All the same, can I hope to approach *Encounters* as dispassionately as if these were stories by some unknown young person, sent to me for an opinion, or a review? I suppose not.

What I remember, chiefly, about the writing is, the newness of the sensation of writing anything. It is, of course, to be doubted whether that sensation does ever become familiar; or, still more, whether the writer ought to desire that it should. The sense of total commitment, of desperate and overweening enterprise, of one's whole self being forced to a conclusive ordeal, remains a constant. What possibly does wear off (or grow through familiarity less acute) is that first uncanny complicity with one's physical surroundings, the objects, sounds, colours and lights-and-shades comprehensively known as 'the writing-table'. The room, the position of the window, the convulsive and anxious grating of my chair on the board floor were hyper-significant for me: here were sensuous witnesses to my crossing the margin of a hallucinatory world.

Embarking upon my first story, 'Breakfast' (not the first I had started, but the first that I had finished), I felt this to be, somehow, a last hope. I was twenty; already I had failed to be a poet; I was in the course of failing to be a painter. My whereabouts was the top of a villa at Harpenden, an attic of which the dormer window was set high – only when I stood up could I see back gardens, apple trees, a blur of Hertfordshire country away beyond. Between the sill of the window and the top of my table intervened a stretch of cream-dotted white wall-paper, lightly mapped by damp – damp which must have filtered in through the outdoor tiling. The map, as I sat at the table, was at eye-level. The short curtains, sprigged with moss roses, had often blown out into the rain; fretting over my head they smelled slightly musty. Now and then a voice from one or other of the gardens could be heard. The main line of the (then) Midland Railway ran along the end of my aunt's road: from time to time an express roared by, or, more intrusively, a slower train rattled towards the Harpenden stop. I wrote by hand, as clearly as seemed possible – as when at school, two or three years before, I had been making a presentable copy of an essay. A bottle of blue-black ink stood in a saucer; I used a ribbed brown pen-holder with a 'Relief' nib. The writing block, which had cost ninepence, had lined pages: this I found an aid to clearness of thought.

The importance to the writer of first writing must be out of all proportion to the actual value of what is written. It was more difficult then than it would be now to disentangle what was *there*, there on the page, from the excitement which had given it birth. There could be but one test of validity: publication. I know I shaped every line in the direction of the unknown arbiter. When I say that had I not written with the idea of being published I should not have written, I should add that I did not so much envisage glory as desire to know that I *had* made sense. I wanted proof that I was not prey to delusions – moreover, publication was the necessary gateway to being read. I know that I wrote then with no less, though also with no more, difficulty than I do today: as an occupation writing enthralled me, which made it suspect, but also killed me, which made it in some way 'right'. The thing was a struggle. I saw no point in killing myself for the sake of anything that was not to become an outright reality. For me reality meant the books I had read – and I turned round, as *I* was writing, from time to time, to stare at them, unassailable in the shelves behind me. (This was my room, containing most things I owned.) I had engaged myself to add to their number.

To retreat upon the short story, when one is a poet *manqué*, is today a decision frequently made. In my youth the short story's position was more anomalous. It had not yet, I think I am right in saying, been recognized as 'a form'. There had been, so far, little constructive-critical interest in the short story's inherent powers and problems. Or were there any such interest, I did not know of it – I could not have been further out of the movement. I had not gone to a university; I formed part of no intellectual group or aesthetic coterie.

I read widely, but wildly. I did not know the stories of Hardy or Henry James; I had heard of Chekhov, but no more. I had not read Maupassant because I dreaded the bother of reading French. . . . Katherine Mansfield was not only to be the innovator but to fly the flag: since *Bliss* the short story had been more prominent. I first read *Bliss* after I had completed my own first set of stories, to be *Encounters* – then, exaltation and envy were shot through, instantly, by foreboding. 'If I ever *am* published, they'll say I copied her.' I was right.

Did I, then, in writing my early stories, imagine I was doing something without precedent? Not quite. I had come on examples, which were incentives – Richard Middleton's *The Ghost Ship*, E. M. Forster's *The Celestial Omnibus*. Both I had read at school.

The *Encounters* stories are a blend of precocity and naïvety. Today, they do not seem to me badly written; the trouble with some may be, they were not well found. But at twenty – twenty-one, twenty-two, twenty-three – where is one to turn? Stories require people (*other* people). At that age one is bound up in one's own sensations – those appear to be new; actually, what is new is one's awareness of them, and one's pleased cultivation of that awareness. Literature, in those particular years, excited me according to its power to reflect, express, magnify and give body to states of feeling of which I came to be conscious in myself. Also, it would not be too much to say that my attitude to literature was brigandish; I could not wait to rifle its vocabulary. I was at the pupil stage, too glad to be shown anything that I had not seen. I perceive, now, how in the *Encounters* stories I was making use (at times) of synthetic language to express what *was* real and true to me nonetheless.

To do myself justice, I was clever in my way of using a story as a device – partly framework for, partly justification of, what I did care truly to gaze upon, or what interested me. The characters in the stories – are they no more than stand-ins, or impatiently jerked-at marionettes? To them, I appear ungratefully harsh. It is the harshness, the quickness to show up, or score off, those helpless *Encounters* 'characters' which today displeases me. Were they called into being to be made a mock of? *Encounters'* author was not so much adolescent as an instance of overprotected childhood. . . . It seems worth remarking (*a*) that with very few exceptions – the child in 'Coming Home', the schoolgirls in 'Daffodils', Laura in 'Sunday Evening' – all these men and women were senior to myself, involved in experiences I did not wot of, often gutted by passions beyond my ken: and (*b*) that not more than three of them bore resemblance to anybody met in my (then) brief life. They all the more impressed me, I do remember, by having a 'realness' for which I could not account. They came it over me, even while I stuck pins in them, by wearing a badge of maturity which was none of mine.

I feel that I had a snobbery with regard to age. For my generation, grown-ups were the ruling class. As an only child I had lived very much among them, noted as closely as possible their habits, and filed what appeared to be their ideas. Motherless since I was thirteen, I was in and out of the homes of my different relatives – and, as constantly, shuttling between two countries: Ireland and England. I was, it seemed, at everyone's disposition. Though quite happy, I lived with a submerged fear that I might fail to establish grown-up status. That fear, it may be, egged me on to writing: an author, a grown-up, must they not be synonymous? As far as I now see, I must have been anxious to approximate to my elders, yet to demolish them. At the same time, I was not yet ready to try conclusions with any world I knew. My story characters, therefore, lived in houses which, in life, I had no more than glimpsed from the outside.

So far, social motive. Dislike of myself being at a disadvantage may have caused me to take it out of my characters at a disadvantage, to snapshot them at a succession of moments when weakness, mistrust, falseness were most exposed. But, one point more: in fairness to the writer of *Encounters* one must allow for intellectual fashion, and for the psychological climate of a decade. The now famous '20s, asceptic and disabused, had already set in, though without a name. If I was *mal elevée* in my attitude to the human race, so were my betters.

The *Encounters* stories have build, style and occasional felicities of expression which I must say I like. They have a striking visual clarity; and though there may occur 'conscious' phrases, sense and feeling seldom bog down in words. And I find in the best of them something better – an attempt to say something not said before. 'Daffodils', 'Requiescat', 'All Saints', 'Mrs Windermere', 'The Shadowy Third', 'Sunday Evening' and 'Coming Home' claim my respect. As a performance, 'The Return' is the most showy, but it has a hollow kernel – a situation I must have thought up, rather than felt. A ring of emotion issues from 'Coming Home' – which, in fact, was transposed autobiography. 'Requiescat' and 'The Shadowy Third' make me, now, clearly see how I used to work: I would posit a situation and then explore it. A more malignant example of that method is, 'The Evil that Men Do –'.

I was still not clear, while writing *Encounters*, as to the difference between a story and a sketch. I did not grasp that, while it could be emancipated from conventional 'plot', a story, to be a story, *must* have a turning-point. A sketch need not have a turning-point, for it is no more than extra-perceptive reportage. ('Breakfast' and 'The Lover' are examples.) When one or two 1923 book reviewers spoke of *Encounters* as 'a collection of sketches', I felt that to be derogatory. It would have been right to describe the volume as 'a collection of sketches and stories'. Today, I imagine few writers, now at the age that I then was, would have a similar blind spot – story-consciousness has gone on maturing.

I claim for *Encounters* one further merit – susceptibility to places, particular moments, objects, and seasons of the year. This shows itself with the naïvety of a natural love. 'Daffodils' overflowed from remembered pleasure in the streets of St Albans one sunny March afternoon; 'Requiescat' released an obsession about Lake Como, and a terrraced garden through whose gates I had peered. Even in the too-ambitious 'Return', I see the genuine love for the emptiness of an empty house; and the setting, if not people, of 'The Shadowy Third' seems to be given frame by emotion. One reason to spring on my characters at their trying moments – their susceptibilities were, then, at the pitch of mine.

I was indebted for the publication of *Encounters* (had it not been published, what would have happened next?) to three persons – an older friend, the 'M.J.' of the dedication, who paid for having the stories typed; Rose Macaulay, upon whose verdict as to whether I was or ever could be a writer I hung my future, and Frank Sidgwick, to whom Rose Macaulay wrote. He not only encouraged me by his confidence, but made my most exorbitant dream come true by issuing *Encounters* in the same format as that of *The Celestial Omnibus*. And the title, to which my collection owed much, was of his finding.

1949

THE LAST SEPTEMBER

This, my second novel, was published in 1929, having been written the year before. I was still young, or at least young as a writer, and, in spite of having accomplished *The Hotel*, still afraid of novels – that was, as an undertaking. Fewer alarms surrounded the short story. Now I have more experience it appears to me that problems, inherent in any writing, loom unduly large when one looks ahead. Though nothing is easy, little is quite impossible. It was a mistake to think of The Novel in the abstract, to be daunted by its 'musts' and its 'oughts', to imagine being constricted by its rules. At the outset, however, one cannot but shrink from anything one feels that one should attempt yet suspects oneself of feeling unequal to. Myself I was most oppressed, in advance, by the difficulty of assembling a novel's cast – bringing the various characters to the same spot, keeping them there, accounting for their continued presence (in real life, people seemed to be constantly getting up and going away) and linking them close enough, and for long enough, to provide the interplay known as 'plot'. In the short story people intersected each other's lines of fate, but for moments only. So far the constituents of my fiction had been encounters, impressions, impacts, shocks. One can see that, generally, in the novel the characters are maintained in the same orbit by some situation which sets a trap for them – some magnetic interest, devilment, quest or passion. My solution was a more childish one: again in *The Last September*, as in *The Hotel*, I used the device of having my men and women actually under the same roof – to remain there, whether by choice or chance, for such time as the story should need to complete its course. To the Italian Riviera hotel of my first novel succeeded the large, lonely Irish house. I am, and am bound to be, a writer involved closely with place and time; for me these are more than elements, they are actors. The impending close of 'the season', everyone leaving, gives climax to the drama of *The Hotel*. *The Last September*, from first to last, takes its pitch from the month of the book's name.

Yet to suggest – if I have suggested? – that I came at *The Last September* as a solution of my major mechanical problem in novel-writing would be gravely untrue. This, which of all my books is nearest my heart, had a deep, unclouded, spontaneous source. Though not poetic, it brims up with what could be the stuff of poetry, the sensations of youth. It is a work of instinct rather than knowledge – to a degree, a 'recall' book, but there had been no such recall before. In 'real' life, my girlhood summers in County Cork, in the house called Danielstown in the story, had been, though touched by romantic pleasure, mainly times of impatience, frivolity, or lassitude. I asked myself *what* I should be, and when? The young (ironically, so much envied) all face those patches of barren worry. In my personal memory, I do not idealize that September of 1920, the month in which this novel chose to be set. But the book, not 'true' (it deals with invented happenings, imagined persons) is at many, many removes from autobiography. Proust remarks that it is those very periods of existence which are lived through, by the writer or future writer, carelessly, unwillingly or in boredom that most often fructify into art.

The Last September is the only one of my novels to be set back deliberately, in a former time. In all others I wanted readers to contemplate what could appear to be the immediate moment – so much so, that to give the sense of the 'now' has been, for me, one imperative of writing. For *The Last September*, that went into reverse – the 'then' (the past) as an element was demanded. The cast of my characters, and their doings, were to reflect the mood of a vanished time. 'All this', I willed the reader to know, 'is done with and over.' From the start, the reader must look, be conscious of looking, backward – down a backward perspective of eight years. Fear that he might miss that viewpoint, that he might read so much as my first pages under misapprehension, haunted me. The ordinary narrative past tense, so much in usage, seemed unlikely to be forceful enough; so I opened my second paragraph with a pointer: 'In those days, girls wore crisp white skirts and transparent blouses clotted with white flowers; ribbons threaded through . . . appeared over the shoulders.' Lois's ribbons, already, were part of history.

When one is young, years count for more, seem longer: to have lived through a few, even, appears a conquest. And in most lives the years between twenty and twenty-eight *are* often important, packed with changes, decisive. When I sat in Old Headington, Oxford, writing *The Last September*, 1920 seemed a long time ago. By now (the year of the writing: 1928) peace had settled on Ireland; trees were already branching inside the shells of large burned-out houses; lawns, once flitted over by pleasures, usefully merged into grazing land. I myself was no longer a tennis girl but a writer; aimlessness was gone, like a morning mist. Not an hour had not a meaning, and a centre. Also changes had altered my sense of space – Ireland seemed immensely distant from Oxford, more like another world than another land. Here I was, living a life dreamed of when, like Lois, I drove the pony trap along endless lanes. Civilization (a word constantly on my 1928 lips) was now around me. I was in company with the articulate and the learned. Yet, onward from the start of *The Last September*, it was that other era that took command – nor is it hard (now that 1928 seems as distant as 1920) to see why. The writer, like a swimmer caught by an undertow, is borne in an unexpected direction. He is carried to a subject which has awaited him – a subject sometimes no part of his conscious plan. Reality, the reality of sensation, has accumulated where it was least sought. To write is to be captured – captured by some experience to which one may have hardly given a thought.

The factual background of *The Last September* – state of affairs round Danielstown, outside happenings which impact on the story – may, for non-Irish readers, need explanation. The action takes place during 'the Troubled Times' – i.e. the roving armed conflict between the Irish Republican Army and British forces still garrisoning Ireland. Ambushes, arrests, captures and burnings, reprisals and counter-reprisals kept the country and country people distraught and tense. The British patrolled and hunted; the Irish planned, lay in wait, and struck. The Army lorry heard in the breathless evening, the purposeful young man glimpsed in the Danielstown woods, the shot in the ruined mill, the barbed-wire fence round the dancers, and the ambush in which the subaltern Gerald, falls – these are fiction with the texture of history. In such an atmosphere, the carrying on of orthodox conventional social life (as they did at Danielstown) might seem either foolhardy or inhuman. One can only say, it appeared the best thing to do. The festivities I have pictured are authentic – they ceased, admittedly, in the more menacing 1921. Irish–British hostilities were brought to an end by the Treaty of 1922; though upon that followed the further chaos caused by the Irish Civil War.

During the Troubles, the position of such Anglo-Irish landowning families as the Naylors, of Danielstown, was not only ambiguous but was more nearly heart-breaking than they cared to show. Inherited loyalty (or at least, adherence) to Britain – where their sons were schooled, in whose wars their sons had for generations fought, and to which they owed their 'Ascendancy' lands and power – pulled them one way; their own temperamental Irishness the other. The Naylors and their kind entertained British officers because this was a hospitable tradition – see most Anglo-Irish memoirs or old-time novels. Though the custom now made for danger, or disrepute, the gentry welcomed the military, as before. But the Troubles troubled everything, even friendliness – see Sir Richard's sombre reaction to Gerald's company. Repugnant became the patrols and raids, the proclaimed intention of 'holding the country down'. If it seem that Sir Richard and Lady Naylor are snobs with regard to Lois's young officers, recall that the uncle's and aunt's ideas dated back to impeccable years before 1914. 'The Army's not what it was' – death had seen to that! Lois's war-damaged gallants of 1920 came of less favoured stock than had Lady Naylor's – nor could they endear themselves by enjoying Ireland: *was* this the time? Lady Naylor's ambivalent attitude to the English, in general, should however be noted; it is a marked Anglo-Irish trait.

Why was Lois, at her romantic age, not more harrowed, or stirred, by the national struggle round her? In part, would not this be self-defence? This was a creature still half-awake, the soul not yet open, nor yet the eyes. And world war had shadowed her school-days: *that* was enough – now she wanted order. Trying enough it is to have to grow up, more so to grow up at a trying time. Her generation, mine, put out few rebels and fewer zealots. Like it or not, however, she acquiesced to strife, abnormalities and danger. Violence was contained in her sense of life, along with dance music, the sweet-pea in the garden, the inexorable raininess of days. Tragedy, she could only touch at the margin – not Gerald's death, but her failure to love. Was it sorrow to her, Danielstown's burning? She was niece always, never child, of that house.

I *was* the child of the house from which Danielstown derives. Bowen's Court survived – nevertheless, so often in my mind's eye did I see it burning that the terrible last event in *The Last September* is more real than anything I have lived through.

1952

STORIES BY ELIZABETH BOWEN

Often, at different times, I thought I should like to select from my own stories – re-read them all, evaluate them afresh. Intermittently I have been writing short stories for what, now, is more than thirty-six years: no wonder a mass of them has mounted. A selection, I felt, should act as a sort of pointer to those which could be considered the most enduring, the most lively, the most nearly good art. Those chosen should be those fit to survive – stories on which my reputation could hope to rest. Also from the first I have had my favourites, dearer, more satisfying to me than others; those, I thought, I should easily single out. The selection (this volume, as I envisaged it) was to have about it an ideality – not that any one story I had written *had* been ideal, but the best should gain, and set one another off, by being no longer crowded by lesser neighbours.

Now it comes to the point, now that I am invited to make my choice and draw up my list, it is not so simple. Choice, for instance, involves judgement; judgement requires a long perspective. Can I stand far enough away from my own work? Also, there cannot but be something alarming about the finality of my own decisions: never shall I be able to appeal against them, for I made them! As I see it, this volume must 'represent' my stories – as though on the assumption that those not in it are due to be blown away on the dust of time. What, exactly, do I want to have represented? What, throughout my life, have I been trying to do, and at which points have I come nearest doing it? Have I, since first I sat down to write, had always the same ideas, or have these altered? – my manner has changed, certainly. (This last is a question I have to raise, as I should with regard to the work of another author. But that is not to say that I can reply to it.) Above all, I am confronted by the question of fairness, justice – I must be fair to the writer, not less so because she has been myself; at the same time, I must do rightly by the reader. The writer pleads to be shown at her best only, the reader might prefer an 'average' view. The fact is, that every short story is an experiment – what one must ask is not only, did it come off, but was it, as an experiment, worth making?

What kind of stories does, or did, Elizabeth Bowen write? This Vintage volume should be the answer. Some idea should be given of the range of subjects, of the technique and its variations, of the imaginative quality, and so on. Misfired pieces, possibly, should go in, alongside those better conceived or more fully realized – as against that, why misuse space when there's not much of it? Stories to be read should be good, as good as they can be: here, even the best show cautionary errors to any student of writing who cares to look for them. I have decided to face criticism by offering stories which certainly do invite it, but which also should, in their ways, stand up to it. These eighteen pieces (the earliest written when I was twenty) can claim to be fair examples of themes and treatments. No, to be candid, though I say 'fair' examples, these are the most hopeful I can produce. If I had written better stories, they would be here.

Not only – now that I settle down to my task – do I confront problems; I sustain disappointments. A number of favourites, for instance, have played me false, failing under the test of austere re-reading. I must have cared for them, I can only think, for some subjective or associative reason, long since evaporated. Alternatively, they were (unbeknownst to me) synthetic; not pure in origin, but inspired, rather, by some intellectual fashion or aesthetic caprice – many of them were written some time ago; because they were of their day, in their day they pleased me. When I was young – and youth in a writer lasts – I was easily impressed myself. Sad as it is, several 'favourites' were among my first discards. What were they but mirages in my memory? I fancied them better than they were.

Equally, I find that I reject stories which reek to me of myself by exhibiting sentiments – or betraying them. In some, I do not seem to have been enough on guard. Such stories seem over-written, or, still worse, yoked to my personality. I am dead against art's being self-expression. I see an inherent failure in any story which does not detach itself from the author – detach itself in the sense that a well-blown soap bubble detaches itself from the bowl of the blower's pipe and spherically takes off into the air as a new, whole, pure, iridescent world. Whereas the ill-blown bubble, as children know, timidly adheres to the bowl's lip, then either bursts or sinks flatly back again.

Total impersonality in story-writing is, for me certainly, impossible – so much so that it would be a waste of time to wonder whether it would be desirable. And I doubt, actually, whether for any writer it is either desirable or possible for this reason: the short story is linked with poetry, and that, we know, cannot but bear a signature. The tale without lyricism or passion desiccates into little more than a document. The poet, and in his wake the short-story writer, is using his own, unique susceptibility to experience: in a sense, the susceptibility is the experience. The susceptibility, equally, is the writer, who therefore cannot be absent from what he writes. The short story is at an advantage over the novel, and can claim its nearer kinship to poetry, because it must be more concentrated, can be more visionary, and is not weighed down (as the novel is bound to be) by facts, explanation, or analysis. I do not mean to say that the short story is by any means exempt from the laws of narrative: it must observe them, but on its own terms. Fewer characters, fewer scenes, and above all fewer happenings are necessary; shape and action are framed for simplification. As against that, there are dangers and can be penalties: essentially, at no point in the story must the electrical-imaginative current be found to fail. Novels legitimately have 'slack' passages, which serve, like intermissions, to ease off the reader between crisis and crisis. But the short story revolves round one crisis only – one might call it, almost, a crisis in itself. There (ideally) ought to be nothing in such a story which can weaken, detract from, or blur the central, single effect.

This, I recognize, has been one idea I have kept before myself. In short-story writing it has been my main aim, and at least as an aim it has been continuous. I state it, though without deluding myself that I have realized it, succeeded in it, in any one story. . . . To return to the matter of the personal, I repeat that one cannot wholly eliminate oneself for a second, and also sufficient, reason: any fiction (and surely poetry too?) is bound to be transposed autobiography. (True, it may be this at so many removes as to defeat ordinary recognition.) I can, and indeed if I would not I still must, relate any and every story I have written to something that happened to me in my own life. But here I am speaking of happenings in a broad sense – to behold, and react, is where I am concerned a happening; speculations, unaccountable stirs of interest, longings, attractions, apprehensions without knowable cause – these are happenings also. When I re-read a story, I re-live the moment from which it sprang. A scene burned itself into me, a building magnetized me, a mood or season of Nature's penetrated me, history suddenly appeared to me in some tiny act or a face had begun to haunt me before I glanced at it.

On the whole, places more often than faces have sparked off stories. To be honest, the scenes have been with me before the characters – it could have seemed to me, even, once or twice, as though the former had summoned up the latter. I do not feel, necessarily, that this is wrong: a story must come to life in its own order. Also, I re-assert what I said when discussing the art of Katherine Mansfield: I do not feel that the short story can be, or should be, used for the analysis or development of character. The full, full-length portrait is fitter work for the novelist; in the short story, treatment must be dramatic – we are dealing with man, or woman or child, in relation to a particular crisis or mood or moment, and to that only. Though (and as to this, law is stern) the crisis must be one in which such-and-such a character would be likely to be involved, or, still more, would be likely to precipitate; the mood must be one to which such-and-such a character would be likely to be prone, or still more, to heighten; the moment should essentially be the one which would, on the given character, act most strongly. Once a story truly germinates in my mind, the inevitable actors in it take form – and not only this, but they also take hold, to the point of remaining after the tale is told. I give, as examples, four stories in this selection: 'The Storm', 'Her Table Spread', 'Ivy Gripped the Steps', 'Mysterious Kôr'. Each of these arose out of an intensified, all but spellbound beholding, on my part, of the scene in question – a fountain-filled Italian garden in livid, pre-thundery light; a shabbily fanciful Irish castle overlooking an estuary; an ivy-strangled house in a formerly suave residential avenue; or weird moonlight over bomb-pitted London. Each time I felt: 'Yes, this affects me – but it would affect "X" more.' Under what circumstances; for what reason? And who is 'X'? In each case, the 'X' I pondered upon became the key character in the resultant story. It could seem to me that stories, with their dramatis personae, pre-exist, only wait to be come upon. I know I do not invent them; I discover them. Though that does not mean that they are easily told. On me devolves the onus of narration.

Fantasy – another important element. One may, of course, say that any story (from any pen) is the exercise or working-out of a fantasy – that any author of fiction, to write at all, must have recourse to his or her dreaming faculty. But in Elizabeth Bowen stories, it may be found, fantasy is often present twice over; part as it is of the fabric of the actual plot, or governor of the behaviour of the characters. Looking through this selection I have made, I find fantasy strongly represented. Critics may possibly say, too much so? Yet these, I still maintain, are my better stories. If I were a short-story writer only, I might well seem to be out of balance. But recall, more than half of my life is under the steadying influence of the novel, with its calmer, stricter, more orthodox demands: into the novel goes such taste as I have for rational behaviour and social portraiture. The short story, as I see it to be, allows for what is crazy about humanity: obstinacies, inordinate heroisms, 'immortal longings'. At no time, even in the novel, do I consider realism to be my forte. Fortunately, however, there are many other writers; taken all-in-all we complement one another – literature is a compost to which we are each contributing what we have. The best that an individual can do is to concentrate on what he or she can do, in the course of a burning effort to do it better.

A full and considerable number of years of life, plus more or less continuous care for writing, ought not altogether to go for nothing. I cannot attempt to outline my development, though I cannot believe there has been none. The fact that this Vintage volume opens with a story about a little girl reminds me how recurrent a subject, with me, have been youth and childhood. I cannot say that I see this to be 'nostalgia'; for one thing, I now enjoy my own adult state. Rather I perceive how much I rely, in art, on immediacy and purity of sensation, and indubitably the young are unspoiled instruments. Many of the greatest writers of short stories, and poets, died before Time had stolen their freshness from them. I have remained in the world dangerously long: I hope there may still be something I need not forfeit.

1959

Orlando
by Virginia Woolf

Virginia Woolf's *Orlando* was first published in London in October of 1928. I remember, the book was regarded with some mistrust by one generation – my own, at that time 'the younger'. We, in our twenties during the '20s, were not only the author's most zealous readers, but, in the matter of reputation, most jealous guardians. Her aesthetic became a faith; we were believers. We more than admired, we felt involved in each of her experimental, dazzling advances. Few of us (then) knew the still-conservative novels of her first period; a minority had informed itself of *The Mark on the Wall* and *Kew Gardens*, hand-printed and issued in 1919 by the original Hogarth Press. She broke full upon us, it would be correct to say, with *Jacob's Room*, 1922, on which followed *Mrs Dalloway*, 1925; then, while we were still breathless, *To the Lighthouse*, 1927. What now, what next? Next came *Orlando*. It was *Orlando*'s fate to come hard on the heels of the third of those masterpieces, of which each had stimulated a further hope. We regarded this book as a setback. Now, thirty-two years later, I wonder why this should have been so.

One trouble was, I imagine, our peculiar attitude to this writer's art. Defending it as we did against all comers – 'stupids', dissidents, or the unseeing critic – we were ready, should so desperate a need arise, to defend it against the artist herself. Never had we foreseen that we might require to. The virtue of the art was, for us, its paradox: sublimating personality into poetry, it had, as art, the chastity of the impersonal. Before we had read *Orlando*, indeed for some time before it was 'out', we scented the book as a transgression. Unofficial publicity was unfortunate, the more so because it was unofficial. This *Orlando* – we did not care for the sound of it. The book was, we gathered, in the nature of a prank, or a private joke; worse still, its genesis was personal. Inspired by a romantic friendship, written for the delectation of the romantic friend, it was likely to be fraught with playful allusion. Nor was that all – a distinguished, sympathetic and 'special' coterie had contributed to the invention known as *Orlando*. That Virginia Woolf should have intimates was a shock.

Most of us had not met Virginia Woolf; nor did we (which may seem strange) aspire to. She did not wish to be met. Her remoteness completed our picture of her, in so far as we formed a picture at all. Exist she must (or writing could not proceed from her), but we were incurious as to how she did. What she looked like, we had not a remote idea; authors' photographs did not, then, ornament book jackets. Our contentment with not knowing Virginia Woolf today would appear extraordinary, could it even be possible. We visualized her less as a woman at work than as a light widening as it brightened. When I say, 'She was a name, to us,' remember (or if you cannot remember, try to imagine) what a name *can* be, surrounded by nothing but the air of heaven. Seldom can living artist have been so – literally – idealized.

Malevolent autumn of '28 – it taunted us with the picture of the lady given to friends, to the point of fondness, and jokes, to within danger of whimsicality. Ourselves, we were singularly uncoordinated, I see now, as generations go. When I hear it said, as sometimes I do today, that Virginia Woolf's reputation was built up by a sophisticated coterie, I ask myself, 'Whom can they possibly mean?' We, the ardent many, were rank-and-file provincials, outlanders, freelances, students (to me, in 1922, reading *Jacob's Room*, Bloomsbury meant University College, London). We ran, if into anything, into floating groups, loose in formation, governed by vague affinities. Then scorning fringes of coteries, we have remained, I notice, unwilling to form their nucleus in our later days – not, I hope, hostile, but non-attachable. Nevertheless, what we heard of *Orlando* galled us. We were young enough to feel out of it.

What we loathed was literary frivolity. So this was what Virginia Woolf could be given over to, if for an instant we took our eye off her – which, to do us justice, we seldom did? Cloak-and-dagger stuff. The finishing touch was the success the book enjoyed with our elders – *Orlando* charmed its way into the forts of middle-aged folly. 'Your Mrs Woolf has so often puzzled us. But *this* book of hers is delightful! We see what you mean!' Betrayed . . .

We, naturally, read *Orlando*. We knew neither how to take it nor what to make of it; it outwitted us. Up to this year, I had never read it again.

The position as to *Orlando* has now changed. Or, better, the book itself has a position it lacked before – it belongs to what is central and main in the writer's work, instead of appearing, as it once did, to hover on the questionable periphery. There has been time, since

Virginia Woolf's death, to stand back and view her work as a whole
– still more, to see the whole as a thing of structure (in so far as an
artist's whole art is like a building) or of inevitable growth (in so far
as a whole art is like a tree). Though what does one mean by 'a whole
art'? Seldom does a writer lay down his pen or a painter his brush
with calculated finality, saying 'This is for ever; I have done!'

Death, other than in very old age, is an arbitrary interruption, the
snipping of a cord at what seems often a fortuitous point. Rather, in
Virginia Woolf's case, say her achievement within her fifty-nine
years of life seems more, rather than less, significant now that we
judge it steadily, *as* a whole. Up to 1941, that is, while she was living
and at work, judgement was bound to be piecemeal, book by book.
Temporary mists, misprisions, prejudices, sometimes intervened.
From those mists' evaporation nothing she did gains more than
Orlando. That *Orlando* was beautiful nobody doubted: what we
now see is that it is important – and why.

It was important to the writer. She was the better, one feels certain,
for writing it; in particular, for doing so when she did. More
irresponsible than the rest of her work in fiction, it has the advantage
of being less considered and more unwary. This book corresponds
with a wildness in her, which might have remained unknown of –
unless one knew her. This was a rebellion on the part of Virginia
Woolf against the solemnity threatening to hem her in. *Orlando* is,
among other things, rumbustious; it is one of the most high-spirited
books I know.

Personal memories of Virginia Woolf cast, for me, their own light
upon *Orlando*, though I certainly never spoke to her of the book,
heard her speak of it, or attempted to find my way back to it while I
knew her. Friendship with her – chiefly laughter and pleasure, and an
entering, in her company, into the rapture caused her by the
unexpected, the spectacular, the inordinate, the improbable, and the
preposterous – filled out nine years of the lengthy interval between
my first and second readings of *Orlando*. From her I learned that one
can be worse than young and foolish; for she was the epitome of the
young and foolish; it is among the glories of *Orlando* that it is in
some ways a foolish book. It is not disorganized – on the contrary, it
is a miracle of 'build' – but it is rhapsodical. Half-way through her
creative life, she desired a plaything – also a mouthpiece. Shyness is
absent from *Orlando*; in what sometimes are rhetorical exclamations, sometimes lyrical flashes like summer lightning, she voices
herself on the subject of art, time, society, love, history, man,
woman. The book is a novelist's holiday, not a novel.

By definition, *Orlando* is a fantasy. What is that? A story that posits 'impossible' circumstances and makes play with them. Fantasy may juggle with time and space, and ignore, for instance, the law of gravity. Infinitely less fortunate is the novel, a work of imagination fettered to earthly fact and subject to dire penalty if it break the chain – one slip on the part of the novelist as to 'reality' and his entire edifice of illusion totters and threatens to tumble down. At the same time, the licence accorded the fantastic is not boundless – the probable must enter his story somewhere. Should it fail to do so, interest is lost. Against extraordinary events, he must balance (in some sense) ordinary, or at least credible, characters. Where would *Wonderland* and *Through the Looking Glass* be without the prim, dogmatic lucidity of the temperamentally *un*adventurous Alice? Virginia Woolf, whom the 'musts' of the novel bored, fell in without complaint with the laws of fantasy. Her Orlando – that is, her central character – though redeemed by grace, genius, and breeding from being 'ordinary', is *as a character* absolutely convincing. To the change of sex, to the mysterious flight of time – centuries slipping by like months in the country – he–she reacts in a manner one cannot challenge – psychologically, all is extremely sound. And the more transitory, lesser cast are touched in, manipulated, with great adroitness. Nothing in *Orlando*, other than the outright impossible, seems improbable. Ironically, fantasy made Virginia Woolf a more thoroughgoing 'straight', one might say assiduous, novelist than she was wont to be. The entire thing was a pleasure – she did not 'have to'; she was out of school.

What a performance *Orlando* is, simultaneously working on amazement and suspending disbelief! At the start, a sixteen-year-old aristocrat, male, proffering a bowl of rose water to the ancient Queen Elizabeth I; at the close, a woman of thirty-six, still Orlando, under an oak tree in the moonlight, in the reign of Britain's King George V – the month October, the year 1928, the exact day probably that of the publication of *Orlando*. The change of sex took place in Constantinople, where Orlando was being ambassador, towards the end of the seventeenth century. The longing to be a poet which consumed the youth has been realized by the woman, who has combined this with giving birth to a son. Exquisite social comedy has enjoyed a run of, roughly, three-and-a-half centuries, partly in London, partly in the great Kentish country house. The Victorian age has been survived. Love has seared its way into a young breast, never to be forgotten, always to be associated with a Jacobean Thames ice carnival lasting a winter. Among the series of grand effronteries with which *Orlando* handles English history, there appear to be a few inadvertent errors – surely St Paul's Cathedral acquires a dome sooner than it did? The enormous sense of release that runs through the book is partly an affair of effortless speed, mobility, action – carriages dashing, whips cracking, mobs swaying, ice islands twirling doomfully down the river. By contrast, I remember Virginia Woolf – back to being a novelist, writing *Between the Acts* – coming down the garden path from her studio, saying, 'I've spent the whole of the morning trying to move people from the dining-room into the hall!'

I have a theory – unsupported by anything she said to me, or, so far as I know, to anyone – that Virginia Woolf's writing of *Orlando* was a prelude to, and in some way rendered possible, her subsequent writing of *The Waves*, 1931. Outwardly, no two works of fiction could be more different; yet, did the fantasy serve to shatter some rigid, deadening, claustrophobic mould of so-called 'actuality' which had been surrounding her? In *To the Lighthouse* (coming before *Orlando*), she had reached one kind of perfection. This she could not surpass; therefore, past it she could not proceed. In *Orlando*, delicacy gives place to bravura, to rhetoric. It was a breaking-point and a breathing-space at the same time, this fantasy. She returned to the novel, to *The Waves*, with – at least temporarily – a more defiant attitude to the novel's 'musts'.

Captive in the heart of the book *Orlando*, in the midst of the splendid changing and shifting scenes, are accounts of the sheer sensation of writing, more direct than this writer has ever given us. For instance:

> At this moment . . . Orlando pushed away her chair, stretched her arms, dropped her pen, came to the window, and exclaimed, 'Done!'
>
> She was almost felled to the ground by the extraordinary sight which now met her eyes. There was the garden and some birds. The world was going on as usual. All the time she was writing the world had continued.
>
> 'And if I were dead, it would be just the same!' she exclaimed.

There is a touch of hallucination about 'reality'; creative Orlando was right, so was his–her creator. Virginia Woolf's vision conferred strangeness, momentarily, on all it fell on; it was, I believe, her effort to see things as they were apparent to *other* people that wore her down. The bus, the lamp-post, the teacup – how formidable she found them, everyday things! Nothing of an ordeal to her, however, were melodrama or panorama – she was at home with, or within, either.

Orlando, about which we who were then young were so stupid in 1928, is, I perceive, a book for those who are young. How does it strike those who are young now?

1960

REVIEWS

Introduction

Some of Elizabeth Bowen's reviews were obviously bread-and-butter work. In the bibliography of her work, there are almost seven hundred entries under the section that includes reviews. Starting in 1935, when she did a fortnightly stint of fiction for the *New Statesman* ('It is a perfectly awful business,' she wrote to Virginia Woolf), Bowen reviewed for the *Spectator*, the *Listener*, the *Saturday Review*, the *Observer, Vogue, Harper's Bazaar* , and more. From 1937 to '38 she covered plays for Graham Greene's short-lived weekly magazine, *Night and Day*, and from 1945 until 1958 she reviewed batches of fiction for the *Tatler*, often for weeks on end. Her last reviews, for the *Spectator* in 1970, were written when she was already ill, three years before her death.

This mass of work impresses, in part, simply for the range of reading it displays. Set with her survey of *English Novelists* for the Collins 'Britain in Pictures' series, her broadcasts on 'Truth and Fiction' and her essays, the reviewing shows a mighty appetite for books. But, as Victoria Glendinning says in her biography of Elizabeth Bowen, she was ambivalent about this time-consuming side-line: 'Like most novelists, Elizabeth felt that it did her no good to write reviews; and like most novelists, she reviewed endlessly.' Her availability was matched by her benevolence: as a critic, she was unusual in being kinder to others than she was to herself. 'She was known in the business as a very soft touch indeed,' her biographer says. Certainly it is difficult to find a harsh review: her disdainful treatment in the *Tatler* in 1949 of Angus Wilson's *The Wrong Set* is unusual. (He had his revenge a year later in his essay for the *Listener* on 'Evil in the English Novel', where she is dismissed as a complacent middle-class lady writer. But they were both to change their minds, as can be seen from Elizabeth Bowen's review of *Anglo-Saxon Attitudes*, and Wilson's recent introduction for Cape to her *Collected Stories*.) A correspondence in 1952 with Terence Kilmartin, literary editor of the *Observer*, shows that she tended only to review when she felt she could praise. He offered her the collected poems of Oliver St John Gogarty, and she returned them:

I can't review them — don't feel qualified to review poetry, to begin with, and, between ourselves, find Gogarty boring and unreadable; though he's nice to meet.

Almost inevitably, she found herself praising her friends, as in reviews of Rosamond Lehmann, Virginia Woolf, Cyril Connolly and William Plomer — though she is acute about their particular qualities. But she is sympathetic, too, to writers with whom she had nothing in common. She is at her best when the book speaks to her of her own interests and preoccupations. The fine pieces about Dublin's history and atmosphere; the intimate feeling for Anglo-Irish families in reviews of books about the Moores and Somerville and Ross; the vivid reconstruction of life in the Blitz, prompted by *The People's War*; the interest of Flaubert's 'poetic objectivity' or Joyce's impersonality; the masterly assessments of her most admired contemporaries, Ivy Compton-Burnett, Henry Green and V. S. Pritchett; and the responsiveness to atmosphere in novels by other women such as Rosamond Lehmann or Eudora Welty (whose Southern Americanness greatly attracted her, and who was to become a close friend): these reviews have an inwardness and confidence for which Elizabeth Bowen, who was severe about dividing her journalism into the lasting and ephemeral, might well have 'wished survival'.

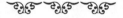

The Weather in the Streets
by Rosamond Lehmann

Miss Lehmann belongs to a generation that, for the most part, finds maturity difficult. Its emotion — congested, one cannot know how synthetic — is, though not pleasant to suffer, easier to suffer than to express; there has come to be perfected, for dealing with emotion, a frigid kind of bravado, irony with a current of mawkishness, in which the public-school spirit has an unhappy counterpart. Many good novels show a muffled dismay. *One* sort of emotional novel is not, unhappily, rare: it is, as a rule, so shocking as to leave one with the impression that only second-rate people are uninhibited now. There is masochistic frankness, but almost no spontaneity.

Miss Lehmann is an exception to all this. The most remarkable, the most natural of her qualities is the power to give emotion its full value and play, to transcribe into prose emotion that is grown-up and spontaneous, fatalistic but not abject, sublime without being high-pitched, infusing life but knowing its own isolation. She attempts to make no relation – necessarily a false relation – between emotion, with its colossal, unmoving subjective landscape, and outside life with its flickering continuity of action and fact. She writes, in fact, to underline this disparity, which is the subject of *The Weather in the Streets*, its plot being the story of a love-affair.

> Beyond the glass casing I was in was the weather, were the winter streets in rain, wind, fog, in the fine frosty days and nights, the mild damp grey ones. Pictures of London weather the other side of the glass – not reaching the body . . . In this time there was no sequence, no development. Each time was new, was different, existing without relation to before and after; all the times were one and the same. . . . Now I see what an odd duality it gave to life; being in love with Rollo was all-important, the times with him were the only reality; yet in another way they had no existence in reality. It must have been the same with him.

Circumstances increase the natural isolation of love. Olivia, sensitive, wary, tentative and a touch defiant, discouraged and in her own view declassed by a futile marriage, now over, becomes the mistress of Rollo Spencer – assured, charming, easy and essentially fortunate. The defensive husk she has acquired irks her a little and does not quite fit. Like most solitary people playing their own hand, she is absorbed, if not always fortified, by an intensive inner life. In any world – with her family, on the night she dances with the Spencers, with her London friends, so gentle, bleak, asexual, intimate – Olivia is alien, uncertain, nostalgic. She is like someone sitting a long way from the fire, but near a mirror reflecting the firelight. Whereas Rollo is more than an inmate of *his* world; his world is part of his nature; she sees in him the strong and happy flowering of it. From this world, now their love affair has begun, she is bound to know him apart; she is conscious that, in being with her, he is dissociated, however happily, from the major part of himself. Their love has for him the exhilaration of island life, whereas for her it is a continent.

The figure of Rollo Spencer, sometimes no more than a big, fatal silhouette, sometimes seen in strong light – with his 'upper-class charm', his intensities of purpose, his confusion of motive – is magnificently put in. Olivia's awareness of her lover never exceeds the bounds of love or art; she apprehends him rather than observes him; in thought, in the narrative of her consciousness, the idiom of love is never departed from – which, pitching the book so perfectly that there is never a drop in it, is in itself very fine art. The changes of person – from the third to the first in Part Two (giving the effect of blurred, too close-up, climactic, subjective vision), then back to the third again in Part Three, for sadder detachment, a sense of brutal collision with the outside world – are very telling. Apart from this, there is not a single intrusion of 'technique'; though technically there are few flaws in the book. As a writer, Miss Lehmann's competence is so great that she has been able to sink her competence in her subject. There is no showing-off – which is too rare. Her style has a sensuous, vital simplicity, to which her brain gives edge.

No one can write better than Miss Lehmann about the aesthetics, the intimate charm – much more than charm – of luxury, the unwary civility of the old world, privilege, ease, grace. She has always been able to place, and to evaluate, glamour. She has also a great command of contrast – between groups of people, settings, seasons of the year, moods, different idioms in talk. Olivia's solitary, though gregarious life in London, her visits home, her times with Rollo Spencer make a strong triangle in the structure of the book. The Curtis family life, with its dialogue, is delicious. There are few 'minor' characters in *The Weather in the Streets*: Kate, now a cool young matron, Kate's children, Mrs Curtis, Lady Spencer, Marigold, Etty and Anna are more than a mere supporting cast; they have an opposing reality of their own, and play a positive part in the plot. Miss Lehmann has accomplished a remarkably difficult thing; she has added, palpably, ten years of age to her characters since their first appearance in *Invitation to the Waltz*. Some features have hardened and others blurred; that first lyrical freshness has left Olivia and Kate.

Everything that went to make Miss Lehmann's three other novels is present in *The Weather in the Streets*, and still more has been added, which is as it should be. This book, which has lovely qualities that are inimitably its writer's, is outstanding as a sheer piece of good work.

New Statesman, 11 July 1936

Dublin under the Georges, 1714-1830
by Constantia Maxwell

Dublin and New York are two standard examples of the grand manner – the eighteenth century's and the twentieth's. Dublin exhales melancholy, the past and the sense of an obliterated purpose that no new world activity can exactly renew: an anticlimactic, possibly endless pause hangs over her large squares, long light streets and darkening Georgian façades. Meanwhile New York, congested on her narrow island, as beautifully brittle-looking as candy in the air, shoots higher yearly, throws out bridges across the Hudson and speedways across the State, tears herself down, re-piles herself in toppling masses and infuses the century with her nervous life. New York grew on a series of impulses; Dublin is rooted in political stubbornness: her great phase had the unity of a social idea.

Miss Maxwell has chronicled what remains – with every salutation of the new Ireland – Dublin's most fully vital, if not her most happy, phase. Under the Georges she was a European capital: as that she has still to find herself again. Strife and complexity, danger and bitter feeling have never released their grip on this unhappy town, but in the eighteenth century, under Grattan's Parliament, the Irish of the Ascendancy turned to them their most nearly unknowing face. Hemmed in by country trouble and shaken by city strife, the aristocratic dwellers each side of the Liffey maintained an almost Venetian level of gaiety. Entertainments were princely. Whatever else happened, they had a good time. Security may have bred, elsewhere, a sounder magnificence, but never magnificence at such fever pitch. Here the great were often shady, but few were shoddy. Trinity College threw out crabbed and mordant wits. The deaneries were headquarters of good company. The Archbishop's wife drove round Dublin in one of the most dashing turnouts on record. The theatre, in spite of the difficulty of keeping the audience off the stage (on one occasion Sheridan had to clear the Smock Alley theatre with firearms), kept, at least to the time of the Union, a notably high form; concert rooms were packed with exacting audiences, and enthusiastic peers composed a private orchestra. The ladies' conversation was full-blooded and snappy, if not always informed. In clubs and drawing-rooms the rate of play was high; the consumption of drink and victuals at dinners was astounding. Elegance in the exact sense may have been rare: spleen and a tough, drink-pickled melancholy underlay much of the glitter: the glitter itself had a tarnish. The scandalous and infinitely regrettable Union struck all this fun in Dublin a fatal blow.

The conditions in which the poor lived were nauseating, even for the period. A certain amount of relief led to some grand building, though even the new Lying-in Hospital seems to have been open to criticism. The other hospitals, the prisons and orphanages were charnel-houses, with an immense mortality. Liffey floods increased the horrors of a very negative sanitation. English policy and foreign wars struck repeated blows at the Dublin industries: the city's distress-pressure was heightened by influxes of futureless, disaffected country workers. Protection – supported by bloodshed, sacked foreign-goods warehouses, burnt effigies and nocturnal howlings – did what it could. The fortunate classes, in so far as fashion and expediency allowed them, stood by what Irish industries there were. The charming and ill-fated Lord Edward Fitzgerald was not alone, though he was the most militant, in espousing a romantic nationalism. A curious and unspoken complicity of spirit between all classes must account for the fact of there not being, in a city of such extremes and such constant feverish pressure, more, or in fact any, sustained, class-hatred.

Miss Maxwell's book, which deals with many more, and more complex, aspects of eighteenth-century Dublin than I have given here, is the fruit of wide, thorough, unbiased and enterprising research. She is admirably documented as to the city's political, social, industrial, academic and artistic life during the period she covers, and she has set out her material most ably. Her style is unaffected, unemotional (though a curious, wry emotion exhales from its matter), concrete, and therefore, I think, excellent.

New Statesman, 25 July 1936

A Biography of Dublin
by Christine Longford

Lady Longford's story of Dublin is tactful and spirited; it cannot
displease the native, it will amuse the visitor. Her book – the first of a
series of city biographies – had to be very short: she has done very
well with it. She rushes through history with rapid discrimination,
making pauses only for anecdote: rightly, for Irish history is a
constellation of anecdotes glittering on a profound and untracked
gloom. Briskness is essential to Lady Longford's manner and to the
form of her book; only two subjects tempt her to potter – the Anglo-
Irish (who first began to make trouble centuries back, while still
called the Old English) and the Dublin theatre. It will be interesting
to see whether other towns in the series – Jerusalem, Moscow, Los
Angeles – offer as much as Dublin to common sense and fun. The
Irish discussing themselves are often boring, long-winded and full of
vanity: they have been given style recently by a new *désabusé* kind of
English wit. It took an Englishwoman – and one with flair – to write
this agreeable, vivid, smooth, un-bitter book. Her style and tone
have their dangers: she comes in places a little too near smartness,
but she gives tragedy place by respectful understatement, honours
the fantastic and the heroic, and shows throughout a sober regard for
fact. Dublin has loomed in art through a haze of native sentiment,
often a tortured sentiment. But taste – of which so great a part is
intelligent and voluntary – better qualifies the biographer. Lady
Longford ably paints the city's portrait and summarizes its past.

Dublin, on the east, the Europe-regarding, coast of Ireland, owes
her vitality and complexity as a city to a continuous influx of foreign
life. The invader, the trader, the opportunist, the social visitor have
all added strife or colour. The Norsemen found her a village – called
Baile Atha Cliath, or Ford of the Hurdles – on the lowest ford of the
Liffey. The river's mouth made a fine harbour, her position was
strategic; since their day until lately she was garrisoned by invaders,
whose ostentation has always been uneasy. Once her walls went up
she became a capital, full of heady passions. The Normans, invited
over, gave a bad deal, but got a worse deal than they had time to see.
Prince John's Lordship of Ireland was not happy; he was frivolous,

tactless and overbearing, offended the older Normans, who had been
settling down, and gave early support to an Irish theory that when
the English come over they go to bits. Richard II found enlighten-
ment did not work. The Fitzgeralds, of Norman origin, made
perpetual trouble; Lord Edward, finally, led a forlorn hope. Dublin,
connected with Ireland by a system of nerves, registered and reacted
to trouble throughout the country: the relation of Paris to France
provides no analogy. She became the headquarters of Protestant
domination, of aristocratic pretension, of bourgeois power. A
minority supported by theoretic authority fled to her at any crisis, to
be fortified. Under Henry VIII, the Protestant aggression had its way
in Dublin: George Browne, the Archbishop, found the greater part of
Ireland unsatisfactory; he complained to Thomas Cromwell: 'The
common people of this isle are more zealous in their blindness than
the saints and martyrs were in the truth.' Puritanism, later, found the
city slippery in its grip. Dublin has always been foreignly irresponsible; an uninformed enthusiasm commands it, and the Stuarts,
attractive and kingly, were warmly supported there. The Restoration
was signalized by a great burst of fun: the theatre (precious to Lady
Longford) first came into evidence, and Roman Catholics were
tolerated. In spite of defeat James II, owing to personal characteristics, became unpopular. Under William and Mary some hanky-
panky over the linen industry brought capitalism into the open as a
declared force. Longer lapses between violence made constitutional
difficulties more apparent. 'The work of the Irish Parliament was
very much obstructed by the fact that certain officials were English,
and only came to Ireland in their spare time.'

Lady Longford makes place for portraits of Swift, Molyneux,
Wolfe Tone, Grattan, Lord Edward Fitzgerald, Emmet, O'Connell
and Parnell. Her desire, which is honourable, to place Swift in the
gallery of enthusiast patriots makes her overlook, or ignore, the in-
turning edge of his wit. To burn for Ireland is not to burn for truth:
Swift never buried for Ireland the quality that he had. Lady Longford, referring to Swift's last charity – the leaving of his money to
found a hospital for lunatics in Dublin – suppresses in her quotation
his next couplet:

> He left the little Wealth he had
> To build a House for Fools and Mad;
> *And shew'd by one satiric Touch,*
> *No Nation wanted it so much.*

The anecdotes are well chosen, pleasant and pithy. There are

pictures of pre-Union Dublin in redundant and crazy flower. The
nineteenth century is summarized, there is a sympathetic family
picture of the Wildes, a broad daylight photograph of the Celtic
Twilight and a respectful résumé of 1916. Lady Longford does
justice to Dublin's present urbanity: the startled and somehow not
yet quite authentic glitter of cinemas and all-night cafés, the
inexhaustible talk with its malice and unfocused uplift, the Grafton
Street animation, the morning coffee, the theatre. Prolonged
European disturbance offers Ireland an opening; she bids fair to
become for the English a more accessible Switzerland, an amiable,
rural country, now that the rifles have cooled there, poetry with the
sting drawn, a country with a decay-glamour, a touch of the Old
South. Dublin may make a bid to be Basle and Berne, the clearing-
house for the sensitive tripper, the intelligent pause on the way to
country house visits, the gateway to bay and bog. For this her
biography, informed and sophisticated, is exceedingly well timed.
But the city is not in tune yet; she is overcast like a yesterday one
remembers with no pleasure; her trams give her away, they have no
Continental brightness; they crawl through the Georgian quarters
with a rasping vibration and the red plush inside gives out a dusty
and charnel smell.

New Statesman, 7 November 1936

Dublin Old and New
by Stephen Gwynn

At the first glance, Dublin nearly always delights the visitor by its
grand perspectives and large light squares, its at once airy and
mysterious look. Then there is a less happy phase in getting to know
the city – when it appears shut-up, faded and meaningless, full of
false starts and dead ends, the store plan of something that never
realized itself. The implacable flatness of the houses begins to
communicate a sort of apathy to the visitor: after her first smile and
her first grand effect, Dublin threatens to offer disappointingly little.
This stale phase in the stranger's relations with the city can only be
cut short by imagination and vigorous curiosity. Dublin is so much
more than purely spectacular; she is impregnated with a past that
never evaporates. Even the recent past, the nineteenth century, leaves

on some outlying quarters of the city a peculiar time-colour. Every quarter – from where the two cathedrals stand in the maze of side-streets, to the latest ring of growth, where red villas straggle into the fields – has, in fact, got a character you could cut with a knife. The more you know, the more you can savour this.

Unlike London, Paris, Edinburgh, the city, at each side of the river, covers flat land. The earth under it forms no romantic contours, and does not thrust the buildings up into different levels: from no point does one get a momentous view of the city. Her position, between the sea and the mountains, is beautiful, but can only be guessed at from her heart. Dublin's grandness, as a capital city, is anti-romantic; it lies in her plan, and her fine buildings, alone. Her interest lies in her contrasts, in the expression she gives to successive different ideas of living. Dublin does not represent Ireland; she is one aspect of it: she stands, or had stood, for wealth, for the imposition of power, for the generally European element that has made itself felt but never been quite absorbed. Not for nothing is she the capital of a country in which blood runs to the head: life here has been always lived at high pressure; everybody is highly articulate; this has always been a city of 'characters', in which nothing gets done impersonally. Emotional memory, here, has so much power that the past and the present seem to be lived simultaneously. In Dublin, as in the rest of Ireland, if you do not know the past you only know the half of anyone's mind.

Mr Stephen Gwynn's *Dublin Old and New* supplies that background which the stranger will need. This is not a guide book, and not a history – though it resumes those parts of the past always most present in the Dubliner's mind. There is information, but no bare information: what we learn is made palatable and given colour by Mr Gwynn's smiling, unhurried style. To the Dublin-born person, this book rings true and is evocative; at the same time, Mr Gwynn has known how to detach, from the web of Dublin's character, facts which will strike the stranger's imagination. He has, chiefly, traced the social growth of the city; he relates its human history in the course of a tour through the streets themselves, picking out here a statue, here a tablet, here a building or corner dark with associations. He also gives, in words, such a vivid plan that the appended map is almost unnecessary.

He is at his best with portraits, and has great command of anecdote. His eighteenth-century Dublin has been knowingly touched in, but, wisely, he has given most of his space to the nineteenth century, assembling a good deal of unwritten history, filling in a tract between fact and gossip. He has taken aspects of

Dublin of which he is most fully qualified to write. *Dublin Old and New* should endow the stranger with a sense of the city's continuous, vivid and far from placid life: the residential quarters, the university buildings will no longer present an obdurate mystery. The best of Mr Gwynn's chapters have the spontaneity of talk, and follow the same compelling, zigzag line. A good deal of the traditional gloom of Dublin (which literature, lately, has reinforced) is relieved by his stories of witty lives. After the Union, Dublin declined from her aristocratic showiness: a good many families left and found their focus in London. But judges, divines, the great doctors, the Trinity College figures continued to enjoy, and to add to, the city's urbanity: there was less wildness, but there was wit, good living and dignity. In Ireland, the nineteenth century showed the best of its mellowness, without the industrial element. It had more grace here, though life was often tragic, never fully secure.

His chapter on the museums and galleries, touches the unhappy subject of the Lane bequest. Here and elsewhere, something more natural than tact guides him through the complex history of a city in which almost every subject is controversial. The great quality of *Dublin Old and New* is its companionableness: it should be carried round with the guide book but not read in the street – its style is too retrospective and leisurely – read, rather, in the intervals of sightseeing, or best of all, in bed in the hotel. It should feed a taste for Dublin – and, also bring to the notice those quiet and atmospheric quarters (along the canal, for instance) that the tourist often overlooks.

New Statesman, 17 May 1938

The Moores of Moore Hall
by Joseph Hone

George Moore, the merchant of Alicante, built Moore Hall when he returned from Spain. The site, on the top of a wooded hill overlooking an inlet of Carra Lake, caught his eye – no doubt it embodied his Irish dreams. He had meant to improve, and to settle at, Ashbrook House, the more modest home of his family, but, like other Irishmen of his period, he could not but deviate into the grand idea. He had the means: he had more than made good during his term abroad –

perhaps his ability came from his mother's side; she had been an Athy of Renville, and the Athys head the roll of the great Galway burgher families. Now, backed by a solid fortune, this first George Moore set out to buy up land at a time when land in Ireland cost more than it does now. He had a right, also, to his wish for the grand, for he had soared out of the Anglo-Irish ambiguity by taking out a patent of nobility in order to attend the court of Spain. He had established, as far as one knows rightly, descent from the Yorkshire family of the Blessed Thomas More. He and his wife (*née* Miss de Kilikelly, or Kelly, reared in Spain and married by him at Bilbao) had thus made part of the aristocratic society of Catholic *émigré* Irish that gathered at Catholic courts. The Catholicism of the Moores – as the fourth and last George Moore was not slow to point out – was recent, and on the whole unimpassioned: that Miss Athy, the merchant's mother, had been a Catholic and brought the religion in. Miss de Kilikelly confirmed the matter, of course. In the clement, propitious Spanish air, the George Moores got from their religious background advancement, poise. But back in Ireland, in Mayo, the position of Catholic gentry was not too good.

However, a chapel was built at the top of the new house, and the family practised its own religion in an easy, unbigoted way. Later, they were to attract Miss Edgeworth and her friend the Dean by their liberalism, their readiness to discuss. With the Moores, there were no mines in this area; their fanaticisms worked out in other ways. The last George Moore's abnegation of Rome and rather wordy embracement of the Protestant faith was the first Moore act of religious fanaticism.

The woods at the top of Muckloon Hill were cleared, and Moore Hall went up. Begun in 1792, the bland Georgian house in its watchful position over the lake and islands was not to live much more than a hundred and thirty years. In 1923 it was burned down – victim, like other Senators' houses, of party violence. Mr Hone shows a dreadful photograph of the shell – not the least indignity is the ivy. While it stood, classic and bare and strong, the house embodied that perfect idea of living that, in actual living, cannot realize itself. The inside, in proportion and decoration, was of Renaissance simplicity. It was (someone said) a house built for hot days; the ceilings must have reflected the lake light. On the first floor, 'the summer room' gave, through a Venetian window, on to balcony over the portico. Had George Moore the First forgotten the rains of the West, the isolation in acres of wet woods? His son, George Moore the Second, the historian, when recalled, to rule here, from

London, from the pleasures of Holland House, added a notable
library. But it was he who said, 'Beautiful as it is, much as I love it, I
have not always been able to exclude ennui from its precincts.'

As the returned merchant found, and as his son the thinker found
later, to dream of Ireland is one thing, to live there another. Ireland
broke each of the Moores, in her oblique way. But being spirited
people, they broke well.

George Moore the First created more than a house. By building
Moore Hall, and by buying much land round it, he saddled his
descendants with that something between a *raison d'être* and a
predicament – an Irish estate. The hold is ghostly as well as material;
there is a touch of 'I have, therefore I am.' And, from the outset,
nothing went very well. The former Miss de Kilikelly moped for
Spain and never quite settled down. The eldest son, John, gave
trouble: reared abroad, he took his transplantation to Ireland in only
too good faith. He detached himself from some squalid troubles in
London to plunge into revolutionary politics. The Moores, already
appalled, next learned that Citizen John Moore had been, immediately after the French landing, proclaimed President of the Republic
of Connaught by General Humbert. John was arrested; tortuous and
expensive litigation ended only with his obscure death. The
unimpeachable Moores had the neighbourhood's sympathy, but
nothing was bad enough for poor John.

Thus, George Moore the Second became the heir; his father's
death recalled him from London to Moore Hall. He married a Mayo
lady, Louisa Browne. This Louisa Moore, with her hard, brilliant
dark eyes and curled upper lip, was a *maîtresse femme*. Women like
this, in every few generations, dominate, in all classes, Irish family
life. Her husband's frail health and his preoccupations made her
master as well as mistress of Moore Hall. In her passionate dealings
with people – most of all with her eldest son – Mrs Moore stopped at
nothing. Anything might be used to implement a quarrel. The letters
she wrote to George Henry were those of a thwarted mistress rather
than of a mother. She took up an impossible position when, her
second son John having been killed in a riding accident, she set
herself against all horses, point blank. With George Henry, love for a
faithless mistress cured itself (no thanks to the intervention of his
aunt, Miss Browne) but horses continued to impassion and dominate
him – as they dominated Mayo and most of Irish society. Augustus,
the third son, precocious and disappointing mathematician, soon
cared for nothing but horses, either. First with the Mayo squireens,
then in England and with the Waterford set (who, jumped their

horses in halls) the two brothers showed indomitable courage and silliness – and George Henry ran up horsey debts. Mrs Louisa Moore lived in that sort of dread that does seem able to magnetize tragedy – Augustus *was* killed, riding at Liverpool. Life for George Henry took a serious turn – he turned to the heartbreak of politics.

It was Mrs Louisa Moore who maintained, on behalf first of her husband, then of her sons, the friendship with Miss Edgeworth. Interchanges of visits and letters between the two households were lively, affectionate, fruitful. In Miss Edgeworth's conversation, in her power to put him back into touch with what should have been his own world, the historian found real solace. Unable to keep back ennui shanghaied in this world of rain and intensive family feeling, with Miss Edgeworth he breathed astringent air. This man wrote, in an unfinished Preface:

> I have had no celebrity in my life. But a prospect of posthumous fame pleases me at this moment . . . we are so made that while we are still living we like to think that we shall not be forgotten after our deaths.

He referred to the promise, solemnly given, that his family were to see through the press his *Historical Memoir of the French Revolution*. For this purpose, £500 was set aside; in this was to lie his posthumous fame. It was good that he found the prospect worth so much. For his *Historical Memoir* was never published, though Miss Edgeworth brought up her failing powers and Louisa and the already distracted George Henry did what they could. It was left to the last George, in an access of family spleen, to bring up the fate of the manuscript.

George Henry Moore's problems as landlord and politician occupy later chapters of Mr Hone's book. *An Irish Gentleman* was the title of George Henry's biography, by Colonel Maurice Moore, his second son. Their father's death left George Moore the Fourth, the writer, and Maurice Moore, the soldier, heirs to the family predicament – and to more, to the family *sense* of predicament. The keen British officer and the Catholic patriot ceaselessly struggled inside Colonel Moore's breast. Also, Colonel Moore loved Moore Hall with passion, his wife had lived there, his children were bred to love it – but Colonel Moore was only the second son and George had broken the entail and could do what he liked – a position George did not fail to make more than clear. George himself was martyrized by a divided wish – to be the free artist, to be the *grand seigneur*. He was plagued by Moore Hall worries wherever he went – fateful letters in dogged handwriting, sure to begin inside, 'Sir, I am sorry to tell you . . .' Letters that make the absentee's heart sink at an Irish stamp. Such letters had harried every reigning Moore; they followed George to Paris, to Ebury Street. The debts, the debts, the roof, the tenants, the drains, the trees. . . . How continue the page of unmarred prose with the Irish stamp sticking out under the manuscript? If George's mincing shoes and town clothes looked funny to his employees, he was nonetheless a just landlord; he rackrented Moore Hall for sensations only – the lake gave him two books. In essence, he wished to return – the Ely Place years had disabused him of Ireland, but he kept the physical feeling for Moore Hall – his ashes repose on one of the lake islands now. His cruelty – an unnerving sprightly sadism – to his over-sincere brother was, I think, neurotic, fruit not only of their over-intensive childhood but of generations of life before them rank with the family myth.

Mr Hone's *The Moores of Moore Hall* covers much ground, in years and experiences, and is at the same time admirably compressed. He has dealt temperately with his material. He quotes just fully enough from letters – family letters, letters from stewards, trainers, debtors, neighbours and friends. Small momentous incidents come out – there was the cook, for instance, who could no longer stand heat. The racing chapters could not be livelier, and seem to me well-informed; the sticky political passages are done with clearness and calm. Here is not only a very welcome pendant to Mr Hone's existing *Life of George Moore*, but a picture, put in perspective and generalized, of an Irish landed family's scope and fate.

New Statesman, 25 November 1939

James Joyce
by Herbert Gorman

James Joyce, European writer owed to Ireland, remained during his lifetime a rather aloof figure. He enveloped himself in no mystery, took up no poses and had no part in promoting the foolish legends that came to settle about his name. After a protracted poverty and obscurity, due to his refusal to make concessions, he became a person almost everyone talked of and many people were anxious to come and see. He sustained with a simplicity that was disconcerting and that appeared cryptic the prominence into which he had been thrust.

He had desired no more – and no less – than the consummation every writer desires: the consummation of his books finding their mark. In his prominent, as in his obscure years, he stood clear of those heated intimacies in which so many writers lose or imperil virtue. He loved his family, liked good company and was subject to the sort of solitary humour that made him dance by himself in a cloak on a Paris bridge, but the atrocities of human communication were unknown to him: he did not hand himself out to disciples in small change. The circle of people with whom he grew familiar was broken up by this present war, and a winter silence hangs over his death.

In days when there is a bad name for detachment, it is hard to assess the detached man. As to the bare circumstances of Joyce's life there has been, up to now, ignorance: by a number of people he has been vaguely seen as an aesthete piqued with his own country, choosing to live abroad. Actually, the detachment Joyce did achieve, the detachment that made it possible for him to go on writing, was a continuous heroic act of the spirit. Nothing was spared him: extreme poverty, repugnant work for a living, frustrations, humiliations, physical pain, sense of exile were by him felt to the full – but they were surmounted. He was reared and educated in a religion from which a deep nature does not without crisis secede, and from which a lonely nature dreads to detach itself. He was adolescent in a provincial capital, Dublin, that ignored or vituperated his vision, a capital whose intelligentsia devoted itself to, as he saw it, a petty and local myth, a national sentiment. In a Paris indifferent to his eager presence the boy of twenty hanging over his notebooks was excruciated by toothache – he had not a franc for a dentist – that at least did him the service of reconciling him to hunger: he would have been unable to masticate the food he was for days unable to buy. Recalled to Dublin, he for five months watched his mother die in an agony only made supportable by the consolation of a Church he knew she knew he had forsworn. Early fatherhood made acute, in a series of foreign cities, that struggle for the very barest subsistence that, apart from art, he accepted as being life. The vacillations of publishers and the *pudeur* of printers blocked, year after year, the publication of his finished works – in fact, the dealings of Joyce's publishers and putative publishers with him could have opened gates to dementia. And his writing, with its immense exactions, could only be done at the weary end of a day: when, in Rome, he wore out the seat of his only trousers, this was not on the writer's chair but on the high stool of the bank at which he worked overtime; in Trieste the precise and burning lover of words drummed commercial English into Berlitz pupils at the rate of tenpence an hour. Landlord after landlord threatened evictions from the minute grilling foreign apartments that were the Joyce homes; he saw his wife humiliated; financial quandaries spoilt his relationship with his brother. All his life he was hampered by eye-trouble, and just when poverty slackened its extreme grip, blindness was found to be imminent – blindness held off him by operations that were ordeals to his whole frame.

To pile up these facts, from the Gorman biography, might seem to be recruiting for Joyce a pity that he certainly never asked, or felt, for himself. Never was there a less pitiable man. The facts should be known, only, because they make his life-history as inspiring as any history of conquest. Also, they invalidate once for all any foolish idea about an Ivory Tower – how many reputed ivory towers would stand the test of an examination of fact? Joyce's equanimity triumphed, through everything: it was a combination of an unmoved belief in his art with a Jesuit-instilled rule of self-discipline. Joyce had that kind of *hauteur*, independent of circumstance, that Stendhal calls *espagnolisme*. He had the Irish qualities shaped and steeled. If his imperturbable manners irritated the bully, they could disarm the bully as well. His gusto for life, his love of round roaring pleasure dictated, during his youth in Dublin, his choice of medical students as his allies: with this pack he ran the city and knew Nighttown.

Mr Gorman's Joyce biography is exciting. I suppose almost every biography *could* be better done: in this the first forty pages – descriptive – move rather heavily, and a few repetitions and *longueurs* come later on. Mr Gorman's writing, however, is admirably impersonal; he is not intrusive and he makes no claims. The Dublin environment and the foreign scenes are well rendered. The book is documented with Joyce's letters – the letter to Ibsen on his seventy-third birthday, written when Joyce was eighteen, is a superb salutation from youthful to aged genius. There are Joyce poems – everything from the doggerel to the lyric – and excerpts from early essays and, most valuable of all, Joyce notes on his own aesthetic, departures from Aquinas and Aristotle, worked on through that first Paris winter of toothache. Joyce's father, that grand old unstable stalwart John Stanislaus, civil servant and tenor, stands out excellently. The vicissitudes of the books with the publishers, the Babel and almost Bedlam years in wartime Zurich, the inauguration of the first cinema in Dublin, are fascinating matter. Through all, Joyce's love–hate relationship with his own city, Dublin, and the crystallization of Dublin inside his art, appears.

Spectator, 14 March 1941

Sentimental Education
by Gustave Flaubert

L'Education Sentimentale stands in the first six, perhaps in the first three, on the great novels nineteenth-century Europe produced. It has not, I think, been translated, at least in England, before, and the appearance of Mr Goldsmith's excellent English version is, therefore, important. The reader who has any French at all would still, of course, do better to read the original: the essence of Flaubert's prose commands so much attention that the very slightly greater difficulty of reading another language becomes immaterial. But for those who cannot or will not read French Mr Goldsmith has lifted a barrier: there is now no reason why anybody's experience should remain incomplete – and to have not read *L'Education Sentimentale* is, I believe, to be in a state of incomplete human experience. Mr Goldsmith has so faultlessly kept, in English, the abruptness and suppleness of Flaubert's prose that his work deserves examination by those who, already familiar with *L'Education Sentimentale*, are interested in translation for its own sake, as an art. The white-heat precision of Flaubert's French and its clearness – he identified style with vision – make translation of it the most exacting test of a man's power to know, and use, his own tongue. Analysis of the shortest sentence is necessary before one is able to render, in English, anything like the equivalent of its content – the very simplicity of each sentence having been achieved by the concentration of Flaubert's entire feeling for art.

And to meet the book, with an English title, in the familiar type and the red covers of the fiction part of the Everyman's Library, is valuable in another way. Flaubert's greatest novel now stands, for the English reader, alongside the classic English and Russian novels with which the Everyman format is associated – and its new position invites a comparison. What makes this latecomer unique – unique even among the other French novels, each in their way outstanding, that are already on the Everyman lists?

Frederic Moreau, whose education in love bears no fruit, for it only finishes when he is capable of no more in life, is a negative, selfish and aimless figure. He is the completely anti-heroic type, not evoking, and not intended to evoke, sympathy. Unlike the heroes of English novels he neither displays prowess nor is endeared to us by humility; unlike the heroes of Russian novels he is magnified by no complexities; unlike the heroes of many French novels he is incapable of exalting any one passion continuously: he is not even consistent in his ambitions. He exists in a series of moments; he does not attempt to synthesize; he reacts nine times for once that he acts. Yet his experience, subject of the novel, is an experience that we behold with awe. The height of the book is the height of the pressure of the emotion through which Frederic moves – and not Frederic alone: there are four women, Mme Arnoux, for whom he feels that ideal love whose nature is that it cannot be realized; Louise, the *gauche* little provincial heiress; Mme Dambreuse, the woman of the world; and Rosanette, the light-hearted courtesan who is too faithful in her relation with him. These four loves, each having not only intensity but in its own way a sort of completeness, cross and recross. And each character, as the book proceeds, comes to carry upon itself the shadows, or one might say the reflections, of the different others. By an art that is consummately Flaubert's own, minutiae and futilities and false starts are used to build up an effect of Fate.

Technically, the novel is on a level that has not been approached again. The plot is elliptic, with scenes moved on and transitions made in a phrase. The method is visual; thought is not analysed, and no consciousness is examined from the inside. Each scene is made to take its peculiar emotional colour from its setting, from the objects surrounding it. From the first page to the last is rendered a beauty that is not to be forgotten – the beauty, immune from feeling, of the thing in itself. Flaubert stands alone as the master of this poetic objectivity. One may say that his characters have been sacrificed to his perception. But it is perception that is the force of the book.

Spectator, 15 August 1941

In My Good Books
by V. S. Pritchett

'If truth is the first casualty in war, the second is the literature of the period, especially the reflective literature,' says Mr Pritchett, opening his Preface to his collected essays, *In My Good Books*. On analysis, the two casualties seem identical – or, at least, the second derives immediately from the first. There is more than war's bringing down 'its medical date-stamp heavily' (and fatally) on every contemporary book. There is at present evidence, in the reflective writer, not so much of inhibition or dulling of his own feeling as an inability to obtain the focus necessary for art. One cannot reflect, or reflect on, what is not wholly in view. These years rebuff the imagination as much by being fragmentary as by being violent. It is by dislocations, by recurrent checks to his desire for meaning, that the writer is most thrown out. The imagination cannot simply endure events; for it the passive role is impossible. Where it cannot dominate, it is put out of action.

Time will give our confusion a perceptible character of its own. When today has become yesterday it will have integrated, into however grotesque a form. Until then, the desire for the whole picture must be satisfied by the contemplation of such whole pictures as already exist – in fact, of works of art that came into being either when there was a present that *could* be got into focus or when time had had time to act on what was already the past. The subsidence of modern prose writing of any power leaves us, says Mr Pritchett, alone with the classics. While nothing can stay our wish that these should be added to – for the incompleteness of art is an endless stimulus, second only to life's felt incompleteness, without the comment of art – we can readjust to the classics in this temporary pause. This release from our claustrophobia is possible – and these essays suggest how great the release can be. If at present we cannot write, and our friends cannot write, we can read. We can add the faculties for one act to the other and, possibly, make better readers than we have been. Any shake-up received by our sets of values may not, in its effects, have been bad. Our susceptibilities may have been heightened; their range has almost certainly increased. The classics have not changed, but we have.

Mr Pritchett writes as a reader – a reader under conditions his Preface shows and I have tried to discuss. The temperament of the last three years has been assimilated into his criticism. In having objectified this temperament and known how to put it to a positive use, he has made an advance on behalf of us all. He is contemporary in the exacting sense. As a critic he has occupied ground not yet touched by the novelists – of whom he is one. Ranging over (roughly) the last two hundred years, he has succeeded, by a series of implications, in throwing the years we are living in into relief. Admittedly, he writes at a period when it is easier to contemplate books than contemplate life, and books are the subjects of his essays. But he goes direct through the form to the living matter. The great novel (he points out) at once attracts and intimidates but above all deludes us with its effect of finality. It may appear to reflect a perfect, synthesized world, of which its author shares the authority. This illusion a closer reading breaks down. The world endorsed in the great French, English and Russian novels proves as complex and shifting, as conflict- and conscience-ridden as our own. The writers have used their power to articulate questions to which no one is qualified to reply. Mr Pritchett, during the interim in which life seems impossible to bring into focus, studies great earlier attempts to focus life. For no artist, as for no insomniac, have the sheep he was trying to count ever stood still. One has to learn, apparently, to count the sheep that keep on jumping about.

Demonstrably, no conditions for writing have ever been really happy. Mr Pritchett is out to define the weakness of a number of different writers' positions. Fielding, Constant, Turgenev, Thackeray, Zola, Lermontov, Gogol, Peacock, Dostoyevsky, Synge and Svevo – to instance a few of the subjects of these essays – each felt equivocally towards his own age. No attempt to create in a book (by means of satire, sentiment, religion, dramatic symbolism or picaresque simplification) the unity of which life is capable ever wholly came off. The autobiographer and the diarist were a degree more happy; they could impose the however crazy unity of the 'I'. For the novelist the task of projection has been at all times, in all countries, differently difficult. Racial or personal make-up, place in society, adverse moral climate or deceptive experience have accounted for those imperfect detachments, those lesions in novelists. On what one might call the English lesions, Mr Pritchett writes particularly well. Fielding and Thackeray made our only two notable attempts to get a grip on society; otherwise, in that direction we have been weak, as the French and Russians were not. Personal relationships, colour-coded by sex and not placed or framed by any clear sense of economic realities have been, too much, the English preoccupation. To an extent, the world of the English novel has remained the provincial, if lively, world of the 'I'.

At the same time – this suggestion runs through these essays – the English have been victims rather than exponents of romanticism. They have been decades behind the rest of Europe in recognizing its inevitable direction, its political dangerousness or its economic spring. To life England contributed Lord Byron, but it was to take the art of Stendhal, Lermontov, Turgenev, to show the romantic hero in play. The barricades as much as the tearful boudoir were to be the theatre of that temperament; today, the mutilated frontiers of Europe show the outcome of the romantic obsession. From the declamation on the eve of the duel to the Nazi monologue it has not really been such a far cry. It may be said (and Mr Pritchett has said) that Fielding, before romanticism had got a name, isolated for notice the man of power; there is a new relevance in *Jonathan Wild*.

These essays, singly known to *New Statesman and Nation* readers, gain by being collected. They assume an important relation to one another, and are in such order as to show the development of Mr Pritchett's critical idea. For its homogeneity as a considered book, *In My Good Books* is not dependent upon its Preface – too many prefaces to collections make rather transparent attempts to 'bind'. Here, the Preface does no more than its proper duty in suggesting the lines, the contemporary nature and the personal object of Mr Pritchett's approach to books read and re-read.

New Statesman, 23 May 1942

Parents and Children
by Ivy Compton-Burnett

'It is the intangibility of the distinction that gives it its point,' says Luce, on an early page of *Parents and Children*, discussing whether her father should join her grandfather, or wait for her grandfather to join him. The residing of Fulbert, his wife Eleanor and their nine children, with Luce at the head, in the house of Fulbert's parents, Sir Jesse and Lady Sullivan, in itself creates a situation in which distinctions are bound to appear. The family fabric of pride and feeling, in which the thirteen Sullivans and their dependants all play their part, has no ordinary groundwork: it starts to rise from the level that Miss Compton-Burnett's novels, in their depiction of living, always assume. There are, that is to say, none of the obvious squalors and enmities. For instance, Lady Sullivan (Regan), of whose three children Fulbert only survives, is a furnace of motherhood, whose interior roar can be heard when some incident opens the door of her nature. But her attitude to Fulbert's wife is not hostile.

She looked at Eleanor with a guarded, neutral expression. She could not see her with affection, as they were not bound by blood; and the motives of her son's choice of her were as obscure to her as such motives to other mothers; but she respected her for her hold on him, and was grateful to her for the children. And she had a strong appreciation of her living beneath her roof. . . . The two women lived in a formal accord which had never come to dependence; and while each saw the other as a fellow and an equal, neither would have grieved at the other's death.

Eleanor's maternity is less positive. In fact, her lack of gift for this rôle is commented on by her children, constantly in her presence and unfailingly when she has left a room. Eleanor Sullivan has, at forty-eight, 'a serious, honest, somewhat equine face, and a nervous, uneasy, controlled expression'. She passes from floor to floor of the house, moves to and fro between the schoolroom and nursery, plucking upon the harp-strings of her young's sensibility with an inexpert but always hopeful hand. Throughout the early part of the book she is attempting to rally the children's feeling – attempting, in fact, to drill the nine Sullivans for climax of a sort of ballet of sorrow – for their father's forthcoming departure for South America. But Eleanor, if she does not captivate, exercises a pull of her own. She enjoys, without intermittence, Fulbert's ironic affection. And, immediately upon Fulbert's reported death, she is wooed by a neighbour, the inscrutable Ridley Cranmer.

The nine children fall into three groups – Luce, Daniel and Graham, young adults; Isabel, Venice and James, the schoolroom party, under the passive control of Miss Mitford, the governess, and Honor, Gavin and Nevill, the nursery children, under the dispensation of the nurse Hatton, her underling Mullet (of the fox-like features and the dramatized youth) and in a state of skirmish with Miss Pilbeam, the nursery governess, whose ingredients are honestness and faith. Actually, Hatton's dispensation extends a good way beyond the nursery bounds: a woman of fewer words than most of the characters, she has the Sullivan make-up perfectly taped. To say that the Sullivans have a Nannie-complex would be to speak on a lower level than the novel deserves. The relationship of the family with the two governesses is – as is usual with Miss Compton-Burnett – perfectly done: it does not cease to be analysed, from both sides, with an imperturbable lack of feeling and zest for truth. 'I like all cold; I like even ice,' says one of the children – though in another context. And an icy sharpness prevails in their dialogue. In fact, to read in these days a page of Compton-Burnett dialogue is to think of the sound of glass being swept up, one of these London mornings after a Blitz. There are detonations in the Sullivan home – Fulbert's departure, his letter to Isabel, the news of his death, his widow's engagement, the show-down with Ridley, the discovery of Sir Jesse's illicit paternity – each creates a momentary shock of dullness, each is measured by this mortality of fine glass.

With each novel, Miss Compton-Burnett adds to her gallery. Figures she has already, in another novel, created, she is content – and content with deliberation – to rename and to put, in *Parents and Children*, to a this time purely formalized use. For the Cranmer family (with the exception of Faith, who is new), for the three mysterious Marlowes and for the three eldest of the nine Sullivans, Miss Compton-Burnett seems to me to rely, and rightly, on our progressive acquaintanceship with one kind of person – what one might call the illustrative rather than the functional character. In *Parents and Children*, these play subsidiary parts. In *Parents and Children* the highlight falls on, and genius is evident in, the younger Sullivan children and their immediate world. Especially James and Nevill. I know no children like James and Nevill; there may be no children like James and Nevill – in fact, the point of this author's genius is that it puts out creatures to which it might defy life to approximate. James and Nevill, of a beauty divorced from senti-ment, *are*, in *Parents and Children* – one cannot question them; they are more living than life. There are also Honor, Gavin, the tearful, complex, articulate Isabel, and Venice – this last more lightly, though as surely, touched in. To say that this book depicts the repercussion of grown-up crisis on children would be incorrect. The children's intensive, moment-to-moment living is for each a solitary crisis, that each maintains: grown-up sense of crisis, grown-up drama do no more than splinter upon these diamond rocks. It is the strength of Lady Sullivan, the strength of Miss Mitford, the strength of Hatton that they recognize the children's inviolability.

In this novel, as in the others, relationships remain static. The dialogue, in less than half of a phrase, in the click of a camera-shutter, shifts from place to place. The careless reader, for instance, must look back twice to discover at which point the departing Fulbert's carriage drives off. Scenes, on the other hand, are played out without mercy, to an attenuation felt by each of the characters. Most notably, the scene of Fulbert's departure. 'Well, it cannot go on much longer, boys,' Fulbert says to his elder sons, as they all stand in the hall. 'If there were any reason why it should stop,' says Graham, 'surely it would have operated by now.' Luce says: 'The train will become due.' The train is the only artificial interference, by Time.

Is this a book for now? Decidedly, yes. And for the 'now' not only of already avowed readers of Miss Compton-Burnett. *Parents and Children*, coming at this juncture, is a book with which new readers might well begin. Miss Compton-Burnett, as ever, makes a few concessions; she has not, like some of our writers, been scared or moralized into attempts to converge on the 'real' in life. But possibly, life has converged on her. Elizabethan implacability, tonic plainness of speaking, are not so strange to us as they were. This is a time for *hard* writers – and here is one.

New Statesman, 24 May 1941

Elders and Betters
by Ivy Compton-Burnett

The great Victorian novelists did not complete their task, their survey of the English psychological scene. One by one they died; their century ended, a decade or two before its nominal close. Then – as after one of those pauses in conversation when either exhaustion or danger is felt to be in the air – the subject was changed.

There came, with the early 1900s, a perceptible lightening, if a decrease in innocence: the Edwardian novelists were more frivolous, more pathetic. Their dread of dowdiness and longwindedness was marked; content to pursue nothing to its logical finish, they reassured their readers while amusing them, and restored at least the fiction of a *beau monde*. They were on the side of fashion: to shine, for their characters, was the thing. Competent, nervous, and in their time daring, they redecorated the English literary haunted house. Their art was an effort to hush things up. Curiously enough, in view of that, almost all the novels I was forbidden to read as a child were contemporary, which was to say, Edwardian. They were said to be 'too grown-up'. (To the infinitely more frightening Victorians, no ban attached whatsoever: a possible exception was *Jane Eyre*.) When, therefore, I did, as I could hardly fail to, read those Edwardian novels, I chiefly got the impression of being left out of something enjoyable. Here was life no longer in terms of power, as I as a child had seen it, but in terms of illusion for its own sake, of successful performance, of display. Yes, and here the illusion bent on the grown-up state, on its stylishness, its esoteric quality. The fashions of the day, that I saw round me – artful silhouettes, intricate mounted hair-dressing, the roses, violets or cherries heaped high on hats – the constant laughter I heard in other rooms and the quick recourses, in my presence, to French, all contributed something to this. The Edwardians, perhaps to mark the belated accession of their King, did, however speciously, build up the grown-up idea. The distant existence of that *élite*, that group of performers that I approached so slowly and who might be no longer there by the time I reached them (a premonition which was to be justified) tormented me, in common with other children. I should like to know how the Edwardian novel affected its grown-up readers. In them too, I suppose, it played on the social nerve, the sensation of missing something.

That the Edwardians were, in fact, on the retreat, that they were fugitives from the preposterous English truths of Victorianism, putting up the best show they could, probably did not appear in their own day. Their shallowness was a policy, however unconscious. We owe it to them to see not only the speciousness but the ingeniousness of their contrived illusion. This was only not stronger because they were poor in artists: it reaches a worthy level in the best of the novels of E. F. Benson; it attains to a sublimation, nothing to do with fear, in the later novels of Henry James.

What, then, was this task the Victorians failed to finish, and that the Edwardians declined to regard as theirs? A survey of emotion as an aggressive force, an account of the battle for power that goes on in every unit of English middle-class life. The Victorians' realism and thoroughness, with regard to what interested them, has perhaps been underrated: where these do not operate, where they are superseded by jocose patter or apparent prudery, I think we may assume the Victorians' interest flagged – for instance, I think it arguable that they were not, imaginatively, interested in sex, and that they were hardly aware of society. Their blind spots matter less than their concentration, from which some few blind spots could not fail to result: they concentrated on power and its symbols – property, God, the family. Of these, their analysis was unconscious: the order was one to which they fully subscribed; they had no idea that they were analysing it, or that, carried far enough, this must be destructive. In that sense, their innocence was complete.

For what they required to work on, for what magnetized them, the

Victorians had no need to look far beyond the family. The family was the circuit: the compulsory closeness of its members to one another, like the voluntary closeness of people making a ring of contact to turn a table, generated something. Society was, for the Victorian novelists' purpose, comparatively negligible: as a concept they could and did ignore it; it might just exist as a looser outside ring, a supplementary system of awards and penalties, or an enlarged vague reproduction of the family pattern. Love was recognized as either promising an addition to the family structure by a right marriage, or threatening damage to it by a wrong one; apart from this, desire was sheer expense, and the lover from the outside, as a latecomer, must be either a nincompoop or a pirate. . . . This would seem to hold good of Dickens and Trollope (whose personal sociability committed them to nothing stronger in writing than a good word for a good time had with good fellows, and left them derisive about any *beau monde*) and of the Brontë sisters, for all their stress on the isolated passion of individuals. As to George Eliot it seems doubtful: her analysis was more conscious, which makes her less Victorian. The most obvious instance is Charlotte M. Yonge, and the major exception Thackeray, whose sense of society was acute, and whose families are in a felt relation to it.

Thackeray was in another sense an exception: in his novels there do exist grown-up people. For elsewhere, with the Victorians, we are in a world of dreadful empowered children. The rule of the seniors only is not questioned because, so visibly, they can enforce it; meanwhile, their juniors queue up, more or less impatiently awaiting their turn for power. The family gradations, though iron, are artificial: inwardly, everyone is the same age. The Victorians could not depict maturity because they did not believe in it. The father of the family was the extension of his youngest son's impotent buried wish, the mother, with her mysterious productivity, that of her daughter's daydream. How far the Victorian family was falsified by the mirror of Victorian art, or how far its characteristics were merely exaggerated, cannot be settled here: it is the art not the family that we study. For that matter, were the Victorian artists influenced by the passionate conjugality, and later equally passionate widowed seclusion, of their Queen? In its subjectivity, in its obsession with emotional power, the age was feminine: the assertions by the male of his masculinity, the propaganda for 'manliness' go to show it. The apron-string, so loudly denounced, was sought, and family life, through being ostensibly patriarchal, was able to cover much. Trollope, in whose own youthful experience family life had stood for debts and deathbeds, and Dickens, in whose it had stood for debts and disgrace, were active in forwarding the ideal.

Or, so it seemed to their readers and to themselves. It can be seen now that Victorian novel-writing, had it continued upon its course, would have endangered, not by frankness but by its innocent observations, the proprieties by which we must hope to live. It can be seen why the Edwardians took fright, and sought refuge in the society fairy-tale. It was certainly not the Edwardians who were the *enfants terribles*. As it happened, the Victorians were interrupted; death hustled them, one by one, from the room. We may only now realize that these exits, and, still more, the nervous change of subject that followed them, were a set-back for the genuine English novel. Its continuity seems to be broken up. Since then, we have a few brilliant phenomena, but, on the whole, a succession of false starts.

Have we, today, any serious novelist who has taken up, or even attempted to take up, at the point where the Victorians left off?

A possible answer might be, Miss Compton-Burnett, whose latest novel, *Elders and Betters*, calls for some fresh discussion of her position. She, like the Victorians, deals with English middle-class family life – her concentration on it is even more frankly narrow. In form, it is true, her novels are ultra-Edwardian; their pages present an attractive lightness, through all the weight being thrown on elliptical dialogue; but, beyond that, their unlikeness to the Edwardian is infinite – to begin and end with, they allow no place for illusion. They are, at the first glance, unlike the Victorian in being static (time is never a factor in them), in being unsensuous and unvisual, in refusing to differentiate between comedy and tragedy, in being without remorse. They resemble the Victorian in their sedateness, and in their atmosphere of physical and social security. Her avoidance of faked, or outward, Victorianism, however, is marked: we find ourselves with this, and more, guarantees that Miss Compton-Burnett is not merely copying but actually continuing the Victorian novel.

She continues it, that is to say, from the inside. Her being in the succession shows in her approach to her subject, rather than in her choice of it – for the family as a subject has never been out of fashion; there is no question of its being reinstated. What Miss Compton-Burnett revives is a way of seeing; she sees, with hyper-acute vision, what the Victorians saw, and what they had still to see. She has been too clever, or too instinctively wise, to set her novels inside any stated time: the idiom of talk is modern, the way of living dates from thirty to forty years back. Costume and accessories play so little part that her characters sometimes give the effect of being physically, as well as psychologically, in the nude, and of not only standing and moving about in but actually sitting on thin air. For some reason, this heightens their reality. In space, they move about very little: they go for short walks, which generally have an object, or advance on each other's houses in groups, like bomber formations. They speak of what they will do, and what they have done, but are seldom to be watched actually doing it – in *Elders and Betters*, we do see Anna burning the will: on examination, we find this to be necessary, for this act she will not admit, and so can never describe. . . . This bareness, which starves the reader's imagination and puts the whole test of the plot to his intellect is, surely, un-Victorian? Miss Compton-Burnett has stripped the Victorian novel of everything but its essentials – which must have been fewer than we thought. Her interest is in its logic, which she applies anew.

As a title, *Elders and Betters* is ironical: everyone in this novel is the same age, and nobody is admirable. In a Victorian novel, the characters fail to impose upon the reader; here, they fail to impose upon each other. The revolution, foreseeable, long overdue, has arrived – without disturbing a single impalpable cup on the impalpable drawing-room mantelpiece. It has been succeeded by this timeless anarchy, in which meals are served and eaten, visits paid, engagements to marry contracted and broken off. Everything that was due to happen in the world the Victorians posited, and condoned, has happened – but, apparently, there is still more to come: such worlds are not easily finished with, and Miss Compton-Burnett may not see the finish herself. For one thing, that disrespect for all other people underlying Victorian manners (as Victorians showed them) has not yet come to the end of its free say, and fear has not yet revenged itself to the full. The passive characters, almost all young men, marvel at the others, but not much or for long; they return to marvelling at themselves. Only the callous or those who recuperate quickly can survive, but in *Elders and Betters* everyone does survive – except Aunt Jessica, who commits suicide after the scene with Anna. In this we are true to the masters; in the Victorian novel people successfully die of their own death-wishes (as Aunt Sukey dies in *Elders and Betters*), but nobody ever dies of an indignity.

Miss Compton-Burnett shows, in *Elders and Betters*, that she can carry weight without losing height. She has been becoming, with each novel, less abstract, more nearly possible to enclose in the human fold. *Elders and Betters* is, compared, for instance, with *Brothers and Sisters*, *terre à terre*; but with that I greet a solid gain in effect. The more she masters what I have called her logic, the more material she can use. Her technique for melodrama has been by degrees perfected, and is now quite superb: I know nothing to equal Chapter X of this book – the duel in Aunt Sukey's death-chamber, after Aunt Sukey's death. Only second to this is the lunch-party, at which two families voice their disgust at old Mr Calderon's engagement to Florence, the governess's young niece. There is an advance, too (again, a logical one), in the articulateness of employed persons: nothing protects the Donnes against Cook and Ethel, with whom even Anna is placatory. The importance of money has not budged, but dependence is now felt by the monied side – also, there is, with regard to employed persons, either a weakening or a belated dawn of grace. In one of the earlier novels, it seemed consistent that a child of the house should laugh every time the governess eats; in *Elders and Betters*, a child suffers because he has left a governess out in the dusk and rain. And religion, the worship in the rock garden, for the first time enters the scene.

The post-Victorian novel, in Miss Compton-Burnett's hands, keeps its course parallel with our modern experience, on which it offers from time to time, a not irrelevant comment in its own language. To the authority of the old, relentless tradition, it has added an authority of its own.

Cornhill, May 1944

The Condemned Playground
by Cyril Connolly

The Condemned Playground is a collection of essays, satires and critical pieces by Cyril Connolly. It offers an open view of the mind, and displays the extraordinary range of powers of one of the most important critics of a generation – the generation now in its young maturity. A generation that has, for a long time, been regarded as one of precocious children – disrespectful, experimental and brilliant – but which must, now, be recognized as having moved forward into its due place, that of the grown-ups.

England – I sometimes feel, in the darker moments – would rather raise, and tolerate, crop after crop of playboys than honour, and take seriously a savagely serious and original mind. There has been a policy – quite, of course, unadmitted and unconscious – of 'Keep the children at play, so long as they don't break anything valuable, until, one morning, they wake up and find they are old men.' England is equally kind to the golden lad and the noble silver head – both voices are listened to with attention. Maturity, and its claims, on the other hand, almost always creates an awkwardness, a predicament. It seems one too many, in almost all fields of action. In fact, there appears to be little demand for it.

Or, there *has* not seemed to be much demand for it. Surely, now, in the crucial days, the demand for maturity – of mind, of judgment, of feeling – has become immediate and pressing? The imperative to be grown-up is upon us all. Those who have hesitated to grow up should pull themselves together and do so; and those who have been grown up for some time, but whose grown-upness has been ignored, should be recognized.

Mr Connolly is by a few years younger than this century – a century whose violences and convulsions have been more noted than, and have perhaps helped to obscure, its accession, by this year, to middle life. He was one of what was collectively called the youth of one post-war period; he represents the maturity of another. The pieces in *The Condemned Playground* cover the years 1927–1944. His first published article, on Sterne, is here; also, critical writing that was his most recent at the time of the book's going to press. What lies behind the selection of the pieces and, at the same time, inspired their arrangement, is significant: read through, *The Condemned Playground* is the reverse of scrappy – the book, in fact, is as continuous as a story. The story is the relation, from year to year, of a mind with its own times.

Of his title, Mr Connolly says:

The Condemned Playground signifies for me the literary scene of the 1930s, the period of ebullience, mediocrity, frivolity and talent during which I wrote most of these essays and my first two books. I also chose the title to refer in a more limited sense to that leafy, tranquil, cultivated *spielraum* of Chelsea, where I worked and wandered. But there is another sense in which *The Condemned Playground* refers to Art itself; for Art is man's noblest attempt to preserve Imagination from Time, to make unbreakable toys of the mind, mud-pies which endure; and yet even the masterpieces whose permanence grants them a mystical authority over us are doomed to decay: a word slithers into oblivion, then a phrase, then an idea . . .

This feeling of evanescence has always been with me as a critic; I feel I am fighting a rearguard action, for although each generation discovers anew the value of masterpieces, generations are never quite the same and ours are, in fact, coming to prefer the response induced by violent stimuli – film , radio, press – to the slow permeation of the personality of great literature.

'Like most critics,' he goes on to say, 'I drifted into the profession through lack of moral stamina.' He suggests that criticism – or, as he at one time felt it to be in his case, 'the interim habit of writing short-term articles about books' – was the outcome of, or the one road left open by, drastic *self*-criticism: the high standards set by his reading made him abandon his own creative work. This cut both ways; it may be remembered that, from the time of his very first appearance, Mr Connolly has been recognized as a creative critic. His earliest book reviews – of which there are examples here – had a richness, force, angle and, above all, unpredictable course which made them works of art in themselves. If they *were* an apprenticeship to writing, they showed no characteristic of 'prentice work. And the two books he did write in the 1930s – *The Rock Pool* and *Enemies of Promise* – show that he did not lower the standards that, at the start, had been so forbiddingly high. Rather, he found himself able to approach them. Since then, there have been rumours of his association with 'Palinurus', of the famous *Unquiet Grave*.

Most of the pieces in *The Condemned Playground* were written concurrently with the writing of the books; and those dating onward from 1940, concurrently with the editing of *Horizon*.

The expression 'literary scene' means something. Literature is like a landscape: its foreground, the present, packed with moving figures, sometimes too close up to be judged; its background, the past, showing those mountain ranges which are the classics – but even these seem to change, seem more or less distant, higher or lower, as mountains do, in the varying, changing lights of our own day. Mr Connolly registers, in his writing, those changing lights. He can also, when his subject is modern writing, fix, by a sort of magnesium flash from his own temperament, figures, here and there, in the chaotic foreground. Where he is concerned, art and life are inseparable: he is fascinated by the interplay between the two. This fascination he communicates to the reader. He does not shun or dread, but rather explores and uses, his own susceptibilities.

The essays in *The Condemned Playground* are at once just and savage, sombre and frivolous – Proust said, frivolity is an intellectual quality. He has a religious regard for 'the saints of art'. *Kind*, he is never – those who have seen salt dropped on a slug may have some image of what he does to the reputation of the middle-brow novelist. The trend of the middle part of this book is to discourage feeling young persons from writing feeling novels unless, absolutely, they must.

The book is in three sections. The first, essays on Sterne, Swift, Chesterfield, and on some of the recognized greater moderns of the inter-war period – Joyce, Gide, Thomas Mann. We have the 'Imitations of Horace'; also, the A. E. Housman controversy, which raised Cain. In the second section, we watch Mr Connolly out with salt after slugs. An exquisite parody of a mid-period Aldous Huxley, and three hair-raising satires – 'Year Nine', 'An Unfortunate Visit' and 'Ackermann's England' supplement the chase. The third section is the most personal, the richest, the most dignified and most interesting: it contains fragments of direct autobiography; the 'Barcelona' piece stands out strongly by having been placed in juxtaposition to the earlier, jaded, blasé 'Spring Revolution'. 'The Fate of An Elizabethan' touches the seat of a malady: and 'The Ant-Lion' is unforgettable. 'Writers and Society' would, for the purpose of wide circulation, merit publication in pamphlet form.

I cannot omit, yet hesitate to embark on, comment on the brilliantly funny 'Where Engels Fears to Tread'. I know of no living English writer, in any field, who commands more admirable, one might say more enviable, prose than does the author of *The Condemned Playground*.

Tatler & Bystander, 23 January 1946

The Wrong Set
by Angus Wilson

Angus Wilson's collection of stories, *The Wrong Set*, is, I understand, his first published book. How, it may be asked, can one tell from a first book whether the writer might or might not have written better? I can only say that *The Wrong Set*, though not a success, makes one feel that here there *is* talent – misused.

'The first thing one notices about these twelve stories,' assert the publishers, 'is how they make one laugh.' This I did not notice: the effect, in the main, is a seediness as to subject, and an out-dated anger, monotonous, in the manner. The drunks and nymphomaniacs and sadists and have-beens who drool through these stories are no more funny than dead flies shaken out of curtains.

What is more, they seem to have lived so long ago that they no longer matter: these stories *date*. If one is to be a satirist, one must be of the moment or of all time: it is fatal to fall between two stools. I do wish Mr Wilson could dislodge from his system the resentments of *circa* 1932; I wish he could eliminate from his style the over-thoroughness of a cement mixer; and I wish he could realize that nauseating physical detail is, apart from other things, an offence against art.

The title story is by far the best: one really does get to like poor old Vi. 'Fresh Air Fiend' is grimly true; and 'Crazy Crowd' and 'Mother's Sense of Fun' have good moments. 'Realpolitik' is lively and efficient. The effect of the stories – the publishers further, hopefully claim, 'is to purge us of our hypocrisies'. If that be the author's object, let him open his eyes and glance at the present-day scene. Hypocrisies have become more rather than less interesting since they acquired the New Look.

Tatler & Bystander, 6 April 1949

The Golden Apples
by Eudora Welty

When one speaks of 'imaginative writing', one may use the term too vaguely and widely. Fiction is often no more than inventive writing – the plot is found, the characters are made lifelike, the scene of the story assumes a short-term reality. All this requires, on the part of the writer, hard concentration and patient ingenuity; the result is entertainment which gives pleasure, and for which thanks should be due. But the fact that much fiction is written to formula cannot be ignored. The formula is created by the wish of the public to be told, yet once again, what it knows already, or to have the same tune played, with slight variation, on a range of feelings of which it is already aware. The inventive writer has to his or her credit a new *story*, but the ideas conveyed by (or feelings contained in) the story have been taken from stock. No new world has been created, no unique vision sheds light, nothing of significance has been laid bare. The reader, having been held for a sum of hours, agreeably, by the inventive novel or book of stories, closes the volume and puts it down again. That is that. He is, as far as he knows, satisfied – nothing disturbs him, nothing haunts him. He has been left, in fact, where he was before. Like a child automatically stretching out its hand for another bun, he heaves himself out of his chair and goes to his book-table, or puts on his hat and goes to his library, in search of another work of fiction which shall resemble the one before.

If imaginative writers were more numerous, the inventive less so, there would be a less rapid turnover of fiction. The work of imagination causes a long, reflective halt in the reader's faculties. It demands to be re-read, to be brooded over, to be ingested, to be lived with and *in*.

Eudora Welty is an imaginative writer. With her, nothing comes out of stock, and it has been impossible for her to stand still. Her art is a matter of contemplation, susceptibility and discovery: it has been necessary for her to evolve for herself a language, and to arrive, each time she writes, at a new form. She has given us two collections of stories – *A Curtain of Green* and *The Wide Net* – a fairyless fairy tale called *The Robber Bridegroom*, and a novel, *Delta Wedding*. Now comes *The Golden Apples*.

The Golden Apples consists of seven stories similar in scene, playing upon the same cast of characters, dramatically different in time, and so placed in relation to one another as to develop a theme and bring out a pattern. The scene is the little town of Morgana, in the southern American state of Mississippi. The characters – whom we see in childhood, in adolescence, in maturity, in love, in death – are dwellers in and around Morgana. We more than see these people; we become identified with them, as though their nerves, senses and thoughts had been, by some operation, spliced into our own. The MacLains, the Starks, the Spights, the Morrisons, the Raineys, and their neighbours, each serve to illuminate for us intense moments of experience, which are at once their own and universal.

From whence has Miss Welty drawn her title? She had in mind those golden apples which, rolled across Atlanta's course as she ran, sent her chasing sideways, and made her lose the race. Outwardly, existences in Morgana – remote, sleepy and past-bound – are conventional: one goes to school, goes to work, marries, raises one's family, dies. Inwardly, each of these human beings gropes his or her way along – perplexed, solitary (in spite of the neighbourliness), and from time to time blinded by flashing illuminations. We have the gentle albino, Snowdie MacLain, and her almost magic relationship with her great, handsome, errant husband. We have hoydenish Virgie Rainey, with her abused music and her miscarried life. And young Loch Morrison, spying on love and insanity in the deserted next-door house. There are the MacLain twins (born of 'the shower of gold') and there is Jinny Love Stark, with her endless girlhood enclosed in a gaunt marriage. Maideen, wearer of dainty gloves, takes her own life after a hallucinated episode of love. Cassie keeps her mother's name written in growing flowers. Old King MacLain, all passion not quite spent, makes terrifying grimaces at a funeral.

This is great, tender, austere stuff, shot through from beginning to end with beauty. Miss Welty does not merely decorate her style with similes and images, she uses them to enlarge it – such as here: '*Behind the bed the window was full of cloudy, pressing flowers and leaves in heavy light, like a jar of figs in syrup held up.*' The seven episodes, or stories, in *The Golden Apples* are not to be separated from one another; they relate at once meaningly and closely: their dramatic total is only to be grasped at the very end – when time, with its action, and change, with its crushing force, seem, with Katie Rainey's burial, to reach full circle. So far as the stories *can* be made to stand apart, *The Shower of Gold, June Recital, Moon Lake* and *The Wanderers* are likely to be judged the most nearly perfect.

In *The Golden Apples*, Miss Welty would seem to have found, for her art, the ideal form. But, for a writer of her stature, nothing is conclusive – what comes next? American, deliberately regional in her settings, she 'belongs', in the narrow sense, to no particular nation or continent, having found a communication which spans oceans.

Books of Today, September 1950

The Anglo-Irish
by Brian Fitzgerald

This book traces the rise to power of what has been called 'a race within a race'. Ascendancy, Mr Fitzgerald shows, cannot be merely inherited or arrived at; neither birth nor careerist achievement quite accounts for it; only by character is it to be maintained. Continuous action and demonstration, morale and energy are required. Those qualities are exemplified by the three persons here chosen as illustrating the central theme – Richard Boyle, first Earl of Cork; James Butler, twelfth Earl and later first Duke of Ormonde, and Dean Swift. In all other aspects no three could be more unlike. Each overlapping a little upon the other's time, the capitalist adventurer, the martial aristocrat and the intellectual succeeded to one another upon a stage left empty when, at the Battle of Kinsale, 1601, the Gaelic, feudal aristocracy of Ireland was swept away.

Anglo-Irish dominance lasted for three centuries – dawned with the seventeenth, entered upon its twilight with the close of the nineteenth. Of this period, Mr Fitzgerald's study covers exactly half: that is, from the start to the culmination. We open with Boyle's arrival in Ireland, close with Swift's death, and watch, through a hundred and fifty years, the first harsh, individual enterprise give place to Protestant nationalism. Grattan is next to come.

The contribution the Anglo-Irish have made to Ireland is now recognized: it is one sign of a happier epoch that the extent, nature and worth of the contribution should be, by general consent, examined. Mr Fitzgerald's relation of characters to history, his threading of continuity through three different lives, is therefore not only skilful but apposite. Boyle came to Ireland, frankly, to make his fortune, and, in consolidating himself and his family, founded something more than was swept away when the 1641 rising ravaged Munster. Antipathetic to many as he can but remain (in spite of Mr Fitzgerald's engaging portraiture), Boyle brought in with him the ideas of the then new world, and imposed one kind of mould on civilization – fruitful land, busy ports, thriving strong little cities, foundries, markets, bridges, and roads.

Boyle *became* Anglo-Irish: Ormonde was born as such. (Of the Butlers, Mr Fitzgerald says: 'Ireland might not be their nation, but it was very definitely their country'.) For centuries his Norman-descended family had ruled from Kilkenny, strong and illustrious: it was for him to meet the crisis caused by revolution in England. 'Out of the feudal wreckage something indestructible survived, something that was vital to him: the habit of service.' From the impact on Ireland of Charles I's breach with his Parliament, total chaos nearly resulted: that it did not was due to Ormond's temperate leadership. He was to live to see re-emergence and, with it, some disillusion: pre-eminently, he justified his class at a time when its worth to Ireland was put to test, by transforming 'faith into honour, morals into manners'. Thanks to the Ormonde prototype, his kind were to befriend as well as to ornament their country for two centuries more.

With Swift comes the voice. The dooming, one might almost say, of the English Dean to become never quite an Irishman but an Irish patriot provides the third, most telling, part of this book, and gives context for a picture of miseries with which Anglo-Ireland failed, till too late, to grapple. Exploitation of land and labour, repetitive, crippling blows to trade and industries, from the English side, make the dire background of these hundred and fifty years. In the Anglo-Irish, those invaders and settlers who came to conquer, stayed to possess and love, national responsibility did come to be born, but social responsibility, alas, not. Where there was benevolence, there should have been reform.

Mr Fitzgerald, whose increasing importance as a historian and biographer is to be noted, gives us a book to be read both sides of the Irish Sea. He writes disinterestedly, and his hope that this analysis of the past may throw light on some of Ireland's present-day problems should, the reader will feel, be realized. And *The Anglo-Irish* has a second possible theme: i.e., the effect of Ireland on English history.

Observer, 16 November 1952

A Writer's Diary
by Virginia Woolf

Virginia Woolf left behind her twenty-six volumes in her hand-writing – her diary, started in 1915, broken off by her death, in 1941. As a diary-keeper, she was irregular. 'There are', says her husband, 'sometimes entries daily for every day; more usually there is an entry for every few days and then there will be a gap of a week or two. But the diary gives for twenty-seven years a consecutive record of what she did, of the people whom she saw, and particularly of what she thought about these people, about herself, about life, and about the books she was writing or hoped to write.'

Upon Leonard Woolf the editorship of the diary has devolved; and with that the onus of decision – a decision more or less certain to be challenged. What he elected to do was to follow through the internal continuity of the writer. That is to say, he has compressed for us, into one volume entitled *A Writer's Diary*, whatever directly refers to his wife's work.

What could have been hoped for was everything which bore on the artist's writing; that is, her sense of existence as an entirety. Mr Woolf's withholding of the bulk of the diary, on the score that it was too personal to be published during the lifetimes of people who figure in it, has already been, if not challenged outright, queried. Something less prying than curiosity may lie behind readers' dissatisfaction. A diary is an inadvertent self-portrait. It is felt or feared that the picture as now it reaches us may be lopsided; or that the editor's judgement as to what *is* continuity may have been arbitrary; or that the excisions sacrifice too much else to the interests of a pain-saving caution. All such objections, it should be said, Mr Woolf at the start did himself foresee. He has, in advance, done his best to answer them. 'At the best,' he declares, 'and even unexpurgated, diaries give a distorted view of the writer, because, as Virginia Woolf herself remarks somewhere in these diaries, one gets into the habit of recording one particular kind of mood – irritation or misery, say – and of not writing when one feels the opposite. The portrait is therefore at the start unbalanced . . . ' His stated aim, as editor, is to correct the unbalance there might have been. As little should be out of the true as possible. One must compute the enormous difficulties of his task. He knew her; the diary, published, was to go out to thousands of persons who did not.

A Writer's Diary, as it has come to us, never shifts from its focus: the writing writer. Such, whether at work or not, was Virginia Woolf. Art was what she was for. In a case of genius, *is* being (existence) ever quite separated from its purpose? Times there may be when divorce appears to occur: in the life, irrelevancies mount up – the more agonising because the writer both sees their nature and feels their power. The chief threat is the threat from what does not matter – hence resentment, protest, the 'irritation or misery'. Into the diary, Virginia Woolf discharged her fury against the consuming futile – interrupters, the over-played social farce, persons whose inner vacuum sucked at her. Great giver out of vitality, she objected – who does not? – to being robbed of it. Who knows what we did to her, we who knew her? If the diary knows, it has kept its secret, largely. Within these selected pages, the rest is silence. And what perhaps was it but a residuum, raged against then forgotten the day after? As a friend she was prodigal with her time and laughter, her teasing, at times her discerning pity. And no word remains in the diary that could mar that memory. Kind to us, the editor has been fair to her – for could *she* wish, through the long run of eternity, to revoke, even impair, any joy she gave? The spring of her art was one kind of joy.

The diary gives an impression of too great sombreness. It does not give an impression of being stripped. It is not spare, as would be a craftsman's notebook. It is full of mood, of tempo; it registers the ups-and-downs of an impassioned relationship. Disliking to be designated 'a woman writer', Virginia Woolf shows herself most a woman in the intensities, crises, panics and exaltations with which her relationship to her art was fraught. Harmony was her happiness. In 1924, 'galloping over' the revision of *Mrs Dalloway*, she notes: 'It seems to leave me plunged into the richest strata of my mind. I can write and write now: the happiest feeling in the world.' To the end of her life, such moments were to recur – though between them what stretches of terror, what troughs of anguish! As one should, she mistrusted her subjectivity: 'Not', she says, 'that my sensations in writing are an infallible guide.' Hence, no doubt, what may astound, even shock, some readers of *A Writer's Diary*: her sensitivity to criticism, her suspense till she knew the result of her book's impact on another mind. There were the phases of dejection, of dereliction, or of an alienating fatigue – 'Thought of my own power of writing with veneration, as of something incredible, belonging to someone else; never again to be enjoyed by me.' And there was the problem of the ordeal presented by the writer's emergence from isolation: the once solitary burner of the writing-lamp on the Richmond table found herself within a widening limelight. Appreciation by an eager few, recognition by an increasing many, fame, threatening 'popularity' – book by book, the situation was to take clearer form. It foreshadowed itself as early as 1921.

Well [she then writes], this question of praise and fame must be faced . . . . How much difference does popularity make? . . . . One wants, as Roger said very truly yesterday, to be kept up to the mark; that people should be interested and watch one's work. . . . One does *not* want an established reputation, such as I think I was getting, as one of our leading female novelists. I have still, of course, to gather in all the private criticism, which is the real test. When I have weighed this I shall be able to say whether I am 'interesting' or obsolete. . . . As I write, there rises somewhere in my head that queer and very pleasant sense of something which I want to write; my own point of view. I wonder, though, whether this feeling that I write for half a

dozen instead of 1,500 will pervert this? – make me eccentric –
no, I think not.

And that poltergeist of her house of the spirit, vanity! – 'Poor Mlle
Lenglen,' she notes, 'finding herself beaten by Mrs Mallory, flung
down her racquet and burst into tears. Her vanity I suppose is
colossal.' Was it, perhaps, latent fear of possible accessibility
through vanity which was at the root of Virginia Woolf's con-
temptuous misprision of the world? 'Brilliant' occasions find her
derisive, hostile. All the time, though with and after each book the
indicator-needle oscillated or faltered, there mounted the pressure
towards success. *The Waves* brought about the height; with *The
Years* a potential drop came. And then it was, most of all, that
absolutely she recognized her own virtue – the untouched ice, the
savage intractability of the spirit which must experiment. To please
she was willing, but never to please at all costs. Never once did she do
the same thing over again.

The question she raises for the reader (that is, the reader of her
novels) is the question that, in one or another form, she for ever poses
to herself – 'What is my own position towards the inner and the
outer? I think a kind of ease and dash are good; some combination of
them ought to be possible. The idea has come to me that what I want
now to do is to saturate every atom . . . to give the moment whole,
whatever it includes.' This was in 1928: *Orlando* is newly glittering
on the world; three major novels are still ahead of her. What
appalled her, as it must still appal others of us, were the non-
moments, the bridge-passages, the 'narrative business of the realist:
getting from lunch to dinner: it is false, unreal, merely conventional.
Why admit anything to literature that is not poetry – by which I
mean saturated?'

The question remains unanswered yet.

New York Times Book Review, 21 February 1954

Anglo-Saxon Attitudes
by Angus Wilson

Impressive novels do, often, turn on questions of conscience. Angus
Wilson's *Anglo-Saxon Attitudes* offers a fine contemporary example. This book carries weight apart from its size; it is of a

Victorian solidity, though the viewpoint is that of the 1950s. Mr Wilson has, apart from anything else, a technical ability rare today; he can afford to tackle both time and space. He handles a large cast of characters, and successfully rounds off a complex plot which has sub-plots in the Victorian manner. And he gives us a hero in the tradition.

Conscience is represented by Gerald Middleton – distinguished, attractive, now in his sixties, and Professor Emeritus of early medieval history. Man of the world, he is nonetheless a man of integrity. Since his youth, and the outset of his career, he has been increasingly troubled by a suspicion. In 1912, he was near the scene of what seemed an epoch-making discovery: an exceedingly rude Anglo-Saxon image was unearthed from the tomb of a Christian missionary – one Eorpwald; who, in the seventh century, had turned the course of religious faith in East Anglia. The conclusion to be drawn was that Eorpwald had been dallying with ancient pagan cults; and Professor Stokesay, who had made the Suffolk find, had not failed to publicise the discovery. Upon it had been founded a whole new school of religious–historic theory, to which a number of scholars had subscribed. Is Middleton to bring the whole structure down, thereby discountenancing his colleagues?

For, the truth now forces itself upon him: the 1912 find *had* been a hoax – the disreputable image had been planted, and around that centres an ugly story of a loved son's animosity to his father. Middleton's tie with the Stokesay family has not ceased, for Dollie, the professor's daughter-in-law, has been Middleton's mistress for many years. And here, in his emotional life, he has again been at grips with an unreality – he has sacrificed Dollie, his true love, to his attempts to keep going a hopeless marriage. Ironically his three children, now grown up, show no signs of having profited by the sacrifice; indeed by their very characters they reproach him. Worst of all, in the life of one of his sons he sees his own mistake repeating itself.

Dollie, since the break, has gone quite to pieces; Ingeborg, Gerald's smug Scandinavian wife, furthers all phoniness, lives in a world of whimsy. Ingeborg is one of those female monsters in whose creation Mr Wilson excels – indeed, all the women in this novel (with the exception of plucky little drunken Dollie and Rose, a dotty woman historian) are blood-curdling – though one salutes Mrs Salad, ex-charwoman and cheery old kleptomaniac. Mr Wilson, to be frank, sees almost all human relationships through a veil of grotesquery. He is a prime constructor of unspeakable scenes, which

I must say one reads about with pleasure. Through *Anglo-Saxon Attitudes* there runs a vein of truly excruciating comedy.

The story gets better and better as it goes on: at the start, the many and not yet fully-connected characters are confusing – in spite of the list provided on the first page. Squalor, exemplified by Mr Rammage and his Earls Court *ménage*, is not spared. But the book derives nobility from its central figure, to whom the following dialogue is a clue:

'You make a lot of your conscience,' Mrs Portway said bitterly. 'It's not *my* conscience,' Gerald cried, 'it's the good faith of a humane study in a world rapidly losing its humanity.'

Tatler, 30 May 1956

The People's War
by Angus Calder

'The chief aim of this book is to describe, as accurately as possible, the effect of war on civilian life in Britain.' So opens Angus Calder's foreword to *The People's War*. And from that aim, be it said at the outset, he has not deviated. The amassing of the facts, social, political, economic, must have entailed a ferocious labour which only a dedicated researcher could carry through: drawn from reports and statistics, they may in general be held to be unassailable. For reasons of morale or security they were withheld from the public during the war; subsequently, they can only not have been brought to daylight because of a lapse in popular interest when war ended: effectively speaking, they were nobody's business. Now Mr Calder has made them his.

Nonetheless, he expects to run into trouble. 'No doubt I shall be accused of wilful debunking. But . . . if a mythical version of the war still holds sway in school textbooks and television documentaries, every person who lived through those years knows that those parts of the myth which concern his or her activities are false.' *Every* person? This last is a sweeping statement; and Mr Calder makes it on what authority? It is unfortunate, in that it shakes one's confidence in generalizations which are to follow, and may inspire misgivings that, here or there, opinion is doing duty for knowledge.

Mr Calder was three when the Second World War ended. He was not, thus, of the generation, any of the generations, that lived through it. To say that this disqualifies him as its historian would be, evidently, most foolish; on the contrary, his relation in time to the time he writes of should make for a greater detachment and objectivity – and does so in the greater part of the book. His coming to consciousness took place during the anticlimactic aftermath. He was, however, sheltered from its contaminating atmosphere – aimlessness, sluggishness, voicelessness and moroseness – by an enviable if somewhat special environment: child of a distinguished intellectual family with a political bent, he grew up in what would have been an *ambiance* of discussion, re-evaluation and diagnosis.

His advantages may have carried a certain handicap; he shows signs of not having broken out, or knocked about, much, among persons other than those who formed, or connected with, his family circle and shared its outlook. Personal memories of the war, spoken or written, on which he draws for documentation, are invariably (or such has been my impression) those of a left-wing élite: and this limits his field. Other types he finds difficult to assimilate, which causes an incomprehension of them that is almost total, and as to which he shows a certain complacency. At times this matters. One may regret, also, outbursts of a youthful censoriousness.

The war on Britain was undergone by all types. Not only The People were people, so were others. For the general run of us, existence during the war had a mythical intensity, heightened for dwellers in cities under attack. The majority of us, living through those years, did not attempt to rationalize them, nor have most of us done so since. War is a prolonged passionate act, and we were involved in it. We at least knew that we only half knew what we were doing.

Exuberance, during the earlier London Blitzes, was not a fake: at the same time, nothing deadened the sense of loss, outrage and horror. There *was* something apocalyptic about the onslaughts. A sort of anarchical pride became the resort as life became more degradingly netted down by restrictions. The drabber years of the war were the real pill; little wonder that, as Mr Calder points out, they have not until now become a subject. (And even he, I note, condenses 1942–45 into a chapter.) Yet the myth, though bedraggled, somehow persisted. How else should we have gone on?

Going its way once it had served its purpose, the myth dispersed. It left behind it, so far as I know, no feeling that we had been bewitched. I know few who reacted against its memory, none in

'Life in the big house . . . is saturated with character.'

'A great cold grey stone house, with rows upon rows of windows.'

Downe House: 'a rather odd and imposing back view.'

Miss Willis rehearsing a play at Downe House: 'We acted a good deal.'

Above: Katherine Mansfield: 'a living writer'; and Alan Cameron: 'a real person . . . in contact with real things.'

Below: William Plomer: 'the most understanding . . . and the dearest of friends'; and Virginia Woolf: 'She illuminated everything.'

Above, left: Rosamond Lehmann: 'a sensuous, vital simplicity.'

Above: Eudora Welty: 'impossible for her to stand still.'

Left: Rose Macaulay: 'Kindness and a touch of imaginative genius.'

Right: Rider Haggard: 'the power of the pen.'

Below: Anthony Trollope: 'a support against . . . *hopelessness.*'

Right: Sheridan Le Fanu: 'a sort of negligent virtuosity in which Le Fanu shows his race.'

Somerville and Ross and
the Somerville-Coghill
tribes: 'a palpable give-
off of Anglo-Ireland.'

Dublin: 'impregnated
with a past that never
evaporates.'

Above: With Cyril Connolly: 'one of the most important critics of a generation.'

Left: Teaching at Vassar

Blitz damage to York Gate, Regent's Park: 'the Regency terraces look like scenery in an empty theatre.'

whom that inspired nostalgia. What, all but twenty-five years later, is there left to 'debunk'? Why should what has vanished be now suspect? Mr Calder desires that there be a non-false picture of civilian reaction to the war, experience in it, behaviour during it. That, as a desire, is shared by all. We cannot have enough, now, of the actualities.

But a picture presented in terms of the actualities *only* would be a false one; inseparable from happenings are the mood, temper and climate of their time. Mr Calder, one may be sure, would concede that. What alarms him is what he holds to be going on – resuscitation of a bygone glory, and exploitation in the wrong interests, for wrong reasons. But what could those be? With the young of the moment, heroics do not seem likely to 'take'. 'It all seems irrelevant now', pronounced a schoolboy, reported on 4 September last.

As a structure, *The People's War* is quite excellent: so it is in method – alternation of statistics with narrative. Packed with matter, the book is not overweight. Mass Observation, by giving the author access to wartime files, provides not only the most living but the most impartial of the documentation; extracts from memoirs and diaries, if more colourful, seem less so. The pre-war suspense (Munich and after), evacuation, the 'phoney war', the collapse of allies, Dunkirk, Battle of Britain and the Blitz (London and provincial), rationing, the extending call-up, the industrial all-out, industrial tensions – the psychological impacts of all are charted. Cold-bloodedly speaking, German invasion of Russia could not, for Britain, have come at a better time – unexpected, spectacular, the new drama, the flare-up of pro-Russian enthusiasm, gave the ruin-strewn summer of '41 a saving lift, a needed shot in the arm. The dire monotony of North African bad results was at least abated. America as a latecomer ally was less popular; the large-scale arrival on our shores of her forces made for an uneasy sense of 'invasion'.

Sagging or shaken morale, the places and times of its nearness to breaking-point, are recorded, *then* for few eyes only; similar secrecy made reports on the devastation of cities as sparing. As bad, often, was the brutalising slowness of their recovery, for which local inefficiency is indicted. Disaffection, a raw black bitterness in the disarmed army back from Dunkirk, was on a scale not to be measured then – limelight rather fell, that 'invasion summer', on the optimism and fervour of LDV (later Home Guard). That force, its organization and its performances, have been rewardingly studied by Mr Calder, as have the different limbs of Civil Defence, their coordination (so far as possible) and the generic temperament each developed: AFS, ARP, the ambulance service, the auxiliary nurses. At off times, harmony did not reign. The indomitable WVS, or green tweed ladies, fell foul, for instance, of us more saturnine wardens: we could not abide the sight of them – why, I wonder? Wardens maintained also a not always tacit warfare with the police. On the whole there was wonderfully little crime.

The war was won on the industrial front. The victory of the factories was the people's: accordingly, it is the epic of this book: as exciting are the decisions behind it, the back-room conflicts, the jockeying for position at top level. Mr Calder's grip on and treatment of this whole section are admirable, and make for compulsive reading; how controversial it may be, *I* cannot tell. In his chapter 'War on the Mind: Science, Religion and the Arts', he may find himself, with regard to some of his readers, on thinner ice. On the whole cautious, he is occasionally provocative – hard not to be! He recalls the predicament of the church – what should be the attitude to belligerence? – and the 'mobilization' of arts, painting and music. There did occur, as we know, a cultural boom which was not without aesthetic reality. But the giant determinants were the mass media: the press, broadcasting. Those two, oracles of the people's war, never had known more power or less freedom: on one hand the dictates of propaganda, on the other the taboos of censorship harried them.

In the main, the voice proved mightier than the pen. Sound made for community of sensation, was emotive (which was required), served entertainment. Genius came to the surface: ITMA began. Most of all, the microphone built up star personalities. The desideratum was not to *address* the masses but speak as one of them; at that, Mr Calder suggests, J. B. Priestley was better than Churchill. Press and radio combined in keeping the people's collective image constantly in front of the people's eyes, and did well in doing so. It was inspirational; one beheld oneself as one had it in one to be. The image was a winner. It perpetuated itself, alter a little though it might as the Churchillian rhetoric lost hold. Churchill projected it, in the first place.

Mr Calder's analysis of 'Churchillianism' is better than dispassionate; there is affection in it, as in his study of the man. The companion-portrait, Bevin, has full dimension: Cripps he has failed to animate – could one? His Beaverbrook is Beaverbrook: enough. No verdict can I pronounce on *The People's War* other than, read it! This is a drastic book, but honourable. There has been room in it, after all, for this:

Sometimes I say if we could stand Monday, we could stand anything. But sometimes I feels I can't stand it any more. But it don't do to say so. If I says anything my girls say to me, 'Stop it, Ma! It's no good saying you can't stand it. You've got to!' My girls is ever so good.

Spectator, 20 September 1969

The Irish Cousins
by Violet Powell

The book jacket of Violet Powell's *The Irish Cousins* is adorned by a family group: a framed photograph. This perfectly sets the tone of what is within. Kinship, or a close degree of affinity, characterizes the features and general attitude of boater-hatted young women in starched white ankle-length skirts and moustached young men, one in a blazer, at rest at the edge of a tennis court, between games. Backdrop, a twinkling shrubbery. There is, to the Anglo-Irish eye, a palpable give-off of Anglo-Ireland; and in its heyday. Conversation, suspended by the camera, leaves heads turned this way or that, alert and waiting. The *personae* are the interknit Somerville–Coghill tribes, soon to be further linked by another marriage. On the periphery may be taken to be either accepted neighbours or summer guests. The locale is Castletownshend, West County Cork, the time circa 1886.

In the forefront, vigorously seated, is Edith Œnone Somerville, 'Top Dog', by virtue of seniority, and more than that, of a generation consisting largely of brothers. Next to her, beautiful in profile, holding her racquet to her chin as one might a fan, is Edith's second cousin, Violet Martin – the 'Ross' of the collaboration to be. *The Irish Cousins* (which takes its title, only a plural added, from the firstfruit novel of that collaboration: *An Irish Cousin*, 1889) introduces itself as a study: 'The Books and Background of Somerville and Ross.' How inseparable the books and the background are, Lady Violet, Anglo-Irish herself, perceives, and goes on to illustrate.

Greater interest must concentrate on what was phenomenal: the collaboration. Interlocking minds, known more to criminal than aesthetic history? No, not that only: this was a rarer case – interlocking creative imaginations. Considering how savagely individual,

how overweeningly solitary, as an activity, is inventive writing, how
could two practitioners unify into one story? – *and* carry this off not
once but again and again? The cousins, we learn, were plagued by
what seemed to them fatuous questions on that subject: 'Who holds
the pen – or pencil, and so on?' Oneself, one retains some sympathy
with the questioners. Leave it, that this was a literary miracle, plus
something other. Result, a superb degree of accomplishment, a
tremendous range.

Lady Violet, too wise to analyse, contents herself with comments,
– on the joint vision, its extra-powerful focus; on the stylishness of
the joint style achieved, likened by her, in its variations, to shot silk.
It may be supposed that Somerville, painter already, charged herself
with that memorable verbal scene-painting, together with *outer*
accounts of action (equine or human), weather, sailing adventures,
meets, funerals, fairs, leaving to Ross, more fine-strung, 'aware' and
tense, the control of dialogue and, where necessary, penetration into
events or persons. Ross's death, in 1915, leaves, in the many
succeeding novels and stories, a lacuna difficult to locate, bravely
though 'communication' was carried on, defiantly though the works
were, still, double-signed.

The answer may be that when the cousins met – which oddly,
given the smallness of Ireland and the high value placed on getting
together, failed to happen till both were in their late twenties – there
occurred one of those fusions of personality which in one way or
another can make history. Their from then on total attachment
incurred no censure, and – still stranger, given the habitual jocularity
of their relatives – seems to have drawn down no family mirth. Nor
was its nature – as it might be in these days – speculated upon.
Absolutely, the upper class, Anglo-Irish were (then) non-physical –
far from keen participants, even, from what one hears of them, in the
joys of marriage.

Edith and Violet loved to travel together, but desired no perma-
nent break-away from parental homes. The Llangollen Ladies,
whose Plas Newydd they viewed on a Welsh tour, seemed to them –
it is recorded – extremely silly. This couple of gentlewomen from
Ireland were encased, armoured, in the invincible heartiness of their
extroverted tribe and specialized class. Round and upon them blew
the prevailing gales of clean fun, anaphrodisiac laughter. Anything
'extreme' was comic: that went for passion, that went for art. Dogs,
jokes, were the accepted currency. Their initial literary endeavours,
daylong disappearances, together, to the neglect of tennis, side-split
brothers and sisters, uncles and aunts. Only when books 'appeared'

did menace begin. The two now ceased to be amateurs: things looked serious. The actual crux, or crunch, was *The Real Charlotte*.

It is owing to *The Real Charlotte* that all this matters: otherwise, who might care? Here, in their third novel, they cut the cable. They made their own a terrain of outrageousness, obliquity, unsavoury tragedy, sexual no less than ambitious passion. *What* fired them into full-stature artists? It is on this masterpiece (which long awaited full recognition) that, as almost unwilling, almost unwitting artists, they do in today's eyes take their stand . . . Secondary in literary glory, toweringly 'the thing' in terms of success, the *Irish RM* stories are less cut-to-pattern in comicality, turn less undeviatingly on blood sports, than anti-blood-sport generations have preferred to suppose. In these tales are no meaningless antic caperings: on the contrary, outsize characters, clashes, crises, realistic in their very delirium. These not only *were* Ireland – they still are Ireland, under the skin.

One would like to know more than there seems to be to be known about Violet Martin: 'Ross,' with her indomitable fragility, her dilated great beautiful hare's eyes – whose near-sightedness had to be aided by *pince-nez*. The Norman-descended Martins of Ross, County Galway, had it less good than the later coming, Scottish-descended Somervilles, County Cork. Their fortunes foundered, under a succession of blows – those intricate troubles known to landowners. Ghosts were the least of the tribulations of the dying house.

Half-way through Violet's childhood, Ross, the mansion, had to be abandoned: her brother went off to seek a living in England; mother and a bevy of spinster girls (Violet the youngest) for some years camped, on the cheap, in Dublin (from whence sprang the rattling good Dublin passages in *The Real Charlotte*). After that, the heroic return to Galway; the struggle, headed by Violet, to rekindle life – such as it had been, never could be again – in the shell of the house. The whole of the wisdom of sorrow was this young woman's; she was early acquainted with wailings, dementia, speechless despairs. She is remembered for her delightful gaiety. Yet can one doubt, it was she who introduced into the Somerville and Ross combination that dark streak – which, at the same time, gave it validity?

Lady Violet is to be thanked for *The Irish Cousins*. Her sense of what *is* relevant to her subject, and her use of that, would seem to me faultless. Moreover, she has read, and assimilated, the Somerville–Ross writings in their entirety: no small task. She summarizes each of the many books, in some detail but without an instant of boringness. The effect is to whet a renewed appetite. How many of the lesser-known works are still in print, available, one would like to know? Could not publishing enterprise strike while the iron is hot? There may not yet be a boom; there *is* a 'revival' ... Did these authors impact on their compatriot, James Joyce? Lady Violet holds that they did, and produces evidence – which is daring and interesting. Their place in the Irish literary Valhalla is accorded, their links with the great native tradition traced. I regret only, in this book, a lack of mention of Joseph Sheridan Le Fanu, with whose novels several outlined here would seem to have a marked, if unconscious, affinity.

Spectator, 31 January 1970

LETTERS

Introduction

Like Virginia Woolf, Elizabeth Bowen was a dedicated letter-writer. A life divided between England and Ireland made for a great deal of correspondence, and she wrote faithfully to her friends – William Plomer, Ottoline Morrell, Virginia Woolf, Sean O'Faolain, Eudora Welty – and family. In 1956 we find her complaining to Plomer that being so busy meant she had no time, as in the thirties, for correspondence – and writing to anyone was 'a great way of making oneself feel in their presence'. I have chosen a selection from the period when she was still writing letters 'copiously'.

Letters are very important in the fiction. Leopold in *The House of Paris*, for instance, learns about himself from the letters he takes out of Naomi Fisher's handbag; Jane falls in love with the past through a cache of letters she discovers in *A World of Love*; Mary, in 'The Happy Autumn Fields', is translated, through old letters and photographs, from bombed London to Victorian County Cork. Letters change people's sense of themselves, and alter plots.

Elizabeth Bowen's own letters are not impressive literary 'set pieces', like Henry James's. Sometimes, perhaps when she is slightly in awe of her correspondent, they tend to be self-consciously descriptive, like an early letter to Virginia Woolf about France, or the youthful travelogue of Italy to Alan Cameron. There is a certain amount of upper-class gushing: 'Yeats was an angel' '. . . Heavenly if you appeared here.' But the letters do give a sense of her character: dry, energetic, observant and generous. There is an admirable letter, written to William Plomer very soon after Alan Cameron's death, which attentively praises Plomer's *Museum Pieces* instead of dwelling on her loss; and the letter to Leonard Woolf sent after Virginia Woolf's suicide, which was a severe blow to Bowen herself, is a model of right feeling and tact. But she can be sharp, too: the letters are brisk with scathing remarks about parochialism, middle-brow writers, people who make a fuss, falsifications of the past, and her own bad behaviour. And they show the same susceptibility to the atmosphere of horrid houses that we find in her stories and novels. She writes to Ottoline Morrell of Tom and Vivien Eliot 'shut up together in grinding proximity', or to Virginia Woolf about the horrors of house-hunting: 'It is impossible to believe that the people . . . are not to be sold with the house, and . . . that it is not necessary to ask oneself whether one likes them.'

The three-way correspondence with Graham Greene and V. S. Pritchett, which began as a broadcast and was published in 1948 as *Why Do I Write?* has, necessarily, a more formal tone. This attractive device of public statement masquerading as private correspondence (which has its roots in the eighteenth century), was embarked on, as Pritchett says in the Preface, partly as a reaction against the prevalence of literary manifestos in the 1930s: they wanted to avoid 'the sterility of debate' and to produce conversation, not polemic. The open letter is not much favoured now, but there were precedents for it then: Leonard and Virginia Woolf, for instance, published a series called the *Hogarth Letters* between 1931 and 1932.

There is no space here for Greene's and Pritchett's side of *Why Do I Write?*, but the main theme of the exchange, an urgent one just after the war when writers had been pressed into service as morale boosters, propagandists and Ministry of Information employees, was the writer's social responsibility. There was a feeling about, as Pritchett says, that writers should be 'putting their shoulders to some wheel or other'. But the writer is in a predicament: he is a citizen, but he also has to be a guerrilla. There is a difference, Pritchett goes on in his first letter to Bowen, 'between the believing and the imagining self'. Bowen replies that she is essentially asocial, but that by writing she makes her own society. There is no guarantee, however, that this creation of relationships will extend outside the written page. Graham Greene writes back that the writer's only duties to society are 'to tell the truth as he sees it and to accept no special privileges from the State . . . Disloyalty is our privilege.' Yes, replies Pritchett, 'the independence of the writer is everything'. But the State, on the other hand, has a duty to the writer: there follows an argument for a public lending right and for subsidies and endowments. Greene disagrees. If the writer is to be a 'piece of grit in the State machinery', he must be left alone to get on with it. Elizabeth Bowen ends the correspondence with a description of the writer as a Resistance leader who must nevertheless maintain a certain level of social decorum. It's a characteristic balancing act between anarchic, romantic individualism and good behaviour.

32 Queen Anne's Gate
January 19th [1923]

Dear Alan,

I am so thrilled, I must tell you – Sidgwick and Jackson are going to publish a book of mine – a collection of short stories. I never really thought anybody would. I interviewed Mr Sidgwick about them the other day; he is so nice. I always imagined publishers were rather snarky and condescending and made a point of crabbing one's work, but he didn't a bit. I haven't signed the contract yet but I suppose they will send it along soon. I don't know when the book will come out. By the time I see you I suppose I shall be suffering from a fearful reaction and feeling I would ~~doing~~ do anything to suppress these stories. Still, Mr Sidgwick is not a fool and I suppose he wouldn't take them if they were rotten. It is fearfully nice to have made a beginning.

I've just heard Walter de la Mare read a paper on 'Wuthering Heights' to the Kings College Literary Society. He is an amazing little man. There is something perfectly distinctive and different about the de la Mare sentence, written or said. 'She had a short life, in the nature of a hasty visit' – he said about Emily Brontë. Talking of short lives, aren't you sorry about Katherine Mansfield. I feel as tho' it were somebody I knew very well, don't you? It is very hard luck on John Middleton Murry – they were so happy. Apparently she had been ill for years – lungs. I wonder if it was that that gave her writing that peculiar vitality. She certainly must have lived up to her means. De la Mare said this evening that very few of us live up to our means – as individuals – intellectually, emotionally ~~and~~ or physically. And as a race, considering the amazing possibilities of our civilized world, he said, we are not living up to our means at all – being thoroughly cramped and unapprehensive. That's rather badly expressed – I wish you had heard him.

I am liking Lucretius awfully. I do like his mind, and the language – as the translation gives it one – is fine: 'the gliding stars' and 'the sunshine crowding the sky' – I am just beginning the fourth book. I have had little or no time for reading.

London really isn't so bad once one's back. But I haven't really detached myself from the country yet – I hope I never shall.

It really is rather much for you, this burst of excitedness about my book. You can only murmur something polite but vague, and hope to Heaven inwardly that you won't be expected to pronounce an opinion on the thing when it appears. I didn't say anything about it at

Christmas – I had sent it off to the publishers just before leaving London, and resolutely put it out of my mind, because it's always better not to think too much about a thing one is keen on but can't do anything further about, don't you always feel that?

By the way, how is Rome? P'raps I'd better not ask.

> Good night.
> Yours B B. [Bitha Bowen]

> Queen Anne's Gate
> Wednesday 14th [Feb. or Mar., 1923]

My dear Alan,

I hope you were sympathetic with H.M.'s Inspector about the earth-closets. Is he the same one who is coming to tea with you on ~~Thursday~~ Sunday? Is he anything like Mr Rupert Birkin, and do you think the Headmistress of the Secondary School will hit him on the head with a paper-weight?

If you get this letter at breakfast do keep it till the evening. You can't ready my disreputable letters in the office, either, all your other papers would curl up their edges in fine scorn and draw away from ~~them~~ it. *Do* send or show me the results of your horoscope. I would like to see it – angel-face, *do*! Yes, do get the kind lady to cast mine. June 7th, 1899, Wednesday (*I think*) – time, 3.p.m. place, (if she wants to know) Dublin. The only thing I'm not certain of is the day of the week, but I'm almost sure it's Wed.

My dear, you're sometimes extraordinarily near me. Not that I believe in telepathy, but I seem to be able to reach out. I don't imagine what you're doing, but I feel you're here. Which is very nice. You are very precious to me – I feel sometimes I am stupid. My love of you seems very childish – I mean sexless and imaginative. You see I have loved you for a long time as a friend, and that feeling still goes deepest and doesn't seem to have changed very much. I have always wanted you – last winter in Italy I thought about you a lot and wondered what you are doing and if we should see each other again ever. I think I loved your *you* long before I saw it in relation to my *me*. At least I don't know – can one? My dear, I do love you so; I am so afraid of hurting you or disappointing you or slipping away from you in this new relationship in which people so often seem to lose each other. Do you realize how – in the worst sense – *young* I am? You are a real person who has come in contact with real things, and I've lived altogether inside myself, all my experiences have been subjective. You are so much bigger than me, I feel inadequate – Am I wrong in writing all this? Angel I don't want you ever to be disappointed. You can make me grow up. There is something in you that can use up everything that is in me and still want more. – I suppose that is why I love you.

If you think I am wrong in writing this sort of letter say so, and I won't again. Angel I have rather got into the way of thinking *into* you, and I have been thinking about all this and wanted you to understand. But perhaps you do. I have only got to know you from a succession of glimpses, like a person walking parallel with one through a wood. I still don't know you very well, only what I don't know of you I am beginning to *feel*. I hope you know me better, and that this isn't only an attraction. That is what has been making me afraid. I sometimes wish we had been *just* friends longer.

Imagine, it's a week tomorrow since I saw you.

Still [Well?], my dear, goodbye for the present.

It is going to be lovely seeing you again

     Your B.B.

                                         32 Q.A.'s G.

[To Alan Cameron]   Saturday 28th [April 1923]

My darling,

It was entirely blessed of you to write so promptly as I found the letter to meet me on the hall table, even returning as I did, a day before I had said. And the book – you dearest thing, how sweet of you⸘ I have been looking through it, and it is going to be a joy – I settle down to it tonight⸘ The first book you have given me – a thing to be very much loved⸘ And why did you only write the inscription in pencil, darling ass? (Good Lord, there were 3 exclamation marks).

I wonder if you will ever get a letter I wrote in the train and posted in Turin – you probably will, but after this. The nice part about our letters is that having no bearing on anything of the slightest importance it doesn't really matter when they arrive. I am looking forward to that one you speak of following me from the Ludovisi. No one, I'm afraid, will ever publish our letters – for no one would ever read them – as the correspondence of two intelligent young Moderns, casting an interesting light on questions of the day – nationalisation, Ireland, population, capitalism. Isn't it a pity. I wish I were engaged to Mr Robins, I'm sure I should maintain a far higher tone in my correspondence with him. We should oscillate between Ireland and sex with a few interjections on the Future of the Theatre. (I could make a few intelligent remarks about *that* at present, having just been to 'R.U.R.' at St Martins. I am boiling over with conversation and criticisms – darling, when can you come up and see it? It's an amazing thing – and a weird swing of the pendulum after Rome, for me.) I'm afraid seriously, angel, that I have got a very unprehensile mind where questions of general and practical interest are concerned. I say it with no complacency, I feel a little small about [it] sometimes. I am too vague and speculative. I love either rushing off into abstractions, or shamelessly talking personalities. You must screw me up about this. It is horrible to yawn inwardly when people discuss Weltpolitik, and think how much nicer it would be to discuss the Short Story. In fact, it is provincial of me, I believe. I spent a long time in the Forum trying to define provincialism, and I couldn't – how would you? No, don't waste a letter on it, say it when we meet.

Well, the circumstances of the journey were pretty hellish – far worse than the one out, but it was enlightened for me by the company of Peter Quennell – my letter from Turin explains him, so I won't say it all over again. The train obliging[ly] lay down in Turin for an hour so we got out and stretched our legs by walking through the town, and ate ices in a café, and I posted your letters. Bar you, Peter Quennell was the most entertaining travelling companion for a forty-eight hour journey, as in the intervals of being really very entertaining he curled up and went to sleep like a dormouse. A decorative and delightful child, altogether. He published 'Masques and Poems' a month or two ago, and was chucked under the chin paternally, I remember, by the London Mercury. Having said so many pretty things about him, it is perhaps infelicitous to remark that he is very like what I would have been at nineteen, if fate had fitted me into the other kind of body. He is a rank young individualist and, except about anything that might happen to interest him, I should think a quite deliberate slacker. You would enjoy him – you must meet him some time.

England does look nasty from the outside, doesn't it? Those dirty white cliffs. I wasn't a bit enthused by it. English twilight is so grubby after the long blue dusk in Italy that rises like water. All the same, I did not go the whole way with Peter Quennel when he pressed his nose against the window (going across Kent where the fruit-blossom was fading into the grubbiness) and said that England was a bloody country, morosely. I was sorry to hear anybody else use that word, because it was not a nice word, also because it was yours. I thought of Northampton forests and said mildly that I did not think even

England was entirely bloody. His remark, meanwhile, sent two ripples of indignation down the two rows of bosoms. It was not a remark one should make in distinct voice in a 2nd class railway carriage closely packed with the [pure?], but I suppose he would not have been inspired to make it anywhere else.

Oh my dear, come up on the 6th. It will be heavenly, and I am glad you're not coming tomorrow, because I shall have longer to anticipate in. That was the worst of Rome, you know, I hadn't long enough to anticipate in. It was almost in the nature of [a] [flaw?] How much better if I had spent my week at Kingthorpe being instructed in Roman history. You might have read me out Gibbons and people, every evening from nine till twelve. You should have told me about Hadrian, and the Lake of Nemi. Ought I really to have known about Nemi? It is a pretty little lake, almost perfectly round, in a cup of hills, slate-grey and syruppy looking, just little wrinkles without the stir of a current.

Darling, I do want you. Fancy, I am only hours away from you, within telephoning distance. But I won't even telephone, because it would establish a precedent, expensive and demoralizing. You are so terribly nice. Goodbye—

B B.

I don't believe, after all this, that I even said 'Thank you' for the book. Thank you very much, dear Alan. The first book I ever give you shall be 'Encounters', for luck. I had a reassuring letter last night from Mr Sidgwick, saying it would soon be out, and thanking me for my patient silence. Apparently lady novelists can be trying to deal with, and the newer the noisier, of course.

Bowen's Court
August 15 [1932]

My dear Lady Ottoline

I have been wanting to write to you for so long, about so much: and *do* forgive me for not acknowledging the copy of the photograph you so very kindly sent: I love having it. I wonder if you are still at Freiburg, and do so very much hope it has done you good: also that you had plenty of sun, which I know you wanted.

I expect David told you that I *didn't* succeed in getting him and Hope Mirrlees to meet, simply because he was convalescing at Hatfield at the end of July when it should have been possible. I was sorry, as I should have liked to have heard what they made of each other. I wonder where *she* is now: I shall look forward to seeing her in the autumn.

I saw the Eliots a good deal before leaving England, and dined there the night before I came over here, so sorry to think I should not see him again – for so long – I mean until after America. There is something about the atmosphere of that flat that I find exceedingly sinister and depressing: my spirits go down with a bump as I go in. Not that the flat itself is so bad, but it's the atmosphere of two unhappy and highly nervous people shut up together in grinding proximity. And that poor little Vivien's wild eyes! But it is a pleasure to see him anywhere: he is so very funny and charming and domestic and nice to be with, besides being so great. I love knowing him.

Here feels a long way from everyone, though at a distance one can think over one's friends, can't one, and it is very spacious and restful and nice. Something about these high bare rooms and empty horizons that does one good. I'm reading with intense pleasure, for the first time, 'L'Education Sentimentale'. What perfect writing, and what a clear painful mind, and what a perfect picture of an enchantment he can produce. And what compass he has: this picture of colour and movement compared to the sad immobility of poor Bovary.

Otherwise, much the same summer life with a few visitors, neighbours and drives and walks. And the thought of London and friends in the autumn makes the contrast of this solitude (which month after month and year after year would be frightening: I can see how people round here go either all vague and sloppy or else take to drink) rather funny and nice.

I do so much look forward to seeing you again: I love seeing you and love your house. How happy you make us all! I'd love to write again later on, if it won't bore you. You must not bother to answer this if you're busy.

My next book is to come out in October: I shall look forward to sending it to you.

> Yours affectionately,
> Elizabeth.

Bowen's Court
August 31 [1935]

Dear A.E.C.

I have been wanting to write for some time, but waiting until I got here to write, to thank you for the *great* pleasure the arrival of *Polly Oliver* and your letter about *The House in Paris* gave me. I am a little worried at Gollancz' prematurity in sending you what I take to have been a proof copy of the H. in P., uncorrected and full of nasty muffling mistakes. I had a copy aside for you with a proper stiff black binding and, better, no sentences inside that make nonsense. I think I'll send it anyhow. I am *very* glad, seriously (I realize that my objections to the proof copies are trivial) that you did like the book. What you said about it moved and pleased me more than I can say – It's funny about the people being hard to visualize – I find I visualize the people I'm writing about in the same terms, with the same blanks and qualifications, as I remember people who have impressed me but that I cannot always see in entirety. I can see all Henrietta except her *features*; Karen's figure, movements and ways but I don't know what kind of nose she had. Max is a portrait of someone I knew quite passingly and superficially once, so of course I do see him; Max [*sic.: read* Leopold] is the same man as a little boy. But if I can't get this across there's something wrong, isn't there. Naomi Fisher I see the whole time, even her clothes.

As for *Polly Oliver*: it gave me the extreme pleasure and sense of amazement and at the same time of actuality your stories always do. I like best *Gone Away – Ring the Bells of Heaven* and *Crippled Bloom*. But then, I liked all of them, startlingly much. I say startlingly because I haven't been able to read much, lately: most print seems to slip over my mind, like water over an oiled surface. And your words don't.

I had read most of the stories before *your* copy came, because I pounced on them as soon as I saw they were out. I read *Gone Away* on the Newhaven–Dieppe boat. After which, shortly after, I did motor for miles in cornfieldy silent August empty France.

How I wish you would come to Ireland. Here – to this house, I mean. You could do what you liked the whole time: there is nothing else to do – I mean, nothing prescribed. I feel sure you won't, but wish you would. It is a pity – for me, I mean – you live on the far side of England.

I shall be here till the end of September, with various odd people – William Plomer for one: do you like his stories? – but also with empty rooms. After that I go back to Oxford, but then we move to London, as my husband has got a new job there. I have found a house in Regent's Park, overlooking the lake, which I like very much. I hope you will see and like it.

> Thank you again.
> Elizabeth B.

> 2 Clarence Terrace,
> Regent's Park,
> N.W.1.
> June 27th [1936]

My dear William

I went away to Dorset for three days, leaving no address, so only found your letter late this evening when I got home. I hope you guessed? If it is now too late to see you on tuesday next, 30th, for tea – I mean if you've made other plans by now, I shall grind my teeth. Yes, I *shall* be in, and I'd love, as you know, to see you. If you've filled up the afternoon, will you come to supper instead. But in a way I'd really rather you came to tea, as I've rather an odd assortment of people coming to supper, and shouldn't see you so much. So if I don't hear to the contrary, I'll expect you to tea.

I can't remember if you have any feeling about or against typed letters. After the extraordinarily nice things you've said about my writing – you once said it was *stylish*, which made a great impression on me – it seems rather a pity to type you one. But the fact is, I've only just, in fact not completely, as you will observe, learnt, and it still gives me a most exhilerating sense of power, in fact feels unlike me, to be doing it at all. I stop to contemplate the most banal sentence with absolute rapture. I suppose you, like everyone else, have been doing it for years.

In case we should not – which would be dreadful – meet on Tuesday, there is one thing I do particularly want to ask you about. In fact, I had been going to write – apart from wanting to say how particularly I liked getting your letter about the waves in the looking-glasses at 4 The Esplanade . . . Mr Eliot, quâ Faber and Faber, has asked me to edit and write a preface to a collection of The Best Short Stories of The Present Day (or words to that effect) to be a companion volume to their Book of Modern Verse. I do *trust* you will let me have one of your's? You'd get a formal proposition from F. and F. later, about terms – which I hope would be in order – and they'd do all negotiations with your publishers. *Conditionally*, which story do you think? Myself, I'd been thinking of the one about the young negro in the mines in *I Speak of Africa*, or else *The Child of Queen Victoria* itself. I know those two are both rather long, but I do like them both so very much.

I know what strong views you have about things, William, so do hope you won't take against this idea. It would discourage me terribly. . . . Do you, also, happen to have struck, in the course of reviewing, any short story, or collection of anyone's stories, that seemed to you in any way *strikingly* good? I feel I really cannot be too snobbish.

I hope, though, that all this will be made superfluous by my seeing you on Tuesday.

Since seeing you, I have been at Hythe (for too short a time to attempt to get near Dover: have you seen Dungeness, by the way; it is more like *Nowhere* than anywhere I have ever seen – a glare of white shingle for miles, and lines of tense-looking vanishing telegraph posts) in Norfolk and in Dorset. But mostly in London. Which has been very hot – I think of settling at Hythe . . . I missed you at that Surrealist opening. What chaos.

How is your mother?

> Till – I hope – Tuesday
> Love from
> Elizabeth

> Bowen's Court
> August 17th [1936]

My dear William,

it was lovely getting your letter this morning. I had been thinking about you specially since getting here, and meaning to write. I wish I had got to Dover, in spite of bad weather: I wanted to see no 4 The Esplanade. The carnaval you describe must have been superb: nutshells in the sea, etc. W. Philipps and B. K. Seymer always do look particularly windblown – how is it – and still more so when together. Rosamond and R. Senhouse are coming here on the 26th or 27th approx, which I look forward to very much.

A sort of belated June is going on here, as owing to the foul summer the hay is only now being cut: they are haymaking, in the intervals of showers, in the field in front of the house, between these clumps of trees, with clankings, voices and very nice smells. Not only the hay but the lime trees smell very strong at nights, which must be because of the damp and steamy heat, then sudden evening chills. At intervals colour and sun break on the country, then the summer goes on being wet again. The sweet peas are very late and the peaches only just ripening.

Yes, indeed I am doing those abominable short stories (the collection, I mean.) As far as I ever do read here, I read nothing else. 4/5ths of what I try out shows a level of absolute mediocrity; arty, they are, and mawkishly tenderhearted. Quite a large number of short stories are told, do you notice, by hikers. 'As I crossed the horizon' they so often begin and the heroine is generally just called 'the woman'. Really they are the hell. The chief break in this (the only break of real pleasure) has been S. O'Faolain's 'Midsummer Night's Madness' stories, which I do think *grand*. I should like to have 'The Small Lady' for my collection, tho' it is about 3 times the length I proposed to allow myself. If I do keep to length, I must have 'The Bomb Shop' which is in its own way nearly as good.

I long more and more to make a collection of *Great Middlebrow Prose*. Would this be actionable? Would you collaborate? I suppose it would ruin one.

Yes, I should simply *love* to have the latest S. O'Faolain, if you can really spare it. How very sweet of you. Have you met him? Is he nice? He might possibly be quite dim.

D. and R. Cecil were here for 10 days, and have just gone to join his family in France. They were very sweet and companionable. Alan got over about 3 days ago, having waited behind to clear off work. I got here on the 31st. Noreen is here, and sends love. Some weekend visitors have just left, and the D. Verschoyles who are touring round about come this afternoon for 2 nights.

I keep losing my voice in a most extraordinary way: for 48 hours together I can only croak or whisper. When I got here I was so very tired that I went to bed for 24 hours and drank bromide.

I am just learning to drive the car: in fact I *can* now, in a sort of way, though I still feel rather terrified at intervals. But I think this tends to make me a safe driver, as I am not at all dashing and take no chances whatever. The feeling of independance is certainly very nice. At present I love driving the car when *alone* in it, but a passenger rather rattles me. Jim Gates taught me: he's certainly very good.

Humphry is having rather an awful time in Calcutta: he's in hospital with flu and dysentery combined: his inside's been awful for 2 months. He says if he goes on feeling as bad as this he thinks he'll have to give it up and come home. He wants, however, to stick a year out if he can, as he hears everything begins to be much better in September, after the rains. The whole job and life sound pretty futile and futureless, and he's getting persecution mania on behalf of those wretched Indians. I rather hope he'll come home. Though to *what* I don't quite know.

Give my love to Stephen when/if you see him.

Oh I do wish you were going to be here, tho' realize it's impossible.

I am afraid this is a rather boring letter, but these short stories have destroyed my brain. However, I feel very happy in a strange, steamy, half-awake way.

The Listener's doing another short story of mine quite shortly, I think.

I *did* love your review of the Priestley book.

Love from Elizabeth.

Will you write again when you have time?

2 Clarence Terrace,
Regent's Park,
N.W.1.
October 21st [1937]

My dear William,

it was lovely to get your letter when I was in Ireland, and I've been meaning to write to you ever since. I adored hearing about all the things you told me. I haven't written because I either had the house full of people, or else was doing literary odd jobbing. The summer at B. Court was lovely, though shorter than usual, as I only got there in mid-August after Salzburg, and had to be back here by the first of October in order to get on with my theatre job for *N. and D.* I hear you are likely to be staying on at Brighton, which selfishly I regret very much as I miss seeing you, though also I can't wonder, as it's a heavenly place and your house is full of charm. How I enjoyed that day there in July. Oh but how I wish I could see you: writing is really most unsatisfactory, as there is so much to talk about that I cannot fit into a letter, especially at the end of a foggy day which I think has got into my brain – the fog, I mean. Can you possibly fit us in on one of your days in London? If not, or even besides that, may I come down and spend another afternoon with you sometime when you're not too busy? I expect you generally always are. Work must be multiplying. I hear Humphry's been corresponding with you about a book.

He really seems to be having a most persecuted time in India, with the police opening his letters. But interesting, I should think.

Salzburg was great fun, and had some funny moments. The Connollys turned up, looking well in mountaineer get-ups. Our party didn't go into those, as we were all either too fat or too small. The weather was heavenly and we drove about in fiacres. There was a great deal of conversation and eating, and the music, which I really did enjoy.

Raymond M. and the Cecils came to Bowen's Court. I also had a heavenly time reading Montherlant. I'm doing a thing on him this week for the N.S.

The Cecils imported some rather nice new paper games – one called Things Left Behind? Do you know it? You have each to give a list of 4 characteristic objects found in a spareroom, and the others have to guess who the person is. And I invented one called Bad Parties – you have to invent a list of the most excruciating eight people (though they may be nice individually) possible to combine. Also to make out a menu of the most repulsive (though it must be credible) dinner you can image. With drinks. And, if possible, the games played afterwards.

The Faber Book of S. Stories is out, with your's figuring largely. *How* good it is!

I really must stop now; I feel so fearfully sleepy. I am back with my novel – going on with it, I mean – which is rather alarming, as I want it to be so good.

So goodnight, William. How I do envy you being at Brighton. London is very much overrated, I think. Do let me see you as soon as is convenient for you.

I am now a member of the Irish Academy of Letters – though you might not think so from this letter.

> Love
> from
> Elizabeth

Bowen's Court
Sunday June 5th [1938]

Dear William,
    it was a joy to get your letter. I do *wish* you were here. I am getting on really quite fast with my novel: I'm now finishing the chapter-before-last, and hope to finish the last before I leave here – only then

it will have (as they do have) to be revised. Tony's portrait of me is also flying ahead: I must say, I do think it's a first-rate piece of work, immensely decorative, energetic, unobvious. It also seems to me flattering, but no sitter, of course, minds that: I shall love to know what you think of it.

I am very glad indeed you are getting on with your novel: I do hope you'll be able to keep Cape work in bounds for it, as I very much want another novel by you. I adored your description of the Cape party and the bitch weasel Miss Riding. How disconcerting that she liked you – be careful, she's most tenacious. Also I'm interested to hear your impression of Madeline House – she looks pop-eyed with anxiety the whole time, poor little creature: I always feel at once sorry for and depressed by her. I thought Humphry much set up by India, really very sweet, now he's back, but I agree with you that I *don't* think he's more than half digested anything he found there. When he went out there, he was a person of so little experience (except of the most hectic and bemusing kinds) that I feel he had too few terms of reference – really no means of sorting anything out. He had, in fact, a rather inadequate stomach, and I feel it's been given lately (in India) too much to digest. It will be interesting to see how he shakes down in England now. I do hope well – he's so nice. I do hope to God he'll take your advice about his book. He's been rather ruined, so far, in what he's written, by this tendency to over-intellectualize things – a form of indigestion (like acidity) I suppose.

I've just been in Dublin for 5 days. I met some of the grand old boys – like Yeats, with whom I spent an evening, who was an angel, in his own house, less showy and more mellow: he has a superb white cat. I spent a day with Frank O'Connor, who's at present living in Wicklow; he's a very nice creature: the most contemporary (I mean, the least up-in-the air) of the younger Irish, at least to talk to, I think. Sean asks to be remembered to you. I wonder what you'll think of his play 'She Had to Do Something' which Cape are publishing. Also of his life of O'Connell.

I shall be back either at the end of this week or the middle of next. *May I really* come down and see you, any day at all (other than in a week-end) after June 20th? Send me a card and say. I should simply love to. Bless you for writing.

Love Elizabeth.

P.S. I took Tony over to tea at the *unstucco* house.

Bowen's Court
Sep 24th [1945]

My dear William

It was very nice *indeed* getting your letter. As a matter of fact, ever since coming over here I had been thinking of you, and therefore thinking I'd like to write to you. I wonder when you *will* 'come out'? I know no one who has been more completely incarcerated and at the same time made less fuss. People who never were doing anything of the slightest importance, interest or value to themselves or anybody have been the ones who have gone on about 'interrupted lives'. However, no criticism even of those who overrate the value of their freedom comes well from me, who have had such a good war – if you know what I mean. I cannot say I'm ashamed of the fact, as I don't think I had a good war at anybody else's expense, but it *is* a fact.

I came over here feeling like death, full of visitations and repugnances, but am feeling much better now. I have worked like a black out of doors (hewing down nettles and undergrowth, clearing woods) which was just what I wanted, and hardly laid pen to paper or finger to type-writer. Which was just what I wanted. I think I have the makings of a better forester than gardener: plenty of brute strength and aggression instinct, but the reverse of green fingers – in fact almost anything I plant dies.

I am now obsessed by the wish to buy a row (4 or 5) of stone statues, for a particular place in the grounds here. [Nubbly?] draped early 19th century goddesses, throw-outs from some house gone to the knackers, would do fine.

I'd been thinking about you in the sense that Alan and I were both wishing you were here. If you suddenly *were* free and came over (no travel formalities now) it would give us both the greatest joy and pleasure. No (private) cars on the roads yet in this country, so it would be very static and dull for you. But if there were anything you wanted to write, or even read, this is not too bad a place. For exercise – forestry. I simply throw this out, as a suggestion, and expression of an entirely (probably) selfish wish on our part. There is plenty of food, space, silence and if one wishes, sleep. We hope to be here up to mid-November.

Alan appreciated very much what you said about his eye trouble. It was the result of the last war (trench poisoning) and has been cumulative. As a matter of fact, ever since he decided to leave the B.B.C. it has been less bad. He used to have a 'good eye' and a 'bad eye'. The good eye has been deteriorating seriously, but the bad eye is now coming into action again. The good eye has, apparently, an operable cataract, to be coped with about 3 years hence.

He has had a terrific tribute of not only affectionate but professionally appreciative letters from a lot of people in the educational world, since his retirement was announced. I'm glad, as he really has worked like a Trojan, and I don't think he ever realises how high people rate him.

Our plans are fluid. We've still got Clarence Terrace, but have sub-let the top floors to a B.B.C. couple, Archie Harding and his wife. The rent they pay covers *our* rent and rates. Our present idea is to move most of our furniture over here and make this place comfortable, and be here more. Alan may do half-time things in England, if salaried. He is obviously wanted, and I'm sure ought to keep irons in the fire. However, there's heaps of time to decide. We shall be spending the main part of the winter, from mid-November to March, at Clarence Terrace, whatever else we do or don't do.

Selfishly speaking I'd much rather live my life here. I've been coming gradually unstuck from England for a long time. I have adored England since 1940 because of the stylishness Mr Churchill gave it, but I've always felt, 'when Mr Churchill goes, I go'. I can't stick all these little middle-class Labour wets with their Old London School of Economics ties and their women. Scratch any of these cuties and you find the governess. Or so I have always found.

I do look forward to seeing you. Heavenly if you appeared here. Otherwise, London in November.

What a long letter.

Love from Elizabeth.

Bowen's Court
9th September [1952]

My dear William

Thank you for your sympathy. You have always been one of the most understanding as well as the dearest of our friends, seeing us in and out of so many scenes and places and times and houses, and I do particularly value your thoughts now. Also, there could not have been a happier time to have had your book – I mean a time at which *Museum Pieces* could be more welcome. The inscription, to both of us, gave me nothing but pleasure; my only wish is that Alan *could* have read the book. To me, it came at a time when I couldn't otherwise read anything, and yet was longing for the pleasure that reading can be – the mental equivalent of nervous hunger coupled with indigestion. To have something of yours – and one of the best I think that you've ever done – and at the same time to be in Tony's company was ideal. Apart from all the praise and reclame *Museum Pieces* is having and will have, remember also that if it had been written, for a special friend at a special moment it could not have brought more happiness – and, in a way I can't explain, consolation.

At any time, William, and speaking objectively (awful word), *Museum Pieces* is a great piece of work. The balanced, apparently casual, up-springing build of the narration is so good. And, you have accomplished what I had always taken to be impossible – the bringing of 'real' people into the dimension of art.

Funny, elegant, tragic, and with the [two?] of them floated in and added to by the element of your sensibility, your perception – oh William, it *is* a beautiful book!

Also, judging it on another (I mean the personally-knowing plane) as a bringing to life of beloved Tony and of his mother, it's quite uncanny. I see all of those changes of his face, the dilation of his eyes, and hear his laughter and the tones of his voice.

So you can imagine that to be both in your company and in his has peopled, has somehow saved, these last otherwise terrifyingly empty days for me.

> All my love
> Elizabeth.

Bowen's Court
6 May [1958]

Dearest William,

I only got back from America a week ago; one of the best things about home-coming was to find your *At Home*. It, I have been reading over these last days, with deliberate slowness, to make it last. Thank you for it twice over: I deeply appreciate having your name, and indeed my name in your hand, inside. This book is really magnificent; the best account of your and my times, and of having such times as one's own times, that I know. And I don't know how to tell you how I admire, and envy, the brilliance *and* depth, suppleness and yet no less precision, of the writing.

Best of all, the book is you, as we know and love you. (I don't know why I use the first person plural instead of the first person singular.) Again and again reading it I felt as though you were in the room: at the same time, I remained rightly in awe of that non-personal greatness one recognizes in a friend. On the whole, I haven't cared very much for most of my contemporaries' autobiographies (such as, though don't tell them) Stephen's and John Lehmann's. Most people do better to keep their traps shut; but you are an exception.

I was grateful, apart from many other things, for the return to life, for me, of Virginia and Tony: they are the only two of the dead whom I *truly* miss. (Alan never seems dead, in the sense that he never seems gone: I suppose that if one has lived the greater part of one's life with a person he continues to accompany one through every moment.)

Only you seem able to bring back Virginia's laughter – I get so *bored* and irked by that tragic fiction which has been manufactured about her, since 1941. As for Tony, I have so often tried (and so invariably felt, tried in vain) to give any idea of him to people who did not know him or barely knew him.

I *can't* believe – though I'd believe it if you say so – that I went to tea at Virginia's, and met you there, on the afternoon of George V's funeral. My cousin Noreen, who was staying with us, and Billy Buchan and I had got up at 4 a.m. to watch the procession in Edgware Road; and I remember nothing else about the afternoon except being anaesthetized by tiredness, plus in vain looking for food for that night's dinner (to which I do remember you and Tom Eliot came) with all shops shut: a condition I'd forgotten to foresee. I remember finally coaxing a large veal-and-ham pie, at black market price, out of [a] little restaurant in the understructure of Baker Street Station where I sometimes ate.

If I were a marker of books (out of sympathy; approbation) I should be drawing constant pencil-marks down your margins. You crystallise things I didn't know I had felt or thought. Also you say intransigent things with which I occasionally disagree; but I couldn't go into those unless I had both you and the book here at the same time, which I fear is unlikely.

What an agreeable life we all had, seeing each other *without* being 'a group'. Perhaps ours was, is, the only non-groupy generation: the younger ones now sound as though they'd started doing that again – or haven't they, really?

I wonder how you feel in the 1950s? Personally I am enjoying this epoch – it is really the first one, it seems to me, in which I've enjoyed being 'grown up' as much as I expected to do when I was a child. The only sad thing is that, owing to the necessity to work so hard, I have altogether ceased to be able to write letters – as I used to do, if you remember, copiously in the 1930s. Not that that's probably a great loss to anyone else; but it *is* a loss to me, because writing to anybody is one great way of making oneself feel one is in their presence. It's unnecessary for me to say, I wish I saw you; say that I greatly miss you. I somehow fatalistically know you'll never come here; yet against all hope I continue to imagine you someday again will. While there's life there's hope – which is the major distinction between one's relations with the living and one's relations with the dead. Here I *am* (I continue to state) with Eddy Sackville-West, who'd also love to see you, living nearby for the summer part of the year. Towards the end of October I'll be going back to New York for another two months.

My reasons for not more often coming to London are of the most banal kind: it's all so expensive. In New York I earn money as well as spend it. And the snag about going to London, but not living there is that it's harder to see those who don't live there either. How well we all do by living elsewhere, all the same.

> Dear William, my best love and, again, thanks.
> Elizabeth.

> Waldencote
> Old Headington
> Oxford
> July 31st [1935]

Dear Virginia

Last Wednesday, the literary dinner went on too long; it turned out to be a very literary dinner at which conversations didn't relax their grip till, when I looked at the clock, it was 11.20 and I knew it was too late to come to you. And I felt very tired and rather degraded, so I went home. The whole thing was a frightening view of literature, and I felt very sore at missing an evening with you.

The part of the summer left still seems very long. I suppose now I shall not see you until October. I do wish you would suddenly come to Ireland again. It is very nice in September even without a car.

I looked for houses in London those five days, promising to myself that I wouldn't take one yet, but I think now we have, which I suppose now was inevitable because they do act on one like madness if one likes them, don't they. But how very alarming and impertinent – feeling this Order to View, walking into people's lived-in houses is.

It is impossible to believe that the people discovered in rooms sitting stiffly about as dolls in a dolls-house attitudes are not to be sold with the house, and to remember that it is not necessary to ask oneself whether one likes them. I had no idea so many houses could be macabre and horrifying.

Now, I am going through all that the other way round: this house is on an agent's books; the agent rings up and strange hostile people with money to lay out are let in and come poking and pottering round. It does feel odd – I suppose because no one who isn't a friend comes into one's house, normally, and these strange mutters, from upstairs and everywhere, of people who have come to look for cracks in the walls is something really not like life at all. It makes the rooms feel unfamiliar afterwards; they begin to look, even, a different shape.

The house we are hoping to take is No. 2 Clarence Terrace, Regents Park. It is about 3½ minutes from Baker St. Station and overlooks the park lake with those coloured-sailed boats and a great many trees. It is a corner house, which is nice, I think, don't you as the windows look different ways. It has high windows and ceilings, and pale-coloured modern parquet floors. The excuse for taking it, and taking it so soon, is that it is a bargain: only just in the market and not very expensive, in fact cheap, because of there being only an eight years lease. The reason to take it is that it is, in a bare plain way, very lovely with green reflections inside from the trees such as I have only seen otherwise in a country house.

Billy Buchan is coming to live with us: that is to say, we are letting him a big bed-sittingroom at the top of the house. He is going to work at Elstree every day, under Mr. Alfred Hitchcock learning to make films. I had always said I would not have anyone else in the house on any account, but when Susan suggested this tentatively Alan and I talked it over and thought it would be a pity not. We are fond of Billy and he is fond of us, we are all very independent and unsociable and not likely to want to sit on top of each other. And, practically speaking, it will be a help with the rent.

May I send you in August – no, what I really mean is, I want to very much and am going to – another book of mine that is coming out, called *The House in Paris*.

I wonder if those people with the caravan have gone to Ireland yet. I do hope they will come and see us, unless they hate the thought of seeing anybody, with which I should perfectly sympathize. We shall not be at Bowen's Court this year till the 20th August; after that I shall be there till the end of September. I hope we are going to Dieppe for a week on Saturday, then must be here for an Educational Conference Alan has got to do with. Then we cross to Ireland on the night of the 19th.

I hope you are having, and will have, a lovely summer at Rodmell.

Love from Elizabeth

Bowen's Court
Kildorrery
Co. Cork
August 26th [1935]

Dear Virginia

I do want you to have a proper copy of this as the other is horrid and full of misprints: I did not mean it (the other) to go to you.

I was awfully disappointed at not being able to go to Rodmell before coming here. The Conference at Oxford was very queer: I wonder if they are all like that. Then there was Wales, a jumbled country with flat light that I do not really like very much, do you. Mountains depend so much on where they are put: in Wales they seem to be in one's mouth the whole time and have a scrubby gritty surface.

Today it is raining, which is nice as it means a fire in the morning legitimately and is good for mushrooms. Do you have mushrooms round you?

I looked inland from Newhaven on our way to Dieppe and imagined that must be where Rodmell was, and thought how very nice it would be to ring you up. But our drive from Oxford to Newhaven was a dash: we only caught the morning boat by ten minutes, when we had left the car in a lock-up garage near the quay, and the return drive was against time too, trying to get back to Oxford in time for the beginning of the Conference, which made a good deal of fuss. One day that week, we took twelve foreign educationists for a drive in a file of taxis across the Cotswolds, rather the way we went with Susan when you were there – I wonder whether you liked the Dutch when you were in Holland. The only really rather dull couple we struck that week were Dutch; their faces were very unmoving and their conversation was very abstract. But perhaps they are better in their own country: anyway it is not fair to judge people by what they are like at a Conference.

Dieppe we did simply love. I wonder whether you know it. I remember years ago reading something of yours called 'To Spain' in the *Nation*: you said that if the traveller behaved instinctively he would get off at Dieppe, to start being abroad at once instead of waiting in a train for more, even if better, to happen – I like the way the steamer comes into the middle of the town, and the train runs about the street with, after dark, a man walking slowly ahead of it waving an oil lamp. And the way the whole town traffic, without warning, falls apart in the middle when that bridge swivels round to let steamers into the inner dock. The Sunday we were there they were blessing the sea, which was very socially done: a holy steamer went out with a great many flags that, waving across its funnels, got very smoky, a pack of choir boys packed tight in the prow, wilting a little in the sun, in crimson surplices, priests etc. with banners, and also all the principle ladies of the town, who managed to look at the same time gay and religious, in large white hats, and a number of officers in their brightest uniforms. At the other end of the ship was the town band, nearly all bassoons, which played a walse as the steamer steamed out of the harbour. Several people, including me, wept, and everybody cheered. They steamed backwards and forwards several times in front of the Casino, then made for the open sea to bless the fish. What I like about the French is that they are never quaint. There was also, the first night we were there, a military procession with a band *and* Chinese lanterns, a combination I have never seen before.

Even the Monday after, the town was still very gay, not at all anti-climatic though the gala was over. They did very imaginative things such as, after dark, floodlighting hedges of pink roses round the foot of the rock. I had not been 'at the seaside' really properly, like that, since I was eleven, so did enjoy it very much. I don't think I had ever before slept in a room facing the sea. The lawn between the hotels and the sea always looks very gay, flying flags, and they mow it at seven o'clock every morning which sounds nice – I hope we shall go there again; it is so easy to get there. I think it would be as good in the autumn, too. The country round is like Maupassant stories: I had seen some of that before, staying with Ethel. I suppose you did, too, when you were there.

I meant to go and see Ethel when we were there, but we got so lazy, sandy dirty and demoralized and spoilt by having nothing to do but look at things. In the afternoon we went for circular drives in char-a-bancs and saw other small towns along in the cracks of the cliffs. There is a strange faded chalk-dusty place that in the eighteenth century must have been very grand, called St. Valery-en-Caux, that we liked very much. And a big embowered villegiaturn village called Veulles-les-Roses, full of roses, hydrangeas and painted balconies, with a crack of strand between two large white cliffs. We liked drinking calvados. I am afraid this is rather like a guide to the Dieppe coast. But places are so very exciting: the only proper experiences one has. I believe I may only write novels for the pleasure of saying where people are. And the advantages of short stories is that that means a different place every time.

I wonder how the caravan party in Co. Waterford are getting on. I am told that *Dunmore* is good: I had never heard of it.

I am so glad you think the Regent's Park house is a good plan. Though the lease is not signed yet, I am living in it in imagination already: I hope this is not what used to be called tempting providence. I do think it would be nice to live by that lake.

I do wish I could have come to Rodmell: I did so fearfully want to. But I am so seldom a useful wife to Alan, and in the course of that conference week it began to appear that it really would be rather mean of me to go away leaving him over-run with people that he had to be genial to. May I come some other time?

My book comes out today: I wonder what that means, exactly – simply that it is being packed into vans and sent to shops? Still, the idea of that is rather exciting – it is a dramatic moment in a book's – I mean a volume's life.

I hope you are having a nice summer. I do wish you were here again. There are an enormous number of sweet-pea which I cannot keep up with keeping picked, and the annual business over lavender – I don't mean you would have to do this when you were here, I mean it is the business of the day. I am not writing anything, but am reviewing novels for the *Statesman* turn about with Peter Quennell for this month and next. It is a perfectly awful business.

Elizabeth

2 Clarence Terrace
Regent's Park
N.W.1.
July 1st [1940]

Dearest Virginia,

Ever since I got back here I have been thinking about Rodmell – this sounds nonsense, but you must know how some part of one's thoughts or one's imagination can go on contemplating a place amost continuously. And when I say Rodmell I mean Monks House and you and Leonard and everything indisassociable from it. It doesn't seem to me that I've ever been so perfectly happy – This seems to me to be all 'I . . . I . . . I . . .', but how impossible, quite wrongly, it is to write about any feeling without identifying oneself, with it. I don't think I'd ever imagined a place and people in which and with whom one felt so perfectly happy that one felt suspended the whole time, and at the same time wanting to smile, *and* smiling, continuously, like a dog.

I still feel very homesick.

At the end of which I can only say, thank you both very much. I loved everything that we did.

I do hope the Co-operative sent the sugar and that Mabel got on well with the currants and raspberries. You will be coming up to London today, I think, so I'm writing to Mecklenburg Square. I wondered if you had any more sirens: there haven't been any here since.

I read your lecture, which I'm sending back in this envelope, coming up in the train, with great excitement. The leaning tower metaphor seemed to me perfect. I'd never thought *into* those young men's position before, and your leaning tower, with the sense at once of unnatural angle and panic, made it (their position) suddenly comprehensible. The element of *fuss* about their work is explained, though not, I think, excused – and you don't excuse it. I didn't think you over-severe – did you think you were? – only deadly accurate. The quotations were damning.

I liked very much the early part – the part about family, books descending from books. I feel sure art ought to breed. The leaning tower people may be imitated (now) but they can breed nothing: they seem to me like mules or something.

I saw Cyril Connolly on Saturday he asked if you liked *Horizon*. I said (I hope truly) you liked his wish that things should be done well. He and Stephen and the young man Watson who finances *Horizon* are all living in a villa in Devonshire, coming up to London just now and then. They don't seem to like it very much.

The cactus travelled very well and had none of its white bloom knocked off. The garlic did well too: I left it with my suitcase and the cactus in the very refined porter's lodge of the English Speaking Union while I was having tea there with my aunt. I think the garlic must have been commented on, as the porter looked at me rather severely when I came to take it away again. I sat in this park on Saturday afternoon and read the Gorky book, notes, about Tolstoi with very great joy, in fact read it twice.

I think I told you I had asked the Ministry of Information if I could do any work, which I felt was wanted in Ireland. On Saturday morning I had a letter from them saying yes, they did want me to go. Now it has come to the point I have rather a feeling of dismay and of not wanting to leave this country. I am to see Harold Nicolson on Thursday and go to Ireland on Friday night next. I don't expect it will be for very long. I shall be at Bowen's Court first, but I expect they will also want me to move about the place. I don't know much till I've seen Harold Nicolson. I hope I shall be some good: I do feel it's important. As far as my own feeling goes I feel low at going away, so can only hope to be some good when I'm there. It will all mean endless talk, but sorting out talk into shape might be interesting. I suppose I shall also finish my book. But Ireland can be dementing, if one's Irish and may well be so now. If there's to be an invasion of Ireland, I hope it may be while I'm there – which I don't mean frivolously – but if anything happens to England while I'm in Ireland I shall wish I'd never left, even for this short time. I suppose the Ministry will give me a come-and-go travel permit.

If I find the letter I began to you at Bowen's Court I'll send it but it will be *very* old.

This letter is already very wandering. If I began to write about affection for you, Virginia, I should degenerate into sheer gush.

I'll write from Ireland, and may I tell you when I come back? Meanwhile my love to you both, and all the thoughts of the most continuous kind, that one can only stodgily call good wishes. Good wishes to you both, at all times and thank you for those lovely two days.

Love from Elizabeth

Bowen's Court
January 5th [1941]

Dear Virginia,

I found the letter I began to you here, but it seemed so faded that I tore it up, and it was like a letter written by someone not me to someone not you. And for months now I have been completely dumb: there seemed to be nothing to add to anything, even in what I said to you. I think about you so much, especially shredding those red currants in the evening up in that top room. And were all those streets that were burnt the streets we walked about? I have never seen them since. When your flat went did that mean all the things in it too? All my life I have said, 'Whatever happens there will always be tables and chairs' – and what a mistake. Clarence Terrace is now perfectly empty, except for ourselves in No 2, and one other, a house with a *reputation*, full of rather gaudy, silent young men who come out in the mornings and walk about two and two, like nuns.

Alan was here for Christmas, but went back two days ago. I am going back to London at the end of this month. I was there in September and part of October, but in a stupefied excited and I think rather vulgar state. To be here is very nice, but I no longer like, as I used to, being here alone. I can't write letters, I can't make plans. The house now is very cold and empty, and very beautiful in a glassy sort of way. Every night it freezes. There are some very early lambs, which at night get through the wires and cry on the lawn under my windows. I am doing the last chapter of the Bowen's Court book: I don't want you to see it till it is done, because the last chapter seems to, or ought to re-write retrospectively all the rest of the book. It is also rather painful and rather difficult, because some of the people in it are still alive. A book of short stories of mine is coming out this month or next: they are mostly rather long ago ones, except one long one called *Summer Night* which I should like very much to know what you think about. I wrote it since I saw you. As soon as I have a copy of the book, may I send it? They made me correct the proofs in a great hurry, but there's no sign of it's coming out yet. I should like to know what you think of all the other stories, but they seem such a long time ago.

Is all the Hogarth Press at Rodmell now? I try and imagine it, and where everyone lives. I wonder if anyone is in the cottage we looked at, with all those oak beams and brass blinkers. I also imagine the hills, and the stretch of your lawn up, in this glass weather. I wonder if the lily pond froze. Have you ever been a whole winter at Rodmell before, I wonder? I would in ways like to be a whole winter here, only I get rather pent-up with no one to talk to. In winter this is a nice house for two. Now *all* the petrol has stopped and we are immobilised, at least immobilised until we get new ideas about time. No motor car ever lived here until ten years ago, so it really is artificial to fuss. I wish now I had a riding horse. I bought a bicycle a year ago but on it I can't think; I keep wanting to get off and sit on the bank to smoke and think and cheer up. I bicycled yesterday morning into the town, Mitchelstown, where one of my aunts lives: she has rooms in the square. It is a beautifully planned but sad little town up under the Galtee mountains: do you remember it – I expect you drove through. The eight miles of road along under the mountains was very raw with wind and I disappointingly hated every mile, except for the pleasure of getting off at my aunt's – having arrived, I mean. This week I am going to Dublin: I take a flat there, very small, the rooms looking on to Stephen's Green. In Dublin I get engaged in deep rather futile talks; it is hard to remember the drift afterwards, though I remember the words. I suppose that (smoke-screen use of words) is a trick of the Irish mind. They are very religious. It is the political people I see mostly: it seems a craggy dangerous miniature world. I can't write any more about that but would like to talk *very much*.

Ever since June I felt I couldn't bear to read French, then I thought I would begin again with someone I liked least, so I bought some collections of Maupassant I hadn't got already, and brought them here. Read in the middle of winter here they are extraordinary. I suppose he had sharp senses but really rather a boring mind. You soon get to know his formula but there is always the fascination; it is like watching someone doing the same card trick over and over again. I did feel the fascination so strongly that I wondered if I were getting rather brutalised myself. There is a particularly preposterous story called *Yvette*, about a young girl whose mother takes a summer villa on the Seine. Looking at the pictures, which are so good and open sort of windows in the writing, I wondered whether illustrations were such a bad thing. Nobody illustrates now, I wonder whether they could.

I wonder if you have snow. I have a card you sent me with Rodmell church with snow on it. This makes me feel very homesick. I feel a sort of despair about my own generation – the people the same age as the century, I mean – we don't really suffer much but we get all sealed up. This letter was interrupted by a telephone call: I got up and was cruel to a neighbour called Mr Gates. I said, 'How can you be so absolutely stupid when you have got an Austrian grandfather?' which is really an unforgivable thing to say to a country neighbour: if one is even a degree more imaginative than anyone else one ought to be nice to them, but how hard it is. And this is certainly no time to be querulous. In principle I feel very humble indeed. I have been cruel to Mr Gates because I made the mistake I so often make, of idealising at the outset a stupid person.

I do long to see you again. I shall be back in February and wish I were back now. Please give my love to Leonard.

Love from Elizabeth

2 Clarence Terrace
Tuesday 18 Feb [1941]

My dear Virginia,

At this moment Lady Jones is having lunch with you (it's 1.45) and I do feel the strongest desire to ring you up – only I expect that, rather than harrying Lady Jones, which is as I should wish, it would be a bother for you. I expect she is really much nicer than one thinks: she has that smoothest Kensington surface but there is a slight rattle in her inside. I hope you'll have a nice afternoon with the Women's Institute, or as we used to call it when I was in the Headington one, the *W.I.* I expect the W.I. will have a nice time anyway. As a matter of fact I do very much miss W.I. dos: since I came to live in London I feel I don't live in England at all.

I was miserable coming away on Saturday. It was absolutely *lovely* at Monks House, all the time. I do hope happiness didn't make me too bouncing: I felt so awfully happy. I still can't see much but your upstairs room with the cyclamens on the window-sill – not actually on the window-sill but on a table, but at window-height – and those two arum lilies, and your embroidery. I mean, even apart from you and Leonard. All I have got to look at are scratches from the beautiful apache cat. The moss is now in the middle of my dinner table, in a sort of white Wedgewood basket dish.

I still haven't written to poor [Sagan?]. Did you?

It was worth while not cutting the theatre with that cousin, because he is obviously very homesick. He is nice, but the chief thing is that his father (long before he *was* his father) was very good to my mother when my father was ill. That is more than thirty years ago, but one has to work out that sort of understanding kindness from one generation to another, like the inverse of a vendetta. This boy, Jack, used to work in Guinness's brewery in Dublin, and has now been drafted to the brewery outside London. He has never been in England before except at school, and it is interesting to hear what he thinks of everything.

Today, this morning, I went and talked to Lord Cranbourne at the Dominions Office about Ireland. I say talked, because he listened with very sympathetic and charming Cecil politeness. I knew he had seen the reports I'd been sending in, and there were things I wanted to say that I couldn't write. So I had asked David to put me in touch with him. Getting into the Dominions Office was such a business: I had had no exact idea where it was, so took a taxi, which didn't know either and aroused far more suspicion than if I had come on my feet. We were challenged by bayonets, and I said each time in a more quavering but more aggressive voice that I had an appointment. Then inside there were forms to fill in, then the long passages that though very hot still manage to smell of stone. There were outer courts of rooms of gentlemen-secretaries and files, then his room, which was nice and long, with boarded-up windows, a stretch of Turkey carpet, a roaring fire. Unfortunately it was just as I had imagined (the scene, I mean) there were almost no surprises. The last time I was in London I went to the War Office, also on an Irish errand, and there, because it was eleven o'clock, they were all drinking glasses of milk, which *was* something that I had not imagined.

Stephen Spender rang up this morning, just when I got in. He is laid up in Mr Worsley's flat, near Sloane Square, with what appeared to be a boil on the knee but what he now thinks must be water on the knee really. So I said I would go to tea with him on Thursday.

Otherwise I have done almost nothing since I came back but try to finish my Bowen's Court book. I have got to the part where my mother and I go and live in Folkestone, which is nothing to do with Bowen's Court except the fact of nobody being *there*, so I am trying to compress Folkestone into a paragraph.

I extremely stupidly left behind at Monks House some things that were on a lower shelf of my dressingtable and that, packing up quickly and absentmindedly, I didn't see. The only point of saying they're there is to say, don't bother about them; they are rather squalid, a green-backed hand mirror (*not* embossed, like Susie's hairbrush) and two rather greasy jars of cold cream. May I make them an excuse to come back to you before I go back to Ireland? I have another hand-glass, and have got to get some more cold cream anyhow, as those two jars were nearly finished.

I told Alan all about your omelette, and he said he would like to have a competition with you. I rather tactlessly said that I thought your omelette would win.

> Thank you very, very much, Virginia and all my love.
> Elizabeth

> Bowen's Court
> April 8th [1941]

Dear Leonard,

It was very good of you to write to me, as and when you did. I do thank you. I have been in Ireland for the last three weeks, so your letter, sent on from Clarence Terrace, reached me here last Saturday. I had not heard anything at all till the Thursday before that, when someone told me what they had heard on the wireless. English papers take nearly a week to come. It meant a good deal, then, to get your letter. You and Virginia and Rodmell had, for those two days, hardly been out of my thoughts – not by day and not much by night. I had begun to imagine what I learned from you to be true – that she had feared her illness was coming back.

You said not to answer your letter, and above all I don't want to trouble you with words now. And it is no time to speak of my own feeling. As far as I am concerned, a great deal of the meaning seems to have gone out of the world. She illuminated everything, and one referred the most trivial things to her in one's thoughts. To have been allowed to know her and love her is a great thing.

I have been thinking so much about you. I hope it is not an intrusion to say this. If there is any practical thing I can do, in the next few months, I know you will be friendly enough to let me know. And if you ever had time to see me, and felt disposed to see me, it would be very kind of you. I am crossing back to London this week, and shall be at Clarence Terrace for some weeks after that.

> Elizabeth

WHY DO I WRITE?

Part of a Correspondence
with Graham Greene and V. S. Pritchett (1948)

[To V. S. Pritchett]
What *do* I think? About the artist, or imaginative writer, and his or her relation to society. About his, her (your, my) response to the challenge of the times. Yes, it is probably something that we should ask each other. When I am asked by an outside person, a non-writer, I do not seem to know what the question means. Or rather, I do see that it must mean something, but almost any answer I can put up or give remains almost totally meaningless to me: bluff or patter. The question – put by an outside person – makes a crook of me, and I resent that. I feel inclined to say: 'Ask no questions and you'll be told no lies.'

But, of course, apart from politeness, one cannot tell intelligent people to go to hell; and the askers of that particular question are intelligent people, who are within their rights. At least I take it they are within their rights: I cannot say with authority what these are, as I do not know exactly what is involved in the being of a full-time intelligent person. I am fully intelligent only when I write. I have a certain amount of small-change intelligence, which I carry round with me as, at any rate in a town, one has to carry small money, for the needs of the day, the non-writing day. But it seems to me that I seldom purely *think*. If I wrote less – I don't mean quantitatively, but with less intensity – I might think more; if I thought more I might write less.

Obviously intelligent people are on the increase: education, I suppose. This sounds supercilious. I do not feel supercilious, but I feel slightly frightened – the intelligent people seem to be closing in on the artist like the rats on the selfish bishop who hoarded corn in famine time. We all know what happened to the bishop; they picked his bones white. The rats were in the right; at any rate they were the instruments of vengeance. The bishop was in the wrong; he had been unsocial. But really nobody could call – and as far as I know nobody does call – you or me Bishop Hattos: we don't hoard. Whatever comes in goes out again. We are not, either, bolted and barred granaries; we are combinations of a mill and a bakery. So I really must get rid of that original rat nightmare, and the idea of that closing-in circle of thousands of avid glittering eyes. The worst it boils down to, really, is that people these days have a mania for being shown round factories.

In fact, I suppose there never has been a time (or has there?) when the public in general, at any rate the Anglo-Saxon public, has been kinder to the artist or more conscious of him. That's what intelligence is doing: breeding this clement air. The very least the artist can do is to come across and be rather less taciturn and farouche. In the face of such kindness, one can't be humble enough – I mean, humble enough with regard to people: it is obviously impossible ever to be anything but humble with regard to art, because of the disparity between what could be done and what one does do. For me personally, as a woman, any sort of kindness or being wished well or thought well of is the breath of life. Nor is that need wholly personal, womanish: it exists in the writing part of me too. I was struck by Osbert Sitwell's saying the other day, in *The Scarlet Tree*, that the artist, like the child, makes the best growth, *does* best, in an atmosphere of affection and encouragement. How I agree.

At the same time, you don't think it possible that things these days may be almost too propitious? And that to let this propitiousness invade us mayn't make for a lowering of internal pressure? We must have something to push against. Oh well, one need not worry: we always shall have. I expect the effects of the present pro-art indoctrination are very much more limited than I'm inclined to feel. A healthy animal indifference to art probably is endemic in human nature, in your crowds in the Lichfield marketplace. If anyone on that wet day had been told they were shouldering up on a writer, they'd probably have thought: 'Lucky to have an indoor job.' It's this virgin indifference on the part of the mass of people, this unspoken individual mystery in each one of them, that they don't propose to trade in, that's lovable and infatuating, that makes you and me write novels and stories. One writes *for* the ideal reader, but not about him. At least, I don't, and you don't. One writes, in so many cases, about the man or woman who would throw a crooked glance at your or my page of prose and groan: 'What is *this* about?' I doubt – though the analogy on my part may be impertinent – whether, for instance, a Proust character could or would have read Proust. Oh yes, Oriane de Guermantes might have – but with a glance up at the clock, from time to time, to see if it was time yet to go and dress for the ball, alternating with a light sigh: 'Ce pauvre Marcel. . . .' Oh yes, and Bloch would have. But how Proust loathed Bloch. Emma Bovary would have dropped asleep over *Madame Bovary* long before she came to anything she could like. But, of course, for Flaubert that was half the pleasure – making 'uninteresting' people (by which one implies, uninterested people) interesting to himself.

Perhaps one emotional reason why one may write is the need to work off, out of the system, the sense of being solitary and farouche. Solitary and farouche people don't have relationships: they are quite unrelatable. If you and I were capable of being altogether housetrained and made jolly, we should be nicer people but not writers. If I feel irked and uneasy when asked about the nature of my (as a writer) relation to society, this is because I am being asked about the nature of something that does not, as far as *I* know, exist. My writing, I am prepared to think, may be a substitute for something I have been born without – a so-called normal relation to society. My books *are* my relation to society. Why should people come and ask me what the nature of this relation is? It seems to me that it is the other people, the readers, who should know.

You, I see, say in better words what amounts to the same thing. Or, do you? 'At some point, he (the writer) splits off from the people who surround him and he discovers the necessity of talking to himself and not to them. A monologue begins. . . . To write is to be naive and one of the strange pleasures of the solitary monologue is the discovery that one has said aloud to oneself what other people are saying silently.' But, of course, your monologue isn't simply a thought-stream; you touch a starter; you set in motion something that never stops (that will never stop so long as a single copy of the story or novel you have written exists) by your 'invention' of people who feel, speak, act. You make a society each time you write a story. In fact, you are in closer relation to the characters in the story than you will ever be to anyone in real life. It is this ideal relationship of intimacy and power which is to fascinate those who read. Fascinate, and delude. They expect this capacity for relationship to be extended outside the written page, to them. To, as they put it, society as a whole.

Actually, isn't it a directive that you seem to give? That you give in writing? And, also, shape. Shape is possibly *the* important thing. Obsessed by shape in art, you and I may forget the importance of shape in life. It could be that your and my non-writing lives are simply margins around the non-stop story, that we are focused internally on writing. But I shouldn't wonder if it were the shape, essentially, that the reader, the mass, the public goes to the story for. The idea of the possibility of shape is not only magnetic, it's salutary. Shapelessness, lack of meaning, and being without direction is most people's nightmare, once they begin to think – and more and more people are beginning to think, clearly. Of course all thought has a tinge of emotionality: it may be greater, it may be less. The pure thinker, capable of thinking without regard to himself, is, I imagine, rare. Isn't the average thinker simply trying to trace out some pattern around himself? Or, to come on, detect, uncover a master-pattern in which he has his place? To the individual, the possibility that his life should be unmeaning, a series of in the main rather hurting fortuities, and that his death should be insignificant, is unbearable. Temporarily, for the reader (or the listener to music, or the looker at pictures) art puts up a buttress against that – or, still more important, makes a counter-assertion. The very arbitrariness of art brings an odd peace. You and I, by writing a story, impose shape – on fictitious life, it's true, but on life that is real-seeming enough to be familiar and recognisable. Every action or word on the part of any one of the characters in the story has meaning (because it's essential for you and me that it *should* have meaning), and the whole trend of the story suggests direction – it may or may not be a tragic one. Even stories which end in the air, which are comments on or pointers to futility, imply that men or women are too big or good for the futility in which they are involved. Even to objectify futility is something.

And couldn't it be that the wish, the demand for shape is more than individual, that it's a mass thing? Or rather, the mass's wish or demand not to have to go on being a mass merely? The difference between a mass and a society is, I suppose, shape. Yes, you, I see, say: 'When I say "society", I mean more than people: I mean people bound together by an end, who are making a future.' Shape, relation, direction. . . . I can't explore this further; I wish you would. I'm only on the edge of a hazy idea that the artist, in these days, is being sought, focused on – *he* may feel, sometimes, beleaguered – because he seems to be a conferrer of shape, an interpreter of direction? If society, at this moment, in this age, *did* exist – as something conscious, authoritative, explicit and realised – I imagine that the artist would be in a more neglected, but for himself healthier, position. At the moment, he's not simply being asked whether he is, feels himself to be, or should be, in relation with society; he's being asked implicitly, to create a society to be in relation with. Or – in so far as society is a sensation as well as a form – to set up in people a sense of society. He seems, from his books, to know the secret: he ought to know how.

Hence, do you think, this demand for journalism about artistry? It obviously must be wanted and will be read, or it would not be commissioned. And the stress is required to be on the social aspect, not the creative one. My view – and, I can see, yours – is that writers should keep out of pulpits and off platforms, and just write. They should not for a moment consider putting their names to petitions or letters to newspapers on matters that they do not know much about and have no reason to know anything about. The temptation to do so is becoming unduly great – why? Obviously, it's a temptation to *amour propre*, but how – I mean, owing to what disordered values and fallacious hopes on the part of the public – does the temptation come to be presented?

All my own discoveries about life have been capricious and inadvertent: I should hesitate to lay down the law about anything. I wouldn't say the same thing about you; but I was fascinated by your story about your story of the X-ray department of the hospital and the nurse who wrote to you. I don't think you and I ought to ignore our own common sense, of which we have the ordinary human modicum. It appears in our writing because it appears in us; but because it is mixed with vision, or whatever else one calls imaginative perception, it sounds Delphic. I could go on about this but had better stop. I meant to shred up the headline about the challenge of our times, but possibly that may come later.

Bowen's Court

[To Graham Greene]

I've read Pritchett's letter to you, and yours to him, with interest. My first reaction would be to say that I agree with you both – not that you and he *were*, as that might imply, having anything particularly in the nature of an argument. No it is more, really, a question of taking up points. His, as to the principal duty of the State towards the writer being that of leaving him alone; yours, as to the duty of (or imperative for) the writer being disloyalty. I do not wish to be organised in any way, either as a writer or a private person. I don't see, referring to Pritchett's point, that we as writers differ in the practical sense – or can expect rightly to be differentiated – from any other freelance makers and putters on the market of luxury, or 'special' goods. Had I not been a writer I should probably have struck out in designing and making belts, jewellery, handbags, lampshades or something of that sort – my aim being that these should catch people's fancy, create a little fashion of their own, and accordingly be saleable by me at a rising price. Had that happened, I should be in about the same rocky, uncertain, incalculable position as I am in now. The putter-across, lucratively, of a presumably enjoyable hobby gets very little sympathy.

No, of course, the analogy doesn't hold good really – the belt- or bag-maker sells his or her goods piecemeal, and does not expect to budget on anything but the specific sums paid down for specific belts or bags; the writer is, or has been, entitled to hope for an income (royalties) from his existing books – those representing, as Pritchett says, his capital. The more books he has written, the larger, theoretically, should be his income. The growing number of written books behind him should (and did once) send his income up, making it possible for him to meet the liabilities which, in all lives, increase with the years. At present, we writers are the victims of a, one must hope, temporary but acute disaster – the complete *non*-existence of all our earlier written books. That is to say, they do not exist commercially: owing to the paper shortage they are out of print – the income, however modest, that we should have expected to be deriving from their continuous sales is lost to us. Twenty or twenty-five years of work is of prestige-value only; not worth a farthing. Oh yes, it leaves us with one asset – reputation. So we have to market that, making good our lost royalty incomes by odd-jobbing.

So frenzying to me is this (it is to be hoped) temporary condition that I cannot see beyond it. If we ever did get the paper back, if we ever could just be reprinted and *kept* in print, it does not seem to me that our position would be so bad. Of course, no publisher could be expected to keep us in print if we failed to sell, if there ceased to be a demand for us. But I am assuming, at once optimistically and for the sake of argument, that there would be.

Writing is a non-competitive profession: there is no question of writers drawing off each other's clients, because readers are not clients. In fact, the better any one writer is, the better becomes the outlook for all writing and, accordingly, for the body of writers as a whole. There cannot possibly be too many good writers, but any kind of subsidy, exemption or protection for the writing trade could easily mean that there were too many *writers*. The idea that writing, as a profession, is risky, ultra-exacting, lonely, dehumanising and unlikely ever fully to be rewarded should, *I* think, be promulgated. There should be no promise of the race being to any but the swift, the battle being to any but the strong. I am sure that in nine out of ten cases the original wish to write is the wish to make oneself felt. It's a sign, I suppose, of life's decreasing livableness *as* life that people should feel it possible to make themselves felt in so few other ways. The non-essential writer never gets past that wish. But actually, as I suppose anybody who *has* written for twenty or twenty-five years knows, that initial wish to make oneself felt evaporates after the second or at latest the third book: after that point writers divide off into those who, honestly planning to make money, have reason to think themselves, now, on to something good, and those who, now, find themselves ridden by an impersonal obsession on the subject of writing for its own sake. The latter, however – one cannot ignore the fact – have got to make money too. Enough money to pay their own and their families' way through life.

I feel that the general public's idea that the writer does, in some semi-sinister way, have himself a very good time, and at the same time grumbles at not being paid at a higher rate for so doing, is in equal measure unjust and correct. Of course, as to this it depends what the writer *is* writing when he is writing. 'Job' writing, under-taken because one must have the money, could, I imagine, beat any other kind of work for drabness – at the same time, because the writer revolts from misusing his faculties entirely, and cannot but heave and drag his best foot forward, however uninspiring the path, he *is* doing hard, specialised and – however reluctantly – honest work, by which he should earn a specialist's pay. On the other hand, there is (as Pritchett says) the writing he wants to do – the creative. In the execution of this – though the strain and the exactions on the whole being are even greater – pleasure predominates: a pleasure elsewhere equalled only in love. Does, one may ask, society, or its organ the State, really owe him anything for this pleasure he has had? It may be taken that a book written in pleasure will transmit it. If it comes to be known that the book is a potential of pleasure, it will be bought: a percentage of its price goes to the author. Leave it at this – the fact that a high percentage of writers kill themselves is ignored by the public. Or, if it be not ignored, there remains an unformulated feeling that such a death is the death of a debauchee.

Yes, to take up another point, I do think conflict essential – conflict in the self (a never quite dislodgeable something to push against), and an if anything hyper-acute sense of every kind of conflict, and every phase of any kind of conflict, in society. I am only not afraid of a conflictless Better World because I am absolutely convinced there will never be one. *I* am convinced, too, that the more outwardly regulated, planned, organised and equitable the world becomes, the stronger will be the unholy (possibly) domination of the artist – no, I mean of art. The artist – particularly the writer, as the most comprehensible – will take on the stature of a Resistance leader. I should, however, say 'would' rather than 'will', as the circumstances seem to me so hypothetical as hardly to matter. Something always seems to happen, something always seems to intervene, something always seems to halt the progress to absolute mediocrity.

As individuals, we writers don't get off any more lightly than any other indidivuals – we have to pay our bills, keep appointments, be or appear to be as agreeable as possible. It seems to me we are threatened by an extra tax which no other working individual would be expected to pay. These days there is a feeling that a writer, or other artist, should contribute to society something other than and in addition to his work. Theoretically, no individual, writer or otherwise, should begrudge anything to the society of which he is a part – of all graceless ugly refusals that seems the worst. But what it has come to, roughly speaking, is that the writer or artist is expected to have no off time – platforms, either actual or metaphorical, claim him as their perpetual due. The vitality, not to speak of the time, demanded by all that sort of thing has got to come from somewhere:

it cannot but be taken from the store intended for his work, his proper work. I regard this as damaging: in his between-times the writer needs to re-charge his batteries by private living, in any one of several possible forms – well does one recognise the dimming lights in the work of the writer who does not. I'm not supporting Skimpolism – I doubt whether any Skimpole could put it across these days. But I don't think society does itself any good by this determination to make oracles out of writers light-headed with exhaustion. It is exceedingly difficult, possibly impossible, don't you think, for the writer to concentrate on anything but what he is writing. It is not easy for him to concentrate on social questions – though he may pick up (in the wireless sense) and transmit some aspect of one. It really is often torment to have the brain picked – picked at – which should I say?

The most that should be asked of him – and it is not so little – is demeanour. He should try not to be too far, personally, below the level of his work. He should discriminate, in his way of life, between the frivolity which may save himself and the frivolity which may damn him for others – *he* might not matter, but what does matter is that he has engaged, however involuntarily, respect. He should not be guilty of impiety. Even to attempt to live up to all that takes quite a lot.

I believe this to be the last letter. So, properly, I should have made a sort of *résumé* of what has been so far said. But the fact is that there is so much more to be said that I don't see why I should try to give an impression that we have come to an end. Perhaps we have all three flown off at our own tangents; perhaps you, I and Pritchett have conducted a sort of Mardi Gras procession, each bearing above us, monstrously enlarged, our own particular King Charles's heads. It is now for society to say what it thinks of us. The relationship between us and society – not defined, I think, in any one of these letters for the good reason that it is indefinable – seems to emerge, from what we have all three said, as a thing of great possibilities and various flaws. I think we have each asserted a sort of recalcitrance, shown a red light: at the same time, I don't think any of us feel ourselves to be unrelatable to *something*. We envisage, we are not passive, and we are not contributing to anarchy: that may be the most to be claimed for us.

BROADCASTS

Introduction

By 1948, when *Why Do I Write?* was broadcast, Elizabeth Bowen had done a good deal of radio work. In spite of her stammer (which she was able to control when broadcasting and lecturing) this was, from the early 1940s onwards, a major source of income. She turned her hand to anything from quiz programmes to interviews. In the 1940s, for example, she did regular book reviews for the B.B.C. Overseas Service and went on a Home Service discussion programme with V. S. Pritchett and Hugh Sykes-Davies; in 1952 she took part in a discussion about traitors with Nigel Balchin and Noel Annan. On March 11 1957 she was the guest on *Desert Island Discs*, for which she chose Paul Robeson singing 'St Louis Blues', a jazz number called 'Hallelujah', Schnabel playing a Beethoven piano sonata (Op. 27 no. 2), Schubert's Unfinished Symphony, Mozart's D Minor Piano Concerto K. 466, an extract from Strauss's *Der Rosenkavelier*, Bach's 'Sheep May Safely Graze' adapted by Walton, and Clarke's Trumpet Voluntary. She told Roy Plomley that the first thing she would do on her island would be 'to make it as civilised and comfortable as I could', and asked to take two packs of playing cards, a kaleidoscope and a copy of *Emma*. In the late 1960s she went on a B.B.C. television literary panel game called 'Take It or Leave it' (other guests included Claire Tomalin, V. S. Naipaul, Cyril Connolly, Peter Porter and A. S. Byatt). One of her last appearances was an interview for a television programme about Virginia Woolf, made in 1970, where she recalled her power for enjoyment and her outrageous laughter ('she laughed in this consuming, choking, delightful, hooting way') and disparaged the myth of Virginia Woolf as a tragic martyr.

Like her lectures and her British Council talks, Elizabeth Bowen's writing for radio was civilised and agreeable, if not very demanding. The talk on Rider Haggard's *She*, for a series about early influences on writers, is a splendidly lively piece of autobiography, as much as of criticism. (She told J. B. Priestley, in a letter of 31 October 1948, that she had nearly chosen Baroness Orczy's *The Scarlet Pimpernel*, which 'was for me as an Edwardian child the first view of a reign of terror'.) As usual in her work, the childish desire to be frightened and excited works against the desire to be consoled. Trollope, as she says in her radio play of 1945, is a consolatory writer whose wartime popularity can be explained by that prevalent longing for a past security on which she writes again and again. The play makes very sympathetic use of Trollope's *Autobiography*: its tracing back of all his themes and characters to his childhood humiliations is highly characteristic.

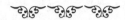

ANTHONY TROLLOPE:

A New Judgement

NARRATOR [*in level, descriptive voice*]: The walls are lined with books. On their backs, the firelight should be playing – but this is war-time: there is an electric radiator, with one bar lit, in the grate. As close as possible to the radiator, the study's owner reclines in an armchair. A fastidious, pleasant, elderly man. He is lost to the world, reading. He holds the book in long fingers. The door opens. A young man in battle-dress hesitates on the threshold before speaking.

WILLIAM: Uncle Jasper?

UNCLE JASPER [*startled*]: Who's that? Why, William! [*warmly*] William . . . Come in, come in, dear boy!

WILLIAM: Disturbing you?

UNCLE JASPER: I like it. Pull up that other chair. Cigarette?

WILLIAM [*in uncertain voice*]: Thanks, I . . .

UNCLE JASPER: Settle down, dear boy, settle down.

WILLIAM: Actually, I haven't got too much time. [*significantly*] Got a train to catch.

UNCLE JASPER [*vaguely*]: Train? [*change of tone – gravely*] Oh. You mean – you're off?

WILLIAM: Very soon – yes.

UNCLE JASPER: One does not ask where?

WILLIAM: We-ell . . .

UNCLE JASPER: But one makes a pretty good guess?

WILLIAM [*audibly grinning*]: One makes a pretty good guess.

UNCLE JASPER [*in tone of controlled feeling*]: Well, I'm glad you looked in, you know: it was nice of you.

WILLIAM [*inarticulate*]: Well, I mean to say . . . [*pause, with audible grin again*] Besides, I wanted to ask —

UNCLE JASPER [*quickly, pleased*]: What — anything *I* can do?

WILLIAM: Well, it's quite a thing to ask — [*with a rush*] Can I take a book?

UNCLE JASPER [*with instinctive reluctance*]: Take a book *away*?

WILLIAM: Well, it comes to that. . . . It *is* quite a thing to ask. And I don't want any old book; I want a Trollope. You know — Anthony Trollope.

UNCLE JASPER [*ironical*]: I know: Anthony Trollope.

WILLIAM: You don't think much of him?

UNCLE JASPER: He doesn't say much to me. That may be my fault: I'm not saying it's not. God forbid *I* should run down any honest man who gives honest pleasure. In fact, who has done so twice. He pleased his own generation — and so he should have done: he had got them taped. And, which seems a good deal odder, he pleases yours — I wish you could tell me why. *I* belong to the generation halfway between: in fact, by a funny coincidence, I was born the year Trollope died — 1882. And frankly, William, by the time I was your age, which is to say in the early 1900s, Trollope was so stone dead, so utterly off the map, that he might just as well not have been born at all. He'd out-stayed his welcome, with his most devoted readers; his reputation went with him down to the grave.

WILLIAM [*thoughtful*]: Funny . . . [*brightening*] It didn't stay there.

UNCLE JASPER [*absently*]: No . . . [*energetically*] Trollope died — in both senses — at the time when the English novel was coming into its own. Hardy, Meredith, Henry James were all in the field. Trollope — by his own admission — wrote for young ladies. Hardy, Meredith, James, wrote for adult minds; or at least, for minds that wanted to be adult. It may seem odd to you, William — in fact, I say this to you with some humility — but we young men, when *I* was a young man, surrounded as we were, to the outward eye, with all the good things of those piping times of peace, *did* look on life as a psychological battle. And into that battle we took our three novelists — Hardy, Meredith, James. Yes, those were the great names when I was your age. And frankly, where I am concerned, they're the great names still. And now? I see *you* go into actual battle carrying Trollope!

WILLIAM [*simply*]: I like him.

UNCLE JASPER: Wherefore, I take off my hat to him. *Not* as a novelist — that would be asking too much. Yes, I *have* tried one or two of his books these last few years, but I couldn't away with any of them. Plum duff, sheer plum duff! No, no, no, no – Henry James, as generous a critic as you wish, said about all for Trollope that could be said, in that essay on him in *Partial Portraits* . . . 'Strong, genial, abundant' . . . 'Something masterly in his large-fisted grip' . . . 'He represents to an admirable degree the natural decorum of the English spirit' . . . 'His complete appreciation of the ordinary' . . . Yes, that – all that. It took James's fine eye to see it. But he, even he, was forced to the last conclusion – and for him, as for me, it *was* the damning one – 'Trollope's imagination had no light of its own.'

WILLIAM: And yet – you take off your hat to him?

UNCLE JASPER [*smile in voice*]: There must be *something* about any writer who lives twice. He's a double man. There's the Trollope his own generation knew, and the Trollope yours has found – or, perhaps, created?

WILLIAM: Created?

UNCLE JASPER: You don't think you give him something he hadn't got?

WILLIAM: I do think he's got something we've never had.

UNCLE JASPER [*reflective, struck*]: That's possible. Something you would have liked? Come to that, old Trollope immortalizes quite a few things I could do with myself. [*shivers*] On a day like *this*, I could do with one of those Plumstead Episcopi roaring fires. . . . The rooks in the elms, the port on the table. . . . [*abruptly*] Which do you want?

WILLIAM [*uncertain*]: Which? –

UNCLE JASPER: Which of the Trollope novels?

WILLIAM [*much relieved*]: Oh, you *have* got some of him, then? I began to wonder.

UNCLE JASPER [*dryly*]: If you move that sofa – which will involve moving the table first – I think you'll find three or four away in the corner, down on the bottom shelf. [*more dryly*] They were your great-aunt Emily's.

WILLIAM [*to sound of moving sofa*]: That old warhorse! Fancy me and Aunt Emily seeing with the same eye! [*pause: voice muffled, as from corner of bookshelves*] Yes, here we are . . .

UNCLE JASPER [*reflective*]: With far from the same eye. Aunt Emily wanted the testimonial –

WILLIAM: Testimonial –

UNCLE JASPER: To her own way of living. Whereas, you want –

WILLIAM [*amused*]: What do *I* want?

UNCLE JASPER: A picture book?

WILLIAM: A picture book . . . [*amused*] Well, I'll look at it in the train.

UNCLE JASPER: Very proper – he probably wrote it in the train.

> *Pause: Fade-in train noises – rather accentuated, as of train taking up-gradient. Gradually fade in, on top of these noises and in their rhythm, voice saying 'A picture book, a picture book, a picture book' . . . The words should gain, slowly, more with each time of speaking, over train noises.*

> *Both Faded Out.*

NARRATOR: William is very tired. He has had quite a day, saying so many good-byes in a short time. Kit stowed in the rack above him, he is dozing, arms folded, in a corner of the compartment – which is surprisingly empty. The book he was holding has slipped to the seat beside him. The mists of William's drowsiness clear and thin as, from time to time, he opens his eyes. Lit by bland winter afternoon sunshine, a landscape streams past the windows. A stone house with white window-frames, basking in the yellow light of a valley . . . A church spire . . . A man on horseback, trotting on the grass verge of a road . . . The lichened roofs of farm buildings . . . In the distance – the smoke of a little city, turned by the sun to gauze . . . And, rising above this – surely? – cathedral towers . . . Now, which cathedral can *that* be?

TROLLOPE [*a very deep voice, at once genial and diffident*]: Barchester, sir.

NARRATOR [*as though surprised*]: William must have slept through the stop at the last station. For, he finds, the seat opposite him, empty last time he looked, is now occupied. A big, clumsy man, with a bushy square beard, sits there, eyeing him over thick spectacles that have slipped some way down on his nose.

WILLIAM [*bewildered*]: This country we're going through – it's familiar. Yet I can't, somehow, place it.

TROLLOPE: Possibly not on the map; no, possibly not on the map. [*with detachment, after clearing throat*] A new shire I added to the English counties.

WILLIAM [*automatically*]: Really sir? [*apologetic laugh*] I'm afraid I'm not very bright today.

TROLLOPE: Much on your mind, no doubt? Well, well. Youth is never an easy time. Not for much would I live through my own again.

WILLIAM: If you'll excuse me, sir, you're the first person of – of anything like *your* age that I've ever heard say that!

TROLLOPE: Oh, heaven endows a number of us old fellows with remarkably kind, false memories. That wasn't so in my case. No, all through my good years – and they were many, for my turning-point came when I was twenty-seven; and I lived to be sixty-eight – I was liable, any night, to wake up sweating from the nightmare that I was young again. Idleness, inferiority, envy. The seamy side. Those are the things, you know, that you don't forget. They don't have to cripple you: they didn't cripple me. But it takes the rest of your remaining days to get up with what they have done to you. Let's say they give you, and leave you with, one particular manner of seeing life. You continue to see life that way, whatever comes. Yes, whatever comes. [*pause*] Industry, success, popularity, well-being. . . . The strong, well-lit desk and my pen flowing well ahead of the clock. . . . The peaches and roses in the garden; my boys' voices out there – my boys had a happy youth. . . . Cheques rolling in, bills paid, the bank balance mounting up. The dinner parties – oh, those dinner parties of the 'eighties!

  Fade In

FIRST LADY [*against general background of tinkling glass, laughter and conversation – her voice flattering, arch*]: Now, Mr Trollope, you wonderful, naughty man, I've got something ever so *serious* to say to you. You really *must* let Lily Dale marry Johnnie Eames! Agatha and I would be *heartbroken*. . . .

SECOND LADY [*more fluttering*]: Mr Trollope, may I just ask you this? I have quite a favourite uncle who's an archdeacon, and he's astounded by your knowledge of clergymen. *I* said that perhaps your father was an archbishop?

FIRST LADY: In confidence – I so wonder – *has* your Lady Glencora any orginal in real life?

SECOND LADY: One can but blame her, of course – though [*wistfully*] Burgo Fitzgerald was *very* fascinating! [*increasingly daring*] Come, Mr Trollope, I know you will never tell me, but how *do* you know so much about ladies' hearts?

FIRST LADY: And peers?

SECOND LADY: And politics?

FIRST LADY: And, even – *quite* – *low* – *life*?

  Fade Out

TROLLOPE [*reflective*]: My glass refilled, camellias, charming bright eyes, warming rustle of silks. And, dearest prospect of all, my return home. . . . And those evenings at the Garrick – of which I became a member in '61. Having up to that time lived very little among men – having hitherto been banished from social gatherings – I enjoyed infinitely the gaiety of the Garrick: it was a festival to me to dine there. [*pause – very modestly*] I think that I became popular among those with whom I associated. I had long, for very long, been aware of a certain weakness in my own character, which I may call a craving for love. The Garrick Club was the first assemblage of men. . . .

Fade Out

Fade-in sounds of men's voices, laughter: a generally prosperous and port-winey background of sound, with a confident Bohemian animation.

FIRST MAN: Ha, ha – very good – excellent. Tell Thackeray.
SECOND MAN [*cutting in*]: You forget, the best of it was, that *The Times* next day . . .
THIRD MAN [*very cordial*]: Aha – *here* comes the real good fellow. Evening, Trollope.
ALL [*to sounds of chairs being pushed back*]: Hello, Evening, Anything new? Was feeling *you* were about due in. Things going on well? Needless to ask *you* that! Dirty evening, out there. Come to the fire. Last come, first served. Whist – bring the table up. Look, Trollope, before you get down to whist – tell me this, Trollope . . . Trollope . . . Listen to this, Trollope . . . (*etc.*).

Fade-out Garrick

Fade-in subdued train sounds.

TROLLOPE [*picking up from point where voice left off*]: The first assemblage of men at which I felt myself to be popular.
WILLIAM [*resigned to the oddness of this, but thoughtful*]: You *are* Anthony Trollope?
TROLLOPE: Well, yes – I know myself by that name. [*pause*] I know myself, that's to say, at least not less well than I know my characters.
WILLIAM [*taken aback*]: Isn't that, sir, a funny way round to put it? Surely one more often hears an author say that he knows his characters almost as well as he knows himself?

TROLLOPE: Indeed? Then you must know some clever fellows. No – [*reflective pause*] It's been t'other way round with me. I've thought more about my characters than I have about myself. To be honest, I like 'em a good deal better. I much prefer their company to my own. For my own company, first, I had no taste – misery, loneliness, wretchedness thrust me into it. I'd escape from it at any moment I could – into daydreams, in which I was a quite different fellow. It was that, no doubt, that set up my first habit of spinning yarns.

WILLIAM [*thoughtful*]: But later, sir, once you'd got thoroughly launched, once you'd got a name, once you had started to do so well?

TROLLOPE: Oh, by then I had no time for my own company, I was a busy man – organised down to each moment of every day. I had a lot to get through, and I got through it. [*simply*] I was a happy man. And a happy, busy man isn't given to thinking about himself. That's an idler's trick – and a wretched, unhappy trick, if you ask me.

WILLIAM [*still perplexed*]: Still, *I* always did understand that all writers, from Shakespeare down, drew their characters out of what they knew of themselves. If that was not so in your case, where *did* your people come from? Archdeacon Grantly, Plantagenet Palliser, old Mr Harding – to mention only a few. Heaven knows, they're foursquare and alive enough!

TROLLOPE: Oh, yes, they're alive all right. [*chuckles*] A sight more alive than I am! [*reflective pause, then vaguely*] Oh, they came along, you know; they just came along. . . .

WILLIAM: But, out of *where*?

TROLLOPE [*with genuine piety*]: Ask the Almighty, my boy. No sense in asking me. I put myself into the habit of steady and rapid writing, set myself to turn out a set number of pages daily – and, moreover, turned 'em out, every day. That being so, my people just – came along.

WILLIAM: You suggest, you know, that a novelist is a sort of medium. Sits down, takes up his pen, goes into a sort of trance –

TROLLOPE [*cuts in – shocked*]: What – spirits? That flimmery-flummery? God forbid!

WILLIAM [*eager, pursuing his own idea*]: Or, better still, a sort of receiving station – picking up and transmitting all sorts of things that are in the air?

TROLLOPE [*not shocked now, merely dubious*]: Oh well, there, you know, we're outside my province. I had – er . . . left England . . . before any of *that* came in. Still, from what I've been able to see – and I watch with interest – there might – 'pon my word, there might – be something in what you say. [*reflective pause*] Scenes, places, people, yes, as I sat there writing, I saw them as sharply as though they *were* going on.

WILLIAM: And so, perhaps, they were, sir?

TROLLOPE [*still dubious; growling*]: Well, I don't know, I'm sure. [*sharply*] Mind, I'm not saying I didn't use my head. It may not have been a bright head, but it was a steady one. I worked out my plot at the start; I stuck to it – and, by Gad, I made the pack of 'em stick to it, what is more!

WILLIAM: Pack of whom?

TROLLOPE: The characters. Once or twice, one or two of 'em kicked their heels up, took ideas into their own heads. Sometimes, the ladies were the devil – as ladies can be the devil in real life. There were chapters, for instance, where I had a bit of trouble with that fine young widow, Eleanor Bold. Yes, writing a novel, my boy, is like driving pigs to market – you have one of them making a bolt down the wrong lane; another won't get over the right stile . . . However [*satisfied sigh*] we all got home in the end.

WILLIAM [*suddenly*]: Sir? May I be a bit impertinent?

TROLLOPE [*with unworried chuckle*]: Go on, my boy, go on.

WILLIAM: Well, you said just now – I don't know if you'll remember – that you knew yourself not less well than you knew your characters. You *then* proceeded to say that, first, you'd fled from yourself as from poison; and that, later on, you'd had no time for yourself. In that case – here's where I'm being impertinent – I don't see how you *can* know yourself at all.

TROLLOPE [*undisturbed*]: Yet I do, you know, yet I do. Yes, I know Anthony Trollope, for what he's worth. I kept learning about myself from my own characters. Some say that to be a father's an education – you may quite often recognize, in your children, bits of yourself you had never known were there. In the same way – and I should say even more so – I found it an education to be a novelist. My characters – the best of them, that's to say – were all more definite, more sure of themselves, more active, and – where they *were* admirable – more admirable than I, myself, had ever been in real life. [*chuckles*] My characters fairly marched in on me – took a look round, took stock, and made use of all that *I* had. Ah, they were cool hands. [*chuckles again*] They commandeered me – my pen, my reasoning powers. And, more than that, they drew on a lot in me – desires, scruples, aspirations, and daydreams – of whose existence *I* had not been aware.

WILLIAM: They stole a march on you?

TROLLOPE [*resignedly*]: Put it that way. [*pause*] The best of them were what, without knowing, I should have liked to be. The worst of them – in the moral sense, that's to say – were what, without knowing, I'd somehow avoided being. My Warden, for instance – old Mr Harding, in the novel, was a personification of my own muddled wish to do right at any cost. Plantagenet Palliser – the political hero whose career reaches its climax in my *Prime Minister* – is not only my political ideal, but personifies my own lost political hopes. I did once, you know, stand for Parliament: at the Beverley elections; I took a sickening knock, and from then on, I buried *my* hopes for ever. But from then on, also, Plantagenet Palliser grew. [*pause: sigh*] Well, well . . . Who was the third you said?

WILLIAM [*eager*]: Archdeacon Grantly.

TROLLOPE [*between sigh and chuckle*]: The Archdeacon . . . A bad, bad man – over-ambitious, hard, self-important, in love with power? A decent fellow, loyal to those he loved, humane, even kindly, in some situations, just? . . . I can pass no judgement, you know, on the Archdeacon. He was the product of my moral consciousness. He raised, for me, questions *I* haven't answered yet.

WILLIAM: I suppose he cared for the world too much.

TROLLOPE [*after reflection, humbly*]: I cannot say *I* never cared for the world. . . . [*with return of confidence*] And I do say, I'd have been a fool if I hadn't.

WILLIAM: For me, it's not quite so simple. My world's in rather a mess.

TROLLOPE: So I understand. You are off to the wars, I see. Off to one of the fronts. War's everywhere – every place that you look.

WILLIAM [*impulsively*]: Do you know, Uncle Jasper says that's why so many people like me are reading your books again? He thinks – at least, I suspect he thinks so – that we're homesick for anything right-and-tight. The whole way of life that this country outside the windows – this country we're running through now – suggests. The whole way of life that is quite, apparently, gone. When he let me take one of your books from his shelves just now, sir, he said – I hope you won't mind? – that I wanted a picture book.

TROLLOPE [*as though leaning forward*]: And you – *was* that what you wanted, eh?

WILLIAM: No, you know, he was wrong! Of course I *do* like, we all like, pictures of the old happy times –

TROLLOPE [*dubious*]: Altogether happy?

WILLIAM: Decent, at any rate. But I don't think, with us, that's the root of the thing. No. I think your novels are a support against the sort of *hopelessness* we're inclined to feel. As you say, the characters in your books are *active*. They keep on the move; and they make decisions. They know what they want, and they want what they want all out. If they don't get it they put such a good face on it, or keep such a flag flying, one is left to feel that they *have* won out, by the end. Your people are stronger than circumstances. Yes, I think I've got to the root of it – *that* must be what we're after in your books. It's essential for us, these days, to believe in people, and in their power to live. Not just in heroes or monsters, but in ordinary people with the knack of living ordinary lives. Now, all of your characters, Mr Trollope – except one or two of the monsters like Mrs Proudie – were ordinary, in a way that sticks out a mile. And you see, we long for what's ordinary.

TROLLOPE: So did I.

WILLIAM: You, sir? But – ?

TROLLOPE: How else could I have painted the ordinary in such sublime colours? Can't you see, my brush was tipped, from the first, with a desire that I could not forget? War isolates *you*, my friend, for the time being, from your proper inheritance as a young Englishman. In my own youth, I knew the same isolation – and that its reasons were different, only made it more bitter. [*shamed half-laugh*] I was a gentleman's son who was, apparently, never to be a gentleman, and who knew of no way to be anything else. My father, consuming himself as he consumed our fortunes, remorselessly confronted me with an ideal which I could not approach. For my failure – which had been his failure – he hated me and made me hate myself. He was at pains to place me where I should suffer most – I enjoyed, I believe, the unique distinction of being miserable – a butt, a failure – at *two* of the greatest English public schools. At the two great schools, my father's story was known – disclosed by his failure to pay my fees. All those years I was surrounded by school-fellows who enjoyed what I should have had – who were poised, successful, assured. Could I fail to romanticise those other lives, those other futures, so unlike mine? At eighteen, I was a shambling usher at a poor school in Belgium. At nineteen, I was a clerk in the Post Office. Yes, in time, I respectably worked my way up; but those first years in the Post Office were – well, well . . . Idleness, debts and squalor, interludes of too well-deserved disgrace. And all that – can't you see it? – made ten times worse by my mirages, my dream-pictures of other lives, built up out of those glimpses that I had had?

WILLIAM [*slightly bewildered*]: I'm sorry, sir.

TROLLOPE [*sharply*]: Thanks, I don't ask for pity. I was merely – explaining. [*pause*] How, once, I yearned for the ordinary like a lover. How I came to depict cheerful, confident people, serene homes, honoured positions, as a lover might depict his beloved's face. However, however ... [*lapse into sudden embarrassment – then abruptly, with complete change of tone*] May I ask which of my novels you've got there?

WILLIAM: *The Small House at Allington.*

TROLLOPE: Eh? My old eyes may deceive me, sir, but I *think* you'll find you are wrong.

WILLIAM: Surely? ... [*pause, then outcry*] Oh, gosh – *oh* gosh! This would happen to *me*! Wrong book! That bottom shelf was dark; and I was in a hurry. Here I am, now, stuck for the duration with some mouldy old autobiography!

TROLLOPE [*dryly*]: Mine, I think.

WILLIAM [*flustered*]: Yours, sir? I'd no idea ...

TROLLOPE [*with amused defiance*]: Well, I did. I wrote one. Cannot regret it, either: did me the world of good. Of course, ruined me, finished my good name. I'd left it with my son Henry, for posthumous publication, so he brought it out the year after I'd – left the scene. Yes, my poor lad Henry, he had to face the music: I felt bad about that – otherwise, I had a hearty laugh!

WILLIAM [*puzzled, diffident*]: Was it – er – scandalous, sir?

TROLLOPE [*chuckling*]: Scandalously honest! Or so it seemed to the lot who read it when it came out: 1883, you know – they were just beginning to have fine feelings. Felt that writers ought to be artists, and so on. Made 'em wince. My own lot, I think, would have understood – Thackeray, for instance; but he'd gone on ahead. And *your* lot, in its turn, I feel somehow, may understand. In fact, my boy, may I say there's no book of mine I would rather see you take with you to the battle? Read it, will you? – and *then* go back to the novels. Maybe I wrote it for you. It's the truth – or as near the truth as man ever came.

WILLIAM: Sir – [*no answer*] Mr Trollope! [*slightly frantic*] Sir! [*pause – bemused voice*] He's – he's not – Have I been asleep then? It's getting dark ...

> *Fade-in train noises for a few seconds, in same rhythm as before, accompanied by voice saying 'The Ordinary! The Ordinary – The Ordinary ... '*

Fade Out

NARRATOR: Yes, it is getting dark. One can just see that the seat opposite William is no longer occupied – if it ever was. Outside the carriage windows the winter country is fading, flowing into the dusk. Perhaps, indeed, we have crossed the Barset border and are back in the numbered English counties again. The sunshine, timeless, mellow, and bland, that fell on Trollope's spires and roofs and roads and manorial gates is gone.

UNCLE JASPER'S VOICE [*as though quoting*]: 'Trollope's imagination had no light of its own.'

NARRATOR: No: only genius sheds light. Faithful talent receives the plain light of nature, holds it, reflects it back. Trollope holds up a mirror in which English faces, seasons, and scenes remain. It is a mirror, not distorting, not flattering; with only one magic quality – retention. Can one wonder it should reassure William to look across the years, and find, in the Trollope mirror, faces so like his own? [*pause*] It was not the clumsy and grubby boy, or the seedy clerk, that the world remembered. The big, burly, genial, likeable chap; the unflagging, successful author; the esteemed Civil Servant; the hard rider to hounds; the prosaically happy husband and father – this was the image left. This was the image that was, in time, to bore Uncle Jasper and his more finely strung generation. *Were* there two Trollopes? Uncle Jasper, off-hand, has thrown us out the idea. The anxious outcast, the successful man of the world – was the first, perhaps, never quite absorbed and lost in the second? Is it the wistful outsider, somewhere in Trollope's writing, who gives that mirage-illusion to the ordinary scene?

Is it the mirage that William seeks? . . .

Yes, it is dark in the railway carriage. The train bears on to his destination William, now sleeping deeply, without a dream – head dropped forward over his folded arms. The *Autobiography* has slipped from his hold again – this time, to the floor. The pages blow over rapidly, in a draught. So the last paragraph is exposed for a moment – it is too dark to read it . . .

TROLLOPE'S VOICE [*from the distance and with a solemn impersonality*]: 'Now I stretch out my hand and from the further shore I bid adieu to all who have cared to read the many words I have written.' . . . Now I stretch out my hand . . .

Broadcast 4 May 1945

RIDER HAGGARD:

She

At the age of twelve I was finding the world too small: it appeared to me like a dull, trim back garden, in which only trivial games could be played. The thunder clouds which were to burst in 1914 were, of course, mounting on the horizon – but unobserved by me. Hemmed in by what seemed to be too much safety, I felt bored and hampered – ungrateful, but there you are: I still can distinctly remember the sensation. Worse still, I had exhausted the myths of childhood. Fairy stories I never had cared for much, but up to now I had revelled in the companionship of violent adventurous book-children. Now, a pall had fallen on them and me. I began to feel it was time we were growing up. Growing up to what?

My ideas of growing up were ambiguous, and sought to have no relation with reality. It was not easy, even in my own thoughts, to pin down my wish for accession to full power – fuller power, really, than I could see at work anywhere round me in the normal scene. Education had, if anything, been discouraging, my own romantic approaches to any subject being rebuffed in favour of quibbling truths. I developed a sort of grudge against actuality. History, for instance, had looked promising; but I soon found it inferior to the historical novel. I sustained, at about this time, a reverse in the matter of my fine essay on the Civil War. I had written:

'Now the Roundheads hated the Cavaliers because the Cavaliers were better-looking than they were. . . .'

'Oh,' *they* said, returning the essay, 'oh, but you can't say that!'

'Why – who says I can't say what?'

'You can't say that because it is not the case. Nothing, alas,' *they* said, with a maddening kindly smile, 'is quite so simple.'

It was 'alas', indeed. Constitutionalism: its first breath blew cold. I wanted the primary motive and the primary colour. So I resigned from history and turned to geography; if there were not a better time there might be a better place? But with geography, also, something shrivelled and shrank: there was no undiscovered country, they told me, now. What a prospect: what an absence of prospect, rather! I was chiefly depressed at that time, I think, by what seemed the sheer

uniformity of the human lot, by its feebleness, arising from some
deficiency. . . .

It was at the height of this, my first winter of discontent, that I
came on the novel *She*, by Rider Haggard. Everything, from the first
glance, made this a book of promise, even its author's name. Rider
Haggard . . . was this some kind of Erl-king or demon horseman –
staring, awful, visionary and pale? Counterbalancing this, where I
was concerned – for I had not a totally gothic taste – was the book's
cover: a solid, homely and edible pink-brown, suggesting cocoa or
milk chocolate. (And, indeed, in time the narrator's style, with its
blend of the jocular and the blood-curdling, was to have on me the
effect of well-sugared cocoa laced with some raw and subtle intoxicant.) It was impossible not to keep looking ahead at the wash
illustrations by Greiffenhagen: a lion and crocodile locked in a
death-grip . . . a savage dance in the dark, lit by human torches . . . a
veiled white form proceeding down endless caves . . . an extinct,
deserted city under the moon. . . .

Whether *She* – which, I see, was written in 1886 – was in the first
place intended for grown-up people, I don't know. It announces
itself as 'a novel of adventure'. It is a story of passion, outsize, direct –
ideally directed, it would appear, to the frustrated, non-moral, pre-
adolescent child. It gains, rather than loses, from the young reader's
indifference to sex. Its soaring unrealism, its very enormities and
deformities as a love-story were for me, really, in my time, its
attraction.

Horace Holly, forty, a Cambridge don, looks ferocious like a
baboon, but is mild at heart. Holly's ward, Leo Vincey, has gold curls
and looks like a Greek god. Leo's twenty-fifth birthday is to be
marked by the ceremonial opening of a family casket: it is revealed
that the Vinceys, good old stock, trace descent from one Kallikrates,
a priest of Isis. This Kallikrates broke his vows to marry, fled to
Egypt, was shipwrecked on the Libyan coast, encountered the white
queen of a savage tribe, and was by her slain – having failed to return
her love for the good reason that he was married already. The
vindictive queen, it remained on record, had bathed in the Fire of
Everlasting Life. We are off – in the turn of a page we are She-ward
bound.

'How different [says Holly, who tells the story] is the scene
whereof I have now to tell from that which has now been told! Gone
are the quiet college rooms, gone the wind-swayed English elms, the
cawing rooks and the familiar volumes on the shelves. And in their
place there rises a vision of the great calm ocean gleaming in shaded

silver lights beneath the beams of a full African moon. . . . Three miles or more to our starboard is a low dim line. It is the Eastern shore of Central Africa – a perilous coast. The night is quiet, so quiet that a faint booming sound rolls across the water to us from the distant land.

'The Arab at the tiller holds up his hand and says one word:- "*Simba* [lion]!"'

'Then it comes again, a slow majestic sound that thrills us to the marrow –'

The overture. Merely lion, but the first premonition – from now on Holly and I are to feel the suction of an inexorable magnetic force. The shipwreck, the unnerving appearance of the Amahagger tribesmen dwelling in cave-tombs inside the mountains, hot-potting their captives, and ruled by She-who-must-be-obeyed.

'*Imperial Kôr is fallen, fallen!*' This is the cry that haunts Horace Holly's sleep. For these marshes and mountain-encircled plains show traces of a vanished civilization – haughty and grandiose. In the rock-chambers honeycombing the mountains lie – still immaculate after six thousand years of death – white-skinned aristocrats. Mild necrophily does, in fact, pervade the pages of *She*: dead beauties set up romantic loves in the dark rude male breasts of the Amahagger; and She-who-must-be-obeyed shares a bedroom-tomb with the preserved corpse of her beloved, the Kallikrates whom she had slain in a fit of pique. . . . But Kôr, Kôr, the enormous derelict city, whose streets the Amahagger dare not tread, is, ever, on the horizon. My impatience to visit it was immense – and my travellers, by this time deeply embroiled with 'She', made, for my tastes, maddeningly slow going. However, here we were at last:

'I wish', gasps Holly, 'it lay within the power of my pen to give any idea of the grandeur of the sight which met our view. There, all bathed in the red glow of the setting sun, were miles of ruins – columns, temples, shrines and palaces of kings. . . . Straight before us stretched away what had evidently been the main thoroughfare of the city, for it was very wide and regular, wider than the Thames Embankment. . . . In the fading light we passed swiftly up the main road, that, I believe I am right in saying, no human foot had pressed for thousands of years . . .'

My spine crept. And, still, the moon was to rise – 'Court upon court, space upon space of empty chambers, that spoke more eloquently to the imagination than any crowded street. It was a wonderful sight to see the full moon looking down on the ruined fane of Kôr. A wonderful thing to think for how many thousands of years the dead orb above and the dead city below had thus gazed upon one another. . . . The white light fell, and minute by minute the slow shadows crept across the grass-grown courts.'

I saw Kôr before I saw London; I was a provincial child. Inevitably, the Thames Embankment was a disappointment, being far, far less wide than Horace Holly had led me to expect. I was inclined to see London as Kôr with the roofs still on. The idea that life in any capital city must be ephemeral, and with a doom ahead, remained with me – a curious obsession for an Edwardian child. At the same time I found something reassuring and comforting in the idea that, whatever happened, buildings survived people. Long, even, before I had read *She*, I would run across any amount of fields to look at any ruin, even the ruin of a cottage. Yes, it seems funny now . . . *She*, the book, glutted my imagination with images and pictures of which I could not, it seemed, have enough.

Can it have been the *mise-en-scène*, rather than the story itself, that, where I was concerned, turned some inside key? No, there was more than that to it. The reincarnation theme, then? – for Leo Vincey, of course, turned out to be re-born Kallikrates, and the whirlwind passion of She-who-must-be-obeyed was, at the first glance at Leo, again unleashed. She took up with Leo exactly where she had left off with Kallikrates. No, it was not *that*, exactly, either. (For one thing, I saw little point in Leo; were I to wait for someone for more than two thousand years, it would not be a jocular athlete with gold curls.) It was the idea of obstination, triumphant obstination, which became so obsessing – want any one thing hard enough, long enough, and it must come your way. This did strike deep: it came up like a reinforcement, because in my day, my childhood, all polite education was against the will – which was something to be subdued, or put out of sight as though it did not exist. Up to now, I had always expected books to be on the side of politeness. *She* contained thoughts and sayings I never had seen in print, and certainly never had heard spoken. Horace Holly, good man, disapproved of 'She' – but how she impressed him! Impressed him? She swept him off his feet. In a fit of what he has set down as 'mad passion' he at one point proposed marriage. Her unsuitability to be a Cambridge don's wife did not have to appear: she was set on Leo. Marriage to Leo, and a return to England to take over the government of that country was her programme. Says Leo: 'But we have a queen already.'

'It is naught, it is naught. She can be overthrown!'

This really does worry Holly, who 'meditated deeply on the awful nature of the problem that now opened before us. What her powers were I knew, and I could not doubt that she would exercise them to the full. . . . Her proud, ambitious spirit would be certain to break loose and avenge itself for the long centuries of solitude. In the end, I had little doubt, she would assume absolute rule over the British dominions, and probably the whole world . . .'

Did *I* then, I must ask, myself aspire to 'She's' role? I honestly cannot say so. 'She' was *she* – outsize absolute of the grown-up. The exaltation I wanted was to be had from the looking-on. She had entered fire (the thing of which I was most frightened). She shocked me, as agreeably and profoundly as she shocked Horace Holly. For me, she continued to have no face – I saw her as I preferred her, veiled, veiled; two eyes burning their way through the layers of gauze. Horace Holly's chaste categoric descriptions of anything further left me cold. The undulating form (even her neck, he told me, undulated at times), the scented raven hair, the rounded arm, the 'tiny sandalled foot' she could – where I was concerned – keep. Or Leo could have them. Enviable? – no, they were mere accessories. She gave me ideas, yes – but not all ideas: I was still twelve.

I read *She*, dreamed *She*, lived *She* for a year and a half. . . . Since then, until almost yesterday, I have not opened the chocolate-pink book again. There are – there can but be – startling divergations between what I remember and what is written. At the same time, surprisingly little of what *was* written has evaporated. All the way there is an echo-track of sensation – just as I find my own childish grubby thumbprints on the pages.

This book *She* is for me historic – it stands for the first totally violent impact I ever received from print. After *She*, print was to fill me with apprehension. I was prepared to handle any book like a bomb. It was – did I realize that all the time? – *Horace Holly*, not ever, really She-who-must-be-obeyed, who controlled the magic. Writing – that creaking, pedantic, obtrusive, arch, prudish, opaque overworded *writing* . . . what it could do! That was the revelation; that was the power in the cave. The power whose inequality dear Holly laments at the opening of every passage. The power of the pen. The inventive pen.

Broadcast 28 February 1947

AUTOBIOGRAPHY

Introduction

Spencer Curtis Brown, Elizabeth Bowen's friend and executor, describes how, early in 1972, when Elizabeth Bowen was already ill with cancer, she showed him two chapters of what was to be a full-length autobiography called *Pictures and Conversations*. In July, her illness got much worse, and she was told that she had only a short time to live. She was still eager to work on the book, but could do very little. Spencer Curtis Brown saw her the day before she died, in February 1973, and asked her if she wanted the fragments of the autobiography published. Speaking 'clearly and firmly', she said: 'I want it published.'

Elizabeth Bowen explains her view of autobiography in an essay of 1951, where she traces a change: 'Whereas autobiography used to be based on statement, now it derives from query, being tentative rather than positive, no longer didactic but open-minded. It is mobile, exploratory.' It makes great use, she says, of sensations, impressions and visual memories. This is borne out by her own autobiographical writings – *Bowen's Court* and the essay on the Bowen housekeeper, Sarah Barry, *Seven Winters* and 'Pictures and Conversations' – which are as much about the landscape and architecture of Ireland and Kent, the atmosphere of her homes and schools and the smell of history, as they are about her actions and feelings. In fact she is expansive and detailed about her childhood inheritance, and reticent about her adult life.

What she wants most to do in 'Pictures and Conversations' is to explain what made her a writer, and what kind of a writer she is. To do this she goes back into Anglo-Irish history, as well as giving a vivid account of her early years (so that there is a close link between the longer work and her affectionate, evocative sketch of Sarah, 'The Most Unforgettable Character I've Met', which though unusually self-indulgent in its tone, gives a powerful picture of Anglo-Irish family life). It's this material which makes up the interior landscape of 'the Bowen terrain', and it's she who is the best equipped to describe it: after all, 'if anybody *must* write a book about Elizabeth Bowen, why should not Elizabeth Bowen?'

THE MOST UNFORGETTABLE
CHARACTER I'VE MET

A great cold grey stone house, with rows upon rows of windows, ringed round with silence, approached by grass-grown avenues – has life forever turned aside from this place? So the stranger might ask today, approaching my family home in Ireland. It is miles from anywhere you have ever heard of; it is backed by woods with mountains behind them; in front, it stares over empty fields. Generations have lived out their lives and died here. But now – everybody has gone away?

No: not quite. A low wing runs out at the back of the house, and from its chimney you see, winter and summer, a plume of wood-smoke rising against the trees. And through one window, as dusk falls, the glow of firelight welcomes you. This fire never goes out; it is Sarah Barry's – or was Sarah Barry's until last spring, when she died. Since then, her son Paddy keeps it alight: he sits beside it in his chair, looking across at hers.

When Sarah, then Sarah Cartey, first arrived at Bowen's Court, County Cork, she was a girl of fourteen. She left her home in County Tipperary to become a kitchenmaid in my grandfather's house. Taking her place in the trap beside her new Master, she had set out one morning upon the fifty-mile drive. She did not know when, if ever, she would see home again. Ireland looks so small from the outside, it is hard to realize how big the distances feel: for the simple people, each county might be a different continent – and way back in the last century this was even more so. Young Sarah, face set towards County Cork, might have been driving off into Peru. Mr Bowen, towering beside her in his greatcoat, and keeping his horse along at a saving trot, was for her the one tie between the old and the new – she already knew him by sight, and by awesome name, for the Master owned large estates in both counties, and drove to and fro weekly between the two. It was on the return from one of these trips that he was bringing back with him Sarah Cartey. In his part of Tipperary, as in his part of Cork, everyone went in dread of Mr Bowen. He was a just man, but he was hard: to his wealth was added the weight of his character – choleric, dynamic and overbearing. In those days, the Protestant Irish landlord exercised more or less absolute power, and was, if he misused it, hated accordingly. Tall and heavy, bearded, genially ruddy but with rather cold blue eyes, my grandfather was typical of his class. Unlike some, he ran his estates like a man of business. Few loved him, but he was a big gun.

But so, in her way, was Sarah. From the first, it seems, they recognized this in each other, which was the reason why they got on so well. Driving along that day, she sat fearlessly upright. When he spoke she answered, cheerfully and forthright. The tears that kept pricking her violet-blue eyes were blinked back: she did not let one fall. At home, her mother and all the neighbours had told her she was a lucky girl, to get such a start – legends of Bowen's Court grandeur were current in Tipperary. So she kept her chin high, as befitted a lucky girl. If this were life, she was going to live it well. It was in the dusk, at the end of the day-long journey, that Sarah saw Bowen's Court for the first time.

When Sarah, as an old woman, told me this story, she looked at me with eyes that had never changed. Their character and their colour were set off by jet-black lashes. Laughing and ageless, these were the most perfect Irish eyes in the world. They were, I suppose, strictly her only beauty – though Sarah was as comely as you could wish. Her complexion kept into old age its vivid bloom. Her hair, curling generously round her forehead, lost no vitality as it turned white – in youth it was, like her vigorous eyebrows, dark. She was short and, since I remember her, broad and stout: she must have been thickset even as a young girl.

The Bowen's Court in which she took up her duties was unlike the silent house of today. Lavishly kept up, it was at the height of its Victorian prime. Mr and Mrs Bowen, their nine children, eight indoor servants and frequent visitors more than filled it. The eldest Bowen daughter was also called Sarah. Perhaps it was something in the tie of the name that made the two girls friends from the first, then lifelong allies. The young Bowens had been rigidly brought up: in the heart of this countryside they led formal lives. Handsome, but overgrown and pale, they lived in fear of their father. They might well have envied Sarah her spontaneity. They adored their gracious mother, but her they too seldom saw. Under the Mistress's calm rule, the household ran like clockwork.

Of the upstairs rooms – with their damasks, marbles, mirrors, mahogany – Sarah Cartey at first saw little: the basement claimed her; over the dark stone-flagged floors she hurried to and fro. At first she was like a kitten, under everyone's feet, but her wits soon gave her command of the situation. Clean, strong, quick, friendly and willing – she was approved. The Bowen's Court servants, from the butler and cook down, were a hierarchy, but a good-humoured one. Some, like Sarah, were Catholics, others Protestants – 'But', Sarah told me, 'we all got on so well together, you'd never know which was which.' In that case, tempers must have been doughty, for the kitchen worked at exacting pressure: if a meal were not on his table up to the minute, the Master would 'roar aloud', at which the whole house-hold quaked.

Except Sarah. She never quaked at the Master: she understood him. He had been out early, poor man, so needed his dinner *now*. As a rule, he ignored the servants, who for their part gave him a wide berth. But whenever he came across Sarah – staggering with her pail from the well, perhaps, or running an errand out to the garden – he would stop and ask her how she was getting on. Was she learning to like her work, did she miss her home? Looking up, she assured the Master that she was happy. The fact was, she refused stoutly to be anything else. Therefore, she kept those dear Tipperary memories locked away in her heart. But there, as a part of her inmost being, they grew in strength and power as years went by. As an old woman, she ached to go back *home*. What kept her? She stayed with us to the end. It was to Bowen's Court that she gave her genius – her genius for making all that she touched live.

Though hers was the most independent mind I have known, Sarah did not question the social order. The injustices (as they would appear now) of my grandfather's household did not strike her. Out of what might have been servitude she made for herself a creative career. Her whole personality went into what she did. I believe that 'class' to Sarah meant simply this – the division of people according to their different duties. Thus, she worked alongside the Bowens, rather than for them. She respected the Bowens because, as she saw it, they played their allotted parts in the proper way. She perceived that the Master, in his estate management, spared himself no more than he spared his men; that the Mistress's life, with so many demands upon it, was selfless; that the young gentlemen lived under discipline like cadets; that the young ladies studied, and practised the piano, as industriously as she, Sarah, scrubbed at the pots and pans. If downstairs you worked like a black, upstairs you had to 'behave' like a Spartan. Life evened up, in the long run. She envied no one, and only pitied those to whom God had given nothing to do. When she was nearly eighty, I told her she worked too hard. 'Thank God, I always enjoy myself!' she flashed out.

Clouds gathered over Bowen's Court. First, the Mistress died of smallpox – her eldest son had brought the infection home from abroad. Then, the Master married again, and his growing-up children resented the woman who had taken their mother's place. Strife and estrangements followed: all over the house one now heard angrily raised voices, or encountered sullenly shut doors. Worse was to come – it became evident that the Master was going out of his mind. The estate, lacking his grip, suffered: it began to run at a loss. When the Master died, it was found that severe retrenchments must be made; labourers were turned away from the farm, and most of the indoor servants were sent away. My father, who as eldest son had now succeeded to Bowen's Court, was hard put to it, even so, to keep things going at all. His sister, Miss Sarah, kept house for him. Need it be said that Sarah Cartey became the new young Mistress's lieutenant?

Together, the two Sarahs schemed and worked to make home what it ought to be for the others. This was always a hard and sometimes a thankless task. Miss Sarah, sensitive to the criticisms of her younger brothers and sisters, relied upon Sarah Cartey to keep her spirits up. The sorrows and terrors of the last few years had left their mark on the young Bowens; also, left will-less without their father's authority, they now hardly knew where to turn. They needed to be rallied, inspired, cheered – and it was here that Sarah Cartey came in. She became the steady dynamo of the house. From her they learned the meaning of zest for life. Her esteem built them up in their own eyes. And she understood them – her devotion was never blind. Short of money, and isolated in the great shabby house, they could easily have dropped out of society. But Sarah insisted that this should not happen; the old Master's children must keep their place. She encouraged the brothers to bring home their friends from college, and compelled the sisters to entertain. She loved to hear laughter. Meanwhile, she was doing the work of six, turning her hand to everything – cooking, laundering, scrubbing. I don't know how many times a day she plied up and down between the basement and attics. But she always had time to joke with the young gentlemen, or to help the young ladies to dress for balls. She, who had left her own mother at fourteen, never ceased to pity the motherless Miss Bowens: she supplied, in her own way, motherly pride and love. It was a lasting disappointment to her that none of the four married.

She herself did not marry till she was over thirty. Her comeliness and her fame as a cheerful worker could not fail to bring many suitors around – but she had literally no time to listen to them. When as last she did give her heart, she chose worthily. This marriage went only in one way against her dreams – it won her away forever from Tipperary. The Barrys were County Cork people: living on the estate, they were trusted employees and friends of the Master's household – and more, between Bowens and Barrys existed the foster-tie, then very strong in Ireland. One after another, the Bowen's Court babies had been sent out to nurse with Mrs Barry, who raised up alongside them a numerous family of her own. I have always heard, and can well believe, that the Barrys were descended from the Kings of Ireland – their ancestors must have been mighty over this very land before my own, Cromwellian settlers, arrived. Certainly, Patrick Barry, who became the husband of Sarah, was tall and distinguished-looking. And he was upright in character as he was in build.

The young couple set up in a colour-washed cottage on the outskirts of the estate: it faced across the road towards distant mountains, but its back window overlooked Bowen's Court, down the fields. So Sarah, even at the height of her own happiness, could still keep an eye on us – and she did. I only hope that calls from the helpless mansion did not break in too often on Sarah's years as a wife. For these, had we only known it, were to be as few as they were ideal.

At Bowen's Court there had again been changes. My father had married; his brothers and sisters had gone their different ways into the world. My mother – charming, dreamy and totally inexperienced as a housekeeper – found her new home an alarming proposition. She had been left by Miss Sarah a parting word of advice – 'Go to Sarah Barry if you are in any trouble.' At this point, I come on the scene – and as far back as *I* can remember, Sarah was with us more or less every day. To escape downstairs to the laundry where Sarah worked became my dominating idea. Happiness stays, for me, about the warm smell of soapsuds. I remember her short strong arms red from the heat of water, and the hilarious energy with which she turned the wringer – as though this were some private game of her own. Under her hand, the iron sped effortlessly over the steaming linen. I suppose all children delight in seeing a thing well done – the craftsman is their ideal grown-up. Sarah, I can see now, was divided between her love for 'the Baba' and her love for her work – one could hardly fail to get in the other's way. When I flopped into her baskets of new-bleached linen, she would haul me out with – 'Come on, now: you're too bold for me altogether!' On the best days, she used to let me 'help'. One of the pleasures of growing older was that of growing more fully into her confidence. And I grew tall fast – it was not so long before her laughter-creased eyes were on a level with mine.

Her vivid plumpness was fascinating – it went with her abundance of warmth and wit. Time was to teach me how comprehending her love could be. In those first years, as the child of a happy home, I suppose I took love for granted – it was, rather, Sarah's *amusingness* that attracted me. Her repartee could be lightning-quick – at that nobody got the better of her. And almost every day she had something for me: a surprise, a story, a secret – only for her and me.

Sarah's cottage home – with the lustre mugs on the dresser, the new-baked bread, the speckless hardwood furniture – seemed to me paradise. But, looking round it again, I found one thing missing: after that I began asking my mother, 'But why hasn't Sarah got any baby?' Other friends must have wondered the same thing – Sarah childless meant a sort of loss to the race. She herself never ceased to believe that God would see to the matter – and so He did. I shall never forget the morning when Sarah called me to her in a particular tone. I could feel at once that something was in the air. She put her arms close round me; her dear breath tickled my ear as she whispered, 'Now here *is* a secret for you – God is going to send me a little parcel!'

We were away when her son was born. My father's illness kept us from Bowen's Court, so that I did not see Paddy till he was two years old. Any child of Sarah's would have seemed beautiful, but this one really was so. The sunshine of her nature seemed to have found its way into his eyes, his glowing cheeks and his golden curls. Her womanhood had been crowned as it deserved. It would have been understandable if Sarah, after her years of waiting, had been unable to bear her darling out of her sight. But in this, as in all, she was generous – she let me make off with this miracle-baby for afternoons together, climb with him up to the tops of hay-ricks, carry him off to the stream to sail paper boats. In our absence – and our visits during those years were brief – she was acting as caretaker at Bowen's Court: with small Paddy clutching her skirts she patrolled the deserted rooms. It seemed unnatural to her, then as always, that 'the Family' should be away – but she could fill the emptiness with her own summer – the radiance in which she lived with husband and child.

Then, while Paddy was still a small boy, Patrick took sick and died. I do not know how she faced out her desolation: she to whom so many had turned could now only turn to herself. Sarah was never meek; there was always a touch of fire about her goodness. Her whole being cried out against this loss. In the end she triumphed; she did not let it warp her. Only, as I grew old enough to be able to read her eyes, I could see behind their gaiety an eternal wound. For a while, her thoughts turned to Tipperary – should she not go home again, taking her child with her? But no; she was wanted at Bowen's Court – she stayed. She continued to live in the roadside cottage, though there were times when its loneliness frightened her. Often, the mountain winds roared through the trees at the back; after holidays, drunken people lurched past her door. One terrible night, she heard one man kill another – as key-witness, she had to attend the trial. Agitation made her evidence contradictory: both the victim and the prisoner had been her neighbours. 'I pitied both the poor fellows,' she said to me.

Sarah's sense of justice was strong, but personal. She felt the Law's aim should be the same as her own – good treatment for as many people as possible. What she detested in crime was its unkindness. The killing at her gate had been exceptional in being a *crime passionel*: most violence in Ireland had a political source. Her girlhood had been in the days of the Land League; she was to live through the repercussions of the 1916 Rising, through 'the bad times' that followed the Great War, through the Civil War after the Treaty, when the British had gone. Lorries crashing along with armed men rocked her house in the night; she saw horizons scarlet with burning mansions and farms; she heard reverberations from blown-up bridges. You never knew what might happen, from day to day. Through all this, Sarah never took sides. Thinking in terms of people, not of ideas, she never examined the ethics either of landlordism or British rule. When, after the Treaty, Ireland was split in twain, it was simply against *all* foolishness that she shook her head. She loved life's decent pattern of love and work – anyone who destroyed this became her enemy.

Through it all, no faction raised its hand against Sarah. Since her widowhood, she had kept herself to herself – on civil terms with all neighbours, she was on close terms with none – and she never talked: her discretion stood her in good stead. In the thick of it all, she did say, 'It would break your heart to see good time squandered away like this.'

I grew from a schoolgirl into a young woman: I married, travelled, became a writer, and enjoyed my fill of big city life. But, each time I returned to Bowen's Court and to Sarah I found that she, who had never in her life left the South of Ireland, could still make circles round me. Nothing I told her surprised her. She liked to hear about London, and, of course, about Rome – I was able to bring her back a rosary blessed by the Pope. She was alarmed when she heard I planned to go to America, for fear I should not come back – so few Irish people did. I don't think she saw much point in travel, really: why should anyone wish to move from their own place? Sarah's scepticism was good for me – like most young people, I bolted ideas whole simply because they were the ideas of my own day. Attempting to argue with her, I was forced to think.

I know that my having no children disappointed her deeply, though she was too delicate in her feeling ever to speak of this. When my father died, at the end of weeks of illness that had been agonising for him and for all of us, it was to her that I turned. Leaving his room, when it was over, I found the staircase full of spring evening light and Sarah standing there looking up, waiting for me. We sat down side by side on the stairs, and she put her arms round me – as she had not done since the day when she whispered to me about her 'little parcel'. 'The poor Master . . . ' she said. Her memories of my father, reaching back, made his life complete. *I* had only known my father as my father. But she, as we sat there, saw the red-headed schoolboy, the anxious young head of the house, the proud bridegroom, the lonely man fighting breakdown for many years. Her sense of his triumphant dignity as a human being passed, without a word spoken, from her to me. It was she, a few hours later, who did the last work for him – 'You must come and see him,' she said proudly, 'He looks lovely.' She took me to see – he did. Her fingers had fluted the linen over his body into a marble-like pattern, a work of art.

I had been the only child: Bowen's Court was now mine. I could not live there altogether; our married home was in England, near my husband's work. So, in order that everything might be taken care of, Sarah and Paddy shut up their cottage and took up their quarters at the back of the house. When we *could* be there, she took charge of us and of everything. What summer holidays she gave us, and what Christmases! And what meals she cooked – once again, the big kitchen range roared, and she stood over it royally. Into those visits of a few weeks on end she helped us pack the feeling of an unbroken home life. Each time, the rooms to which we returned might have been left only yesterday. Fires burned, flowers were in the vases, and our beloved possessions (preserved by Sarah as might be the toys of children) lay where we had put them down last time.

As of old, she was all for company: to please her we could not invite too many guests. Beaming, she watched me re-open what had been dismantled bedrooms at the top of the house. She declared, 'We're like a palace again!' Sarah's idea of company, I remembered, had been formed in the stately days of my grandfather – gentlemen in tailcoats and high collars, ladies whose rustling silks swept the ground. What would she make of my friends – creatures of a changed society, of an outside world that she did not know? But at bare-limbed young women in brief skirts, at young men in slack and colourful country clothes – sunning themselves on the steps, calling out of the windows, playing wild games on wet days – she did not bat an eyelid. They were happy, they liked the house and us and her cooking – so they were all right with her. Because she loved human nature, she could move with the times. Each new guest, on arrival, came downstairs with me to be introduced to Sarah – and there were few who did not find their way down again. One was safe in tracing a missing guest to the kitchen. As one of them said to me, 'She's an education.'

What Sarah felt in her heart of hearts about my becoming a writer I do not know. Books could teach her nothing, and played no part in her life. She was used to seeing a gentleman at his desk – my grandfather at his accounts, my father over his legal documents – but she might well have considered a typewriter inhuman company for a woman. I think it was always a shock to come on me, rooted there, indoors on a fine morning or late on into the night. But her philosophy with regard to work held good: happy in hers she could not begrudge me mine. Also, I had explained to her how my affairs stood – since my grandfather's death finances had not improved: I could only afford to keep Bowen's Court if I earned money. So she saw that what I did, along with the much that she did, followed the same ideal – to keep things going.

Sarah refused to believe that this war would come. She still held that the Great War had taught us the needed lesson – she was not a student of European affairs. Her optimism had kept so much trouble at bay that I think I almost believed it could stop Hitler. After Munich, she was all triumph – 'Didn't I tell you, now?' When, on that sunny Sunday morning, 3 September 1939, I switched off the radio after Chamberlain's voice, I hesitated at the head of the kitchen stairs. How was I to tell Sarah she had been wrong? When I had done so, she shrugged her shoulders, opened the front of the range and poked the fire. The she flashed round on me – 'Well, it won't last!'

I wish she could have lived through it. Shadows of change, anxiety, deprivation crept up on the house in her last years. I don't think she set much store by Ireland's neutral safety while my husband and I

were in London, 'among those bombs'. She knew I knew she would
have given the world for me to have stayed at Bowen's Court, out of
it all. But her comprehension of things was too fine to allow her once
to suggest that I should do so. My husband's work was in London,
and my place was beside him: people she loved did not desert their
posts. Beyond that, this war had for her no definable rights and
wrongs, any more than a senseless family quarrel. She hated war as
unkindness; she mourned it as waste.

Our visits were shorter, fewer: no friends came with us. From
rooms no longer in use Sarah packed away the hangings and pictures
– 'Till the good times come back.' The wing behind Bowen's Court,
in which she lived with Paddy, is a row of rooms overlooking the
grass-grown yard. From them in the old Master's day one had heard
the clatter of horses, in my day cars being run in and out of the
garage. Now all was silence. Sarah's parlour had been my grandfather's estate office: with its barred window and iron safe in the wall
it was not home-like – but somehow she made it so. She hung it
round with pictures that had been in my nursery, and on the hearth
kept burning that constant fire. Again, she patrolled the empty block
of the house, on the watch for any suspicion of damp or damage.
Every day Paddy switched on the library radio, and, among sheeted
furniture, he and she heard the news. Paddy, now grown up into a
clever man, explained the war to his mother – but could not explain
it away. Things began to run very short – coal, tea. And you had to
think twice before you lit a candle.

It was in the fourth year of the war that the final assault on her
came. A growth formed in her body. To her, who always had been
sound from top to toe, this at first seemed a nightmare from which
she must surely wake. It was weeks before she nerved herself to tell
Paddy. When she did, she bound him to secrecy: *I* must not be
worried – wasn't the war enough? Things got worse: she consented
to see a doctor. Radium treatment in Dublin was his urgent advice.
Very well: she would go, she would try it. She was not in pain, thank
God.

Sarah, now nearing eighty, left Bowen's Court in the spirit in
which she arrived there at fourteen – chin up, heart high, ready for
what might come. Before she left she was busy: she had a great deal
to see to. She went over every inch of the house – yes, it was fit for us
to come back, if we chose, tomorrow. In the larder, she checked over
the bottled fruit, and re-covered some dozens of jars of jam. She
wished she could have made more strawberry, that was our favourite
kind. The evening before she started, friends from far and near came

in to bid her Godspeed. Sarah, the Tipperary woman who had always kept her heart a little detached, had to realize how well County Cork loved her. Even those who only knew her by sight, driving her donkey trap up the hill to Mass on Sundays, sent good wishes. Everyone, shyly, promised Sarah their prayers. *She* – as they all remember – was in great spirits. 'Oh, I'll be back', she laughed, 'before you can miss the time. And too grand for you altogether, after my trip to Dublin.'

She had only once – and that years ago – been to Dublin before. She said she would be a poor thing if she couldn't enjoy a journey. She and Paddy made their way down the train to the tea-car, where they declared a feast. The line, as though specially laid for her, runs through County Tipperary – all the way she sat entranced, looking out of the window at the landscape flying past in the spring light; also, she had all the fun in the world observing her fellow-passengers and their ways. But the journey's end held pain: at the Dublin hospital she and Paddy had to say goodbye.

I reached Dublin from London two days later. Sarah's treatment, with its alarming strangeness, had started – but as I walked down the ward to her bed her smile came to meet me, gay as ever. Lying there in a striped jacket, with sun falling on to the fluffy curls round her face, she looked young, almost schoolgirlish. At the same time, she was already the queen of her surroundings. She sent me up and down the beds, distributing the flowers and fruit I had brought her among the other patients. From left and right, I saw poor exhausted faces turned her way, as though imbibing strength. 'Mrs Barry's a treat for us all,' said the nurse to me. Sarah praised the hospital, saying she could not have run it better herself. During my daily visits we never, by her clear wish, spoke of her ordeal: instead, we chatted and laughed over little things. She said, 'Don't you want to know how I like Dublin?' I reminded her I still owed her a Christmas present, and she said she'd like a length for a new dress – 'with a nice little clever pattern; not too bold'.

I brought the stuff, but she never wore the dress. Just when everyone was most optimistic, when plans for her return journey had begun to be made, her heart gave out under the treatment: Sarah died. It was now, at last, that she realized her wish to return forever to Tipperary. As she had asked her son, she was buried there. Her funeral drove past the farms and gates and hedges whose picture had always been in her heart. Through Paddy's mind, as he followed, ran all those Tipperary stories she had told him over their fire in County Cork.

At the start, I pictured Bowen's Court standing empty. But that is not the picture Sarah would want you to see – and more, it is not a true one. Her presence is still to be felt there, and from no place where Sarah reigns can life turn away for long. I believe in her power to magnetize people home again: in the rooms will be heard again the laughter she liked to hear. You may say she gave her genius to a forlorn hope – to a house at the back of beyond, to a dying-out family. But I think no gift goes for nothing. She never lowered her flag; and by that she alone could make me believe in greatness. If we can play our parts in building a better world in Sarah's spirit, we shall not do too badly.

1944

PICTURES AND CONVERSATIONS

I

ORIGINS

The day this book was begun I went for a walk. The part of Kent I am living in has wide views, though also mysterious interstices. It can be considered to have two coastlines: a past, a present – the former looks from below like a ridge of hills, but in fact is the edge of an upland plateau: originally the sea reached to the foot of this. Afterwards, the withdrawal of the sea laid bare salty stretches, formerly its bed; two of the Cinque Ports, Hythe, New Romney, consequently found themselves high-and-dry, as did what was left of the Roman harbour under the heights of Lympne. . . . The existing coastline, a long shallow inward curve westward from Folkestone to the far-out shingly projection of Dungeness, is fortified for the greater part of its way by a massive wall, lest the sea change its mind again. Inside the sea-wall, the protected lands keep an illusory look of marine emptiness – widening, west of Hythe, into the spaces of Romney Marsh, known for its sheep, its dykes, its sunsets and its solitary churches. On a clear day, the whole of this area meets the eye: there are no secrets.

Not so uphill, inland. The plateau, exposed to gales on its Channel front, has a clement hinterland, undulating and wooded. It is cleft by valleys, down which streams make their way to the sea; and there are also hollows, creases and dips, which, sunk between open-airy pastures and cornfields, are not to be guessed at till you stumble upon them: then, they are enticing, breathless and lush, with their wandering dogpaths and choked thickets. Into a part of such a region, rather to the east, my Saturday morning walk took me – looking for a road I had known sixty years ago. There seemed no reason why it should no longer be there.

It was. Slanting upward from Seabrook, it zig-zags across the face of a steep slope, finally to emerge from a tunnel of greenery, and terminate, at a high-up point where once stood Hythe's railway station. The ascent is continuous, but gentle.

On your left, as you mount from Seabrook, is the sea – even farther below, out there beyond the Military Canal. Also below you, but mostly tree-hidden, runs the trafficky main thoroughfare, A 259. On your right, you are accompanied by the derelict cutting of what was a single-track railway line – first above you, then on the same level, then, as the road rises, risen above. Where it used to deepen, the cutting has silted up and become a jungle, overhung by vertical woods, invaded by saplings. Here and there, buttresses of South Eastern & Chatham brickwork, darkened by moss and time, remind you that this primitive-looking landscape is in origin structural and was man-made. The road shows signs of being of the same epoch as the vanished railway, and of surviving only because *it* was impossible to remove. Each side, it is encroached upon by its grassy verges; remnants of some attempt to 'surface' it adhere, in macerated tar-dark patches, to what elsewhere is gutted as though by tropical torrents, fins of rock bespeaking unthinkable cruelty to motor-cars. Accordingly, contrary to my fears, there has been not more than half-hearted residential development. Late-coming villas and bungalows peter out still not far from Seabrook; on the Channel side, for a little way farther up, costlier homes in the Spanish manner (patios, ironwork) cliffhang on slithery pine-clad slopes, but there are but few of them. Not a soul to be seen, or as much as heard; the road that morning was as unfrequented as when I frequented it first. Nothing of its character was gone. The May Saturday morning was transiently, slightly hysterically sunny, with a chill undertone.

When there had been nothing for some time, I came to – or was come upon, as one might be by an apparition – a garden created by someone in the fertile, leaf-mouldy bed of the cutting. No house was near it, only a shack in which to camp for a night. This less was a garden than a flowering glade, glimmering and sensuous. Young 'weeping' birches trailed veils of foliage golden rather than green;

white rhododendrons were in bloom like white lamps in daylight; magnolias dropped upon their chalice buds. . . . Having ascended past this, the road made later, as ever, a sharp turn in order to cross a bridge.

The bridge's command of the line it was built to span enabled us – once, long ago, as children – to watch the train coming romping out of the distance, loudened by the acoustics of the gulley. . . . What had been the perspective was now blocked by the falling across it of a huge tree, whose deadness accentuated the hush. Weeds sprouting between its torn-up roots, brambles matting its shattered branches, the tree stayed wedged there; nobody's business. Among my pictures of here was a corpse of another kind: a sheep, come upon by me and another girl. Its body hideously torn open, bowels gushing forth, blood rusting its clotted wool, flies walking about on its open eyes, it lay as though nested in the deep, springy grass edging the road. We skirted it, sliding glances at it but saying nothing. I imagine that floundering downward, as sheep do, through the trees from a grazing patch on the skyline – there *were* sheep up there – into the trap of the cutting, it had been hit by a train, then been dragged by somebody up the embankment and cast away. The day after, in silent, dreadful accord, we went back to look: it was still there – but the next gone, as though it had walked away. But that was far from the last of it. 'I know where there's a wood with a dead sheep in it,' Sheikie Beaker announces in *The Little Girls*, adding, 'Some boys showed me.' No boys showed us. No wood hid our sheep, it lay at the roadside. Also, Sheikie's sheep – though, from what she hints, some way into decomposition – was not mutilated; otherwise she'd have said so. Who, though, *was* my fellow-conspirator in that entire silence? (We never reported the sheep, being ashamed.) All my companions of that year are as clear as day to me, or at least as yesterday; her only I cannot identify, either by face or name. She is blotted out.

*

There was, or we held there to be, only one train. Indefatigably (if that were so) in motion, it shuttled to-fro over the short track between Sandling Junction and the terminal, Sandgate, its purpose being in some part military, for on top of the bluff over Sandgate station (which was in Seabrook) is Shorncliffe Camp. A poor day when soldiers were not aboard! Soon after passing under the bridge, on its way to Sandling, the train underwent a personality-transformation: woods began, giving it, as it tailed away into them to at last vanish, the flickering secretiveness of a reptile. . . . The road, once over the bridge, said goodbye to the railway and struck off on a course of its own.

Nothing was banal round here. Inland, the steep overhanging scenery took on the look of a painted backdrop: one had the sensation of gazing up not so much at trees, rocks and bastions of evergreen as at depictions of them. Yet with this went a suggestion of Alpine danger. Here or there, creeper-dimmed gabled houses sat, as it were perilously, on brackets; while above tree-level was that bald skyline, on which (as said) were isolated some few sheep. And what was *behind* this canvas? – the rest of England.

For all that, it was the foreground I stood upon that possessed me. Underfoot, it lost nothing by being *terra firma*: actual and tangible, it remained magic. Able to be rambled about on, in, into, and, one might have thought, penetrated to the depths of their being, these scanty backwoods, road, bridge, cutting, eluded familiarity, keeping about them the magnetism of things, or scenes, on some other, aloof planet. . . . The road over the dropping-away sea smelled of sunshine and warmed lichen on rocks. Flowers erratically scattered their way along it: never was there a plethora of anything – a tuft or two of yellow flowering broom, and in turfy ditches scarlet-tipped lady's-fingers, rare harebells, and, later, the mauver blue of wild scabious. Vetches wove themselves into the longer grass.

I knew the place for less than a year, never in autumn: by the middle of that one summer we had gone. And seldom did I make my way up there by myself. Nobody stopped me; no danger attached in those days, or was thought to, to the solitary, unrestricted movement of little girls. But, it seems, I safeguarded myself against any onset of what could possibly disturbingly be poetic by being perpetually (and, I must say, enjoyably) in company – that of boon companions. So the road came to be fraught with rowdy dramas of the kind children can and do manufacture and would rather die than exist without; throughout which I registered what I loved with such pangs of love (that is to say, registered what was round me) only out of the corner of an eye, only with an unwilling fraction of my being. This was the beginning of a career of withstood emotion. Sensation, I have never fought shy of or done anything to restrain.

*

My mother and I, that year, were living at Seabrook, that I might share a governess with the little Salmons, daughters of the rector of Old Cheriton. This still being in the nature of an experiment, our existence was tentative, temporary, the villa we occupied having been taken furnished – our own belongings, lately brought over from Ireland, remained behind at Lyminge, in another villa we had called Erin Cottage. Seabrook, an early example of ribbon-development, consisted, and still does, mainly of smallish early-Edwardian dwellings strung out along the Hythe–Folkestone road. There had been strategic reasons for each of our many moves, in the last few years, to and fro in the triangle formed by Hythe, Folkestone and Lyminge. Seabrook stood for one of the intermissions from Lindum, my Folkestone day-school, where – while thinking as highly of the school as ever – my mother feared lest I suffer from overwork. That was the least of my troubles, for I was lazy, but such were her periodic dreads. 'Overwork' had officially been the cause of my father's breakdown. My mother's family, the Colleys, had had misgivings as to her marriage to Henry Bowen, on the ground that the Bowens of Bowen's Court, County Cork, were rumoured to have an uncertain mental heredity. My paternal grandfather, Robert, had died in the throes of a violent mania brought on by a continuous quarrel with his heir (Henry); and there had been other cases of instability, due, it was understood, to first-cousin marriages back through the Bowen pedigree. To the Colleys, undeviatingly sane, ensconced, since their arrival in Ireland, in that central and civilized part of it known as The Pale, there could have seemed to be something fey and outlandish about those unpopulated stretches of County Cork with their unforgotten battlefields and abounding ruins. Also, Bowen's Court, architecturally solid enough, was the residence or at least the abiding headquarters of my father's large brood of brothers and sisters, who, whether or not Henry brought home a bride, would continue to see the mansion in that light: that is, they perceived no reason for moving out. Nor had my father very much money, the enraged Robert having left all that he possibly could away from him. The house and lands could not, to the chagrin of Robert, be diverted from Henry, being entailed.

However, this being clearly a case of love, optimism prevailed; the marriage went through. I, born nine years later, was the one child of it. The young couple shelved the Bowen's Court problem by setting up house in Herbert Place, Dublin, he being a member of the Dublin Bar. All was happiness till the blow fell – his 'breakdown', which was in fact the beginning of an agonizing mental illness. Repressed forebodings now came again to the surface. Certified, by his own wish, he was sent for treatment to a mental hospital outside Dublin; my mother and I were ordered away by the doctors. Better for us to be across the sea, for even the idea of our nearness agitated him. She was told, also, that in going away, taking me with her, she was doing not only the best for him but the best for me. So we took off for England when I was seven. A heartbreaking decision for her to make: she must have been torn by the rights and wrongs of it. She showed me no signs, however, of what she was going through, and I asked no questions. Here we were, adventurers in this other country. Of her constant, underlying, watchful anxiety with regard to me, as my father's child, I have only had knowledge afterwards. Her advice, 'You must never tire your brain,' the concern when I had a fever and ran a temperature, together with the periodic removings of me from Lindum, seemed to me little more than a gentle fad, which occasionally had pleasing outcomes – such as the extension of summer holidays. She would not have me taught to read till I was seven (so that I should not burn out my eyes, she said) and even after that used to read aloud to me, a delight so great that it has spoiled me for being 'alone with a book'. She besought me not to get freckles on my hands – 'All Bowens get freckles on their hands.' . . . I in no way connected anything with my father's plight.

Otherwise she was altogether without fussiness. I was let run wild, to an extent at which other mothers lifted their eyebrows – falling off horses, flopping about in the sea (made dangerous for non-swimming children along these beaches, by shelving shingle), plunging dementedly round and round till I fell smack down on the roller-skating rink, or death-diving on the precipitous Folkestone switchback railway, when money was to be found. I was a tough child, strong as a horse – or colt. I had come out of the tensions and mystery of my father's illness, the apprehensive silences or chaotic shoutings (while he was still there with us in the Dublin house) with nothing more disastrous than a stammer. Not 'nervous', I was demonstrative and excitable: an extrovert.

Arriving in England, with our way to make and our destiny uncertain, my mother and I were not so alone as might be supposed. A grapevine of powerful Anglo-Irish relatives instantly took us into their keeping, passing us from hand to hand. We settled in south-east Kent (after a round of exploratory visits elsewhere) under the aegis of Cousin Isabel Chenevix Trench, widowed daughter-in-law of the late Archbishop of Dublin, who lived with her striking-looking growing-up family in Radnor Park, Folkestone, and Cousin Lilla Chichester, a childless dowager who commanded Sandgate from an ilex-dark eminence. (Enfield, her Victorian-Italianate home, reappears in one of my stories, 'The Inherited Clock'.) Without those two, our position – in those days, when everything was rather more right-and-tight – might have been ambiguous: it was not the thing for a woman other than a widow to be without a husband, and my mother was suspiciously lovely-looking, in addition to being accompanied by me. I learned not how the land lay but how it might have from a chance conversation, when I was about nine. 'What is "blackmail"?' I asked her, out of the blue. We were wandering about Hythe, near the canal. She thought, then said: 'That would be, if somebody came to me and threatened to spread horrible stories about us unless I gave them money.' 'Oh,' I said, knowing how little money we had. 'But,' she went on, not only with her usual serenity but with an air of distinct triumph over the putative situation, 'that would not matter, because I should simply go to Cousin Isabel and Cousin Lilla, and they would tell everybody that those were lies.' This impressed me, not in terms of respectability (which I don't imagine I'd ever heard of) but as proof of the dominance of my more or less synonymous race and family: the Anglo-Irish – with their manner of instantly striking root into the interstices of any society in which they happened to find themselves, and in their own way proceeding to rule the roost. One could perpetually be vouched for.

Which benefactress put us in touch with the Salmons, or initiated the plan of sharing the governess, I am not certain. We had had, already, one unofficial view of the Salmons when, out of a blend of spiritual and geographical curiosity, we had strayed from Hythe and attended mid-morning church at St Martin's, Old Cheriton. It being a summery summer, a June Sunday, the two girls were wearing white muslin frocks, together with large floppy leghorn hats from beneath which fell cataracts of well-brushed hair, the elder's honey-yellow, the younger's dark. Story-book children. One was one size larger, one one size smaller, than I. Coming out, when the service was over, they smiled at us, newcomers to their father's flock – but we did not at that time expect to know them. Of their mother nothing was to be seen but a handsome back: she was animatedly talking to some parishioners. Mr Salmon, from whom we had had an invigorating sermon, had features of an initial harshness lit up by originality and engaging charm: it was by resembling him that his little girls were redeemed from more ordinary childish prettiness. . . . My mother would have been as carried away as I was, had she not been in trouble with her conscience: my father, whose ethics continued to rule us, disapproved infidelity to one's parish church – we'd had no right to desert from St Leonard's, Hythe. This was an escapade we must not repeat. The Salmons bade fair to remain an attractive memory.

Fate spun her wheel, and things turned out otherwise. Now, at a quarter-to-nine every weekday morning, I and the governess, Miss Clark, met at a corner in Seabrook, outside the Fountain Hotel – she coming from Sandgate, where her father was senior curate. She was an able young woman, trim in outline. In spite of a touch of the Gallic about her style – quick-moving, bright, rather prominent dark eyes, an alternately ruby and amethyst velvet ribbon threaded between the frizzy puffs of her hair – Miss Clark transpired to be more English than anyone I had yet met. Her manner was incisive. She could, I imagine, have gone far in any career – and perhaps did, subsequently? I disliked her only when she was sarcastic, or when she picked on me about my stammer, which in her view was due largely to faults of character: over-impatience, self-importance. 'You try and get too much out at the same time,' she would point out. 'Concentrate on *one* thing, draw a deep breath, then say it *slowly*.' Together we went under the railway bridge (a lofty arch supporting the single line) and then on up Horn Street which, said to be prehistoric, shared the trough of a valley with the Seabrook brook, on its way to the sea. One ended by taking a short-cut up a steep field made marshy by many springs: when those overflowed then froze, as in the course of that winter they once or twice did, one had the extra sensation of ascending a glacier.

At the top stood the atmospheric rectory.

Contrary to my story-book notion of English parsonages, this one did not ramble and was not rose-clad. In shape it was like a domino on end. Behind (where was the hall-door) it looked into a wood in which was a rookery; but on *this* side three rows of sky-reflecting windows beamed on one as one squelched up the short-cut. Benevolently, the place looked haunted. In this house I remained with the Salmons throughout the day, Miss Clark dropping me back in Seabrook towards evening.

I felt a familiarity with the place from the first moment, and still do, and always shall – though it is no more. Between then and now it went through varying fortunes, not always clerical: it became, for instance, the residence, at one time, of one of the baroque relatives of my friend Tony Butts. Ultimately left empty, camped in now and then by a passing tramp, it caught fire and was burned to the ground. The wood behind it was felled. Yet, gone, it is not as though it had never been. The front rooms had in their nature – for all their ample windows and wide outlook – an inherent duskiness, comfortable and congenial; those at the back were intriguingly gloomy at any hour. At the back was situated 'the parish room', with its resonant bare floor, hard chairs, upright piano. Two staircases, many-doored landings, blind closets, cavernous cellars, attics and, above all, weirdly misleading echoes made this house ideal for hide-and-seek – best of all in the dark, in the short days: winter. Rushing about was the nearest to violence we ever came.

Whether or not for that reason, I hit it off better with the rectory than I did with its tantalising inhabitants. I reacted, in some obscure way, against unfamiliarly liberal surroundings. This was my first view, from close up, of genuinely idyllic family life – and it was too much for me. Veronica and Maisie never fought. There seemed no way of driving a wedge between them. My Fiennes first cousins (Aunt Gertrude's children), to whom I was habituated, fought each other like demons, and I took part. (I learned, later, that owing to me the fighting grew worse.) No sooner was I happily into harbour with the Salmons than I started behaving like a yahoo: I sulked – lagging behind on walks, feigning loss of appetite at midday dinner. I bragged and exaggerated. Miss Clark considered me a typical only child, and said so. Mrs Salmon, an acute, maternal, educated and resourceful gentlewoman, showed more patience: she observed me, thoughtful but with a knowledgeable twinkle in the eye. Occasionally she joined us in the schoolroom, augmenting or even taking over that day's lessons, and stimulating and fruitful those sessions were. *I* enjoyed them. I was at my best at lessons at that age – woolgatherings and abeyances came later. Between-times, we constructed a wonderful toy theatre, and staged a performance of *A Midsummer Night's Dream* (or, at least, of the Titania parts) with a cast of penny dolls glamorized by gauze. Or we sing-songed around the parish piano. Or Mrs Salmon read aloud *The Talisman*. I could not have had less to complain of, one way and another: nothing was lacking – yet it was those very diversions which caught me out. A rift in the lute, a flaw in the crystal. . . . How trying *did* they find me? Probably they never allowed themselves to know. Mr Salmon, whom I continued to idolize, sometimes swivelled upon me, from under jutting black eyebrows, a look of sardonic appreciation – satanic behaviour being, I suppose, in his line of country.

Possibly I was jealous of the whole family?

The sisters, with their animated, differentiated faces inside those contrasting cascades of hair (mine never grew longer than my shoulders), leaning together to look at the same book, strolling with arms interlaced, tying each other's sashes to go to parties (Veronica's sash sky-blue, Maisie's coral-pink). . . . While exasperating, they continued to charm me. I was told they felt an affection for me: *now* I see that, miraculously, they somehow did. But the fact was, sensibly or insensibly, I was missing Lindum, that larger, cruder theatre of action. There, we girls did not live actually the lives of gladiators, but by contrast with Old Cheriton we could seem to. Though a small school, it was a roomy world. One was not impinged upon. With notice-boards, hockey sticks, creaky desks, smelly inkpots, white mice stowed away in the cloakroom, catchwords, crazes and clatter, I was in my element: I was at that level. I was not fit, yet, to intake sweetness and light; the Old Cheriton foretaste came too early. This being either perceived by Mrs Salmon and indicated to my mother, or perceived by my mother and indicated to Mrs Salmon – or, possible, dawning on both of them simultaneously? – lessons at the rectory terminated, in an atmosphere of unclouded amicability. I returned to Lindum; and my mother, there no longer being reason to live at Seabrook, began to meditate a return to Hythe, which would involve disengaging the furniture from Lyminge.

*

My belligerence, to a degree given an outlet, to a degree neutralised by school life, was inborn, a derivative of race. Irish and Anglo-Irish have it in common. It stood out, possibly, more strongly in the placidity of England. At times a tiresome trait, it is not a detestable one, being poles apart from aggressiveness – which as we know is engendered by some grudge, spite or bias against the rest of the world. Your belligerent person has no chip on his shoulder, and tends to sail through life in excellent spirits. He likes fighting. He distinguishes between a fight and a quarrel, on these grounds: a fight, soon over, purifies the air and leaves no one the worse (unless they are dead), whereas a quarrel, unlikely to be ever wholly resolved, not only fouls the surrounding air but may set up a festering trail of lifelong bitterness. That distinction has always been clear to me. I would go miles out of my way to avoid a quarrel.

Sir Jonah Barrington, to whose *Personal Sketches of His Own Times* I owe as all-round an account as I hope to find of the manners, tenets and general outlook on life of my ancestors, his compatriots and contemporaries, witnessed the regrettable decline of duelling in Ireland – where, as a manly practice, it had survived its all but extinction across the water. Cease to be lawful it might: a blind eye was turned to it. It was in the tradition, generic to that society which gave Sir Jonah and my relatives birth: the Ascendancy, with its passion for virtuosity of all kinds, not least sword-play or mastery with a pistol. In the best days, apparently, almost everyone fought:

Earl Clare, Lord Chancellor of Ireland, fought the Master of the Rolls, the Right Honourable John Philpot Curran, with twelve-inch pistols. The Earl of Clonmel, Chief Justice of the King's Bench, fought Lord Tyrawly, about his wife, and the Earl of Landaff, about his sister; and others, with sword or pistol, on miscellaneous subjects. The Judge of the County of Dublin, Egan, fought the Master of the Rolls, Roger Barrett, and three others; one with swords. The Chancellor of the Exchequer, the Right Honourable Isaac Corry, fought the Right Honourable Henry Grattan, a privy counsellor, and the chancellor was hit. He also exchanged shots or thrusts with *two* other gentlemen. A baron of the exchequer, Baron Medge, fought his brother-in-law and two others – a hit. . . . The Judge of Prerogative Court, Doctor Duigenan, fought *one* barrister and frightened *another* on the ground. The latter was a very curious case. . . . The Provost of the University of Dublin, the Right Honourable Hely Hutchinson, fought Mr Doyle, Master in Chancery: they went to the plains of Minden to fight. . . . The Right Honourable George Ogle, the Orange Chieftain, fought Barny Coyle, a whisky distiller, because he was a *papist*. They fired eight shots wihout stop or stay, and no hit occurred: but Mr Ogle's second broke his own arm by tumbling into a potato-trench. . . .

Sir Jonah abridges, he says, 'this dignified list', which, even so, takes up two of his pages: and I have further abridged it – his point is made. His attitude is, if nostalgic, reflective also: 'It is nearly incredible what a singular passion the Irish gentlemen (though in general excellent-tempered fellows) had for fighting each other and immediately becoming friends again.' Actually (we have it on his authority) a duel frequently served to cement a friendship. And why not? Did not the prestige date back to the chivalric tradition, to knightly jousting? – not really more honourable, and (should you not care for that sort of thing) just as futile? Semi-sacredness came to attach to family weapons: 'Each family had its case of hereditary pistols, which descended as an heirloom.' The Barringtons' were 'included in the armoury of our ancient castle of Ballynakill in the reign of Elizabeth (the stocks, locks and hair-triggers were, however, modern). . . . One of them was named "*sweet lips*" the other "*the darling*".' (One must not allow Sir Jonah to grate on one.) Sheridan, loosing Sir Lucius O'Trigger, in *The Rivals*, on to the modish – but in the Irish baronet's view, half-hearted – society of Bath, adds credibility to the Barrington jottings. Heiress-hunting (another national sport) does not occupy all Sir Lucius's time: he is master-minding Bob Acres into a duel. He is, however, riled by technical hitches – 'I don't know what's the reason,' he cries aloud, 'but in England, if a thing of this kind gets wind, people make such a pother that a gentleman can never fight in peace and quietness.'

Horsemanship apart, the Anglo-Irish, together with what was left of the indigenous autocrats, would subsequently have been in a poor way were it not for writing. To that we have taken like ducks to water. Accommodating ourselves to a tamer day, we interchanged sword-play for word-play. Repartee, with its thrusts, opened alternative possibilities of mastery. Given rein to, creative imagination ran to the tensed-up, to extreme situations, to confrontations. Bravado characterizes much Irish, all Anglo-Irish writing: gloriously it is sublimated by Yeats. Nationally, we have an undertow to the showy. It follows that primarily we have produced dramatists, the novel being too life-like, humdrum, to do us justice. We do not do badly with the short story, 'that, in a spleen, unfolds both heaven and earth' – or should. There is this about us: to most of the rest of the world we are semi-strangers, for whom existence has something of the trance-like quality of a spectacle. As beings, we are at once brilliant and limited; our unbeatables, up to now, accordingly, have been those who best profited by that: Goldsmith, Sheridan, Wilde, Shaw, Beckett. Art is for us inseparable from artifice: of that, the theatre is the home.

Possibly, it was England made me a novelist. At an early though conscious age, I was transplanted. I arrived, young, into a different mythology – in fact, into one totally alien to that of my forefathers, none of whom had resided anywhere but in Ireland for some centuries, and some of whom may never have been in England at all: the Bowens were Welsh. From now on there was to be (as for any immigrant) a cleft between my heredity and my environment – the former remaining, in my case, the more powerful. Submerged, the mythology of this 'other' land could be felt at work in the ways, manners and views of its people, round me: those, because I disliked being at a disadvantage, it became necessary to probe. It cannot be said that a child of seven was analytic; more, with a blend of characteristic guile and uncharacteristic patience I took note – which, though I had at that time no thought of my future art, is, after all, one of the main activities of the novelist. At the outset, the denizens of England and their goings-on inspired me with what a hymn epitomises as 'scornful wonder' – protective mechanism? – but I was not a disagreeable child, so any initial hostility wore off.

Lacking that stimulus, my attention wandered: society not being by nature interesting, or for long interesting, to the very young, I transferred my gaze from it to its geographical setting. Thereafter, England affected me more in a scenic way than in any other – and still does. It was the lie of the land, with that cool, clear light falling upon it, which was extraordinary.

Well for me, that we pitched our camp where we did! Fortunate, I mean, that 'England' was Kent, and, above all, Kent's dramatizable coastline. Suppose, for instance, some Cousin Lilla or Cousin Isabel had siren-sung us into the Midlands, with their soporific monotony? Or, for that matter, into the West Country, with its rainy semi-resemblances to Ireland? As it was, where we *were* stood out in absolute contrast to where we came from. Gone was the changing blue of mountains: instead, bleached blond in summer, the bald downs showed exciting great gashes of white chalk. Everything, including the geological formation, struck me as having been recently put together. Trees were smaller in size, having not yet, one could imagine, had time for growth. 'Thunderbolts' – meteorites? – to be collected along the slippery dogpaths of the Warren might have rained down from the heavens the night before. And this *newness* of England, manifest in the brightness, occasionally the crudity, of its colouring, had about it something of the precarious. *Would* it last? The edifices lining the tilted streets or gummed at differing levels above the Channel seemed engaged in just not sliding about. How much *would* this brittle fabric stand up to? My thoughts dallied with landslides, subsidences and tidal waves.

England's appearance of youth was, however, gainsaid by evidences of history. Those were all over the place. In Ireland, history – because, I suppose, of its melancholy, uneasy trend – had on the whole tended to be played down; one knew *of* it, but spoke of it little. Here, it burst from under the contemporary surface at every point, arousing enthusiasm. A success story – or, in these days one might say, a gigantic musical. Everyone figured, including the Ancient Romans. Nor had any of the stage-sets for the performance – or, indeed, any of those rigged up for performances which had not, after all, taken place, such as a Napoleonic invasion – been cleared away: east of me Dover Castle, shored up on tier-upon-tier of fortification, flew its triumphant flag; west of me, martello towers diminished into the distance, more than one of them pounded down into massive jumbles of broken masonry, not, after all, by enemy cannon-fire but by the sea, which had also breached the sea-wall, for the elements had also taken a hand. Our Military Canal was not the less seductive for boating-picnics for having as yet served no military purpose. Foundations of circumspect-looking buildings were (I heard) riddled with secret passages. The Cinque Ports' navy had torn up and down the Channel harassing any marauding French; smugglers had cat-and-moused with revenue men over the marshes, into the woods. To crown all, there had been terrific marine pageantry, spectacular arrivals and departures, monarchs, brides, envoys and so on – a constant, glittering, affable come-and-go between here and France. Not a dull moment.

'History' inebriated me, and no wonder. Moreover, *here* was where it belonged: Kent-England had a proprietary hold on it. So it was this landscape, with everything it was eloquent of and compre-hended, which won me (the newcomer to it) over – filling me, at the same time, with envy and the wish to partake. Not long after my eighth birthday, celebrated at Folkestone, I entered upon a long, voluptuous phase in which I saw life as a non-stop historical novel, disguised only thinly (in my day) by modern dress. I saw myself, even, in an historic light, which gave at once a momentousness and a premonition of their possible consequences to all my doings. And the same attached to anyone who attracted me. When or how I divested myself of this daydream, I do not remember – did I entirely do so ever? Becoming a writer knocked a good deal of nonsense out of my system. But always there is a residuum. (I detect in my betters, the giants of my profession, a magnificent, self-exonerating silliness: would or could anybody become a novelist who was not internally silly in *some* way?) As a novelist, I cannot occupy myself with 'characters', or at any rate central ones, who lack panache, in one or another sense, who would be incapable of a major action or a major passion, or who have not at least a touch of the ambiguity, the ultimate unaccountability, the enlarging mistiness of personages 'in history'. History, as more austerely I now know it, is not romantic. But I am.

*

Another lure of this region's was architectural. When we got here, Edwardian villa-building, superimposed on the also pretty but stodgier late-Victorian, had for some years been at its most volatile and prolific. Dotted over hills in sight of the sea and in valleys out of it, villas came in all shapes – a phantasmagoric variety – and sizes. And not only were there villas but one could live in them – in Ireland one could not: habit, fatalism or piety bound my people either to inherited homes or homes they had inherited ideas about, and almost unfailingly those were Georgian, box-square in the country, strait-and-narrow, with high front-door steps, in town. Onward from my birth (which took place in an intended back drawing-room at 15 Herbert Place), there had been an all but unbroken procession of similar rooms. Repetitive eighteenth-century interiors with their rational proportions and faultless mouldings, evenly daylit, without shadow, curiousness or cranny, not only said nothing to my imagina-tion; they, if they did anything, repelled it. In so far as I found them anything I found them 'sad', associating them perhaps with my father's illness. Outdoors, the uniformity of façades in Dublin (along streets terminated only by the horizon), and the inevitable alikeness of one landowner's mansion to another throughout the South, bespoke to me nothing but uninventiveness. I was surfeited with the classical when we sailed for England – where release, to the point of delirium, awaited me. I found myself in a paradise of white balconies, ornate porches, verandahs festooned with Dorothy Perkins roses, bow windows protuberant as balloons, dream-childish attic bedrooms with tentlike ceilings, sublimated ivory-fretwork inglenooks inset with jujubes of tinted glass, built-in overmantels with flight upon flight of brackets round oval mirrors, oxidized bronze door-handles with floral motifs, archways demurely to be curtained across, being through-ways to more utilitarian or less mentionable parts of the dwelling, and so on. . . .

These were now to be mine. The prospect was heady. Villas we actually came to occupy were few (though, as already said, we did not do badly) in comparison with the hosts we viewed. This we mainly did, as my mother put it, 'on chance'. Any empty premises that we liked the look of we entered, whether at that time requiring or contemplating a change of residence or not. Part of the fun of the game was to obtain the key from the house agent without the house agent; occasionally our entrances were unauthorized – I became as adept as a Fagin pupil at snaking in through some forgotten little back window, then finding a door to unbolt to admit her. The deserted rooms, downstairs in summer often embowered in shadows of the syringa embowering the bewildered gardens, of which the lawns had grown high in hay, smelled intoxicatingly of wallpaper, sunshine, mustiness. With the first echo of our steps on the stripped floors, or of our voices excitedly hushed by these new acoustics, another dream-future sprang into being. We took over wherever we were, at the first glance. Yes, what a supposititious existence ours came to be, in these one-after-another fantasy buildings, pavilions of love. In the last of the villas in which it came about that we did actually live, she died.

Wobbly rustic steps led, often, up to a sagging terrace or down to a dried-out pool. Who *had* been the inhabitants, so mysteriously gone? I cannot wonder villas gained such a hold on me, waiting only a few years more to become the dominants of the stories I started to write. It being necessary there should be people to put in them, I summoned up 'people': men, women, children. Much of my 'creation' of character has, rather, been evocation, borne out by guesswork. Guesses have hit the mark, by a miracle.

How, though (at the time I am speaking of), did I reconcile my craze for – my infatuation with – villas, unhistorical gimcrack little bubbles of illusion, with my history-fed passion for the mighty, immortal and grandiose? I cannot say. The two ran concurrently.

And, of course, villas were part of the exoticism of Kent-England. They stood for an outing, a total contrast. Their frivolity chimed in with my fundamentally frivolous, semi-sceptical attitude to this 'other' land. If you began in Ireland, Ireland remains the norm: like it or not. Looking through *Seven Winters*, which is about my earlier, Dublin childhood, I find I have said this: 'I never looked up Sackville Street without pleasure, for I was told it was the widest street in the world. Just as Phoenix Park, grey-green distance beyond the Zoo, was the largest park in the world. These superlatives pleased me only too much: my earliest pride of race was attached to them. And my most endemic pride in my own country was, for some years, founded on a mistake: my failing to have a nice ear for vowel sounds, and the Anglo-Irish slurred, hurried way of speaking, made me take the words "Ireland" and "island" to be synonymous. Thus, all other countries quite surrounded by water took (it appeared) their generic name from ours. It seemed fine to live in a country that was a prototype. England, for instance, was "an ireland" (or, a sub-Ireland) – an imitation. Then I learned that England was not even "an ireland", having failed to detach herself from the flanks of Scotland and Wales. Vaguely, as a Unionist child, I conceived that our politeness to England must be a form of pity.

'In the same sense, I took Dublin to be the model of cities, of which there were imitations scattered over the world.'

I had yet to see London, when first we settled in Kent. I had once or twice crossed it, for that was necessary, but there had not been anything particularly metropolitan about our cab drives, usually after dark and in a darkness which was generally foggy, from one terminal railway station to another. In transit, we had called in on

Cousin Bella Guise, my mother's godmother, living in Cliveden Place: but as Cousin Bella came from County Wexford and had brought Wexford belongings and their ambience with her, hers hardly was to be called a London interior. How successful an imitation of Dublin London was, I had not, therefore, so far been able to judge. Then, what about Folkestone? True, not a city but really a quite large town, my first English one. Folkestone, self-christened 'Queen of the South', had hardly yet overdrawn on what had been a highly fashionable reputation. Henry James characters, for instance, had stayed there (though that I was not to know). Admittedly, Folkestone was *the seaside* – formerly associated by me with Anglesea lodging-houses, autumn changes-of-air. In the course of acclimatising to Folkestone, I looked round at it from the 'imitation' angle. The place had wide, lengthy, raying-out avenues, tree-planted. The Leas – laid out as a high-up, sea-viewing promenade, up and down which sailed scarlet or pink silk parasols, tilted by owners glancing to see if one *could* see France – were handsome. Inland from the Leas was a hive of flourishing schools, of which mine was one. The shops were showy, and hummed with custom. Hotels were many, and some were gorgeous. Buildings either were of rubicund brick, with yellow-stone trimmings, or stucco, white, cream, pearl or dove-grey. Everywhere were hanging baskets of pink geraniums. Everything went well. In fact, I adapted to Folkestone (only to learn, alas, that my mother detested it). We removed to Hythe. I perceived in Folkestone an absolute, insulating self-contentment. Nothing other than Folkestone did it aspire to. An English 'resort' versus the Irish Capital. The blotting-out of all my visual past was so total as to become giddying. What had to be bitten on was that two entities so opposed, so irreconcilable in climate, character and intention, as Folkestone and Dublin should exist simultaneously, and be operative, in the same lifetime, particularly my own.

II

PLACES

Few people questioning me about my novels, or my short stories, show curiosity as to the places in them. Thesis-writers, interviewers or individuals I encounter at parties all, but all, stick to the same track, which by-passes locality. On the subject of my symbology, if any, or psychology (whether my own or my characters'), I have occasionally been run ragged; but as to the *where* of my stories, its importance in them and for me, and the reasons for that, a negative apathy persists.

Why? Am I not manifestly a writer for whom places loom large? As a reader, it is to the place-element that I react most strongly: for me, what gives fiction verisimilitude is its topography. No story gains absolute hold on me (which is to say, gains the required hold) if its background – the ambience of its happenings – be indefinite, abstract or generalised. Characters operating *in vacuo* are for me bodiless. Were I to meet a writer, living or dead, whose work had so percolated into my own experience as to become part of it, his places would be what I should first want to discuss. How many – I should desire to ask him – were 'actual', how many composed of fragmented memories (some dating so far back as to be untraceable) organized into shape? How many (were such a thing possible) were '*imagined*' purely? How many structural alterations in a house, town or landscape otherwise 'actual' had to be made, to meet some unforeseen exigency of the story's? And how often? Exactly where are, or were, the originals (partial or in entirety) of places in this writer's narratives to be found?

To me, questions of this kind are seldom put.

One reason may be I am not a 'regional' writer in the accredited sense. Novelists being so various and so many, it is necessary to assemble them under headings, and under the 'regional' heading I am not placed: I do not qualify. The Bowen terrain cannot be demarcated on any existing map; it is unspecific. Ireland and England, between them, contain my stories, with occasional outgoings into France or Italy: within the boundaries of those countries there is no particular locality I have staked a claim on or identified with. Given the size of the world, the scenes of my stories are scattered over only a small area: but they *are* scattered. Nothing (at least on the surface) connects them, or gives them generic character of the kind found to claim or merit consideration. Failing to throw a collective light on my art, my places tend to be thought of as its accessories, engaging enough to read of but not 'meaningful'. Wherefore, Bowen topography has so far, so far as I know, been untouched by research. Should anyone give it a thought after I am dead, that will be too late. To it, only I hold the key.

When I say I am not a 'regional' writer in the outright sense, do I mean that I am one in any other? Internally, yes. Since I started writing, I have been welding together an inner landscape, assembled anything but at random. But if not at random, under the influence of what? I suppose necessity, and what accompanies that. A writer needs to have a command, and to have recourse to, a recognisable world, geographically consistent and having for him or her a super-reality.

Lacking that, his or her art would be unconcrete, insulated and unconvincing – most fatal of all! – to the writer himself. For the 'regionalist' proper, such a world is to hand: his native territory, plus its pre-natal hold on him. Acceptance, for him, is in itself inspiration; what could have been subjugation becomes victory. But it is necessary for him to be gigantic, as were for instance Hardy, Mauriac, Faulkner – and with that, stoical. Apart from not being on, or anywhere within sight of, the scale of those three, I have not in me the makings of regionalism as forged by them. Imagination of my kind is most caught, most fired, most worked upon by the unfamiliar: I have thriven, accordingly, on the changes and chances, the dislocations and (as I have said) the contrasts which have made up so much of my life. That may be why 'my' world (my world as a writer) is something of a mosaic. *As* it is, it is something that assembled itself. Looking back at my work, I perceive that the scenes of my successive, various stories predetermined themselves. And not only that but they predetermined the stories to a greater extent than I may have known at the time.

A Quotation from 'Notes on Writing a Novel'

Nothing can happen nowhere. The locale of the happening always colours the happening, and often, to a degree, shapes it. Scene, scenes . . . give the happening the desired force. . . . Scene is only justified in the novel where it can be shown, or at least felt, to act upon action or character. In fact, where it has dramatic use.

Where it is not intended for dramatic use, scene is a sheer slower-down. Its staticness is a dead weight. It cannot make part of the plot's movement by being shown *in play*. (Thunderstorms, the sea, landscape flying past car or railway-carriage windows are not scene but happenings.)

The deadeningness of straight and prolonged 'description' is as apparent with regard to scene as it is with regard to character. Scene must be evoked. . . . Scene must, like the characters, not fail to materialise. In this it follows the same law – instantaneous for the novelist, gradual for the reader.

Though the 'Notes' were contributed by me to John Lehmann's distinguished *Orion II* so far back as 1945, they contain nothing that now, years later, I would want to unsay (though I don't, now, like their peremptory tone). There are one or two statements I should be glad to expand, together with others I ought to qualify. The staticness of scene *is* a dead weight. Yes, indeed it can be; but there are ways round this. For instance, one can exploit the staticness – underline it, dramatize it effectively. That I had already done in *The House in Paris* (1935). Here is Mme Fisher's sick-room as reacted to by the child Henrietta:

> Mme Fisher's bedroom, though it was over the salon, had two windows, not one. Jalousies were pulled to over the far window, so that no light fell across the head of the bed. A cone of sick-room incense on the bureau sent spirals up the daylight near the door; daylight fell cold white on the honeycomb quilt rolled back. Round the curtained bedhead, Pompeian red walls drank objects into their shadow: picture-frames, armies of bottles, boxes, an ornate clock showed without glinting, as though not quite painted out by some dark transparent wash. Henrietta had never been in a room so full and still. She stood by the door Miss Fisher had shut behind her, with her heart in her mouth. Her eyes turned despairingly to a bracket on which stood spiked shells with cameos on their lips. The airlessness had a strange dry pure physical smell.
>
> 'Here is Henrietta,' Miss Fisher said.
> 'Good morning, Henrietta,' said Mme Fisher.
> 'Good morning, Mme Fisher,' Henrietta replied. The hand she saw in the shadows did not stir on the sheet, so she stayed where she was on the parquet beside the door.

Staticness: the all-out of the dead weight. Yet this passage makes contradictory use of four vigorous anti-static verbs: 'sent spirals up', 'fell', 'drank', 'turned'. It brings into the picture three (anti-static) lately completed acts: jalousies pulled to, quilt rolled back, door shut behind Henrietta. Further, there is an evocation of action thwarted (or withheld energy): light (because of the jalousies) does *not* fall across the head of the bed; ornate clock, glassy bottles, etc., show but 'without glinting'; Mme Fisher's hand does *not* stir on the sheet – though it could have. The one thing in action here is the incense cone

consuming itself by its slow burning (and *it* is a sickness symbol). The
room, felt by the child as 'so full and still', is a case not of mere
immobility but of immobilization. In a terrible way, it is a *bois
dormant*. What has brought this about? Mme Fisher: on the bed in
the centre.

> Mme Fisher was not in herself a pretty old lady. Waxy skin
> strained over her temples, jaws and cheek-bones; grey hair fell
> in wisps round an unwomanly forehead; her nostrils were wide
> and looked in the dusk skullish; her mouth was graven round
> with ironic lines. Neither patience nor discontent but a passion-
> ate un-resignation was written across her features, tense with
> the expectation of more pain. She seemed to lie as she lay less in
> weakness than in unwilling credulity, as though the successive
> disasters that make an illness had convinced her slowly, by
> repetition. She lay, still only a little beyond surprise at this end to
> her, webbed down, frustrated, or, still more, like someone cast,
> still alive, as an effigy for their own tomb.

She is the hub of the scene.

Alternatively, one can break the staticness down by showing scene
in fluidity, in (apparent) motion. For that, the beholder must be in
motion himself, on foot or on or in a conveyance of whatever kind, at
whatever speed. The greater the speed, the more liquefying the
process. He may be airborne – which is least satisfactory, for altitude
flattens what is beneath. Better, he is traversing *terra firma*, by any of
the many means, or on shipboard, moving across or along water: in
both cases he then has the illusion of movement past him, or (should
a ship be approaching a coast or a car making towards a range of
mountains) towards him. He does not merely – as he would were he
at a standstill – *see* scene, he *watches* its continuous changes, which
act upon him compulsively like a non-stop narrative.

Here, for instance (again, from *The House in Paris*) is a ship, and
on it, amongst others, a young woman. The crossing from a Welsh
port has been overnight; just after dawn the ship turned in from the
open sea, and is now making its way inland up the Lee River towards
Cork city, where it will dock.

> While Karen sat at breakfast in the saloon, trees began to pass
> the portholes; soon she went back on deck. The sun brightened
> the vapoury white sky but never quite shone: both shores
> reflected its melting light. The ship, checking, balanced
> uncertainly up the narrowing river, trees on each side, as though

navigating an avenue, leaving a salt wake. Houses asleep with their eyes open watched the vibrating ship pass; against the woody background those red and white funnels must look like a dream. Seagulls, circling, settled on mown lawns. The wake made a dark streak in the glassy water; its ripples broke against garden walls. Every hill running down, each turn of the river, seemed to trap the ship more and cut off the open sea.

On the left shore, a steeple pricked up out of a knoll of trees, above a snuggle of Gothic villas; then there was the sad stare of what looked like an orphanage. A holy bell rang and a girl at a corner mounted her bicycle and rode out of sight. The river kept washing salt off the ship's prow. Then, to the right, the tree-dark hill of Tivoli began to go up, steep, with pallid stucco houses appearing to balance on the tops of trees. Palladian columns, gazebos, glass-houses, terraces showed on the background misted with spring green, at the top of shafts or on toppling brackets of rock, all stuck to the hill, all slipping past the ship.

Someone remarked, Bowen characters are almost perpetually in transit. Arguably: if you are to include transitions from room to room or floor to floor of the same house, or one to another portion of its surroundings. I agree, Bowen characters are in transit *consciously*. Sensationalists, they are able to re-experience what they do, or equally, what is done to them, every day. They tend to behold afresh and react accordingly. An arrival, even into another room, is an event to be registered in some way. When they extend their environment, strike outward, invade the unknown, travel, what goes on in them is magnified and enhanced: impacts are sharper, there is more objectivity. But then, is this not so with all persons, living or fictional? Simply, it may be, it is at such moments that men, women and children are by me most often portrayed.

I may, too, impart to some of my characters, unconsciously, an enthusiastic naïvety with regard to transport which in my own case time has not dimmed. Zestfully they take ship or board planes: few of them even are *blasés* about railways. Motor-cars magnetize them particularly. Bicycling, which is a theme-song in *A World of Love* and part of *The Little Girls*, began for me only when I was thirteen, after my mother's death. It had been the one activity she withheld me from, her professed reason being that child cyclists grew up with bandy legs – her inner one could have been the fate of Aubrey, one of my early confederates at Hythe, flung to his death in an accident one fine morning. . . . Aunt Laura, with whom I went to live at

Harpenden, was herself seldom off a bicycle, so was calmer: once she considered me competent, she procured for me a glittering brand-new Raleigh. 'Now *this* is yours,' she said. First riding the Raleigh, I dismounted, often, simply to stand and look at it. This, my first machine, had an intrinsic beauty. And it opened for me an era of all but flying, which roads emptily crossing the airy, gold-gorsy Common enhanced. Nothing since has equalled that birdlike freedom.

In a way, as a writer I may be at an advantage in being born when I was. Not born, that is, into the age of speed, I was there while it came into being round me: much that went on was new not only to me, but wholly new in itself, by its own right. About motor-cars and their offspring motor-bikes there continued, for longer than may be realized now, to be something mythical and phenomenal – even hostile? 'Flying machines' at the start were less ill-seen: few and freakish, they constituted a threat only to aeronauts who took off in them. Motor-cars, which spawned at a greater rate, looked at once Martian and caddish. Their colour spectrum and flashing fittings of brass were themselves offensive. The combustion engine, with its splutterings and roarings, was at once disagreeable and enigmatic. . . . The age of speed, thus exemplified, was not – at least by Folkestone and its surroundings, fair cross-section of *rentier* civilization – cordially welcomed in: recollect that it superimposed itself upon an existing age, a state of society, which *had*, already, all it consciously wanted. Thanks to the previous century's revolutionizing discovery, steam power, there by now was suave, trustworthy, comfortable locomotion, rapid enough: trains, steamers. And existence was further enhanced by a host of amenities: telephones, electric light, electric bells, lifts, gramophones, pianolas. There were occasional moving-picture shows. The twentieth century, therefore, dawned on a world which already had cause to regard itself as completely modern, and congratulate itself thereupon. Enough was enough. Anything further, one felt, might annoy God.

Propaganda against speed went out to children. One line of attack called it 'against nature'. Its intensifications, however, *we* were to discover, were good for art. As I say, speed is exciting to have grown up with. It alerts vision, making vision retentive with regard to what only may have been seen for a split second. By contrast, it accentuates the absoluteness of stillness. Permanence, where it occurs, and it does occur, stands out the more strongly in an otherwise ephemeral world. Permanence is an attribute of recalled places.

*

Schools – as I knew them – crystallized place-feelings.

Harpenden Hall, second of the three I went to, was the most comely. Built, I should think, in the late seventeenth century, low, long, graceful and solid, 'The Hall' stood a short way back from the bicycling Common, on to which its windows gazed calmly out. In front, a paved path led to it, across lawns. It looked like a picture in a romantic novel with a historic trend. (I did, in fact, and while I was still there, come on a black-and-white of it in a *Louis Wain Annual*, the great cat artist having resided in Harpenden during at least some of his years of fame.) Indoors, the panelling of the main rooms was a dimmed ivory, the steps of the dark polished staircase were shallow. Where there was not panelling there were Morris wallpapers. This did not look like a school.

But then, neither had Lindum done so, nor would Downe House. Never had I the misfortune to be educated in any building erected for that purpose. Each of my schools being small (I believe, by choice), each had established itself, with minimal changes, in what had till recently been a private house. The effect was a genial air of make-do – reassuring to an anti-scholastic child. At Harpenden Hall, the now desk-filled ivory parlours and bare-floored dining-room with 'gym' apparatus fitted around its walls kept the climate of earlier, 'ordinary' occupation. Or here and there vanished tribes left frivolous traces, or sentimental ones – names cut on the glass of windows. . . . This did not distract our attention, which was demanded. We *learned*: the classrooms were brisk, the teaching was thorough. No one of the schools I went to was amateurish.

On the surface only – that touch of improvisation – did any resemble St Agatha's, in *The Little Girls*:

Thick cream glazed blinds were pulled most of the way down. Failing to keep out the marine sunshine, they flopped lazily over the open windows in the hot June breath rather than breeze haunting the garden. St Agatha's had been a house, IV-A classroom probably the morning-room. The blinds were lace-bordered. There was a garlanded wallpaper – called to order by having on it a bald, pontifical clock, only a size or two smaller than a station one, a baize board clustered with lists and warnings, and sepia reproductions of inspiriting pictures, among them 'Hope', framed in oak. Of oak were the desks, to which were clamped high-backed seats. An aroma of plasticene came from the models along the chimneypiece, and from jars of botanical specimens near a window whiffs of water slimy with rotting greenery were fanned in – the girl in charge of the specimens being absent with one of her summer colds. Chalk in the neighbourhood of the blackboard and ink thickening in china wells in the desks were the only other educational smells.

A dozen or so girls, most of them aged eleven, some ten, some twelve, sat at the desks. All wore their summer tunics of butcher-blue.

St Agatha's is imaginary, in that it has no physical origin. No link, for instance, with real-life Lindum, apart from both being girls' day-schools in a Kent seaside town. St Agatha's, you recall, had its own beach, together with uphill 'grounds'; Lindum, built in to a close residential area, was neither in view nor in easy reach of the sea. . . . Yet I perceive fictitious St Agatha's with the same detailed, stereo-scopic clearness as that with which I recollect solid Lindum. In the long run, art is realler than life? St Agatha's *has* one link with Harpenden Hall, for a school garden in Hertfordshire (not Kent) was the scene of an act that survives in *The Little Girls*.

*

I entered Harpenden Hall, at mid-term, still in a state of shock. It was something to find myself making a fresh start. The less said the better: I had what I see can go with total bereavement, a sense of disfigurement, mortification, disgrace. The more people who had never met me before, the better. Though inevitably a number of Harpenden people would know *about* me: my popular uncle and aunt's having a little niece coming to live with them, and the reason for that, would have been broadcast. ('Little', I had come to notice, was part of the vocabulary of pathos – if a baby died, it was always a 'little' baby.) Would the Harpenden Hall girls have been told about my disaster? As to that I did not know what to wish. Sometimes I wanted nonentity, sometimes celebrity.

Those wishes came uppermost alternately. Result, ambivalence in the matter of the school uniform. The uniform itself I particularly liked – I was all for it, and saw it likely to be a becoming one: brown tunic box-pleated into a square yoke (exactly as today) with a blue-and-white striped shirt to be worn under it, and a brown tie to be knotted over the shirt.

This outfit was, thanks to forethought, ready for me when I arrived at Harpenden, and I could not wait to be into it, to be 'merged'. But I insisted on wearing a *black* tie. I did not, now it came to the point, wish to be stripped of my insignia. Since my mother's death, in September, I had worn mourning, of the euphemistic kind permitted for children; black, while not ever total, had not ever been missing and had spoken out, like the ink of a notice-board, from whatever part of my person it was on. *Now*, and so soon, was I to be shorn of that? 'My black' was the last I had of my mother. *That* gone, there would be nothing, so far as I knew, ever again. For I could not remember her, think of her, speak of her or suffer to hear her spoken of.

Aunt Laura, no less in a state of shock, said, 'Just as you like'; 1912 (which this still was) had been an unbearable year. The closeness of the Colleys to one another, the depths of their involvement with one another, magnified anything that might happen: and see what had! That March handsome clever Constance, the woman doctor, consumptive, had died in a Folkestone nursing home, on her way back from an unavailing Swiss sanatorium. That April Eddy, the youngest and dearest brother, had gone down with the *Titanic*. That summer Florence, my mother, was told by a Dublin doctor, to her delight, that she would be in Heaven six months hence. (It was to be less than six months.) We returned to Kent where my father joined us. That September the evenings at Hythe, even up on the hill, were stuffy and bodeful. The sorts of evenings which later one associated with the thrummings of a bomber, circling, coming brutally nearer each time. She died, at Clyne House on the —— of the month. I was staying next door.

The problem I represented had been solved in advance: I was to go to Aunt Laura. My mother had made the arrangement with loving optimism, and Aunt Laura accepted it as a vocation. Considering all she had been through, that three-death year, might not having me to cope with have been the finish? As against that, may the challenge have braced her up? At all events, the energy, ingenuity and briskness with which she rose to the occasion did her credit in the eyes of the rest of the family, inclined till then to refer to her as 'poor Laura', on the grounds of her being a shade sentimental, unmarried, and muddle-headed, and of having been down-trodden by her more brilliant sisters – not least Florence. . . . The actual sufferer under the arrangement could have been Uncle Wingfield, the angelic unmarried clergyman brother for whom, at this time, at Harpenden, she kept house. His prolonged bachelor state was said to be due to her zealous chaperonage. He, a winning, delightful man, was with regard to some aspects of life pathologically shy, bashful, prone to cramping embarrassments. Still being a curate, though an important one, he did not as yet qualify for a parsonage: South View, a semi-detached villa, already contained, to a nicety, his entourage: Aunt Laura, their 'working housekeeper' Miss Kilby, and the dog Susan. The wedging-in, on the top of these, of a girl supposedly on the verge of puberty, could have spelled for him more than spatial discomfort. His sweetness of nature, however, triumphed. He was forever devising 'surprises' for me: treats, gifts, jokes, outings. All of these were accompanied by an understanding speechlessness, which I valued. If any gout or driblet of love – of affection, even – was during that time to be wrung from my petrified heart, it was for him. . . . But South View was in great part wasted on me. I did not desire 'a home life', the fact was. It would have been better to send me straight to boarding-school. I made do by devoting myself to Harpenden Hall, where I spent about ten hours of each day.

Getting me in there had been a coup of Aunt Laura's. The school did not want to take any more day-girls: in intention, since it began, it had been a boarding-school, and Miss English wished it to keep that character. However, her objections were overborne. Two or three weekly boarders were there, from neighbouring parts of Hertfordshire; *the* boarders all, but all, came from London. At Lindum, day-school pure and simple, my fellow-girls had necessarily been 'locals': one could track any one of them back to her home surroundings – which in the end could wither one's interest.

Londoners were birds of another feather. In uniform, they had the look of being in disguise – who knew what they wore in the capital city? Collectively they were characters in the stage sense, or in the novel's, of whom the entirety never is to be known – or, if known, told. They were a breed I had not been among before. I attributed to them foreign splendours and miseries, and why not? At this juncture, this lifeless time in my own life, something outstanding and startling was what I needed: these girls *had* to be out of the ordinary run. Whether they were or were not, I cannot now say. They were ever so slightly sophisticated, compared to me and my fellow Harpenden day-girls, but not depraved. They were known in the village, drifting shopping around in their Hall tunics, as being old-for-their ages. They had as models, probably, social mothers. Two were nascent beauties: Dorothy Lewis, of mysterious (and, it was to transpire, sensational) parentage, whose short, dazzling subsequent life and terrible death outdid the utmost I could have foreseen for her; and Agatha Kentish, 'a big girl', golden to the tips of her eyelashes, serene but given to the loveliest blushing – where is *she* now? Also among our numbers were two foreigners: Lili, my first German, from Düsseldorf, Junoesque, pink-and-white, good-humoured though with a disparaging smile; and Françoise, from where in France I do not remember, bilious complexion, darting berry-dark eyes, sharp elbows, topknot of hair upheld by a vast black bow like a flapping raven. *Her* smile was quizzical, rallying, just not cynical. When the First World War broke out, in 1914, those two were my prototypes of the warring nations. The War had the tact to break out during school holidays.

Harpenden Hall, as said, was a good school. The teaching was calm and authoritative. We were kept abreast of what went on in the world. What I learned there has – as by now, how could it not? – subsided into the compost which is the base of one's mind; but I know I did learn. Unhappily there was at that time little to show for it. At Lindum, I had been on the whole a bright child: quick answerer, fluent if moralistic essayist, comer-out-top at spelling, general knowledge, even mental arithmetic. Now the bright child gave place to the dunce girl. When, every Monday morning, after school prayers, Miss English read out to the assembled school the form-orders of the preceding week, I came out bottom or bottom-but-one of mine. To save my face, I adopted a pose of being 'lazy'. This must have been chagrinning for Miss English, upon whom, I suspect, I had been imposed by Aunt Laura as eager, intelligent and 'promising'. She had the grace to show herself as less vexed than puzzled. One or two of the mistresses took against me, saying I sulked. My defection did me little harm with the girls, one of whom said, 'But you must be clever in *some* way.'

My stupidity may have been due to denied sorrow. Officially, since I was then thirteen, it could have been charged – as it certainly would be these days – to an overpowering onslaught of adolescence. That would have been incorrect. I never did have adolescence at all badly, either at Harpenden Hall or at Downe House. Chicken-pox, measles, German measles, mumps, whooping-cough in turn took their toll of me, and heavily, but with the last of those my afflictions ceased. Adolescence apparently by-passed me – or if I ever did have it, I got off light. Towering periods of silliness, oh yes. And I made vile scenes with unfortunate Aunt Laura, but those were, rather, instances of protracted childhood, which a furious selfishness reinforced. At around sixteen I dabbled in introspection, but hardly more. Tormenting nameless disturbances, conflicts, cravings were not experienced by me. I had never heard of them.

I would have been more galled by intellectual failure had I not had an alternative foot to stand on. I'd become a high-ranking initiator of school crazes, for which there was constant demand at Harpenden

Hall. One or two had been going when I arrived, at mid-term, but showed signs of being upon the wane. Further ideas and impetus were needed: mine filled the bill. In a short time I had zealots excavating for secret passages, one at least of which was said, I can't say by whom, to run from The Hall cellars to the doubtless bone-strewn vaults of the parish church away off at the other end of the village. The cellars were tortuous, endless, musty and, at a first reconnaissance, unrewarding: evidently our end of the passage had been blocked up, by some malignant hand. We first tapped then beat about with our trowels along the walls, dislodging segments of scabrous plaster, harkening for 'hollownesses'. I carried a tottering candle: the London boarders were to a girl equipped with electric torches, procured by them for nightly reading in bed – lurid histori-cal romances – after Lights Out. This (had we known) not really very original Gothic experiment of ours was put a stop to: our bangings-about had been audible upstairs; the cobwebs and coal dust in which we emerged coated caused unfriendly remarks. So next we moved onward to the occult. Marjory Bowen's *Black Magic* became our bible, though we gleaned what we could about witchcraft, demonic possession and the technique of cursing also from lesser works. At first we were at a loss for anybody to curse; the least popular member of the staff, an aggressive carrot-haired Scotswoman, was at length decided on, and the ceremonial of wax-image modelling, then pin-sticking, gone through. Miss X promptly came out with a 'runny' cold, which she gave to us all – for fuller results we had needed fingernail clippings, plus one or two of her dreadful hairs. Lack of major ingredients, bats' blood, etc., also told against the potions we brewed, though we moaned incantations. Dorothy Lewis wanted to woo the Devil, but he remained away – which was as well, for cumulatively this thing was making us nervous: one of the girls began to shriek in her sleep, two or three who were about to be confirmed developed scruples and I began to have qualms about Uncle Winkie. So we gave over and started collecting perchy-birds. A village shop had an aviary-full of them: they were miniature bright-painted celluloid imitations of exotic species from many parts of the world. Each cost a penny. Each had a weight in its tail, enabling it to perch upright wherever placed – table-edge, bedhead, taut cord or outstretched finger. Flicked at, they swayed to and fro, not ceasing to perch. Their delicate equilibrium besotted us. Borne round in a dandified manner, as though falcons, they were caressed and murmured to: banished, inevitably, from classrooms they were all the more a feature of school walks: we sported them, when we filed from Harpenden Hall – semi-transparent in sunshine, brilliant as emblems – stuck rail-down into the rims of our knitted caps. . . . Then *they* ceased: *they* might never have been. We had had enough of them.

Gambling with death was instigated by Eileen Carver, whose unwilling lieutenant I became. We entered upon a carnival of bravado, or alternatively incipient commando training, wall-top running, roof-top running, roof mountaineering (the roofs of the Hall were steep) and blindfold bicycling being the early stages. She was a small, taut, pale, wiry London girl, alarmingly taciturn, demon at basketball (at which she captained us) and not basketball only. She had ruthlessly slighted the rest of our crazes, so far. A withheld personality, apt to become a searing one. Afternoon 'nature rambles' over Harpenden Common or through hitherto friendly Hertford-shire thickets and lanes became, that autumn, darkened by appre-hension: what might not she challenge us to do next? When it came to balancing, at a run, *eyes shut*, along the sky-high parapet of a railway bridge, several defaulted. She did not so much as look at them. Worst was to be the day of the deadly nightshade – for as that a spray of berries glistening under a hedge was identified by two embryonic botanists. 'If *you* eat those, if you even touch those, you die!' 'Rot,' returned our Leader, in her most languid tone. 'How do you know it's rot?' She flickered those summing-up eyes from face to face, then said: 'Well, all right – at least *I* am.' She plucked a palmful of berries and gulped them down.

Throughout school tea, choked, we awaited the onset of the convulsions: after-tea prep, clamped in rows to our desks, captive spectators, spying upon the stealthy advance of the wall clock, glancing away from the clock at her bullet-head, *we* were the immolated ones. 'What's the *matter* with you all?' thundered Miss X, our invigilator that evening – 'eh?' So we acted writing, scratch-scratch-scratch with our pens, or reading, holding books up to our faces. Then a girl clapped a hand to her mouth and ran out, to vomit. I was the only day-girl in that classroom: at six-thirty Miss X ordered me home. So I deserted: back on the Raleigh to South View.

'Is deadly nightshade fatal?' I asked Aunt Laura. She said, so she had always supposed, adding: 'Why?'

Next morning, Eileen was very well.

We then switched to collecting crêpe-de-Chine hankies, of every colour, these costing sixpence each. At Harpenden Hall (I repeat) took place the 'burying' which centralises *The Little Girls*. The real-life proceedings were less impressive, more scatterbrained, and had a tinge of facetiousness. A smallish biscuit tin, sealed, containing some cryptic writings and accompanied by two or three broken knick-knacks, was immured in the hollow base of a rough stone wall dividing the kitchen garden: this taking place, I think, at about the time of our failure to uncover the secret passage. Foiled of the past, we at least might make a fool of the future. This attempt I had completely forgotten till it was returned to me by *The Little Girls*.

III

PEOPLE

No one of the characters in my novels has originated, so far as I know, in real life. If anything, the contrary was the case: persons playing a part in my life – the first twenty years of it – had about them something semi-fictitious. Born with no idea what people are like, I was slow to learn, therefore made guesses at them. A guess is an exercise of inventiveness. Some of my guesses may not have been quite wide of the mark – but if that was so, it was so by fortuity. Those concerned, whether grown-ups or children, either did not perceive what was going on or did not object to it: it is something to have 'character' attributed to one, of whatever kind. For a main trait of human nature is its amorphousness, the amorphousness of the drifting and flopping jellyfish in a cloudy tide, and secret fears (such as fear of nonentity), discouragement and demoralizing misgivings prey upon individuals made aware of this. There results an obsessive wish to acquire outline, to be unmistakably demarcated, to *take shape*. Shape – shape is the desideratum: hence the overlordship of characters in novels, who have it, over the desirous reader who has it not. Fictional characters stand out, enlarged by doing so. That their power is given them by art does not (indeed, must not) appear. They *are*: thereby, their effect is tonic.

I do not think my make-believe about people was peculiar as a future novelist: friends I have who have never written a line tell me, as children they did the same. But I ask myself, could those early dodges of mine queer the pitch for me as an autobiographer? What *was*, as opposed to what I chose to imagine, is what I want to unearth: long-ago actualities are the exciting thing – the more so for their being hard to discern clearly thanks to patchy surviving mists, the debris of childhood. To the fraction of the past that is in my keeping, I should like to give the sobriety of history: facts, events, circumstances demand to be accurately recorded: that is my aim.

But, people? – the denizens of those times and places? With people, the impossibility of 'accuracy' begins. Those I lived among and therefore know to have lived, after all and by the end of it all, what were they? Many, and by now I suppose most of them, having taken their mysteries to the grave with them, I cannot ask them. Gone, they remain – elusive as ever.

With the characters in my stories it has been otherwise. Between them and me existed, exists, no gulf. I could say, they have made themselves known to me – instantly recognizable, memorable from then on. From the moment they hove into view, they were inevitable. Nominally 'imaginary'; these beings made more sense, were more convincing, more authoritative as humans, than those others, consisting of flesh-and-blood, that I had wasted years in failing to know. These newcomers (for their visitations began only when, at twenty, I began to invoke them by writing stories) inspired me with what had been a lacking confidence: I gained, I grew, I assimilated much from being on terms with them, for they were adult as compared to myself – in experience, for instance, far, far ahead of me. They enlightened me, I believe, as to many things. I became, and remain, my characters' close and intent watcher: their director, never. Their creator I cannot feel that I was, or am. Yet in spite of all that, they were my servitors, for it was within *my* stories (stories conceived by me) that they existed, being in being only that they might play their assigned parts. I thought of stories first, of characters afterwards. . . . For some time, I did not draw heavily on my characters, for the reason that I kept to writing short stories, some of them very short, hardly more than sketches: I was a visual writer, with no taste for analysis, so those suited me better – my first two books, *Encounters* and *Ann Lee's*, were collections of them.

[*Here* (Spencer Curtis Brown notes) *the manuscript breaks off. Elizabeth Bowen had, however, prepared, some while earlier, notes about the book for her publishers and these give some idea of the themes she at that time had in mind for the later sections.*]

It is not easy to make a synopsis of this (projected) book – of which the title is drawn from page 1 of *Alice's Adventures in Wonderland*. Much of the life, or liveliness, of the book should derive from its sparking its way along by free association – 'recalls', and the ideas a recall brings with it.

The book is *not* to be an autobiography. It will differ from an autobiography (in the accepted sense) in two ways. (1) It will not follow a time sequence. (2) It will be anything but all-inclusive.

The underlying theme – to which the book will owe what it is necessary that a book *should* have, continuity – will be the relationship (so far as that can be traceable, and perhaps it is most interesting when it is apparently not traceable) between living and writing. Dislike of pomposity inhibits me from saying, 'the relationship between life and art' (meaning my own).

The book is to be illustrated by quotations.

Some, from books by other people. So far as I am able to foresee, these will be very largely from 'old' books, of which the copyright has expired. If there are exceptions, they will be brief.

Other quotations will be from books by me. The use of quotations from my own books will not be a sign of laziness on my part. The quotations will be used to give point and relevance to, and to illustrate, what in this new book I shall be in course of saying. It would seem to me stupid, and in a way dishonest, to rewrite, or paraphrase, anything I have already written – and published.

One of my reasons for wishing to write this book (*Pictures and Conversations*), and one, also, why I think it should be a fairly good or at least an engaging book, is: books, lengthy critical studies, theses are perpetually being written about writers, novelists in particular. I, inevitably, have been the subject of a certain number of these. While appreciative of the honour done me and of the hard work involved, I have found some of them wildly off the mark. To the point of asking myself, if anybody *must* write a book about Elizabeth Bowen, why should not Elizabeth Bowen?

Structure of Pictures and Conversations

I foresee the book as dividing itself into five sections.

I. ORIGINS. My own: Anglo-Ireland and its peculiarities. The infiltration – I believe? – of at least some of these peculiarities into my books. This documented by the Jonah Barrington memoirs, Le Fanu and Edgeworth novels, and others.

II. PLACES. Their sometimes fateful influence. The sometimes contrasts, sometimes affinities between them. The topography of Elizabeth Bowen fiction.

III. PEOPLE. (a) in 'real life': some famous, others obscure.
(b) in novels and stories I have written.

The inevitable question, where do 'characters' come from?

IV. GENESIS (of a book, in particular of a novel or long short story). Remarks on the growth a book makes while being written. Remarks, also, on the subsequent growth a book makes when, having been published, and the cable having been cut between it and the author, it enters upon an unforeseeable life of its own.

V. WITCHCRAFT: A QUERY. Is anything uncanny involved in the process of writing? General conclusions drawn by the author, with regard in part to her own work, but also no less, if anything more, to that of the hierarchy of other writers.

Added to this, a page or so winding up *Pictures and Conversations*.

I can think of nothing further to add to this – I can see – rather sketchy forecast of *Pictures and Conversations*. I shall know more about this book when I am under way with it. A considerable – in fact, probably the greater – part of what it *is* to be about is still fairly deep down in my consciousness, waiting to be brought to the surface.

1975

Notes

ESSAYS

Page

30 *general note to 'Eire':* This report on Ireland's neutrality came out of Elizabeth Bowen's wartime work for the Ministry of Information, which took her to Dublin in 1940 and 1941 to ascertain Irish attitudes to the war (see letters to Virginia Wolf).

31 *de Valera:* First President of the Irish Republic, founder of Fianna Fail, and Prime Minister since 1932. In 1938, in return for control of the 'Treaty' ports held by the British Navy, he promised to refuse their facilities to foreign powers in the event of war. Ireland was the only nation in the Commonwealth not to declare war on Germany in 1939, and de Valera maintained this policy of neutrality in spite of Roosevelt's attempts to make him join the Allied cause.

32 *the exodus of young men:* Thousands of Irishmen crossed to England to enlist in the British forces, in spite of the official policy of neutrality.

33 *The Dictator:* Presumably Charlie Chaplin's *The Great Dictator* (1940) which was showing in London at the beginning of 1941.

33 *Boule de Suif:* Maupassant's cynical wartime story. I can find no mention of this adaptation by Lennox Robinson, Irish playwright and manager of the Abbey Theatre, Dublin.

33 *Picture Post:* The popular illustrated magazine (1938–57), founded by Sir Edward Hulton and edited by Tom Hopkinson.

33 *The IRA bomb affair:* In 1938 the I.R.A. had declared war on Britain, and begun a bombing campaign in January 1939. On Friday 25 August 1939 at 2.30 p.m., in Broadgate, Coventry, a bomb went off killing five people (including an old man and a young boy), badly injuring twelve and hurting forty. There was enormous public outrage. Two men were executed.

34 *Heimkunst (sic):* *Heimat kunst*, regional or local art.

38 *the flat character:* in E. M. Forster's *Aspects of the Novel*, 1927.

42 *by Henry James:* in, for instance, the preface to *The Portrait of a Lady*.

50 *bare ruined choirs:* Shakespeare, *Sonnets*, 73.

51 *Millions of strange shadows on you tend:* Shakespeare, *Sonnets*, 53.

52 *Sir Percy:* In *The Scarlet Pimpernel* (1905) by Baroness Orczy, the hero is Sir Percy Blakeney, an English aristocrat who rescues French nobility, victims of the Reign of Terror, from the guillotine.

52 *E. Nesbit:* (1858–1924), children's writer, whose books include *The Story of the Treasure Seekers* (1899) and *The Railway Children* (1906). Her London family, the Bastables, occur in several of her books.

53 *Kipps:* (1905), by H. G. Wells.

60 *Graham Greene:* see '*Why Do I Write? An Exchange of Views between Elizabeth Bowen, Graham Greene, and V. S. Pritchett*'.

65 *general note to 'On Not Rising To the Occasion':* for Elizabeth Bowen's childhood, see also 'Rider Haggard: *She*' and 'Pictures and Conversations'.

69 *general note to 'A living Writer':* This passage is taken from a much longer essay on Katherine Mansfield's life and characteristics as a

writer, which was a Preface to a collection of her stories published in 1957. Katherine Mansfield (1888–1923) came from New Zealand to England in 1908. Her writing life was overshadowed by her search for a cure for tuberculosis. After her death her edited journals were published, in 1927, by her husband John Middleton Murry.

86 *E. F. Benson:* (1867–1940), son of the headmaster of Wellington and educated at Marlborough (which produced the juvenile *Sketches from Marlborough*), best known for his 'Lucia' novels.

86 *Compton Mackenzie:* (1883–1972), *Sinister Street* (1914) is his low-life London novel.

87 *Baroness Orczy:* see 'Out of a Book'.

87 *E. V. Lucas:* (1868–1938), well-known essayist, journalist, biographer and novelist.

87 *Edith Somerville:* (1858–1949), second cousin of Violet Martin, with whom, as 'Somerville and Ross', she wrote the *Irish R.M.* series and other Anglo-Irish novels including *The Real Charlotte* (1894) and *The Big House at Inver* (1925). See review, '*The Irish Cousins* by Violet Powell'.

87 *Stephen Gwynn:* (1864–1950), author and nationalist, M.P. for Galway City 1906–18, whose books include *The Case for Home Rule* (1911), *Henry Grattan and his Times* (1939) and *The History of Ireland* (1923). In 1918, six years after the death of Elizabeth Bowen's mother, her father married Stephen Gwynn's sister, Mary.

87 *A great-aunt in Queen Anne's Gate:* Lady Edith Allendale, widow of Sir George Colley, who had been killed in the Boer War.

88 *London Mercury:* a monthly literary periodical founded in 1919 by J. C. Squire, incorporated into *Life and Letters* in 1939.

88 *The Poetry Bookshop:* Harold Monro, the Georgian poet, founded this centre for publishing and poetry in 1913.

88 *Rose Macaulay:* (1881–1958), novelist and travel writer, who had been at Oxford with Olive Willis, and helped Elizabeth Bowen when she first came to London.

88 *Naomi Royde-Smith:* (d. 1964), literary editor of *The Westminster Gazette* and hostess of celebrated weekly parties at 44 Princes Gardens, Kensington, much disliked by Virginia Woolf: 'I detest the mixture of ideas and South Kensington' (*Diary*, 5 June 1921). Rose Macaulay was a protégée of hers. I have not identified Mary Hope Allen.

89 *John Strachey:* (1860–1927), cousin of Lytton Strachey, editor and proprietor of the *Spectator* from 1898 to 1925.

89 *Cyril Connolly:* (1903–74), a close friend of Elizabeth Bowen, who began his long career as a literary journalist reviewing for the *New Statesman*. See review, '*The Condemned Playground* by Cyril Connolly'.

89 *Ethel Sands:* (1873–1962), American-born painter, hostess and patron of the arts. Lived in the Château d'Auppegard near Dieppe, and with

Nan Hudson at 15 The Vale, Chelsea. See reference in letter to Virginia Woolf, 26 August 1935.

89 *Regent's Park:* Elizabeth Bowen and her husband Alan Cameron moved from Oxford to 2 Clarence Terrace, Regent's Park in 1935. See letter to Virginia Woolf, 31 July 1935.

PREFACES

94 *magazines or papers:* the stories were published, while *The Heat of the Day* was being written, in *Horizon, The Listener, The Bell, Cornhill, Penguin New Writing, Argosy* and the *New Yorker.*

100 *Sheridan Le Fanu:* (1814–73), Dublin writer of ghost stories and mysteries, published *Uncle Silas* in 1864. The novel had a strong influence on Elizabeth Bowen (see 'Pictures and Conversations'); her guess that it was 'an Irish story transposed to an English setting' is correct, as the novel expanded on an earlier story, 'Passages in the Secret History of an Irish Countess'. She also wrote an introduction to Le Fanu's *The House by the Churchyard* (1861–63).

113 *Mrs Radcliffe:* Ann Radcliffe (1764–1823), author of 'gothic' novels such as *The Mysteries of Udolpho* (1794) and *The Italian* (1797).

114 *general note:* Frost in May (1933) is the first volume of the quasi-autobiographical four-volume novel by Antonia White (1899–1979): the others are *The Lost Traveller* (1950), *The Sugar House* (1952) and *Beyond the Glass* (1954). She appears first as Nanda Grey and then as Clara Batchelor. *Frost in May* tells of her education at the Convent of the Sacred Heart, Roehampton.

114 *Tom Brown's Schooldays:* (1857), an evocation of Rugby under Dr Thomas Arnold by Thomas Hughes (1822–96).

114 *Stalky and Co:* (1899), school stories by Rudyard Kipling (1865–1936), based on the United Services College at Westward Ho!

114 *E. F. Benson:* see 'Coming to London'.

114 *H. A. Vachell:* (1861–1955), educated at Harrow, author of about a hundred books, including novels and short stories.

114 *The Backward Son:* (1940), Stephen Spender (b.1909) was educated at University College School, London.

115 *Susan Coolidge: What Katy Did* (1873), the very popular American girls' story, was followed by *What Katy Did At School* (1874) and *What Katy Did Next* (1887).

115 *Colette:* (1873–1954). *Claudine à l'École* (1902) was translated by Antonia White in 1956.

118 *general note to 'Encounters':* Elizabeth Bowen began writing stories when she was twenty, while studying for two terms at the L.C.C. School of Art in Southampton Row, and living with her Aunt Laura, her mother's unmarried sister, who kept house for her brother William

Wingfield Colley, a curate, in Harpenden, Hertfordshire. See her letter to Alan Cameron, 19 January 1923, for the acceptance of these stories.

120 *Katherine Mansfield: Bliss and Other Stories* was published in 1920. See 'A Living Writer: Katherine Mansfield'.

120 *Richard Middleton: The Ghost Ship* (1912) included fairy stories and school stories.

120 *E. M. Forster: The Celestial Omnibus* was published in 1911.

REVIEWS

143 *Constantia Maxwell:* (1886–1962), Professor of Economic History at Trinity College, Dublin, Lecky Professor of History in 1945, and author of many books on Irish history.

143 *Grattan's Parliament:* Henry Grattan, great leader and orator, entered Parliament in 1775 where he led the movement for Irish independence. In 1782, after the English defeat in the American War of Independence, Irish parliamentary independence was formally recognized, and for a short time (1782–98) Ireland became, in Grattan's words, 'a nation', with its own post office, bank, custom house, courts and defence force (the 'Volunteers').

143 *Sheridan and Smock Alley:* Smock Alley, the rival theatre to the Theatre Royal in late eighteenth-century Dublin, was managed by Thomas Sheridan, father of Richard Brinsley Sheridan the playwright, and friend of Swift. There were a number of notorious theatrical riots under his régime.

143 *the Union:* in 1798, after the French Revolution and the attempted uprising of the United Irishmen under Wolfe Tone, William Pitt, the British Prime Minister, decided on a Union of the British and Irish Parliaments. A majority was secured (by bribing a large number of peers and M.P.s) and the act was passed in 1800. Ireland became part of the United Kingdom in January 1801. Like most of the Anglo-Irish, Elizabeth Bowen laments the Act of Union as a 'bad deal' and as spelling the end of Anglo-Irish self-respect. See *Bowen's Court*, especially Chapter VII.

144 *Edward Fitzgerald:* (1763–98). One of the leaders of the 1798 uprising, a popular hero, a romantically handsome young aristocrat, descendant of the ancient Fitzgerald earldoms, married to an illegitimate daughter of the House of Orleans, he was fatally wounded while resisting arrest and died in Newgate Prison.

145 *Old English:* the early, fourteenth-century, colonizers of Ireland were known by this name. The term Anglo-Irish did not come into general use until the eighteenth century.

146 *Fitzgeralds:* the Earls of Desmond and Kildare, put into power by

Page

Richard II, and a strong threat to the English kings in the fifteenth and sixteenth centuries.

146 *George Browne:* Archbishop of Dublin, who supported the Reformation and voted Henry VIII supreme over ecclesiastical matters.

146 *James II:* his reign is described by Lady Longford as 'an interlude of Catholic ascendancy in Ireland'.

146 *some hanky-panky over the linen industry:* a mild reference to the English Parliament's stifling of the burgeoning woollen industry in Ireland, by prohibiting (in 1699) the export of woollen goods from Ireland to any country except England, from which heavy duties in any case debarred them. The Irish Parliament had attempted to placate English opinion in 1698 by promising to encourage the linen industry.

146 *Molyneux:* William Molyneux (1656–98), philosopher and patriot, author of *The Case of Ireland's being bound by Acts of Parliament in England stated* (1698).

146 *Wolfe Tone:* (1763–98), leader of the United Irishmen and of the 1798 Uprising, which sought to establish a free Irish Republic on French principles. Died in prison.

146 *Emmet:* Robert Emmet (1778–1803), a revolutionary leader following the aims of Wolfe Tone, executed at the age of twenty-five in 1803.

146 *O'Connell:* Daniel O'Connell (1775–1847), 'the Liberator', great leader for Catholic emancipation and Irish independence.

146 *Parnell:* Charles Stewart Parnell (1845–91), Protestant leader of the Land League and Home Rule M.P, discredited in 1890 by the Kitty O'Shea divorce case.

147 *He left the little Wealth he had:* Swift, *Verses on the Death of Dr Swift*, 1731.

147 *Stephen Gwynn:* See 'Coming to London'.

149 *the Lane bequest:* Sir Hugh Lane (1875–1915), supported by Yeats and Lady Gregory, proposed in 1904 that a fund should be raised to buy a large collection of modern French paintings, as the basis of a National Gallery of Art in Dublin. Lane acquired the collection and housed it temporarily in Harcourt Street, but what Gwynn called 'an ugly ignorant press attack' hindered the building of a gallery. The disappointed Lane went to London, taking the best pictures with him, and left thirty-nine of them to the National Gallery in London. Eventually a Municipal Gallery was built in Dublin (see Yeats's poem, 'The Municipal Gallery Revisited').

149 *general note:* see 'The Big House'.

149 *Joseph Hone:* (1882–1959), biographer of Yeats (1943), also author of books on George Moore, Henry Tonks and Bishop Berkeley. President of the Irish Academy of Letters in 1957.

150 *Miss Edgeworth:* Maria Edgeworth (1768–1849), Irish novelist, author of *Castle Rackrent* (1800) and *The Absentee* (1812).

Page

150 *party violence:* for the Troubles, see introduction to 'The Last September'.

151 *Holland House:* George Moore the historian, while reading for the law in London, became an habitué of Holland House, which under the 3rd Baron Holland (1773–1840) became an important political, literary and artistic centre.

151 *Citizen John Moore:* Hone writes: 'In 1798, a force of Frenchmen under General Humbert landed at Killala on the North coast of Mayo. John Moore rode off with a large number of the Moore tenantry and committed himself to Humbert's cause . . . They surprised the English army at Castlebar . . . but were surrounded and defeated at Ballinamuck on September 1798.'

153 *the lake gave him two books:* George Moore (1852–1933) used his home setting most in *The Untilled Field* (1903) and *The Lake* (1905).

153 *Herbert Gorman:* also wrote books on Hawthorne (1927), Dumas (1929) and Longfellow (1927).

155 *Nighttown:* Dublin's brothel area, scene of the 'Circe' section of *Ulysses*, which begins at 'the Mabbot Street entrance to nighttown'.

156 *general note to 'A Sentimental Education':* see her reference in the letter to Ottoline Morrell, 15 August 1932, to her reading of *L'Education Sentimentale*.

157 *V. S. Pritchett:* (b.1900), had been reviewing and writing short stories and novels since the 1920s, and became a director of the *New Statesman* in 1946. See 'Why Do I Write?'

160 *Ivy Compton-Burnett:* (1884–1969), whose first published novel *Pastors and Masters* came out in 1925.

168 *Cyril Connolly:* see 'Coming to London'.

171 *Angus Wilson:* (b.1913) began his long career as a novelist with the short stories of *The Wrong Set* (1949) and *Such Darling Dodos* (1950). This is a rare example of Elizabeth Bowen's giving a bad review; she was kinder to *Anglo-Saxon Attitudes*.

172 *Eudora Welty:* (b.1909), novelist and short story writer, has lived most of her life in Jackson, Mississippi. She and Elizabeth Bowen were close friends from the 1950s onwards.

174 *Brian Fitzgerald:* also wrote books on Defoe (1954), the Duchess of Leinster 1731–1814 (1949) and Lady Louisa Connolly 1743–1821 (1950).

175 *Richard Boyle:* an English adventurer who had built up a vast estate in Munster in the seventeenth century, whose political influence was severely undermined by Wentworth in 1635, and who was one of the leaders of the 1641 attack on Wentworth.

175 *James Butler:* (1610–88), Earl of Ormond, Protestant monarchist, leader of the Irish army that opposed Cromwell, and head of a family that had been settled in Ireland since the reign of King John. He governed Ireland as Lord Lieutenant after the Restoration.

Page

176 *general note to 'A Writer's Diary:* extracts from Virginia Woolf's *Diary*, since published in full, posthumously edited by Leonard Woolf and first published in 1953.

181 *general note to 'The People's War':* Angus Calder's book about the civilian experience of the Second World War in Britain referred to *The Heat of the Day* as a brilliant evocation of London between 1940 and 1942. See 'London, 1940'.

183 *Mass Observation:* The pre-war and wartime diaries and 'anthropological' records of the British way of life, begun in 1937 (prompted by reactions to Edward VIII's abdication) by Tom Harrisson, Charles Madge and the photographer Humphrey Spender (see *Speak for Yourself: A Mass-Observation Anthology 1937–1949*, eds. Angus Calder and Dorothy Sheridan, Cape, London, 1984).

185 *Somerville and Ross:* see 'Coming to London'.

186 *The Llangollen Ladies:* Lady Eleanor Butler (1745–1829) and Sarah Ponsonby (1755–1831) left their Anglo-Irish families to live together in seclusion in Llangollen for fifty years.

188 *Sheridan Le Fanu:* see preface, *'Uncle Silas* by Sheridan Le Fanu'.

LETTERS

General note: spelling in all letters as in Elizabeth Bowen's original.

193 *general note:* these letters were written in the year of Elizabeth Bowen's engagement to Alan Cameron, a friend of her cousin Audrey Fiennes, who had been gassed and wounded in the war and was working as Assistant Secretary for Education for Northamptonshire. During the courtship, Elizabeth was living with her great-aunt Edith Allendale at 32 Queen Anne's Gate; after the marriage, on 4 August 1923, she and Alan moved to Northampton, where they lived for two years before moving to Oxford. See Victoria Glendinning: *Elizabeth Bowen* (1977) Chapter 3, for an account of the marriage. Elizabeth stayed with Alan until his death in 1952, but had several love affairs, notably with the critic Humphry House and the Canadian diplomat Charles Ritchie.

193 *a collection of short stories: Encounters*, published 1923. See preface, *'Encounters'*.

193 *Katherine Mansfield:* she had died on 9 January 1923.

193 *the fourth book:* of *De Rerum Natura*.

194 *Bitha:* Elizabeth Bowen's family pet-name.

194 *Mr Rupert Birkin:* D. H. Lawrence's *Women in Love* (in which Rupert Birkin is a school inspector, and gets hit on the head with a paperweight by Hermione Roddice) was published in 1921.

195 *the Ludovisi:* the Ludovisi collection, in the Museo delle Terme in Rome, was begun by the nephew of a pope, Cardinal Ludovico Ludovisi, whose uncle reigned as Gregory XV from 1621 to 1623.

Page

195 *Mr Robins:* not known.

196 *'R.U.R.' at St Martins:* 'Rossum's Universal Robots' a 'fantastic melodrama' by Karel Capek, (1890–1939), published in 1923. Capek was a Czech novelist and dramatist involved with Czech nationalist politics and very interested in scientific discoveries. 'R.U.R.' was a drama on the mechanization of the proletariat, which anticipated Huxley's *Brave New World*, and gave to the English language the word 'robot' (from Czech 'robota', compulsory service).

196 *Weltpolitik:* world politics.

196 *Peter Quennell:* (b.1905), poet and man of letters, who in the 1930s alternated weekly fiction reviews in the *New Statesman* with Elizabeth Bowen. The description of this encounter on a train journey from Italy to England strikingly anticipates the first chapter of *To the North* (1932), the first meeting of Cecilia and the Satanic Markie.

196 *the London Mercury:* see 'Coming to London'.

197 *Kingthorpe:* Alan was living at 73 Knights Lane, Kingthorpe, Northampton.

197 *Gibbons (sic):* a joke, or a mistake, for Gibbon.

197 *the Lake of Nemi:* A lake in the Alban hills near Rome, a famous beauty spot. Elizabeth Bowen had spent the winter of 1921 in Italy and was to return many times. Several of her stories, and an early novel, *The Hotel*, are set in Italy, and much later she wrote an impressionistic guide book, *A Time in Rome* (1960).

197 *general note:* Ottoline Morrell (1873–1938), famous hostess and patron of artists at Garsington Manor from 1915 to 1927, at 44 Bedford Square and now at 10 Gower Street, was ageing and ill when Elizabeth Bowen came to know her.

197 *David:* Lord David Cecil (1902–85), scholar and biographer, and a close friend of Elizabeth Bowen from their first meetings in Oxford in 1926.

197 *Hope Mirrlees:* (1887–1978), writer, old friend of Virginia Woolf (who described her as 'eccentric impulsive ecstatic odd' in *Diary*, 12 November 1934) and of T. S. Eliot.

198 *the Eliots:* 1932 was the last year of the Eliots' disastrous marriage. They were still living at 68 Clarence Gate Gardens and seeing friends such as Ottoline and the Woolfs, but Eliot had decided to leave Vivien and in September he sailed for America.

198 *my next book: To the North* (1932).

199 *general note:* Alfred Edgar Coppard (1878–1957), short story writer and poet, was a long-term friend and correspondent of Elizabeth Bowen.

199 *Polly Oliver:* (1935), stories.

199 *The House in Paris:* according to Victoria Glendinning, the novel is based on Elizabeth Bowen's love-affair with the critic Humphry House, and Naomi Fisher is a 'portrait' of his wife Madeline House.

Page

199 *William Plomer:* see letters to Plomer.

200 *new job:* Alan Cameron had been appointed secretary to the Central Council of School Broadcasting of the B.B.C.

200 *House in Regent's Park:* Elizabeth Bowen found 2 Clarence Terrace in 1935; see 'Coming to London' and letters to Virginia Woolf.

200 *general note:* William Plomer (1903–73), novelist, poet and publisher's reader, was one of Elizabeth Bowen's closest friends. He grew up in South Africa, taught for two years in Japan, settled in England in 1929 and in 1937 succeeded Edward Garnett as Jonathan Cape's principal reader, with a wartime interim as editor of intelligence reports for the Admiralty. His first novel, *Turbott Wolfe* (1928) was published by the Woolfs. He edited the diaries of Francis Kilvert, a Welsh border clergyman, between 1938 and 1944, and wrote libretti for several of Britten's operas. His autobiography, put together from *Double Lives* (1943) and *At Home* (1958) was published posthumously in 1975. He was homosexual, and lived for much of his life with the painter Anthony Butts.

200 *4 the Esplanade:* In 1936, William Plomer spent a year in Dover in a flat at the west end of the Promenade. In July 1937 E. M. Forster and his mother stayed in lodgings rented by Joe Ackerley. Isherwood and Auden also visited Dover.

200 *the best short stories: The Faber Book of Modern Short Stories*, with an introduction by Elizabeth Bowen, was published in 1937. The Plomer story included was 'Ula Masondo'.

201 *Wogan Philipps:* (b.1902), eldest son of Sir Laurence Philipps, painter, farmer, communist, married Rosamond Lehmann in 1928. The marriage broke up in the late thirties. Philipps drove an ambulance in the Spanish Civil War and was wounded.

201 *B. K. Seymer (sic):* Beatrice Kean Seymour, a minor novelist writing between the 1920s and 1950s, whose novels included *Intrusion* (1921) and a trilogy about a domestic servant, Sally Dunn: *Maids and Mistresses* (1932), *Interlude for Sally* (1934) and *Summer of Life* (1936).

201 *Rosamond Lehmann* (b.1901), novelist. Plomer describes meeting her through Stephen Spender in Chapter 4 of *At Home*. Elizabeth Bowen had known Rosamond since going to Oxford in 1925. This visit of Rosamond to Bowen's Court in the summer of 1936 was to prove an eventful one, as during it Rosamond fell in love with Elizabeth Bowen's current boyfriend, Goronwy Rees, who was to be the model for Eddie in *The Death of the Heart*.

201 *Roger Senhouse:* (1900–70), translator of Colette and Simone de Beauvoir, publisher at Secker & Warburg, old friend of Harold Nicolson and lover of Lytton Strachey.

202 *those abominable short stories:* see reference to *The Faber Book of Modern Short Stories* in the previous letter.

Page

202 *Sean O'Faolain:* (b.1900), Irish short story writer. His first collection, *Midsummer Night Madness*, was published in 1932. Elizabeth met him in 1937 and he became a friend. The story she chose for her anthology was 'The Bombshop'.

202 *D. and R. Cecil:* David Cecil had married Rachel MacCarthy, daughter of Desmond, in 1937.

202 *Noreen:* Noreen Colley, Elizabeth's cousin, then in her teens, was the daughter of Edie and George Colley. She later married Gilbert Butler.

202 *the D. Verschoyles:* Derek and Evelyn. Derek Verschoyle worked for the *Spectator* and edited *The English Novelists* (1936), in which Elizabeth Bowen had an essay on Jane Austen.

202 *Jim Gates:* manager of the creamery at Kildorrery, next to Bowen's Court; his mother had been Elizabeth Bowen's mother's great friend, and he was a life-long friendly neighbour.

202 *Humphry House:* scholar and teacher, with whom Elizabeth Bowen was in love between 1933 and his return from India in 1936.

203 *The Listener:* 'Tears, Idle Tears', published in *The Listener* on 2 September 1936 and reprinted in *Look At All Those Roses*.

203 *Salzburg:* Elizabeth Bowen visited the Salzburg festival with Sean O'Faolain, Isaiah Berlin, Stuart Hampshire and Sally Graves, and wrote it up for *Night and Day*, the magazine edited by Graham Greene from 1937 to 1938, for which she contributed theatre criticisms. (The magazine was ruined by a libel action brought against it by Shirley Temple.)

203 *Brighton:* Plomer lived for two years in the late thirties in a furnished house in Brighton, which he described as 'only a suburb of London but agreeable to live in, especially in the winter'.

203 *one of your days in London:* Plomer was now principal reader for Cape.

204 *Raymond Mortimer:* (1895–1980), critic, essayist, Bloomsbury figure, and literary editor of the *New Statesman and Nation* from 1935 to 1947.

204 *Montherlant:* Henri de Montherlant (1896–1972), a right-wing Catholic French novelist and dramatist. Elizabeth Bowen reviewed translations of *Pity for Women* and *The Young Girls* in the *New Statesman* for 30 October 1937.

204 *my novel: The Death of the Heart* (1938).

205 *Tony:* Anthony Butts (1900–41), wealthy painter, son of an old Norfolk family, Etonian, friend and companion of William Plomer, fictionalised by him in *Museum Pieces* (1952), and vividly described by Stephen Spender in *World Within World* (1951).

205 *Miss Riding:* Laura Riding (b.1901), poet and critic, who lived and worked with Robert Graves from 1927 to 1939.

205 *Madeline House:* see note to letter to A. E. Coppard, 31 August 1935.

Page

205 *Frank O'Connor:* (1903–66), Irish short story writer, novelist and critic.

205 *Sean:* see note to letter to William Plomer, 17 August 1936. O'Faolain's life of Daniel O'Connell, 'the Liberator', was published in 1938.

206 *a good war:* Elizabeth Bowen was able to travel between London and Ireland during the war because of her work for the Ministry of Information (see notes to 'Eire'). Though her house in London was bombed, she relished living in London during the war years, and wrote some of her best fiction out of the experience. The war was also the context for her love affair with Charles Ritchie.

206 *stone statues:* see P. N. Furbank, *E. M. Forster: A Life*, Secker & Warburg, London, 1978, Vol II, p. 178, for William Plomer's 'collector's passion' for public statues.

207 *Churchill:* at the General Election of 5 July 1945, Churchill's Conservative government was overwhelmingly defeated by Attlee's Labour party. Churchill resigned on 26 July.

207 *your sympathy:* Alan Cameron died at Bowen's Court in August 1952.

207 *Museum Pieces:* (1952), described by Plomer in his autobiography as 'a novel which would commemorate a certain residuary and unstandardised way of living in a London sphere of which I had intimate knowledge during the war', a fictional version of Anthony Butts and his mother Mary Colville-Hyde, who appear in the novel as Toby d'Arfey and Susannah Mountfaucon.

208 *America:* from the early 1950s onwards Elizabeth Bowen was a regular visitor to America as guest lecturer and visiting fellow at several American universities.

208 *At Home:* the second part of Plomer's autobiography.

209 *Stephen's and John Lehmann's:* respectively, *World Within World* (1951) and *The Whispering Gallery* (1951).

209 *George V's funeral:* Plomer describes this in his autobiography: 'In the afternoon I went to the Woolves, where I found Elizabeth Bowen and Iris Origo and Ethel Smyth. . . I went to Elizabeth's to dinner, and Eliot was there. His gravity seemed decidedly male in comparison with those exceptionally quick-witted women. . .' See also Virginia Woolf's *Diary* for Tuesday 28 January 1937.

209 *Noreen:* see note to letter to Plomer, 17 August 1936.

209 *Billy Buchan:* son of Susan and John Buchan, old friends of Elizabeth Bowen, and a protégé of hers.

210 *Eddy Sackville-West:* (1901–65), Vita Sackville-West's cousin and heir to Knole and the Sackville titles, an old friend of Elizabeth Bowen, who bought a house in County Tipperary partly to be near her.

210 *general note:* Elizabeth Bowen met Virginia Woolf through Ottoline Morrell in 1932 and they became friends. She first went to tea with Virginia Woolf on 18 March 1932 (the *Diary* reports her as 'stammering, shy, conventional', but says she is 'improving' on 29 October

1933). The Woolfs visited Bowen's Court in May 1934 (a vivid description is given in the *Diary* for 2 May 1934) and Elizabeth Bowen visited Rodmell twice, on 25–27 June 1940 and on 13–15 February 1941, shortly before Virginia Woolf's suicide. In the summer of 1940 the two women went walking together through London.

211 *Billy Buchan:* see note to letter to Plomer, 6 May 1958. The Buchans went to Canada in 1935 where John Buchan was to be Governor-General.

211 *The House in Paris:* 1935.

212 *copy of this: The House in Paris.*

212 *conference:* Elizabeth Bowen had had to turn down an invitation to Rodmell in order to attend an educational conference with Alan at Oxford.

212 *Susan:* Buchan.

212 *To Spain: Nation & Athenaeum,* 5 May 1923. Virginia Woolf's essay begins with a description of the Channel crossing to Dieppe.

213 *Ethel:* Sands. See note to 'Coming to London'.

214 *Dunmore:* not identified.

214 *Peter Quennell:* see note to letter to Alan Cameron, 28 April 1923.

214 *Rodmell:* see Virginia Woolf, *Diary,* 27 June 1940, for Elizabeth Bowen's visit ('we talked very on the whole congenially'). On 5 July they went walking through the City.

215 *your lecture:* 'The Leaning Tower', delivered 27 April 1940 and published 1940, in which Virginia Woolf continued her argument in 'Letter to a Young Poet' (1932) with contemporary poets.

215 *Horizon:* Stephen Spender had agreed to help Cyril Connolly co-edit *Horizon* in 1939. Virginia Woolf felt she could not contribute to *Horizon* out of loyalty to John Lehmann, who thought that his magazine *New Writing* was threatened by the new publication (see Virginia Woolf, letter to Stephen Spender, 16 December 1939). Victor William ('Peter') Watson (1908–56), who had inherited a fortune made from margarine in the First World War and was an art collector, gave financial support to *Horizon.* In the summer of 1940 Watson, Spender and Connolly edited *Horizon* from Thurlstone in Devonshire.

215 *the Gorky book: Reminiscences of Tolstoi,* translated by S. S. Koteliansky and Leonard Woolf, 1920.

216 *your flat:* On 17 August 1939, the Woolfs moved the Hogarth Press from Tavistock Square to 37 Mecklenburgh Square. In September 1940 Mecklenburgh Square was badly bombed. On 18 October 1940 they saw 52 Tavistock Square in ruins. For the atmosphere of London in wartime, see 'London, 1940', *The Heat of the Day* and *The Demon Lover* short stories.

217 *the Bowen's Court book:* published in 1942.

217 *short stories: Look At All Those Roses* (1941).

217 *Hogarth Press:* on 23 September 1940 the Hogarth Press was moved to

Page

Letchworth in Hertfordshire where it operated under John Lehmann's supervision. On 14 December 1940 the printing machine was delivered to Monks House, Rodmell.

218 *Dublin:* see note to 'Eire'. Elizabeth Bowen's war 'talks' were undertaken to ascertain Irish attitudes to the 'Treaty' ports.

218 *Mr Gates:* see note to letter to Plomer, 17 August 1936.

219 *Lady Jones:* Enid Bagnold, Lady Jones (1889–1981), the writer, lived at Rottingdean. On 26 January 1941 Virginia Woolf wrote to invite her to lunch with Vita Sackville-West on 18 February, when Vita was addressing the Rodmell W.I. about Persia.

219 *poor Sagan:* not identified.

219 *homesick cousin:* son of George and Edie Colley, brother of Noreen?

219 *Lord Cranbourne (sic):* Lord Cranborne, David Cecil's brother.

220 *Mr Worsley:* Thomas Cuthbert Worsley, author of *Education Today and Tomorrow* (1939) with W. H. Auden, *Behind the Battle* (1939); on the Spanish Civil War which he went to with Stephen Spender, *The End of the 'Old School Tie'* (1941) and *The Fugitive Art: Dramatic Commentaries 1947–1951* (1952).

220 *general note:* Virginia Woolf killed herself on 28 March 1941.

221 *general note:* These two letters are from a three-way public correspondence between Elizabeth Bowen, V. S. Pritchett and Graham Greene about the relation of the artist to society, broadcast in short form on the B.B.C. on 10 July 1948 and published by Percival Marshall in November 1948. See 'Disloyalties', first published in 1950, which developed the train of thought raised by Graham Greene's contention in the correspondence that a writer has a duty to be disloyal. All three insisted on the writer's need to be independent from the State.

225 *X-ray department:* The nurse had written to praise Pritchett for exposing a social evil in his story, but he had only been concerned with its aesthetic merits.

228 *Resistance leader:* see preface, 'The Demon Lover'.

229 *Skimpolism:* after Harold Skimpole (supposedly based on Leigh Hunt) in Dickens' *Bleak House*, notorious for his faux-naif belief that the world would somehow provide for the artist while the artist was free to contemplate beauty.

BROADCASTS

236 *Partial Portraits:* contains James's essay on Trollope, first published 1883.

236 *Plumstead Episcopi:* Archdeacon Grantly's parsonage and church in the Barsetshire novels.

237 *Barchester:* Trollope's imaginary cathedral town in the West Country shire of Barset, setting for the Barsetshire novels (*The Warden, Barch-*

ester Towers, Doctor Thorne, Framley Parsonage, The Small House at Allington and *The Last Chronicle of Barset*).

237 *Youth is never an easy time:* Elizabeth Bowen has taken all the material about Trollope's life from his *Autobiography* (1883).

238 *Lily Dale:* heroine of *The Small House at Allington* (1864), who never does marry her childhood sweetheart Johnny Eames.

238 *Lady Glencora:* the beautiful heiress who marries Plantagenet Palliser, the future Prime Minister, in *Can You Forgive Her?* (1864–65), and is romantically entangled with the reckless Burgo Fitzgerald.

240 *Archdeacon Grantly* and *Mr Harding:* the combative and ambitious archdeacon and his mild, decent father-in-law, the Warden, in the Barsetshire novels.

241 *Eleanor Bold:* Mr Harding's widowed daughter in *Barchester Towers*.

243 *Mrs Proudie:* the domineering and manipulative wife of the Bishop of Barchester.

243 *Two English public schools:* Harrow and Winchester.

245 *Now I stretch out my hand:* last words of Trollope's *Autobiography*. 'Now I stretch out my hand, and from the further shore I bid adieu to all who have cared to read any among the many words that I have written'.

246 *general note to 'She':* Rider Haggard's novels, including *King Solomon's Mines* (1886), *She* (1887), *Allen Quartermain* (1887) and *Ayesha, The Return of She* (1905) were enormously popular children's books in the first half of this century.

247 *Greiffenhagen:* Maurice Greiffenhagen, who illustrated many of Rider Haggard's books, and also Edward Fitzgerald's *Rubaiyat of Omar Khayyam* (1909).

248 *Kôr:* Rider Haggard's ancient city also inspired Elizabeth Bowen's wartime story, 'Mysterious Kôr'.

AUTOBIOGRAPHY

254 *general note:* This manuscript is given the alternative titles 'Tipperary Woman' and 'Sarah Barry'.

254 *my grandfather:* Robert Cole Bowen (1830–88), whose Victorian reign over Bowen's Court, estrangement from his son and deepening instability is described in Chapters 9 and 10 of *Bowen's Court*, where the Victorian atmosphere of the house is very fully evoked.

257 *the Mistress died:* see *Bowen's Court*, Chapter 9. Henry Bowen went to London in 1881 as part of his Grand Tour, caught smallpox, and was nursed at Bowen's Court by his mother Elizabeth, who died of the disease, aged forty-five. In 1882 Robert Cole Bowen remarried his first wife's cousin, Georgina Mansergh, who was ostracised by Elizabeth's children and died in 1885. After Robert's death in 1888, Sarah, the eldest daughter, ran the house.

Page

258 *my father:* Henry Bowen married Florence Colley, daughter of a large and distinguished Anglo-Irish family living at Mount Temple, Clontarf, in 1890. See Chapter 1 of *Seven Winters* (1942) for an account of their marriage.

259 *my father's illness:* See Chapter 10 of *Bowen's Court*, and the end of *Seven Winters*. Henry Bowen, a lawyer for the Land Commission, developed anaemia of the brain from overwork in 1905. From 1906 to 1911 Florence and Elizabeth lived with relatives in England, as doctors advised that Henry should live apart from his family. Henry recovered, but Florence died of cancer in 1912.

260 *Land League:* the movement for land reform in Ireland led by Michael Davitt and Parnell in the 1870s and 1880s.

261 *when my father died:* in 1930, after a recurrence of his earlier illness.

262 *my . . . finances:* Bowen's Court was a constant drain, and after Alan Cameron's death in 1952, it became so much of a burden that in 1959 she had to sell it, to a local farmer who promised to maintain it, but who, in fact, demolished it soon afterwards.

265 *a forlorn hope:* see 'The Big House'.

265 *general note:* early in 1972 Elizabeth Bowen showed Spencer Curtis Brown, her literary executor, the draft of the first two chapters of her autobiography. By July she was in hospital with cancer and she died on 22 February 1973, having asked him to publish the unfinished chapters. They were included in the posthumous collection, *Pictures and Conversations* (1975).

267 *The Little Girls:* (1964) returns three women friends, 'Dicey', 'Mumbo' and 'Sheikie' to their school days at 'St Agatha's, Southstone' in 1914, which is a combination of Elizabeth Bowen's three English schools, including the Downe House of 'The Mulberry Tree'.

268 *my mother and I:* see notes to 'The Most Unforgettable Character I've Met', and also Chapters 9 and 10 of *Bowen's Court*, for the history of Robert Cole Bowen's mania, her father's illness and her 'exile', from the age of seven to twelve, in Kentish schools, living with her mother and her mother's relatives. Elizabeth Bowen's semi-orphaned itinerant childhood lies behind the characters of Portia in *The Death of the Heart* and of Eva Trout.

269 *the Pale:* the eastern triangle around Dublin governed by England in the fifteenth century; hence the phrase 'beyond the Pale' for what lay outside the 'civilised' boundaries (like County Cork!).

269 *Herbert Place:* see *Seven Winters* for Elizabeth Bowen's description of her childhood winters at 15 Herbert Place.

272 *the atmospheric rectory:* see the opening chapters of *Eva Trout*.

272 *Tony Butts:* see note to letter to William Plomer, 5 June 1938.

273 *The Talisman:* (1825), novel of the Crusades, by Walter Scott.

274 *Sir Jonah Barrington:* (1760–1834), Anglo-Irish lawyer and landowner who entered Parliament in 1790, was strongly opposed to the

Act of Union, and wrote an autobiography in 1827 full of robust and violent anecdotes.

275 *Sheridan's The Rivals:* first produced in 1775.

276 *the Bowens were Welsh:* the Bowens, originally 'ap Owens', came from the Gower Peninsula.

288 *Louis Wain:* illustrator of such children's books as *The Adventures of Friskers and His Friends* (1907), *Madame Tabby's Establishment* (1909) and *Louis Wain's Animal Book* (1928).

290 *Aunt Laura:* see preface, '*Encounters*'.

291 *Dorothy Lewis:* not identified.

293 *Marjory (sic) Bowen:* Marjorie Bowen (1886–1952), whose novel *The Viper of Milan* (1906) profoundly influenced Graham Greene.

296 *Encounters:* (1923).

296 *Ann Lee's:* (1926).

297 *Le Fanu and Edgeworth novels:* see preface, '*Uncle Silas* by Sheridan Le Fanu', and notes to '*The Moores of Moore Hall*, by Joseph Hone'.

BIBLIOGRAPHY

Works by Elizabeth Bowen in chronological order

Encounters, Sidgwick & Jackson, London, 1923.
Ann Lee's and Other Stories, Sidgwick & Jackson, London, 1926.
The Hotel, Constable, London 1927.
The Last September, Constable, London, 1929.
Joining Charles, Constable, London, 1929.
Friends and Relations, Constable, London, 1931.
To the North, Gollancz, London, 1932.
The Cat Jumps, Gollancz, London, 1934.
The House in Paris, Gollancz, London, 1935.
The Death of the Heart, Gollancz, London, 1938.
Look at all those Roses, Gollancz, London, 1941.
Seven Winters, Cuala Press, Dublin, 1942 (limited edition of 450 copies);
    Longmans, London, 1943; Knopf, New York, 1962.
Bowen's Court, Longmans, London, 1942.
English Novelists, Collins, London, 1945.
The Demon Lover, Cape, London, 1945.
The Heat of the Day, Cape, London, 1949.
Collected Impressions, Longmans, London, 1950; Knopf, New York, 1950.
The Shelbourne, Harrap, London, 1951.
A World of Love, Cape, London, 1955.
A Time in Rome, Longmans, London, 1960.
Afterthought, Longmans, London, 1962.
The Little Girls, Cape, London, 1964.
The Good Tiger, Knopf, New York, 1965; Cape, London, 1970.
A Day in the Dark, Cape, London, 1965.
Eva Trout, Cape, London, 1969.
Pictures and Conversations, Cape, London, 1975 (posthumous: edited and
    with a foreword by Spencer Curtis Brown); Knopf, New York, 1975.
Collected Stories, Cape, London, 1980; introduction by Angus Wilson.
Bowen's Court and Seven Winters, Virago, London, 1984; introduction by
    Hermione Lee.

Other works

Glendinning, Victoria, *Elizabeth Bowen: Portrait of a Writer*, Weidenfeld & Nicolson, London, 1977, Penguin, 1985.

Lee, Hermione, *Elizabeth Bowen: an Estimation*, Vision Press, London, 1981.

Sellery, J'nan and Harris, William. O., *Elizabeth Bowen: A Bibliography*, University of Texas, Austin, 1981.

Index